MW01591774

POLITICAL DECISION-MAKING, DELIBERATION AND PARTICIPATION

RESEARCH IN MICROPOLITICS

Series Editors: Michael X. Delli Carpini,
Leonie Huddy and Robert Y. Shapiro

Recent Volumes:

Volumes 1–3: edited by Samuel Long

Volumes 4–5: edited by Michael X. Delli Carpini, Leonie Huddy and Robert Y. Shapiro

POLITICAL DECISION-MAKING, DELIBERATION AND PARTICIPATION

EDITED BY

MICHAEL X. DELLI CARPINI
The Pew Charitable Trusts and Barnard College, USA

LEONIE HUDDY
Department of Political Science, SUNY – Stony Brook, USA

ROBERT Y. SHAPIRO
Department of Political Science and Institute for Social and Economic Research and Policy, Columbia University, USA

2002

JAI
An Imprint of Elsevier Science

Amsterdam – Boston – London – New York – Oxford – Paris
San Diego – San Francisco – Singapore – Sydney – Tokyo

ELSEVIER SCIENCE Ltd
The Boulevard, Langford Lane
Kidlington, Oxford OX5 1GB, UK

First edition 2002

Library of Congress Cataloging in Publication Data
A catalog record from the Library of Congress has been applied for.

British Library Cataloguing in Publication Data
A catalogue record from the British Library has been applied for.

ISBN: 0-7623-0227-5
ISSN: 1041-5858 (Series)

♾The paper used in this publication meets the requirements of ANSI/NISO Z39.48-1992 (Permanence of Paper).
Printed in The Netherlands.

CONTENTS

v

PART 3: POLITICAL PARTICIPATION

LIST OF CONTRIBUTORS

Eugene Borgida Department of Psychology,
University of Minnesota, USA

Karen Callaghan Political Science Department,
University of Massachusetts, USA

Michael X. Delli Carpini The Pew Charitable Trusts and Barnard College,
Columbia University, USA

James Farr Department of Political Science,
University of Minnesota, USA

Martin Gilens Department of Political Science,
University of California, Los Angeles, USA

Beth Haney Children's Defense Fund, Minnesota, USA

Leonie Huddy Department of Political Science,
State University of New York at Stony Brook,
USA

William G. Jacoby Department of Government and International
Studies, University of South Carolina, USA

Mark Lindeman Department of Political Science,
Columbia University, USA

Tali Mendelberg Department of Politics,
Princeton University, USA

Naomi Murakawa Department of Political Science,
Yale University, USA

David K. Park   Department of Political Science and The
                          Institute for Social and Economic Research
                          and Policy, Columbia University, USA

Robert Y. Shapiro   Department of Political Science,
                          Institute for Social and Economic Research
                          and Policy, Columbia University, USA

Nayda Terkildsen   Unaffiliated

Carlos Vargas-Ramos   Center for Puerto Rican Studies,
                          Hunter College, USA

INTRODUCTION: POLITICAL DECISION-MAKING, DELIBERATION AND PARTICIPATION

Michael X. Delli Carpini, Leonie Huddy and Robert Y. Shapiro

This volume of *Research in Micropolitics* is the sixth in a series dating back to 1989. It is also the third and final volume under our editorship. As with previous volumes our goal is to publish essays on a variety of substantive, conceptual and methodological issues of relevance to political psychology, with particular emphasis on promising new areas of theory and research. While the specific topic of each essay varies, all authors provide interpretive reviews of recent and important research in their fields. Several also present original or updated findings from their own research.

As the title of this introduction (and the subtitle of this volume) suggests, the essays in this collection address three important and interrelated themes in the theory and practice of democratic politics. They also draw on a well established body of theory and findings from within psychology, including research on information processing and intergroup relations, to critique and enrich current political research.

Understanding the ways in which citizens make political decisions – and the kind of information that is used in this decision-making process – has long been a topic of study in political psychology. Given the complexity of many political choices and/or the relatively low levels of public interest in politics, citizens often rely (consciously or not) on information short cuts in deciding

Political Decision Making, Deliberation and Participation, Volume 6, pages 1–11.
Copyright © 2002 by Elsevier Science Ltd.
All rights of reproduction in any form reserved.
ISBN: 0-7623-0227-5

where they stand or whom they support. The three essays in Part One of this volume explore three important decision-making cues: elites, race and ideology.

Political elites are often the subject of citizens' opinions and the target of their actions. But as Martin Gilens and Naomi Murakawa argue in their essay, elites also serve as a mechanism through which opinions are formed. As they note, democratic governance requires citizens to make decisions about a wide range of complex issues about which most Americans are woefully uninformed. As a possible escape from this "democratic dilemma" heuristics offer informational shortcuts that enable political decision making without comprehensive knowledge. One common heuristic is the elite cue, in which individuals make political decisions by considering not the details of the political issue but rather the positions taken by trusted elites, including politicians, experts and interest groups.

In their essay Gilens and Murakawa review the logic of elite cueing, the empirical evidence that bears on citizens' use of elite cues in political decision making, and the consequences of cue taking for American democracy. Drawing from cognitive models of central and peripheral processing they begin by describing the psychology of cue taking. They then examine the characteristics that make political issues attractive for cue taking, finding that individuals are more likely to rely on elite cues in deciding low-involvement issues and new or technically complex issues. Furthermore, individuals with lower levels of political knowledge and interest are more likely to use cues in political decision making. The authors next turn to a consideration of how people select cue givers, highlighting "like-mindedness" and "truthfulness" as potential criteria. As a way of assessing the effectiveness of cue-based decision making, the authors ask whether elite cues enable relatively uninformed citizens to make the same political judgments they would make if fully knowledgeable about the given issue. While a review of the literature suggests that a firm conclusion on this matter is premature, Gilens and Murakawa do conclude that members of the public are generally capable of discerning cue givers' political predispositions and of identifying their endorsements, two factors that are essential to cue-based decision making.

Late in their essay the authors turn their attention from the capacity of citizens to the adequacy of the cue-giving environment itself. Here they provide a valuable sketch of an ideal cueing environment – one that provides cues that are credible, comprehensive in terms of both breadth across the political spectrum and depth within issues, and balanced in the frequency of presentation in the mass media. Gilens and Murakawa conclude that "[e]lite cues are important, but imperfect, elements of democratic participation" and that future research should "address both citizens' propensities to use elite cues and the availability of such cues in the political environment."

What is clear from Gilens and Murakawa's interpretive review of the literature is that the role of elites as cue givers is a complex one that depends upon characteristics of the elites in question, the issue under consideration, the decision maker and the larger information environment. This theme is taken up in Karen Callaghan and Nayda Terkildsen's exploration of the impact of candidate race on citizens' vote choice. The authors' central theme is that despite the well-developed literature on how citizens decide whom to vote for, mainstream models largely ignore the role of candidate race, especially as it affects white voters. Callaghan and Terkildsen begin their essay with a brief overview of the history of "bi-racial" elections, emphasizing the relative recency of such elections, the growing but still few number of such races and the resulting under-representation of African Americans in elected office. They then provide an overview of mainstream research, concluding that this literature tells us little about whether the models used to explain vote choice apply when one candidate is black.

After exploring possible reasons for this gap – ranging from the historically few number of bi-racial elections to the effects of racism on the profession – Callaghan and Terkildsen turn to an examination of the literature that does exist on the effects of candidate race. While their review suggests that "race matters," they also find that the existing literature is replete with data and measurement problems that make drawing generalizable conclusions difficult. Central to these problems are an over-dependence on case studies, the limited availability of appropriate survey data, sample bias and the tendency of white respondents to "self-monitor" their responses when they involve race. They also argue that little is known about how "individuation" (i.e. focusing on the individual characteristics of a candidate) and/or "categorization" (i.e. focusing on perceived group characteristics and applying these characteristics to an individual) come into play in assessing African American candidates. Finally, they conclude that little is known about the ways in which "candidate" categorizations (e.g. trustworthiness or honesty) and "racial" categorizations (e.g. work ethic or intelligence) interact with each other when the candidate being evaluated is black.

Callaghan and Terkildsen begin to explore some of these largely unanswered questions by presenting data from their own experimental research. While they acknowledge that this research suffers from some of the same limitations found in the larger literature, they do present suggestive evidence that white voters directly and indirectly draw on racial stereotypes in their evaluations of black candidates and do so in ways that work against their prospects of being elected. The authors conclude that the race and ethnicity of candidates and voters need to be integrated into mainstream models of vote choice – a point that is especially important given the growing diversity of the American electorate.

Callaghan and Terkildsen make a compelling appeal for including a too often ignored variable in our models of citizen decision making. In the third essay in this volume William Jacoby is equally convincing in arguing that an often studied and commonly criticized variable – ideology – remains an important organizer of how citizens interpret the political world. Jacoby reviews the scholarly research on ideology within the American electorate, emphasizing the resurgence of attention to liberal-conservative thinking that occurred from the 1970s until the early 1990s. According to Jacoby, studies of ideology in the 1950s and early 1960s focused largely on the presence or absence of ideological thinking in the American electorate ("levels of conceptualization"). When these studies concluded that the vast majority of Americans do not think in explicitly ideological terms, the concept of ideology lost much of its cache in subsequent studies of mass beliefs.

News of the death of ideology was premature, however. The re-emergence of this concept in scholarly research was driven in part by the availability of data – starting in 1972 the National Election Studies began to regularly include its now standard seven-point ideological self-placement measure. It was also driven by the greater visibility of ideological schisms between the Democratic and Republican parties in 1968 and 1972. But Jacoby convincingly argues that the return of ideology as a central variable has occurred mainly because of three major changes in how the concept has been used. First, ideology has become more clearly differentiated from other related but ultimately distinct concepts such as rationality, issue voting, attitude stability, democratic norms and civic competence. Second, the theoretical, empirical and methodological underpinnings of ideology as a concept have been refined. And third, the focus of research has shifted from how many citizens think ideologically to what impact ideology has on the political beliefs, opinions and actions of citizens.

As these changes have occurred, evidence has grown that ideology is an important filter, organizer and/or shortcut for many aspects of citizens' political decision making, influencing their beliefs and opinions about parties and candidates, vote choice, stance on issues and political participation. In short, ideology, once properly conceptualized and measured, was found to matter to citizens in important ways. In addition, ideology matters to elites, who continue to define themselves and the issues they deal with in largely bi-polar, liberal versus conservative ways. Thus, to the extent that the political environment is defined in ideological terms, citizens are likely to use this concept as a way of understanding and acting in this environment. Jacoby concludes that while the concept of ideology has proven to be a resilient one and that our understanding of its meaning and role in the formation and expression of mass beliefs has come a long way, there is still room for further refinements in how it is defined and measured.

All of the first three essays in this volume build implicitly from a model of mass politics that assumes citizens who are only marginally informed and interested and who make decisions as relatively autonomous, even isolated individuals. While much of citizen politics in large representative democracies adheres to this model, there has been a growing interest in the communal and deliberative aspects of democratic politics. This research has been driven by both normative and conceptual arguments about the public benefits of collective decision making. The two essays in Part Two of this volume address the strengths and weaknesses of this emerging research agenda.

As Tali Mendelberg notes in her essay, the theory of deliberative democracy assumes that egalitarian, reciprocal, reasonable and open exchanges among citizens about public issues will lead to a number of individual and collective benefits. Among these are greater empathy and tolerance, a better understanding of one's own views and those of others, the building of consensus, a more engaged, active citizenry, and decisions that are more reasoned and attuned to the larger public good. As she also notes, however, there is a dearth of systematic, empirical research, testing this assumption as it applies to political decision making. Since most deliberation does or would occur in small groups she posits that a review of existing experimental research on the dynamics of small groups may provide useful findings that could be extrapolated to the real world of politics.

To this end Mendelberg provides a comprehensive review of social science research on small groups, deftly drawing conclusions that both support and challenge much of the theory of deliberative democracy. For example, she argues that discussions of important "social dilemmas" can lead to greater cooperation and genuine consensus among participating *individuals*. When discussions involve *groups* with clearly defined identities, however, the impact is more variable and contingent, sometimes resulting in cooperation and consensus and sometimes in increased conflict and polarization. The impact of deliberative group interactions appears to depend on a number of factors, including the degree of interdependence and/or shared values, the equality of representation, the amount and quality of information provided, and the relative status of the groups involved. In general, higher status or dominant groups can dominate discussions, leading either to greater conflict and polarization on the one hand, or acquiescence by the subordinate group on the other. Even this conclusion is contingent however. Certain settings (for example, where subordinate groups have the opportunity to provide novel or persuasive arguments, speak in a uniform voice and/or base their views on norms that are consistent with the dominant group) can result in opinion shifts in favor of the minority view. Mendelberg also finds that consensus and cooperation is more likely to emerge when the discussions center on objective facts rather than deeply held, but conflicting group values.

Mendelberg's review also uncovers a number of other factors that help determine the impact and outcomes of small group deliberations. Systematic differences in the propensity to talk and the ability to argue associated with race, gender, income and education can exacerbate conflict or lead to false consensus. Language can be used to either build bridges across individual and group differences or increase these divides. Emotional arguments can either derail the deliberative process or, when combined with reason, make for more engaging and persuasive exchanges. The structure in which deliberation occurs (for example, the role of discussion leaders or the rules by which decisions are made) are important, but the effectiveness of particular structures depend heavily on the nature of the issue and the make up of the participants. And, while there is some evidence that citizens either have the skills and information necessary to deliberate effectively or that they can acquire these skills and information as part of the deliberative process itself, it remains an open question whether most citizens *want* to engage in such a process, especially involving issues of politics and policy.

In what is arguably one of the greatest challenges to deliberative theory uncovered by Mendelberg, she argues that existing research on small group dynamics suggest that the "quality" of decisions made in groups is not better and is often worse than those made by individuals or experts. Even here, however, she notes that the presence of reliable, objective information and effective group leadership can reduce this tendency. Taken as a whole, Mendelberg's consistent message is that while deliberative processes in and of themselves are no guarantee of a more participatory, communal and rational democracy there is enough evidence in support of these ideals to warrant further research that focuses explicitly on political deliberation. The key, both to refining the theory of political deliberation and understanding its dynamics, is developing a richer understanding of the specific contexts in which deliberation is most likely to be effective.

As noted above, Mendelberg laments the lack of systematic research on the nature and consequences of political deliberation. In his essay Mark Lindeman begins to close this gap through a thoughtful discussion of the role of deliberative research in better understanding the quality of public opinion and the policy preferences of citizens. One of the central purposes of deliberation is to allow citizens to come to greater clarity about their policy preferences and provide a vehicle for them to express these preferences. In theory, deliberation can alter opinions by increasing and improving citizens' factual base; shifting the norms, values and evaluative criteria used to form and express preferences;

providing opportunities to better understand one's self interest and its relationship to the common good; and creating greater consistency and stability across preferences and over time. All these qualities should produce collective opinions that more accurately represent the public's "true" policy preferences.

Unlike many researchers falling in the deliberative democracy camp, Lindeman does not see either deliberation or a consideration of the common good as emerging solely from collective, face-to-face discussions. Rather, he argues that citizens can "deliberate" about issues and their collective implications on their own. In addition, while he argues that traditional survey research by its very design is ill equipped to discern the "true" policy preferences of citizens, he believes that the benefits of deliberation can be realized through opinion surveys, albeit ones that are designed explicitly to do so. Face-to-face forums and deliberative polls each have their own strengths and weaknesses, both as vehicles for the formation of preferences and as methods for tapping these preferences. Rather than choose between them, Lindeman appeals for the use of multiple formats by practitioners and multiple methods by researchers.

While Lindeman believes that deliberation can be a valuable mechanism for unlocking the public's policy preferences, he is well aware of the potential pitfalls and opportunities for distortion discussed in the Mendelberg essay. A key to better understanding the relationship between deliberation and policy preferences is the development of better definitions and measures of "quality" opinion, an issue he addresses in some detail. Throughout his essay Lindeman supports his views with a careful review of relevant literature. In addition, he mines a number of data sets, case studies and reports based on real world applications of deliberative forums and polls that have rarely been tapped by academic researchers. Finally, he presents two brief case studies – on health care reform and environmental regulation – which effectively illustrate the potential benefits of deliberative research.

Although the study of public opinion and decision making is important in its own right, for public preferences to play a role in the political process citizens must ultimately act upon them – through voting, contacting public officials, participating in political organizations and the like. The two essays in Part Three of this volume explore the dynamics of political and civic engagement in the United States.

Spurred in part by growing if controversial evidence of declining levels of political participation, political and social trust and social capital in the United States, there has been a renewed interest in citizenship and civic engagement, both in the academic community and among a range of non-profit organizations, educational institutions and foundations. In their essay Beth Haney, Eugene Borgida and James Farr explore this growing interest. While noting that recent research and practice has identified various causes and potential solutions to this perceived problem they argue that much of this work lacks the specificity required to provide effective remedies. In particular, academic research lacks a well-developed conceptualization of the political psychology of civic engagement. In addition, real world interventions designed to increase citizens' participation in public life seldom systematically assess their impact on participants in ways that could provide valuable lessons about what works and what does not.

Building on these critiques the authors outline a model of the psychology of civic engagement that provides a mechanism for potentially increasing such engagement. Underpinning this emerging model are four interrelated assumptions, drawn from and supported by existing literature. First, individuals hold conceptions of what citizenship and/or being a member of a community means. These conceptions can vary with age, generation, education, region and a host of other contextual factors, but an important distinction is the degree to which they are based on "active" or "passive" notions of what citizenship and being part of a community entail. In turn, the degree to which these roles are viewed as active or passive is linked to the inclusion or absence of political efficacy as part of their definitions.

Second, while conceptualizations of citizenship and community membership help determine whether someone will become engaged, this relationship can operate in reverse. That is, how one defines these roles can be changed through experience, including specific interventions designed to give citizens the opportunity to participate in public life. However, the likelihood of this change occurring and the direction of this change depend on the quality of the civic experience. Third, individuals hold multiple self-identities, including a sense of one's "civic self." The centrality of this identity and the extent to which it involves "action" as a key component depends both on how citizenship and community membership have been defined as well as on one's prior civic experiences. Fourth and finally, one's sense of civic self directly affects future perceptions, interpretations and participation in the political world.

To test the utility of their model and its underlying assumptions, Haney, Borgida and Farr provide findings from a field experiment designed to measure the impact of a high school civic engagement program on participants' definitions of citizenship and community membership, their political efficacy and their political and civic participation. While the authors' research produces mixed findings regarding the impact of this particular program, it does suggest that their four assumptions could play a valuable role in both understanding the psychological roots of civic engagement and in designing and assessing ways to increase levels of civic engagement over time.

As with political decision making and deliberation, the dynamics of political participation are complex and context dependent. In the final essay in this volume, David Park and Carlos Vargas-Ramos review existing literature on an important and often understudied aspect of this dynamic – race and ethnicity. Driven in part by the growing number and percentage of minorities in the United States and the resulting diversity of the population, political candidates, parties and organizations have devoted greater attention to mobilizing this portion of the electorate.

Research on minority and immigrant participation has lagged behind, however. Survey data and aggregate statistics generally show that African, Hispanic and Asian Americans engage in most forms of political participation at lower rates than non-Hispanic whites. But why is this the case? Park and Vargas-Ramos review existing literature on this question. They argue that the dominant explanation for who participates and who does not – which they label the "SES model" – while accounting for much of the difference between whites and minorities is ultimately inadequate. For example, while much (though not all) of the difference between levels of Hispanic and non-Hispanic participation can be accounted for by socioeconomic factors such as income and education, African American participation, controlling for SES, often exceeds that of whites. In addition, SES appears to be a poor explanation for many Asian Americans' lower levels of participation. Clearly some other factors are at play.

More recent research has refined the SES model in valuable ways by clarifying the pathways by which socioeconomic status affects participation. For example, the "civic volunteerism" model argues that higher socioeconomic status increases the psychological predispositions, skills and resources and opportunities necessary for participation. However, even these refinements fail to fully explain racial and ethnic differences in participation rates. The authors argue that such an explanation is unlikely to emerge until mainstream researchers include race and ethnicity more explicitly in their theories and analysis.

Park and Vargas-Ramos next turn to research that does focus on race and ethnicity, identifying two dominant approaches. The first, labeled the "pan-ethnic model," agrees that race and ethnicity are important explanatory variables, but downplays differences within and across minority populations, focusing instead on broader majority-minority differences. The second, labeled the "nationality model," argues that to truly understand the impact of race and ethnicity one must disaggregate minority groups, not only by broad categories such as African American or Asian American, but by more finely-grained categories such as specific nation of origin. Each model has its own strengths and weaknesses. Given its simpler design and more limited assumptions, the pan-ethnic model is more easily tested. It is also consistent with theories that argue minority group identities form in part in relationship to majority-group status and perceptions. However the nationality model, while more complex and difficult to test systematically, is arguably more consistent with the realities of inter and intra group differences within the minority community. Park and Vargas-Ramos see benefits to both models, but ultimately conclude that existing research is too incomplete to assess which if either comes closest to capturing the realities of minority participation in the United States.

The authors conclude by calling for more and more refined research in this area. In particular they note the need to consider the impact on minority participation rates of the increasing geographic dispersion of minorities; the national, regional and local (including urban versus suburban) contexts within which minorities live; and the cultural, social and economic heterogeneity within and across minority populations. They also suggest that racial and ethnic participation may be a fruitful area of study for rational choice theorists, at least for participation other than voting. And they suggest that more research on the role of political and communal mobilization on minority participation is needed.

Taken together the essays in this volume offer a valuable contribution to our understanding of the complex and context-dependent dynamics of mass politics in the United States today. As the authors show, existing research on the psychology of political attitudes, opinions and action has much to offer to both the theory and practice of democratic politics. They also show, however, that many questions remain to be answered. We hope these essays – as well as those from earlier volumes in this series – help to point the way for this ongoing research.

The last three volumes of *Research in Micropolitics* have, as we stated in the first volume under our editorship, cast a wide net in emphasizing new directions in political psychology and research on the "cutting edge." In attempting to do this, we benefited greatly from our participation in the New York Area Political Psychology Seminar that has been held each semester at Columbia University. We thank the many presenters and participants in the seminar, who have helped us keep abreast of exciting new research in political psychology. We are especially grateful to the Paul F. Lazarsfeld Center and the Institute for Social and Economic Theory and Policy (the successor to the Center for the Social Sciences) at Columbia, and their current and past directors, Peter Bearman and Harrison White, for support of the seminar. We thank Samuel Long again for inviting us to succeed him as co-editors of the series, and the editors and publishers of the *Research in Micropolitics* series for their ongoing guidance. Finally, we would like to thank our respective institutions – Barnard College, Columbia University and the State University of New York at Stony Brook – for their general support over the seven years of our editorship.

PART 1:
POLITICAL DECISION-MAKING

ELITE CUES AND POLITICAL DECISION-MAKING

Martin Gilens and Naomi Murakawa

INTRODUCTION

For most Americans, most political issues are complex and remote. Recognizing the prohibitive costs of becoming well informed on a wide range of issues, Anthony Downs (1957, p. 233) notes that the average citizen "cannot be expert in all the fields of policy that are relevant to his decision. Therefore, he will seek assistance from men who are experts in those fields, have the same political goals he does, and have good judgment."[1] As a resource-saving device, individuals will rely on trusted experts and political elites to form their opinions on political issues without having to work through the details of those issues themselves.

Citizens have clear incentives to take political cues from those more knowledgeable, typically experts or elites whose views are conveyed by the media. But while the incentives for elite cue taking are clear, the process and the implications are not. How do citizens make use of elite cues in their political decision-making, and are elite cues effective in guiding citizens toward the political choices that a more "informationally demanding" process would produce?

Much is at stake in answering these questions. It is well established that the American public is woefully uninformed on political issues (Campbell et al., 1960; Delli Carpini & Keeter, 1996), and many fear that this widespread political ignorance threatens democratic processes. Yet despite their lack of information, Americans do express opinions on a wide range of political issues. Moreover,

Political Decision Making, Deliberation and Participation, Volume 6, pages 15–49.
Copyright © 2002 by Elsevier Science Ltd.
All rights of reproduction in any form reserved.
ISBN: 0-7623-0227-5

these opinions – in the aggregate at least – appear to respond in sensible and predictable ways to changes in social and political conditions (Page & Shapiro, 1992).

One mechanism that has been offered as a bridge between the public's general ignorance of relevant information and the "rational" behavior of its collective opinions is the use of informational shortcuts or heuristics. Heuristics enable people to "be knowledgeable in their reasoning about political choices without necessarily possessing a large body of knowledge about politics" (Sniderman, Brody & Tetlock 1991, p. 19). As suggested above by Downs, a common heuristic is the elite cue.

This article reviews the logic of elite cueing, the empirical evidence that bears on citizens' use of elite cues in political decision-making, and the consequences of "cue taking" for American democracy. We understand elites to include a potentially wide range of individuals and organizations, including politicians and political officials, policy experts, interest groups, religious leaders, and journalists. Personal acquaintances can also serve as cue-givers to the extent that the decision-maker sees them as being more knowledgeable about a particular question than he or she is. Although the process of gaining exposure to the cues of personal cue-givers may differ from the process through which elite cues are acquired, we expect that the psychology of cue-based decision-making is largely the same. In this paper, however, we concentrate on the more visible influence of elite cue-givers – that is, those whose views are communicated through the media.[2]

In the first section below we describe the psychology of cue taking, drawing from cognitive models of central and peripheral processing. The second section examines the characteristics that make political issues more or less attractive for cue taking and the characteristics that make individuals more or less likely to use cues in political decision-making. In section three, we turn our attention to citizens' selection of cue givers, exploring the criteria by which potential cue-giving elites are judged. Section four asks how effective cue-based decision-making is in enabling relatively uninformed citizens to make the same political judgments that they would make if fully knowledgeable about the topic at hand. The final section addresses the implications of elite cue taking for American democracy, examining the conditions necessary for effective cue taking and the characteristics of the existing cue-giving environment.

THE PSYCHOLOGY OF CUE TAKING: CENTRAL VERSUS PERIPHERAL PROCESSING

In their Elaboration Likelihood Model, Richard Petty and John Cacioppo (1981, 1986) develop an account of persuasion with particular usefulness for understanding cue-based decision-making. Petty and Cacioppo identify two paths to persuasion. The central route to persuasion entails consideration of substantive content, including evidence and the soundness of an argument's logic. The primary determinant of persuasion through central processing is argument strength and if attitude change occurs through this route it is expected to be relatively stable and enduring. The peripheral route, in contrast, entails consideration of factors external to message content, such as the credibility and attractiveness of the message source. The primary determinants of peripheral-route persuasion are "persuasion cues" which produce attitude change *"without any active thinking about the attributes of the issue or the object under consideration"* (Petty & Cacioppo, 1981, p. 256; italics in original). Attitude change through peripheral processes is more superficial and less stable than central-route persuasion (see Chaiken, 1980, 1987 for a description of her similar dual-process "heuristic-systematic model" of persuasion).

Petty and Cacioppo identify two factors that influence whether individuals use central rather than peripheral processing: motivation and ability. Individuals with greater involvement or concern with an issue are more likely to be motivated to use central-route processing (which requires greater cognitive effort than cue-based peripheral processing). For example, Petty and Cacioppo (1986) asked college undergraduates to evaluate a proposal for new comprehensive examinations. They provided their subjects with either strong or weak arguments and attributed the arguments to either a high-status or low-status source. They found that students who expected to be affected by the proposed exams disregarded source credentials and based their evaluation of the exams on the strength of the arguments they were given. However, students who were told that proposed exams would not begin for ten years were uninfluenced by argument strength but responded instead to the credibility of the arguments' alleged source.

The greater cognitive demands of central-route processing mean that not only motivation but also the ability to judge an argument on its merits will influence the way information is evaluated. When a topic is very complex or requires specialized knowledge, decision-makers will be more likely to rely on peripheral cues such as source credibility. In addition to characteristics of issues and decision-makers, the decision-making context can also influence a decision-maker's ability to evaluate the merits of an argument. For example, Petty and Cacioppo (1979) found that time pressures or distractions decreased subjects' information processing abilities and led to greater reliance on peripheral-route cues in decision-making.

There are many possible peripheral-route heuristics that citizens might employ to simplify the process of political decision-making. Contemporary discussions of cognitive heuristics originate in Kahneman and Tversky's pioneering work (Kahneman & Tversky, 1972, 1973; Tversky & Kahneman, 1973, 1974). Sniderman, Brody and Tetlock (1991) apply these concepts to the study of mass politics, and expand the set of heuristic processes to include "availability" (drawn from Kahneman & Tversky), "likability," and "desert." Mondak (1994b) provides a valuable discussion of heuristic-based political decision-making, adding the "representativeness" heuristic to the list above.

We believe that all of these (and no doubt many other) heuristics play a role in shaping citizens' views of political issues. Among political scientists, however, the heuristic that has attracted the greatest attention is the use of elite cues as aids in political decision-making. In this paper we examine only elite cueing as a decision-making shortcut.

Motivation and Opinion Formation

An overarching assumption in the literature on dual-process decision-making and political cue taking is that a decision-maker's primary motivation is to "get it right," in the sense of arriving at a decision that is most consistent with her values and interests. But other decision-making motivations may come into play. For example, quite independent of the merits of the case, a decision-maker might prefer that his position on an issue be consistent with his spouse's position. Moreover, political preferences are rarely acquired in one dramatic moment, but are more often formed over time as an individual's pool of relevant information accumulates. Research on "motivated reasoning" shows that people have a strong tendency to evaluate new information in a manner biased toward maintaining their pre-existing preferences (Ditto & Lopez, 1992; Lodge, McGraw & Stroh, 1989; Lodge, Steenbergen & Brau, 1995). In short, the desire to "get it right" is only one of the motivations at work in political decision-making.

Given that individual decision-making can be guided by multiple motivations, cue taking can not only help a decision-maker in forming a preference on an issue, but can also serve to defend or justify an already existing preference. In this case, an existing preference for one or another position on an issue might guide a decision-maker in his or her choice of cue-givers.

The discussion of cue taking offered below assumes that the decision-maker's primary motivation is to identify the position most consistent with his or her values and interests. This focus reflects the dominant orientation of this literature and responds to the question "Do elite cues enable citizens to arrive at the same preferences that a more demanding, substantively focused decision process would produce?" It is important to keep in mind, however, that other decision-making motives also exist, and that the dynamics of elite cue taking (like the dynamics of substantive deliberation) will differ depending on the mix of motivations at work.

WHEN ARE CUES USED?

Based on dual process models of persuasion we would predict that citizens are more likely to rely on elite cues in forming opinions on new or technically complex issues (reflecting a lesser ability to reason through the substance of the issue), or on issues with low levels of involvement or concern (reflecting lower motivation to do so). Similarly, we expect to find greater reliance on elite cues among citizens with lower levels of political knowledge and interest (reflecting lower levels of ability and motivation, respectively). In this section we review the empirical literature on citizen use of elite cues with an eye toward these predictions.

What Issues are Most Likely to be "Cueable"?

Cues and shortcuts are available on every political issue and cue-taking incentives are high. For most Americans, politics is a sideshow in the circus of life. Most political issues seem complex and remote, so following politics generally becomes a hobby that competes for time with the more tangible demands of work and family. In this context, why would a person opt to forego a cue in lieu of substantive information and arguments? Are there particular issues that make a person more likely to invest the time and cognitive resources necessary for central-route processing?

Hard versus Easy Issues
Carmines and Stimson (1980) provide a useful distinction between easy issues, which are ends-oriented, emotional, and relatively familiar, and hard issues, which are means-oriented, technical, and unfamiliar. A law against flag burning, for example, is an easy issue – not because the "correct" position seems obvious but because it involves values and ideas that are familiar and accessible to most people. Hard issues, on the other hand, typically require specialized knowledge that might range from environmental science (on issues like acid rain or environmental carcinogens) to social or economic dynamics (e.g. the impact of immigration on the U.S. economy) to foreign affairs (e.g. the strategic importance of Middle Eastern allies). Some issues are clearly "easier" or "harder" than others in a general sense. But the diversity of special-ized knowledge across individuals suggests that different issues are likely to be more or less difficult for different people.[3]

Empirical findings generally support the prediction that citizens will look to source cues more when evaluating hard issues. Ratneshwar and Chaiken (1991) found that when study participants have difficulty comprehending a message, they are more likely to use source credibility to infer level of agreement with the message. Conversely, high comprehensibility leads participants to overlook source credibility. For example, Carmines and Kuklinski (1990) found that cues from trusted legislators increased respondents' certainty more for the hard issue of a new missile defense system than for the easy issue of compensation for racial discrimination. Lupia (1994) showed that voters who were poorly informed about the complex details of five competing insurance-reform initiatives on a California ballot used elite cues (in this case, the endorsement or opposition of the insurance industry). On this "hard" issue, poorly informed voters who had elite cues to draw on were able to emulate the voting behavior of their better-informed peers. Finally, in the absence of source cues, Cobb and Kuklinski (1997) report that hard arguments about national health care generally have less influence than easy arguments.

Perhaps the clearest cases of "easy" issues are those in which the empirical components are simple and undisputed and citizens' evaluations of the issues turn primarily on their value commitments. In such cases, the public may feel little need for the assistance of elite cues in coming to judgment. The 1993 confirmation hearing of Zoe Baird, nominated by President Clinton for U.S. Attorney General, provides a good example.

When news broke that Baird had employed two Peruvians living illegally in the United States, the near-consensus among political leaders and media commentators was that this posed no threat to Baird's confirmation. By contrast, the mass public condemned Baird, phoning in words of protest to members of Congress and to radio talk shows. Page and Tannenbaum (1996) found that the public's "mass condemnation" of Baird preceded the appearance of anti-Baird sentiment in the mainstream media, and survey data showed that public rejection was large and not confined to any particular demographic group (Page & Tannenbaum, 1996). In evaluating Baird's behavior and her fitness for the office of Attorney General, the public apparently had little need for elite cues.

The public's response to revelations of President Clinton's affair with a 23-year-old White House intern similarly shows that the public will ignore elite cues on some issues. In this case, the near-unanimous elite opinion that the Lewinsky affair meant big trouble for Clinton and the widespread calls for his resignation in the opinion pages of the nation's newspapers seemed to have little effect on public opinion (Zaller, 1998; Kagay, 1999). While the evidence is still thin, it appears that citizens behave in the political realm much as they do in the psychology lab. At least at the extremes, the public relies more on elite cues in evaluating technical and unfamiliar issues.

High-Involvement versus Low-Involvement Issues. Experiments in social psychology generally confirm that high personal involvement in an issue makes participants less likely to rely on source cues and more likely to consider argument strength (Hample, 1985; Morley, 1987; Petty & Cacioppo, 1986). In the political world, however, personal involvement in an issue rarely matches the level found in these experiments (Zaller, 1992, p. 46). While the stakes in political decision-making are potentially high, the connections between any specific policy choice and the life conditions of any given citizen are typically nebulous and opaque (Edelman, 1985). Even policy proposals on such "doorstep" issues as health care, taxes, and family leave have multiple, tenuous links from policy options to suspected effects on everyday life.

While the characteristics of an issue can make it "easy" or "hard," involvement necessarily reflects the relationship *between* a particular issue and an individual decision-maker.[4] Although we are not aware of any research that explicitly compares citizens' political decision-making with regard to high-involvement versus low-involvement *issues,* there is some evidence that central-route processing is more prevalent among those *individuals* who are more involved with a specific issue. For example, van Knippenberg and Daamen (1996) presented survey respondents with an array of factual information about alternative ways of generating electricity. They found that both higher educated respondents and those who expressed greater involvement with energy policy expressed more stable and consistent policy preferences. The authors interpreted these results as reflecting the greater use of central-route processing among respondents with higher levels of ability (as measured by education) and motivation (as measured by issue involvement).

Van Knippenberg and Daamen's study suggests that at least a subset of citizens will reason through the specifics of a complex public policy issue if asked to do so. But the respondents in this study were given only raw information about alternative energy proposals, and therefore did not have the option of using elite cues as a shortcut in their decision-making. How these results correspond to the real-world context of political decision-making remains unclear.[5]

Even at extreme levels of political involvement – for example, on issues where an individual's livelihood is clearly and directly at stake – people may be more likely to use cues than to reason through the substance of a complex issue. For example, doctors evaluating health care reform are less likely to wade into the literature on health care financing than to turn to their professional organizations for cues about what reforms to support or oppose. Thus even for high-involvement issues, and all the more so for issues of lesser concern, cue taking is likely to be a more common means of evaluating political issues than substantive assessment of competing evidence and arguments.

Who is Most Responsive to Elite Cues?

Converse (1962) suggested that political persuasion depends on the two separate processes of exposure to a political message and acceptance of its contents. McGuire (1968), focusing not on political communication but on the personality correlates of susceptibility to persuasion, developed a similar model in which the probability of opinion change is a function of the probability of receiving a message times the probability of yielding to the message if it is received. For McGuire, message "reception" meant more than exposure however; a potentially persuasive message was considered to be received only if it was both *attended to* and *comprehended by* a decision-maker.

McGuire (1969) used this model to account for the variety of different functional relationships between individual characteristics and the probability of opinion change in response to a persuasive message. McGuire noted, for example, that self-esteem is curvilinearly related to influenceability, with low- and high-esteem individuals exhibiting the smallest probability of opinion change, and average esteem individuals exhibiting the greatest probability of opinion change. The curvilinear form of this relationship, McGuire argued, results from the positive association of self-esteem with message reception (due to greater sociability) and the negative association of self-esteem to yielding (due to higher confidence). Thus individuals with low self-esteem are unlikely to receive the message in the first place, while those with high self-esteem will receive it but resist its persuasive influence.[6]

The flexibility of McGuire's two-stage model allows it to account not only for curvilinear relationships with opinion change, but for negative and positive relationships as well. For example, McGuire (1968) notes that lower intelligence scores are generally associated with higher levels of opinion change due to the greater tendency of those scoring lower on intelligence scales to yield to a persuasive message. But in circumstances where message reception is difficult (e.g. a message that is hard to comprehend), intelligence scores may be positively related to opinion change.

Applying the Converse-McGuire model of opinion change to the context of political cue taking, Zaller (1992) highlights the roles of political awareness (i.e. knowledge about and cognitive engagement with politics) and message congruity or incongruity with a decision-maker's pre-existing political orientations. Awareness, Zaller argues, is positively related to political message reception, but negatively related to acceptance of messages that are inconsistent with pre-existing political orientations. The combination of political awareness, political orientation, and message environment determine the likelihood of opinion change in response to elite cues. In a message environment in which essentially all elites support the same position on an issue (e.g. the Vietnam war during the early 1960s), citizens' political awareness will be positively related to the mainstream position. In cases where elites disagree, on the other hand, the pattern of public opinion will depend on the nature of the dominant message flow at a given point in time.

For example, during the first two years of the Reagan presidency, elite messages regarding defense spending (as conveyed through the mass media) were predominantly opposed to further spending increases (Zaller, 1992, p. 128). As a result, the relationship between political awareness and preferences on defense spending differed for Democrats (whose political predispositions were consistent with elite messages) and Republicans (whose political predispositions were inconsistent with those messages). Among Democrats, greater political awareness led to a higher probability of receiving the anti-defense spending message, while resistance was low at all awareness levels. Consequently, awareness among Democrats was positively and monotonically associated with opinion change in opposition to defense spending.

Among Republicans, on the other hand, the relationship between political awareness and opinion change was curvilinear: Republicans with low levels of political awareness did not receive the elite cues about defense spending, while those with high levels of political awareness received but resisted them. For Republicans, the greatest responsiveness to elite cues occurred among those with moderate levels of political awareness.

Zaller's model of political opinion formation focuses exclusively on the psychologically "peripheral" process of cue taking. Other researchers have sought to compare the use of cue-driven and information-driven decision processes for citizens with varying levels of education or political information. Their findings are not inconsistent with Zaller's work, but they suggest that while the politically engaged may be most capable of effective cue taking, they may also be – at least under some circumstances – the least dependent on source cues and the most likely to make use of more demanding central-process decision-making strategies.

In a study of public preferences on a California anti-nuclear energy initiative, Kuklinski, Metlay and Kay (1982) found that well-informed and poorly-informed respondents made similar use of cues from groups like labor unions, environmentalists, business leaders, utilities, and so on.[7] However, the preferences of the better informed were more strongly influenced by their assessments of the specific costs and benefits of nuclear energy and by their ideological orientations. Thus better informed citizens *responded to* elite cues like those with less information, but because they made use of a wider range of information, the better informed *depended less* on elite cues in forming their preferences.

Using a very different approach, Mondak (1994a) compared responses to three questions about the Reagan administration's defense build-up in the early 1980s. The "control" version stated that "The federal government has undertaken a major build-up of our military defense during the past several years." Respondents were then asked "Do you feel this military build-up has been necessary or unnecessary?" In the "cueing" condition, an identical question was asked except that in place of the federal government, the military build-up was attributed to "The Reagan administration." Finally, a "policy information" version of the question contained both the cue to the Reagan administration and the additional information that the defense build-up involved $2.4 trillion, "more money than has been spent in any comparable period since World War II."

The close and obvious connection between the defense policy of the "federal government" and that of the "Reagan administration" might lead us to expect the Reagan cue to have its largest impact on the least politically aware. This is indeed what Mondak found. The only group that responded differently to the cueing and control versions consisted of Reagan opponents who had low levels of education. For this group, replacing the reference to the "federal government" with the "Reagan administration" led about one-quarter of those who would otherwise be expected to support the defense build-up to oppose it instead.[8]

Mondak found cueing alone to have its largest impact among the least educated respondents. In contrast, policy information most strongly influenced the preferences of the best-educated respondents, at least among those who generally disapproved of Reagan's performance as president. Adding policy information to the question on the defense build-up reduced by half the number of well-educated Reagan opponents who supported the build-up, but among poorly educated Reagan opponents, the addition of policy information made virtually no difference.

Existing research suggests that there is no simple and universal relationship between political sophistication and the use of elite cues. When cue-taking depends on both attentiveness to information and responsiveness to that information (as in observational studies such as Zaller, 1992), cue taking appears to be most common among the most politically sophisticated. In experimental studies, however, in which cues are (or are not) provided to respondents, cue taking has been found to be equally important to more and less sophisticated respondents (Kuklinski, Metlay & Kay, 1982), or to be more important to the least sophisticated (Mondak, 1994a). These latter studies in particular suggest that differences in the use of elite source cues across education or political information may well depend on the complexity of the issue and the informational value of the cue. Simple cues, like the association between the incumbent president and federal policy, may have their largest impact on the least politically involved both because they are easy to understand and because they contain information (or remind cue takers of connections) that better informed citizens are already aware of.[9] In contrast, well-educated respondents' use of source cues on nuclear power may reflect both the complexity of the issue and the information contained in the cues. These two studies were consistent, however, in finding that policy-relevant information had the strongest influence on the policy preferences of those with the highest levels of education or political information.

Studies of individual differences in political cue taking have focused solely on political knowledge or engagement. This research has yet to offer a definitive account of the conditions under which citizens with different levels of political knowledge will be more or less likely to use elite source cues in forming preferences on political issues. But it does offer insight into the multiple factors that affect the relationship between political knowledge and cue taking. Among the important factors in this relationship are the partisan flow of cueing information (that is, whether elite cues exclusively favor one side of an issue or are politically divided), the accessibility of elite cues, the complexity of the issue, and the level of information contained in a given set of source cues.

FROM WHOM ARE CUES TAKEN?

By what criteria do citizens choose the elites from whom to take cues? Downs suggests two criteria: knowledge and "like-mindedness." As noted above, Downs indicates that the average citizen "will seek assistance from men who are experts in [their] fields, have the same political goals he does, and have good judgment" (1957, p. 223). Clearly, if a potential cue giver is thought to lack knowledge of the relevant issue or to have poor judgment in the relevant domain, citizens are unlikely to follow his or her advice. The role of shared political goals, however, is more complex.

Cue Taking from Like Minded and Non-like Minded Elites

Some students of elite cueing share Downs' view that cue takers respond to persuasive messages from those they deem like minded and disregard messages from those they believe to have differing goals, values, or interests with regard to the issue at hand. For example, Page and Shapiro write that "Ordinary citizens . . . can learn enough to form intelligent preferences simply by knowing whom to trust for a reliable conclusion. If the public lacks like-minded and trustworthy cue givers . . . collective deliberation breaks down" (1992, p. 365).

This conceptualization of "cue choosing" focuses on the characteristics of a message source that make the message persuasive to a given recipient. Typically, these characteristics are viewed as some form of perceived similarity of interests or values between the message source and the message receiver. Effective cue givers are often taken to be political elites that share the same ideological or partisan orientation as the member of the public. Thus, liberals will find a message from liberal leaders more persuasive than the same message coming from conservative leaders. Similarly, conservatives are more likely to follow the lead of conservative elites.

In Zaller's model, citizens with low levels of political awareness are fairly undiscriminating about who they will take cues from. But as political awareness grows, the tendency to dismiss cues from non-like-minded elites increases. Describing what he labels "partisan resistance" to elite cues, Zaller argues that "Democrats and Republicans tend to reject messages from the opposing party, and liberals and conservatives reject persuasive communications that are inconsistent with their ideologies" (1992, p. 267).

This conceptualization of elite cues is the least demanding on the public. All it requires is that citizens attend to the elite source of a potentially persuasive message and accept the message only if the source is deemed "like minded." But what happens if the source of the message is not "like minded"? This first conceptualization of cue taking suggests that in such cases the message is rejected and the receiver's policy preferences remain unchanged.

A second model of elite cueing suggests a slightly more complex process. From this perspective, elite messages can have not only persuasive effects, but dissuasive effects as well. A Republican identifier might respond to a message from Democratic elites not by rejecting the Democratic endorsement, but by adopting the opposite position. For example, the endorsement by Democratic leaders of a particular campaign finance reform bill might lead Democratic identifiers to increase their support for the bill, but might also lead Republican identifiers to decrease their support (or increase their opposition). In the first model, source cues serve as a perceptual screen, allowing some persuasive messages to "penetrate" and keeping others at bay. In the second model, message recipients are somewhat more sophisticated in their use of cueing information, adapting potentially persuasive messages to their own purposes on the basis of source cues.

Carmines and Kuklinski (1990) adopt this second version of elite cueing in their discussion of legislators as elite source cues. They suggest that citizens' policy preferences can be shaped by cues from both like-minded and non-like minded elites:

> In the simple (and perhaps common) case where trusted congressional members take one side of the policy debate and untrusted legislators the other, the institutionally generated

information is reinforcing and gives citizens a firm basis on which to form an opinion (p. 254).

Formal models of cue taking from sources with varying degrees of like mindedness are developed by Calvert (1985, 1986), McKelvey and Ordeshook (1985, 1986), and Grofman and Norrander (1990). Although differing in focus and intent, these models identify a range of theoretical conditions under which cue taking can effectively substitute for substantive knowledge about political candidates or issues.

In an empirical demonstration of this process, Lupia (1995) told random subsamples of respondents that Jesse Jackson either favored or opposed no-fault automobile insurance, while other random subsamples were told that Patrick Buchanan either favored or opposed such insurance. As this second model of elite cue taking would suggest, Lupia found that Democratic respondents who heard that Buchanan favored no-fault insurance were less likely to favor it themselves compared to those who heard that Buchanan opposed it. Buchanan's endorsement apparently provided "dissuasive" information to Democratic respondents. In Lupia's experiment, the same pattern held for Republican respondents, who took Jackson's endorsement as a reason to oppose no-fault insurance. Interestingly, in both cases the message from an elite member of the opposite party actually had a larger influence on respondents' policy preferences than the message from an elite member of the respondent's own party. That is, Democrats were more influenced by Buchanan's purported position on no-fault insurance than by Jackson's, while Republicans were more influenced by Jackson's position than by Buchanan's (Lupia, 1995, p. 14).

A similar dissuasive influence of elite cues was also found in Mondak's (1994a) study of attitudes toward the Reagan defense build-up discussed above. Consistent with Lupia's findings, Mondak found that the effect of the "Reagan administration" cue (in comparison to "the federal government") was greater for Reagan opponents than it was for Reagan supporters (Mondak 1994a, p. 177; see also Mondak, 1993).

Truthfulness and Cue Taking

Lupia and McCubbins (1998) discuss elite cues within the broader context of political persuasion. They argue that the necessary and sufficient conditions for persuasion are: (1) that a speaker is knowledgeable about the issue at hand, and (2) that the speaker can be trusted to truthfully reveal what he or she knows. The perception of trustworthiness, Lupia and McCubbins point out, can result either from perceived common interests between the speaker and the cue taker, or from external circumstances such as penalties for lying. Based on their analysis of the conditions of persuasion, Lupia and McCubbins argue that like-mindedness is not a necessary condition for persuasion. Indeed, they view it as irrelevant to persuasion except inasmuch as it sheds light on a speaker's knowledge or trustworthiness (1998, p. 64).

For decision-making based on raw information, we might well be indifferent to the values or interests of a potential information source; whether like minded or non-like-minded in their political orientations, they are equally useful as long as they are knowledgeable and can be trusted to reveal what they know. As Lupia and McCubbins put it "You do not necessarily learn more from people who are like you, nor do you necessarily learn more from people you like" (1998, p. 63).

But what about decision-making based on elite source cues rather than substantive information? In this case, the information needed is precisely the cue giver's political orientations and his or her policy endorsement. A Republican citizen, for example, might encounter opposing endorsements on a given policy from Democratic and Republican elites. The citizen might well believe both elite sources to be equally knowledgeable about the issue and both to have equally compelling incentives to speak truthfully. But the cue-taking citizen would respond very differently to the advice (or endorsement) of the two different sources.[10]

Faith in the truth of elites' messages is as important in cue taking as it is in information-based decision-making. But the relevant messages for cue takers are the predispositions (i.e. the values and interests) of a cue giver and his or her policy endorsement. It is unusual for cue givers to purposefully misrepresent their true policy preferences, but perhaps not so unusual for cue givers to misrepresent their true values and interests. For example, many elites who endorse income tax cuts claim to have the interests of the middle class at heart. While this is likely true for some of these potential cue givers, others who endorse tax cuts may do so out of concern not for the middle class but for the wealthy. By misrepresenting their underlying political orientation, such duplicitous elites try to entice cue takers to adopt their policy preferences out of the mistaken belief that they share a set of political values.[11]

For effective cue taking to occur, a cue taker need not share the same political values and interests as a potential cue giver. But the cue taker does need true information about the cue giver's values and interests, as well as knowledge of the cue giver's policy preferences.

Cue Taking Decision Rules

Like other heuristics, elite cues can greatly simplify political preference formation. But the extent of this simplification varies depending on the cue-taking decision rules an individual cue taker employs. The simplest form of elite cue taking consists of an unreflective acceptance of whatever elite communication one happens to encounter. Zaller attributes this style of cue taking to citizens with the lowest level of political awareness. Most citizens, however, appear to discriminate at least to some degree among potential elite cueing sources. At the extreme, we would expect few Americans to adopt the policy endorsements of Saddam Hussein or the American Communist Party.[12] How, then, do citizens decide from whom to take cues?

As discussed above, one consideration is whether the potential cue giver is like-minded or non-like-minded, with the most general and oft-noted criteria for judging like-mindedness being partisanship and ideology. One reason that the relationship between cue taker and cue giver in partisan or ideological orientation serves as a useful criterion is because it is relatively easy to assess. That is to say, information identifying elites' partisan affiliation and (to a lesser degree) ideological orientation is comparatively easy to come by. Political actors appearing in the media are almost invariably identified by a partisan label, and many potential cue-giving groups are classified by reporters as "liberal" or "conservative."

Cueing sources identified by their partisan and ideological orientations are also useful because they provide guidance across a multiplicity of issues. Simply by attending to the cues of Democratic or Republican leaders, a citizen can form opinions on the wide range of "party cleavage" issues – that is, those issues on which the two major parties take opposing stances (Page, 1978).

But partisan and ideologically-based cueing has its limitations. For one thing, issues sometimes arise that cross cut traditional cleavages. The North American Free Trade Agreement (NAFTA), for example, was a contentious issue that had both supporters and opponents among leaders of both political parties. Moreover, the fit between the political orientations of any given cue taker and such broad groups as Democrats or Republicans, liberals or conservatives, is bound to be imperfect. This suggests a second and somewhat more complex decision rule for cue taking. For some citizens, the decision of who to take cues from may depend on the specific issue at hand. For example, some individuals may find that they share the Democrats' orientations on social issues and the Republicans' values on fiscal issues. In this case, effective cue taking would require a more complex calculus that divides up the world of elite cueing sources by issue type.

Following this same logic, a third model of elite cueing suggests not a few broad cue givers, but a multiplicity of elite cueing sources each identified with specific issues. For example, Lupia (1994) showed that the insurance industry served as a (negative) cue giver on the topic of automobile insurance reform in California. But we would not expect the public to turn toward the insurance industry for cues on welfare, or foreign policy, or racial set-asides. A host of other groups likely serve as cue givers within particular policy domains: the Sierra Club on the environment, the AARP for retirement issues, unions and business groups on labor and trade policy, and so on.

By turning to alternative sources for cues in specific policy areas, citizens can better match their political values and interests with those of the cue givers they rely on. But such specialization in cue taking comes at a cost. Although certainly easier than evaluating the substance of every new issue, the amount of information needed to identify the appropriate cue givers for any given issue domain, and then to ascertain their position on new issues, is considerable. Consequently, we would expect the habitual use of multiple cue givers to be more common among more politically engaged citizens.

A final complication in the process of matching a cueing source with a set of issues is that a cue-takers' use of a particular cue may depend not only on the connection between the source and the issue, but on the three-way fit between the source, the issue, and the source's endorsement of a specific policy. One example of this three-way process is the "Nixon-to-China" phenomenon (Cukierman & Tommasi, 1998). Because President Nixon was widely viewed as a fervent anti-communist, his endorsement of normalizing relations with communist China was highly effective. Many citizens no doubt felt that their own orientations were less anti-communist than Nixon's. Consequently, they would not have been swayed by an *anti*-communist cue from the President. But for that same reason, Nixon's endorsement of normalization served as a strong signal that conditions in fact warranted a softer stand toward China. Thus, who a decision-maker takes cues from may depend not only on the issue under consideration but on the relationship between the potential cue giver's endorsement and his or her perceived political orientations.

Thus far we have discussed cue taking as if the decision-maker's objective were to identify *the* cue-giver appropriate to a particular issue. In fact, citizens may often draw upon more than one cue giver in forming an opinion on a particular policy choice. In some cases multiple cue givers may be consistent and reinforcing in their endorsements, either because all like-minded cue givers express the same opinion, or because like-minded and non-like-minded cue givers express opposite opinions. In other cases, elite cues from broadly like-minded cue givers may be contradictory. If so, cue takers can either: (1) weigh the various cues and arrive at some intermediate opinion, (2) seek further information about the political values and interests of the cue givers which might explain the discrepancies in their endorsements, or (3) throw up their hands and fail to form any clear opinion on the issue.

Finally, we note that decision rules for identifying cue givers vary not only in the number of cue givers any individual turns toward on a single issue or across many different issues, but also the kind of criteria by which cue givers are selected. Kuklinski and Hurley (1994), for example, contrast race and ideology as characteristics of potential cue givers that might be used by a cue taker to judge similarity of political values or orientation. In responding to policy cues on a racial issue from Jesse Jackson, Clarence Thomas, Ted Kennedy, and George Bush, Kuklinski and Hurley found that black subjects relied more on the race than the ideological orientation of the cue giver (responding more positively to cues from Jackson and Thomas than from Kennedy or Bush).

The decision process for choosing cue givers is itself a potentially demanding exercise. Consequently, it is not surprising that a second level of heuristic reasoning is often used. That is, rather than assessing the appropriateness of (say) a specific Democratic member of Congress to serve as a cue giver, a citizen might use the heuristic decision rule that Democrats in Congress generally share (or don't share) his or her political values. Similarly, characteristics such as race and sex can serve as fairly crude (but perhaps reasonably effective) *cues* about a potential cue-giver's political orientations.

HOW EFFECTIVE IS CUE-BASED POLITICAL DECISION-MAKING?

Some see informational shortcuts like elite cues as an escape from the democratic dilemma of mass decision-making power combined with mass ignorance. Using decision-making heuristics, individuals who have little incentive to educate themselves about an array of complicated issues can nevertheless contribute meaningfully to democratic governance (Sniderman, Brody & Tetlock, 1991; Page & Shapiro, 1992; Popkin, 1991). But others fear that citizens who use such shortcuts are likely to end up at very different destinations than they would if fully knowledgeable about issues (Kuklinski & Quirk, 1998; Bartels, 1996; Althaus, 1998; Delli Carpini & Keeter, 1996).

Effective cue-based decision-making requires first that citizens are able to distinguish between potential cue givers who share their political orientations and those who do not, and second that citizens are able to identify cue givers' policy endorsements. The research reviewed above provides some evidence on each of these points, but a firm conclusion is premature.

Discerning Cue Givers' Political Predispositions
Studies described above show that members of the public do indeed distinguish between like-minded and non-like-minded cue givers (Lupia, 1994, 1995; Kuklinski & Hurley, 1994; Kuklinski, Metlay & Kay, 1982). Further, while these distinctions are more common among citizens who are more politically

knowledgeable (Zaller, 1992), even poorly informed Americans distinguish among cue givers under the right circumstances (Mondak, 1994a; Kuklinski, Metlay & Kay, 1982). Finally, citizens at all levels of political engagement sometimes reject not specific cue givers but specific cues on particular issues, as in the Monica Lewinsky and Zoe Baird examples discussed above.

It is clear that the American public is attentive to the different political orientations of alternative cue givers, although the degree of this attentiveness appears to vary considerably both among individuals and across cueing sources. Further, even the endorsements of "trusted" cue givers will sometimes be rejected if they are obviously at variance with the public's evaluation of the issue at hand. Further research is needed to clarify the extent and circumstances under which citizens succeed in matching their political predispositions to the elites from whom they take political cues.

Identifying Cue Givers' Endorsements
Even if citizens do distinguish sufficiently between like-minded and non-like-minded cue givers, they must also correctly identify the policies that those cue givers endorse. Kuklinski, Metlay and Kay (1982, p. 628) found that the most well informed 20% of their sample was almost perfect in identifying the policy endorsements of six elite groups relevant to the nuclear energy initiative they studied. The bottom 80% of their respondents did not perform as well in this regard, but even so were able to correctly identify the endorsements of these groups about three-quarters of the time. Lupia's (1994, p. 73) insurance initiative voters did not do as well. Averaging across the five insurance reform measures, voters were correct in identifying the insurance industry's position only 57% of the time (a slim improvement over random guessing).

How does the public fare in the perhaps more common task of identifying the policy positions of prominent political figures or of the Democratic and Republican parties? A direct answer to this question is elusive because the views of specific elites cannot easily be mapped onto a survey question (Conover & Feldman, 1989; Krosnick, 1990, p. 1978). It is not obvious, for example, what the "true" position of the Democratic party is on the standard NES 7-point scale for government services and spending.

A less demanding criterion of "correct perception" is available, however. At a minimum, effective cueing requires the ability to place different political figures or parties relative to each other on a given issue dimension. Even if the exact position of the Democratic party on government services is unclear, for example, it *is* clear that the Democrats are more supportive of government services and spending than are the Republicans.

Using this less demanding "relative placement" approach, Krosnick (1990) examined Americans' perceptions of the two 1984 presidential candidates' positions on: (1) whether government should provide more services and increase spending or fewer services and decrease spending, (2) whether government should see that everyone has a job and a good standard of living or just let each person get ahead on their own, and (3) whether government should become more or less involved in Central America. He found that between 18% and 31% of respondents failed to identify Reagan as more conservative than Mondale on these three issues (1990, p. 168). However, if we include in the calculations respondents who said they didn't know where to place one or the other candidate, the percentage failing to identifying Reagan as more conservative increases to between 31% and 42% (American National Election Study, 1984).

As a general rule, political parties are more enduring source cues than individuals, a feature that might facilitate perceptions of issue stances. On the other hand, parties are more heterogeneous and therefore more difficult to associate with a particular policy position. As these countervailing factors suggest, Americans in 1984 were about equally able (or unable) to identify the relative positions of the Democratic and Republican parties as they were the two presidential candidates: between 32% and 47% failed to identiy the Republican Party as the more conservative on these three issues (with respondents saying "Don't Know" for one or the other party included in the analysis; American National Election Study, 1984). In interpreting these results, it is worth considering that some respondents arrived at the correct placement of the two candidates or parties by guessing, and that respondents who declined to place themselves on these scales were not even asked to place the candidates or parties.

In sum, it appears that substantial proportions of the public are unable to identify the relative positions of the most visible political cue givers on some very central issues. Despite this unimpressive performance, cue taking from parties and candidates might be a very important part of preference formation for that segment of the public that is able to identify the policy positions of political elites. Further, existence of "issue publics" among the citizenry suggests that even those who are unable to identify the policy positions of potential cue givers on most issues may be able to do so for the few issues about which they care most (Converse, 1964; Iyengar, 1990; Krosnick, 1990).

Global Evaluations of Heuristic Decision-Making

The effectiveness of elite cueing has been addressed from another angle as well. If the public is successful in using elite cues *and other informational shortcuts* then we should find that the political judgments of poorly informed citizens resemble those of the well informed who share their political orientations.

In evaluating the overall effectiveness of political heuristics, we need to distinguish between two criteria of success. Heuristics can be judged both by their efficacy for individuals and by their effectiveness for a collectivity (Page & Shapiro, 1992). If shortcuts lead some citizens to support a policy which, if they spent the time to study it, they would oppose, then heuristic reasoning has failed those citizens. But if relying on shortcuts leads some "true opponents" to support a policy and also leads an equal number of "true supporters" to oppose that policy, then aggregate opinion on that issue would not differ from what would be found if everyone based their position on a thorough substantive investigation.

We focus here on the effectiveness of heuristics for collective (i.e. aggregate) opinion formation, both because we have more evidence on this score and because it is of greater importance for democratic governance. Despite the limited power of individual citizens, the public as a whole does appear to have substantial influence over government policy (Monroe, 1979; Monroe & Gardner, 1987; Page & Shapiro, 1983; Stimson, MacKuen & Erikson, 1995). If heuristics lead to aggregate preferences that are strongly at variance with what an informed public would desire, then democracy is at risk.

A growing literature attempts to make global evaluations of the effectiveness of the public's political decision-making processes, asking how closely citizens come to the choices they would make if fully informed about the issues or vote choices at hand. The most straightforward way to address this question is to inform a representative sample of the public about a set of issues and see whether their preferences change as a result. If citizens are already using heuristics effectively, their issue positions should not change much as a result of the new information.

James Fishkin has done just this in a series of "deliberative polls" conducted both in the United States and abroad. For example, the National Issues Convention (NIC), conducted in January of 1996, brought 466 participants, selected at random from the U.S. population, to Austin, Texas (Fishkin & Luskin, 1999; Luskin & Fishkin, 1998). Participants spent four days reading briefing materials on various economic, foreign policy, and family issues, discussing those issues in small groups, and participating in question-and-answer sessions with experts. When initially contacted, and once again at the end of their stay in Austin, NIC participants answered identical questions concerning their policy preferences in these three issue areas. To provide a comparison group, members of the initial sample who elected not to come to Austin completed the same surveys. Like the Austin participants, the control group answered identical questions twice (when initially contacted and once again when the Austin group completed their second questionnaire).

On many of the issues examined, substantial numbers of participants changed their preferences during the course of the study. For example, when initially surveyed, 44% of participants expressed support for a flat tax but after four days of deliberation, only 30% still thought the flat tax was a good idea (Fishkin & Luskin, 1999, p. 25). On other items, however, changes were minimal. Further, if non-participants' attitudes changed as much as participants' then we should attribute those changes to random fluctuations in response tendencies or to the experience of being interviewed twice rather than to the influence of information or deliberation on the substance of the issues.

Rescaling the 48 policy questions to the same 0-to-1 scale reveals that the aggregate preferences of NIC participants did change more than non-participants, but not by much. Across all 48 items, the absolute change in aggregate score for participants averaged 0.05 units, while the aggregate change for non-participants averaged 0.03 units.[13]

Although it appears that the average aggregate change in response to the education and deliberation of the National Issues Convention was small, a firm conclusion about the efficacy of existing heuristics in allowing citizens to identify the positions they would take if better informed is elusive. Perhaps some *other* information than that provided would have led the participants to change their minds. Or, to put the matter another way, perhaps not all of the 48 policy questions were sufficiently relevant to the information provided. In this case, we would not expect to see changes on all of the policy questions examined, and the changes that did take place would be diluted by the stability of responses to the less relevant items.

Another approach to the global evaluation of heuristic decision-making statistically simulates "fully informed preferences" by comparing the preferences of the highly informed to those of less informed respondents with the same demographic characteristics (Delli Carpini & Keeter, 1996; Bartels, 1996; Althaus, 1998; see Gilens, 2001 for an experimentally-based alternative to this approach). For example, examining presidential vote choice for 1972 through 1992, Bartels (1996) found that the aggregate vote share for Democratic candidates would have been about two percentage points lower if the entire electorate was as well informed as his best informed respondents. Incumbent presidents running for re-election appear to be even more advantaged by the public's lack of information; Bartels estimated that the vote share for incumbent presidents would have been almost five percentage points lower in a fully informed electorate.

Althaus (1998) used a similar approach to model policy preferences. He found that the aggregate issue preferences of a fully informed citizenry would be more dovish on foreign policy, more willing to pay for government services, less willing to pay for defense, more supportive of the free market, slightly more progressive on most social issues, and slightly less progressive on some racial issues. Across the 45 policy preference questions he examines, Althaus found an average difference of about seven percentage points between actual and hypothetical fully informed opinion.[14]

How Successful is Heuristic-Based Decision-Making?

The research discussed above allows us to begin to evaluate the public's success in compensating for its lack of political information. But we must be clear about what any such evaluation can and cannot reveal. First, the studies by Fishkin, Bartels, and Althaus are silent about what heuristic decision-making processes (if any) the public employs. These studies simply ask how better informed preferences might differ from those currently expressed. Small differences could reflect the extensive use of shortcuts by the American public, but we have no way of judging what those specific shortcuts are.

A second consideration in assessing the findings reported above is that they reflect not the *potential* of heuristics to substitute for in-depth information, but only the extent to which the public does *in fact* make effective use of heuristics. Large differences between "actual" and "informed" opinions could reflect either the failure of heuristics or their lack of use by the public. Either is important, to be sure, but they lead to very different conclusions about the efficacy of informational shortcuts and the implications for democratic governance. Lupia's (1994) study of insurance reform provides a case in point. Although knowledge of the insurance industry's policy endorsements was spotty at best, those poorly informed voters who *did* correctly perceive these cues were able to emulate the voting behavior of voters with substantive knowledge of the competing insurance initiatives.

Furthermore, as we discuss below, either the failure of heuristics to lead decision-makers to the "right" conclusions or the lack of use of heuristics by the public could result from one (or both) of two conditions. First, an indifference to political issues or lack of effort among the public could explain citizens' failures to make use of available cues. On the other hand, a lack of available cues from appropriate elites could also explain both the failure to use cueing information and the poor outcome that would result if citizens substituted more easily available but less appropriate cueing sources. In short, ineffective citizen decision-making suggests shortcomings in the use of political heuristics, but does not reveal the extent to which those short-comings should be attributed to decision-makers or to the decision-making environment.

With these limitations in mind, we can draw some tentative conclusions about the effectiveness of compensatory strategies of political decision-making. In broad terms, the National Issues Convention (Fishkin & Luskin, 1999; Luskin & Fishkin, 1998) demonstrated only modest changes in participants' policy preferences. Bartels' analysis of presidential vote choice found a very modest difference in party preference (of about two percentage points) and a more substantial (five percentage point) advantage for incumbent presidents due to the failures of heuristic decision processes. But as Althaus (1998:552) points out, none of the outcomes of the six elections that Bartels examined would have changed had the electorate voted in accord with Bartels' "fully informed" predictions. Finally, Althaus' (1998) analysis of policy preferences reveals the largest discrepancies between observed and "fully informed" opinions. On nine of the 45 policy questions Althaus looked at, the public's predicted fully informed preference order (i.e. favor, oppose, or evenly-split) differed from the public's existing preference order.

Finally, any assessment of the efficacy of elite cues must acknowledge the unavoidable necessity of cue taking in a democratic system that involves innumerable and often complex issues. If, for example, we find that cue takers express preferences on the Comprehensive Nuclear Test Ban Treaty that differ from their hypothetically fully informed preferences, what conclusions should we draw? We might investigate the cue-taking process in an effort to identify how the public was led astray. But we would surely not suggest that citizens must read the treaty themselves. Such demands on the public are unrealistic. Even people who devote their lives to politics cannot become experts in all matters. In a complex political system with a seemingly boundless array of issues, both the most and the least engaged must rely on cues for at least some issues.

THE CUE-GIVING ENVIRONMENT AND DEMOCRATIC GOVERNANCE

Skeptics claim that ordinary citizens are ill suited to the demands of democracy. These critics frame the democratic dilemma – public ignorance combined with public decision-making power – as the responsibility and burden of the ordinary individual, implicitly asking "What kind of citizens do we need to make democracy work?" The bulk of this paper is an exploration of one aspect of this question – the use of elite cues by ordinary Americans to compensate for limited substantive information. But effective cueing requires both cue takers and cue givers, and so in this final section we turn our attention to the latter, asking, in essence, "What kind of cueing environment do we need to make democracy work?" In doing so, we follow Lupia's (1994, p. 72) suggestion that instead of chancy and high-cost endeavors to broadly educate the public,

> a deeper understanding of how people adapt to the uncertainty that characterizes many of their important decisions suggests that directing our efforts into the provision of credible and widely accessible "signals" may be a more effective and cost-effective way to ensure the responsiveness of electoral outcomes to the electorate's preferences.

In this spirit, we highlight the major attributes of and barriers to an effective cueing environment.

Basic Attributes of an Effective Cueing Environment

Page and Shapiro (1992, p. 356) suggest that "authentic" or "enlightened" public opinion can emerge when "the public receives useful interpretations, and correct and helpful information – information and interpretations that help it move toward the policy choices it would make if it were fully and completely informed . . ." The obstacles to this state of affairs, Page and Shapiro go on to say, are a lack of trustworthy cue givers or an information flow that is distorted or monolithic (see also Bartels, 1998, Shapiro, 1998, and Zaller, 1992 for further discussion of "enlightened" public opinion). The ideal environment, then, should provide cues that are credible, comprehensive in terms of both breadth across the political spectrum and depth within issues, and balanced in the frequency of presentation in the mass media.

Credible Cue Sources

Decision-makers will take cues only from certain sources. As delineated above, decision-makers must believe that cue givers are knowledgeable and truthful. Since effective cueing hinges on the matching of predispositions (i.e. values and interests), cue givers must be credible in the sense of being trusted to reveal their true political predispositions and policy preferences. The term "credible" does not imply that the cue giver is like-minded, virtuous, knowledgeable, or trustworthy in any universal sense. Rather, a credible cue giver is one that a cue taker perceives to be knowledgeable about the issue at hand and honest in revealing his or her predispositions and policy preferences.

There are thousands of potential cue givers, and determining whether each one is knowledgeable and truthful carries impossibly high informational costs – costs so high that cue taking would no longer be a shortcut. Therefore, decision-makers are more likely to take as credible those cue givers who are identifiable either as individuals or organizations. Identifiability facilitates the assessment of credibility by providing a reputation for honesty and expertise (or their lack) based on past experience.

Comprehensive Range of Cues
The "range of cues" spans two dimensions. One dimension is the breadth of cues across the political spectrum, the other dimension is the depth of specialization for each issue. For example, a narrow breadth of cues might include only messages from leaders of the two political parties. By contrast, a wide breadth of cues would provide messages from leaders across the political spectrum, including socialists, communists, libertarians, anarchists, and so on.

Yet the range of available cues could span the political spectrum while still having a shallow depth of specialization. For example, a proposal for greater expenditure on prison construction could have cues from a broad range of political interests, from retribution-seeking conservatives to rehabilitation-minded liberals. But without cues from issue-specialists, the cue environment is still shallow. Issue-specific depth might include cues from private prison corporations, members of the Prison Moratorium Project, union leaders representing prison guards, and University of Pennsylvania criminologist John DiIulio. Note that depth of specialization includes not only academic or expert specialists, but also citizens and activist organizations that mobilize around a particular interest.

We expect that a broader and deeper range of cues would disproportionately help the most politically engaged. First, the politically engaged are more likely to actually receive a fuller range of specialized political ideas, as they generally devote more time to pursuing political information. Second, the politically engaged are generally more adept at identifying the political values of the cue giver and are therefore more likely to accept the message best matched to their own values. The key benefit is precision – with more specialized cues across a broader political spectrum, the politically engaged are more equipped to find the cue giver that most accurately approximates their own interests and values.

Balance of Voices
Balance refers to the frequency distribution of cues across the political spectrum available in the mainstream media. While a comprehensive range of cues is likely to help the most politically engaged, we suspect that a balance of cues is likely to help the least politically engaged. For example, if the mass media contain predominantly centrist cues from public officials, and cues from alternative and minority voices are infrequently heard, only the most engaged will receive these alternative cues; the least engaged will miss them entirely. Imbalance renders some cues less visible, and this lower visibility means that some decision-makers, particularly the least engaged, will miss the cue that best fits their predispositions.

A broad representation of cue givers in the media would facilitate involved citizens' cue-based preference formation. But if the media were to give equal representation to all potential cue givers including "fringe voices" whom few citizens would turn to for policy guidance, many would find it harder, not easier, to identify the appropriate cue givers and discern their policy endorsements. Either of these extremes would ill serve both cue giving and democratic decision-making more generally.

A Limited Assessment of the Current Cueing Environment

In closing, we briefly touch on some major forces and potential problems in the current cue environment, considering both the factors shaping cue "production" and the dissemination of cues by the mass media.[15]

Cue Production

Are cues from politicians and government officials credible, comprehensive, and balanced? Competition among elected officials ensures some variation in political perspective and provides politicians with strong incentives to give accurate information. As Carmines and Kuklinski (1990, p. 266) write:

> By its very nature, the competitive legislative process ensures alternative voices and signals from which citizens can choose. Moreover, most congressional members intend to remain in the "market," which greatly reduces – although, unfortunately, does not eliminate – the likelihood of their betraying or pulling the wool over the public's eye. Facing re-election and internal competition supposedly collars the potentially recalcitrant and/or deceitful legislator.

Furthermore, electoral incentives encourage reputation building through ongoing policy leadership and entrepreneurship. A handful of legislators – mostly Senators and some House members – develop reputations, become easily identifiable for particular value and policy stances, and establish known track records of reliability. For example, Claude Pepper, the long serving U.S. Representative from Florida, was widely recognized as an advocate for the elderly.

Party structure can also facilitate trusted cue giving. In a system of single-member plurality districts, candidates have an incentive to coordinate policy positions with the party. Coordination helps to create a reliable party "brand name." Furthermore, party leaders can establish penalties for lying (Cox & McCubbins, 1994). These factors can make party a precise and trustworthy cue, so that when individuals hear a Democratic senator's policy preference, even if they do not recognize that particular Democrat, the label conveys a specific history of ideology and reliability (analyses of congressional voting suggest that the two major parties have become more homogeneous, and therefore more useful as cueing sources, since the late 1970s; Poole & Rosenthal, 1997, 1999).

The structural incentives we have highlighted may be credibility promoting, but they may also be scope truncating. In some ways, the demands of credibility and identifiability tradeoff with the benefits of a broad range of cues. For example, a reliable party "brand name" may promote precise and trusted cue giving, but only at the expense of diversity within parties. Moreover, the demands of electoral competition in a two-party system work to push the parties toward the middle of the political spectrum (Page, 1996; Downs, 1957). While this moderating effect of party competition appears to have diminished in recent decades (Jacobs & Shapiro, 2000; Poole & Rosenthal, 1999), the political spectrum in the United States remains quite narrow in comparison to the multi-party European democracies.

The tensions between credibility and scope extend beyond elected officials and party politics to the broader universe of cues. When the requirements of credibility trump scope, the implication is that obscure groups will be ignored, mostly because they have no history of reliability and trustworthiness (Lupia & McCubbins, 1998, p. 207). Like the logic of accepting cues based on political party, "obscure" individuals probably have a better chance of becoming accessible cue givers if they are affiliated with credible institutions such as prestigious universities, well-known research institutes, or a handful of other long-standing, well-funded organizations. Consistent with this observation, Page, Shapiro and Dempsey (1987) found that media reports of experts' opinions have substantial influence over public preferences on a range of policy issues. This responsiveness of the public to experts' opinions underscores the importance of media "gate keeping" and interest group resources in determining who is an "expert" and which experts' views are heard by the public.

Cue Dissemination
Information about political issues rarely comes directly from political actors; rather, news media and professional communicators select, filter, and frame the information dispersed to the mass public.

In evaluating the cueing environment, perhaps the most consequential media norm is reliance on official government sources (e.g. Hallin, 1986, Bennett, 1990, Mermin, 1999, Page, 1996). Reliance on official sources stems from both professional norms of credibility and newsworthiness, and from the normal routines of news gathering. Public officials meet journalistic standards of source legitimacy, and officials' power to shape events makes their opinions more newsworthy (Bennett, 1990; Zaller & Chiu, 2000). Furthermore, the routine of "beat" reporting means that journalists establish ongoing relationships with their sources (Gans, 1979).

Reliance on official sources has a mixed impact on the cueing environment. On the one hand, it may be relatively easy for an individual to identify an official's political ideology and history of reliability; an "authoritative" source by journalistic standards is probably an identifiable source for cue takers. If the speaker is well known or affiliated with a prominent institution, then a potential cue taker may be more capable of recognizing whether the speaker is trustworthy and knowledgeable.

On the other hand, when journalists rely on a limited number of similar kinds of official sources, they transmit this imbalance to the public. Reliance on official sources not only creates cue imbalance, but it also truncates the range of cues through a process referred to as "indexing." As Bennett (1990, p. 106) argues, the mainstream media " 'index' the range of voices and viewpoints in both news and editorials according to the range of views expressed in mainstream government debate about a given topic." Indexing allows official sources to determine the parameters of debate as presented in the mass media, limiting the range of available cues and favoring the institutionally mainstream, the powerful, and the organized.

Trends in media corporate ownership also limit the range and balance of cues and information dispersed through the mass media. Media concentration and the rise of large media conglomerates raise concerns that ownership shapes coverage in the interests of American business in general (Herman & Chomsky, 1988) and corporate media owners in particular (Alger, 1998; Bagdikian, 1992; Pratte & Whiting, 1986; Snider & Page, 1997; Gilens & Hertzman, 2000). As Page and Shapiro (1992) emphasize, the quality of public decision-making reflects the quality of the information available to the public. Media biases that limit the available cueing messages (just like media biases that limit substantive policy information) undermine the public's ability to participate in democratic decision-making.

CONCLUSIONS

Normative theories of democracy often make demands on citizens that far surpass what the American public seems able to fulfill. As Berelson, Lazarsfeld, and McPhee wrote in their landmark study *Voting*:

> The Democratic citizen is expected to be well informed about political affairs. He is supposed to know what the issues are, what their history is, what the relevant facts are, what alternatives are proposed, what the party stands for, what the likely consequences are (1954, p. 308).

Based on this lofty standard, the American public falls far short. But decision-making heuristics seem to offer a less demanding alternative by which citizens can form meaningful policy preferences. If elite cues and other decision shortcuts lead citizens to the same aggregate preferences that they would form if they had the time, interest, and expertise to reason through the substance of each issue, then the public can fulfill its democratic role while remaining largely ignorant of the substantive complexity of government policy.

In the preceding pages we sought to clarify the process of elite cueing and summarize the existing literature. Citizens' use of elite cues in political decision-making is well established. Moreover, we argued, cue taking can sometimes constitute a fairly nuanced and sophisticated process in which decision-makers take into account not only the like-mindedness of a cueing source, but the relationship between their own predispositions, the predispositions of the cueing source, and the substantive content of the cue on a particular issue (e.g. Nixon's overture to communist China).

Yet while elite cues *can* provide an efficient shortcut to political decision-making, the extent to which they are used and their effectiveness as a substitute for substantive knowledge remain unclear. The inability of large numbers of Americans to identify the positions of the major parties and presidential candidates on basic policy issues does not bode well. Even more significantly, "ignorance-induced" aggregate biases in public preferences appear to exist in a number of issue domains as well as in presidential voting.

An overall assessment of the American public's democratic decision-making depends on the benchmark we choose to apply. Elite cues and other heuristics clearly facilitate citizen participation. Without such shortcuts, meaningful democratic participation would be impossible in a society as large and complex as our own. It is equally clear, however, that citizens' political decision-making falls short of traditional democratic norms, with negative consequences for both individual preference formation and aggregate opinion as well. Yet we do muddle through, with the public – for better or for worse – playing a significant role in shaping government policy.

Elite cues are important, but imperfect, elements of democratic participation. Future research on heuristic decision-making will need to address both citizens' propensities to use elite cues and the availability of such cues in the political environment in order to further illuminate the strengths and weaknesses of the American public's political decision-making.

NOTES

1. When Downs wrote this selection in 1957 it was standard practice to use language which assumes that cue seekers and cue givers are exclusively male. We of course reject this assumption.

2. For a discussion of the role of personal networks in political decision-making, see Huckfeldt and Sprague (1991, 1995).

3. As Converse (1964) suggested, citizens can be divided into "issue publics" based on their apparent concern or involvement with specific topics. Iyengar (1990), for example, reports that, net of general levels of political attentiveness, Jews are more knowledgeable

about the Middle East and blacks are more knowledgeable about civil rights. Furthermore, as Iyengar also shows, those who already possess relatively high knowledge about a particular issue are more likely to gain knowledge about that issue when exposed to new information in the news. See also Krosnick (1990) for a discussion of issue publics.

4. We do not explore the processes that account for differences across individuals in issue involvement. *Ceteris paribus,* we would expect individuals who perceive themselves to have a larger stake in an issue to be more psychologically and cognitively involved in that issue. Given the infrequency with which material self-interest is strongly connected with issue preference (Citrin & Green, 1990; Sears & Funk, 1990, 1991), perceived "stakes" in an issue may be symbolic as often as material (e.g. the higher involvement of American Jews with Middle-Eastern politics; Iyengar, 1990).

5. It should be noted that van Knippenberg and Daamen's objective in this research was not to assess citizen decision-making in a "real-world" context, but to evaluate the potential contribution of an "artificially" informed representative sample of the public. This project closely parallels James Fishkin's "deliberative polls" discussed below (e.g. Fishkin, 1995; Fishkin & Luskin, 1999; Luskin & Fishkin, 1998).

6. Meta-analysis confirms McGuire's hypothesis that self-esteem is curvilinearly related to persuasibility (Rhodes & Wood, 1992).

7. Kuklinski, Metlay and Kay (1982) find a slightly but non-significantly larger impact of elite cues on the policy preferences of the less knowledgeable; they find nearly identical impacts of elite cues on the cost-benefit analyses of the two information groups (Table 5, p. 631).

8. Among respondents with the lowest education who disapproved of Reagan's performance, about 22% fewer expressed support for the defense build-up in the cueing condition than the baseline condition; among the most highly educated respondents, the difference between the cueing and control conditions was negligible. See Mondak (1994a), Fig. 1.

9. Zaller's research suggests that citizens with the lowest levels of political awareness should be the least likely to distinguish between cues from "like-minded" and "non-like-minded" elites. This may well be true, but Mondak's (1994a) study shows that under the right circumstances, even low-education respondents make use of elite cues by discriminating between cue givers who share their political orientations and those who don't. The circumstances that allowed Mondak's low-education respondents who disapproved of Reagan's performance to use the association of the Reagan administration with the defense build-up as a dissuasive cue were, first, that Mondak used an experimental design in which exposure to the elite cue was equalized across educational levels and, second, that the cue in question (i.e. the incumbent president) was familiar to even the least politically attentive respondents.

10. Contrast this account with Lupia and McCubbins' explanation of a decision-maker's proper response to communication from a non-like-minded source:

> Explanations of persuasion based on *ideology, affect,* and *partisanship* suffer the same fate as reputation. None of these factors is necessary or sufficient for persuasion in our model. To see why, consider the following example. You might really *like* Mr. A or know him to be a conservative like yourself but believe that he knows nothing whatsoever about policy B. In this case, you should not follow Mr. A's advice. Alternatively, you might believe Mr. A to be a knowledgeable, non-conservative, and unlikable person who nevertheless faces a strong incentive to reveal what he knows. In this case, you should follow his advice (1988, p. 63, italics in original).

Lupia and McCubbins' recommendation makes sense if what Mr. A reveals is raw information relevant to policy B. But if "following Mr. A's advice" means adopting his position on policy B, then clearly a cue-taker's judgments of ideological or partisan like-mindedness are critical in knowing whether to follow Mr. A's advice, ignore it, or adopt the opposite position on policy B to that endorsed by Mr. A.

11. Cue givers might also misrepresent their true preferences on a given policy in order to mislead cue takers about their true values or interests. For example, a strategic politician might publicly oppose an upper-class tax cut that she truly favors in order to credibly maintain the perception that she shares the interests of the middle class. In this case, she is using dishonesty about her preferences on one policy choice in order to shape the public's perceptions of her political orientations which in turn will enhance her ability to successfully cue the public on a related policy choice (say, a tax cut that appears more friendly to the middle class).

12. This is true unless they paid so little attention that they didn't recognize the source of the endorsements they encountered.

13. These figures are calculated from Luskin and Fishkin (1998), Table 3, columns 5 and 6.

14. Delli Carpini and Keeter (1996, pp. 241–251) use a similar approach to that of Bartels (1996) and Althaus (1998). However, because Delli Carpini and Keeter compare the predicted policy preferences of their best informed and worst informed respondents, it is difficult to assess the difference of interest here – the gap between actual preferences and the expected preferences of a "fully informed" citizenry.

15. "The media," of course, represent a diverse array of information sources, and less popular perspectives are often found in less popular media sources. Our focus here is primarily on mainstream media because of its particularly central role in facilitating (or failing to facilitate) cue-based decision-making. Our interest, after all, is in elite cues as shortcuts, and shortcuts are supposed to be easy and readily accessible. Furthermore, mainstream sources are often viewed as more credible and therefore more likely to be more influential cue givers. For example, Druckman (1998) found that an article attributed to the New York Times could change respondents attitudes about a KKK rally, while the same article attributed to the National Inquirer wielded almost no persuasive power.

ACKNOWLEDGMENTS

The authors' names are listed alphabetically. The authors would like to thank Leonie Huddy, James Kuklinski, Mark Lindeman and Robert Shapiro for helpful comments and the Institute for Social Science Research at UCLA and the Center for the Study of Race, Inequality, and Politics at Yale University for financial support.

REFERENCES

Alger, D. (1998). *Megamedia: How Giant Corporations Dominate Mass Media, Distort Competition, and Endanger Democracy.* Lanham, MD: Rowan and Littlefield.

Althaus, S. L. (1998). Information Effects in Collective Preferences. *American Political Science Review, 92*, 545–558.

Bagdikian, B. H. (1992). *The Media Monopoly*. Boston: Beacon Press.

Bartels, L. M. (1996). Uninformed Votes: Information Effects in Presidential Elections. *American Journal of Political Science, 40*, 194–230.

Bartels, L. M. (1998). Democracy with Attitudes. Unpublished manuscript, presented at the Columbia University Political Psychology Seminar, New York, May 9.

Bennett, L. W. (1990). Toward a Theory of Press-State Relations in the United States. *Journal of Communication, 40*, 103–125.

Berelson, B. R., Lazarsfeld, P. F., & McPhee, W. N. (1954). *Voting: A Study of Opinion Formation in a Presidential Campaign*. Chicago: University of Chicago Press.

Calvert, R. L. (1985). The Value of Biased Information: A Rational Choice Model of Political Advice. *Journal of Politics, 47*, 530–555.

Calvert, R. L. (1986). *Models of Imperfect Information in Politics*. Chur, Switzerland: Harwood Academic Publishers.

Campbell, A., Converse, P. E., Miller, W. E., & Stokes, D. E. (1960). *The American Voter*. Chicago: University of Chicago Press.

Carmines, E. G., & Kuklinski, J. H. (1990). Incentives, Opportunities, and the Logic of Public Opinion in American Political Representation. In: J. A. Ferejohn & J. H. Kuklinski (Eds), *Information and Democratic Processes*. Urbana, IL: University of Illinois Press.

Carmines, E. G., & Stimson, J. A. (1980). The Two Faces of Issue Voting. *American Political Science Review, 74*, 78–91.

Chaiken, S. (1980). Heuristic Versus Systematic Information Processing and the Use of Source Versus Message Cues in Persuasion. *Journal of Personality and Social Psychology, 37*, 1387–1397.

Chaiken, S. (1987). The Heuristic Model of Persuasion. In: M. P. Zanna & J. M. Olson (Eds), *Social Influence: The Ontario Symposium* (Vol. 5). Hillsdale, NJ: Lawrence Erlbaum Associates.

Citrin, J., & Green, D. P. (1990). The Self-Interest Motive in American Public Opinion. *Research in Micropolitics, 3*, 1–28.

Cobb, M. D., & Kuklinski, J. H. (1997). Changing Minds: Political Arguments and Political Persuasion. *American Journal of Political Science, 41*, 88–121.

Conover, P. J., & Feldman, S. (1989). Candidate Perception in an Ambiguous World: Campaigns, Cues, and Inference Processess. *American Journal of Political Science, 33*, 912–940.

Converse, P. E. (1962). Information Flow and the Stability of Partisan Attitudes. *Public Opinion Quarterly, 26*, 578–599.

Converse, P. E. (1964). The Nature of Belief Systems in Mass Publics. In: D. E. Apter (Ed.), *Ideology and Discontent*. New York: Free Press.

Cox, G. W., & McCubbins, M. D. (1994). Bonding, Structure, and the Stability of Political Parties: Party Government in the House. *Legislative Studies Quarterly, 19*(2)(May), 215–231.

Cukierman, A., & Tommasi, M. (1998). When Does It Take a Nixon to Go to China? *American Economic Review, 88*, 180–197.

Delli Carpini, M. X., & Keeter, S. (1996). *What Americans Know About Politics and Why It Matters*. New Haven: Yale University Press.

Ditto, P. H., & Lopez, D. F. (1992). Motivated Skepticism: Use of Differential Decision Criteria for Preferred and Non-preferred Conclusions. *Journal of Personality and Social Psychology*, 568–584.

Downs, A. (1957). *An Economic Theory of Democracy*. New York: Harper Collins.

Druckman, J. N. (1998). Who Can Frame?: Source Credibility and Framing Effects. Prepared for the annual meetings of the American Political Science Association, Boston, September 3–6.

Edelman, M. (1985). *The Symbolic Uses of Politics*. Urbana: University of Illinois Press.

Fishkin, J. S. (1995). *The Voice of the People: Public Opinion and Democracy*. New Haven: Yale University Press.

Fishkin, J. S., & Luskin, R. C. (1999). Bringing Deliberation to the Democratic Dialogue. In M. McCombs & A. Reynolds (Eds), *A Poll with a Human Face*. New York: Lawrence Erlbaum Associates.

Gans, H. J. (1979). *Deciding What's News*. New York: Pantheon Books.

Gilens, M. (2001). Political Ignorance and Collective Policy Preferences. *American Political Science Review, 95*, 379–396.

Gilens, M., & Hertzman, C. (2000). Corporate Ownership and News Bias: Newspaper Coverage of the 1996 Telecommunications Act. *Journal of Politics*, forthcoming.

Grofman, B., & Norrander, B. (1990). Efficient Use of Reference Group Cues in a Single Dimension. *Public Choice, 64*, 213–227.

Hallin, D. C. (1986). *"The Uncensored War": The Media and Vietnam*. Berkeley: University of California Press.

Hample, D. (1985). Refinements on the Cognitive Model of Argument: Concreteness, Involvement, and Group Scores. *Western Journal of Speech Communication, 49*, 267–285.

Herman, E. S., & Chomsky, N. (1988). *Manufacturing Consent: The Political Economy of the Mass Media*. New York: Pantheon.

Huckfeldt, R. R., & Sprague, J. (1991). Discussant Effects on Vote Choice – Intimacy, Structure, and Interdependence. *Journal of Politics, 53*, 122–158.

Huckfeldt, R. R., & Sprague, J. (1995). *Citizens, Politics, and Social Communication: Information and Influence in an Election Campaign*. Cambridge: Cambridge University Press.

Iyengar, S. (1990). Shortcuts to Political Knowledge: The Role of Selective Attention and Accessibility. In: J. A. Ferejohn & J. H. Kuklinski, *Information and Democratic Processes*. Urbana, IL: University of Illinois Press.

Jacobs, L. R., & Shapiro, R. Y. (2000). *Politicians Don't Pander: Political Manipulation and the Loss of Democratic Responsiveness*. Chicago: University of Chicago Press.

Kagay, M. R. (1999). Presidential Address: Public Opinion and Polling During Presidential Scandal and Impeachment. *Public Opinion Quarterly, 63*, 449–463.

Kahneman, D., & Tversky, A. (1972). Subjective Probability: A Judgment of Representativeness. *Cognitive Psychology, 3*, 430–454.

Kahneman, D., & Tversky, A. (1973). On the Psychology of Prediction. *Psychological Review, 80*, 237–251.

Krosnick, J. A. (1990). Government Policy and Citizen Passion: A Study of Issue Publics in Contemporary America. *Political Behavior, 12*, 59–92.

Kuklinski, J. H., & Hurley, N. L. (1994). On Hearing and Interpreting Political Messages: A Cautionary Tale of Citizen Cue Taking. *Journal of Politics, 56*, 729–751.

Kuklinski, J. H., Metlay, D. S., & Kay, W. D. (1982). Citizen Knowledge and Choices on the Complex Issue of Nuclear Energy. *American Journal of Political Science, 26*, 615–628.

Kuklinski, J. H., & Quirk, P. J. (1998). Reconsidering the Rational Public: Heuristics, Cognition, and Mass Opinion. Presented at the University of Chicago American Politics Workshop, April 15.

Lodge, M., McGraw, K. M., & Stroh, P. (1989). An Impression-Driven Model of Candidate Evaluation. *American Political Science Review, 87*, 399–419.

Lodge, M., Steenbergen, M. L., & Brau, S. (1995). The Responsive Voter: Campaign Information and the Dynamics of Candidate Evaluation. *American Political Science Review, 89*, 309–326.

Lupia, A. (1994). Shortcuts Versus Encyclopedias: Information and Voting Behavior in California Insurance Reform Elections. *American Political Science Review, 88*, 63–76.

Lupia, A. (1995). Who Can Persuade?: A Formal Theory, A Survey and Implications for Democracy. Prepared for the Annual Meetings of the Midwest Political Science Association, Chicago, IL, April 6–8.

Lupia, A., & McCubbins. M. D. (1998). *The Democratic Dilemma: Can Citizens Learn What They Need to Know?* Cambridge: Cambridge University Press.

Luskin, R. C., & Fishkin, J. S. (1998). Deliberative Polling, Public Opinion, and Democracy: The Case of the National Issues Convention. Unpublished manuscript.

McGuire, W. J. (1968). Personality and Susceptibility to Social Influence. In: E. F. Borgatta & W. W. Lambert (Eds), *Handbook of Personality Theory and Research*. Chicago: Rand McNally.

McGuire, W. J. (1969). The Nature of Attitudes and Attitude Change. In: G. Lindzey & E. Aronson (Eds), *Handbook of Social Psychology* (Vol. 3). Reading, MA: Addison-Wesley.

McKelvey, R. D., & Ordeshook, P. C. (1985). Elections with Limited Information: A Fulfilled Expectations Model Using Contemporaneous Poll and Endorsement Data as Information Sources. *Journal of Economic Theory, 36*, 55–85.

McKelvey, R. D., & Ordeshook, P. C. (1986). Information, Electoral Equilibria, and the Democratic Ideal. *Journal of Politics, 48*, 909–937.

Mermin, J. (1999). *Debating War and Peace: Media Coverage of U.S. Intervention in the Post-Vietnam Era*. Princeton: Princeton University Press.

Mondak, J. J. (1993). Source Cues and Policy Approval: The Cognitive Dynamics of Public Support for the Reagan Agenda. *American Journal of Political Science, 37*, 186–212.

Mondak, J. J. (1994a). Question Wording and Mass Policy Preferences: The Comparative Impact of Substantive Information and Peripheral Cues. *Political Communication, 11*, 165–183.

Mondak, J. J. (1994b). Cognitive Heuristics, Heuristic Processing, and Efficiency in Decision-Making. In: M. X. Delli Carpini, L. Huddy & R. Y. Shapiro (Eds), *Research in Micropolitics* (Vol. 4). Greenwich, CT: JAI Press.

Monroe, A. D. (1979). Consistency Between Public Preferences and National Policy Decisions. *American Politics Quarterly, 7*, 3–19.

Monroe, A. D., & Gardner, P. J. (1987). Public Policy Linkages. In: S. Long (Eds), *Research in Micropolitics*. Greenwich, CT: JAI Press.

Morley, D. D. (1987). Subjective Message Constructs: A Theory of Persuasion. *Communication Monographs, 54*, 183–203.

Page, B. I. (1978). *Choices and Echoes in Presidential Elections: Rational Man and Electoral Democracy*. Chicago: University of Chicago Press.

Page, B. I. (1996). *Who Deliberates? Mass Media in Modern Democracy*. Chicago: University of Chicago Press.

Page, B. I., & Shapiro, R. Y. (1983). Effects of Public Opinion on Policy. *American Political Science Review, 77*, 175–190.

Page, B. I., Shapiro, R. Y., & Dempsey, G. R. (1987). What Moves Public Opinion. *American Political Science Review, 81*, 23–43.

Page, B. I., & Shapiro, R. Y. (1992). *The Rational Public: Fifty Years of Trends in Americans' Policy Preferences*. Chicago: University of Chicago Press.

Page B. I., & Tannenbaum. (1996). Zoe Baird, Nannies, and Talk Radio. In: *Who Deliberates? Mass Media in Modern Democracy*. Chicago: University of Chicago Press.

Petty, R. E., & Cacioppo, J. T. (1979). Issue Involvement can Increase or Decrease Persuasion by Enhancing Message-Relevant cognitive Responses. *Journal of Personality and Social Psychology, 37*, 1915–1926.

Petty, R. E., & Cacioppo, J. T. (1981). *Attitudes and Persuasion: Classic and Contemporary Approaches*. Boulder: Westview Press.

Petty, R. E., & Cacioppo, J. T. (1986). *Communication and Persuasion: Central and Peripheral Routs to Attitude Change*. New York: Springer-Verlag.

Poole, K. T., & Rosenthal, H. (1997). *Congress: A Political-Economic History of Roll Call Voting*. Oxford: Oxford University Press.

Poole, K. T., & Rosenthal, H. (1999). D-NOMINATE After 10 Years: A Comparative Update to *Congress: A Political Economic History of Roll Call Voting*. Unpublished manuscript, Carnegie Mellon University, September 27.

Popkin, S. L. (1991). *The Reasoning Voter: Communication and Persuasion in Presidential Campaigns*. Chicago: University of Chicago Press.

Pratte, A., & Whiting, G. (1986). What Newspaper Editorials Have Said About Deregulation of Broadcasting. *Journalism Quarterly*, *61*, 56–65.

Ratneshwar, S., & Chaiken, S. (1991). Comprehension's Role in Persuasion: The Case of its Moderating Effect on the Persuasive Impact of Source Cues. *Journal of Consumer Research*, *18*, 52–62.

Rhodes, N., & Wood, W. (1992). Self-Esteem and Intelligence Affect Influenceability: The Mediating Role of Message Reception. *Psychology Bulletin*, *111*, 156–171.

Sears, D. O., & Funk, C. L. (1990). Self-Interest in Americans' Political Opinions. In: J. J. Mansbridge (Ed.), *Self-Interest*. Chicago: University of Chicago Press.

Sears, D. O., & Funk, C. L. (1991). The Role of Self-Interest in Social and Political Attitudes. *Advances in Experimental Social Psychology*, *24*, 1–91.

Shapiro, R. Y. (1998). Public Opinion, Elites, and Democracy. *Critical Review*, *12*, 501–528.

Snider, J. H., & Page, B. I. (1997). Does Media Ownership Affect Media Stands?: The Case of the Telecommunications Act of 1996. Prepared for the Annual Meetings of the Midwest Political Science Association, Chicago IL, April 10–12.

Sniderman, P. M., Brody, R. A., & Tetlock, P. E. (1991). *Reasoning and Choice: Explorations in Political Psychology*. Cambridge: Cambridge University Press.

Stimson, J. A., MacKuen, M. B., & Erikson, R. (1995). Dynamic Representation. *American Political Science Review*, *89*, 543–565.

Tversky, A., & Kahneman, D. (1973). Availability: A Heuristic for Judging Frequency and Probability. *Cognitive Psychology*, *5*, 207–232.

Tversky, A., & Kahneman, D. (1974). Judgment Under Uncertainty: Heuristics and Biases. *Science*, *185*, 1124–1131.

van Knippenberg, D., & Daamen, D. (1996). Providing Information in Public Opinion Surveys: Motivation and Ability in the Information-and-Choice Questionnaire. *International Journal of Public Opinion Research*, *8*, 70–82.

Zaller, J. R. (1992). *The Nature and Origins of Mass Opinion*. Cambridge: Cambridge University Press.

Zaller, J. R. (1998). Monica Lewinsky's Contribution to Political Science. *P.S.*, *31*, 182–189.

Zaller, J. R., & Chiu, D. (2000). Government's Little Helper: U.S. Press Coverage of Foreign Policy Crises, 1945–1999. In: B. L. Nacos, R. Y. Shapiro & I. Pierangelo (Eds), *Decision-Making in a Glass House: Mass Media, Public Opinion, and American and European Foreign Policy in the 21st Century*. Lanham: Rowman and Littlefield.

UNDERSTANDING THE ROLE OF RACE IN CANDIDATE EVALUATION

Karen Callaghan and Nayda Terkildsen

INTRODUCTION

Any observer of U.S. politics would agree that racial prejudice is one of the nation's most enduring problems. Race "helps define the ideologies of liberals and conservatives . . . shapes the presidential coalitions of the Democratic and Republican parties . . . [and] dramatically changed the course of the 1980, 1984 and 1988 presidential elections" (Edsall & Edsall, 1991, p. 53). The political role of race is both subtle and complex. Directly or indirectly, race is embedded in the politics of the nation as well as of each of her citizens. In short, race "as much as we might like to deny it, or wish it away, or ascribe to it a diminished role" still matters. Its effects still pervade all aspects of our political system with voters and politicians "perpetually caught up in an explosive chain reaction of race, rights, and values" (Edsall & Edsall, p. 54).

While the impact of race on American life is well documented, its repercussions in the voting booth remain unclear. Social science research has largely ignored whites' evaluation of non-white candidates. This leaves a serious gap in our knowledge. To the extent that African-American candidates are defined by their race and thus evaluated differently than white candidates, voters view race as instrumental to their political assessments of minority candidates. But exactly how traditional voting models differ for minority candidates remains ambiguous. It is unclear whether the universal vote elements (e.g. partisanship, issue positions, ideology) that serve to shape the electability of white

Political Decision Making, Deliberation and Participation, Volume 6, pages 51–95.
Copyright © 2002 by Elsevier Science Ltd.
All rights of reproduction in any form reserved.
ISBN: 0-7623-0227-5

candidates also influence voters' evaluations of minority candidates. Put another way, are black candidates who run in biracial contests subject to specific racial biases and constraints that are either directly or indirectly related to their race? As increasing numbers of African-Americans seek political office, the answers to these questions remain of vital interest to students of both political behavior and democratic theory.

In this essay we synthesize the literature on race, candidate evaluation and voting, focusing on white voters' evaluations of minority candidates.[1] The primary question we explore is: "How does the race of a candidate influence the type of voting model that comes into play?" Our essay is divided into five parts. First, we briefly explore the historical and political context of biracial elections. Then we briefly explore the research on candidate evaluation, providing a general picture of the terrain. The most striking feature of this research is that mainstream models of candidate evaluation fail to include candidate race. We discuss the major reasons for this neglect, and acknowledge another crucial weakness in the voting behavior literature: the absence of the black voter from electoral research. But even with the systematic inclusion of candidate and voter race, we would still be oversimplifying the puzzle. A properly specified model would include an assessment of other racial and ethnic groups' attitudes toward African-American candidates, not just white voter stereotypes. We recognize this gap even within our own research, as well as in the current literature.

In the third part of this essay, we review the literature that most directly addresses the evaluation of African-American candidates in the context of biracial or "mixed" race contests (i.e. contests in which at least one candidate is black). We pay particular attention to the role that different categories of factors – electoral, social-psychological, and candidate-based – play in polarizing biracial elections. What will become especially apparent from our discussion is the lack of a discernible consensus concerning the role of race or the systematic impact of racism. We also discuss important methodological problems inherent in race research, and explore how some scholars have handled them. This is not a methodological search-and-destroy mission; rather our goal is to build upon past critiques to develop a systematic agenda on race. In particular we investigate three major problems that hamper our understanding of the role of race in biracial elections: (1) sample bias; (2) self-monitoring biases; and (3) individuation versus categorization processes.

In our discussion of "self-monitoring" we explore the way that investigations into the impact of race in biracial elections have also been hampered by the complicated and often deceptive nature of race and "racial" issues. Some white voters, specifically the prejudiced, misrepresent their true views about

African-American candidates with "politically correct," but behaviorally hollow responses. This masking of offensive but critically important political attitudes – "self-monitoring" – presents a conundrum for political behaviorists interested in biracial elections: how can we best identify and separate genuine racial tolerance from the "self-censored" kind?[2]

In our discussion of individuation and categorization processes we are interested in how variations in the attitude object (in this case the issue positions and qualifications of minority candidates) increase or decrease the role of racial stereotypes in candidate evaluation processes. To illustrate the importance of individuation processes, consider the following facts. In the aggregate, reported levels of white prejudice have declined substantially since the 1970s (Schuman, Steeh, Bobo & Krysan, 1997; Sigelman & Welch, 1991). Throughout this period increasing numbers of African-Americans have been elected in majority white districts, including in the deep South (Swain, 1990) with white voters more frequently supporting black candidates than in the past. However, in some electoral contests white voters are still unlikely to vote for an African-American candidate over a white candidate. In fact in some contests, black candidates are unable to win even a minimal level of white voter support.

What are we to make of this? Is prejudice not a uniform factor in biracial elections? Or, are some black candidates better able than others to attract white voter support? Is a black politician's ability to offset the racially-biased assessments that some white voters make about her related to voter perceptions about how well she fits elements of the black stereotype? We believe so, at least in part. Three factors seem to play a role: (1) the general propensity for an individual (voter) to stereotype blacks as a group; (2) the extent to which the group member under assessment (candidate) varies from her group; and (3) the level of personal interaction between the evaluator (voter) and the individual (candidate) being judged.

In the fourth section of this essay we extend our discussion of the methodological difficulties inherent in research on biracial elections by focusing on candidate (as opposed to overtly racial) stereotypes. This dimension has been excluded from models of black candidate evaluation. A systematic analysis of candidate stereotyping is needed. That white candidates are appraised partly in terms of character traits is well documented (Kinder, 1986; Miller et al., 1986). But which sets of personality traits and beliefs are central and which are peripheral to minority candidates? Are domain-specific "subgroup" stereotypes (i.e. stereotypes about black politicians) more likely to come into play? Scholars have largely ignored the function of racial traits and racial beliefs in voters' judgments about African-American candidates.

In the fifth part of this essay we present empirical data – based upon an experimental study of white voters' responses to fictitious black and white candidates for office – that demonstrate the advantages of integrating candidate stereotypes into models of minority candidate evaluation. Finally, in our conclusion we suggest some directions for future research. Stepping back from the analyses of particular studies and measures, we outline a systematic agenda on race. The question we address is: "What would a well-defined, fully integrated model of black candidate evaluation look like?"

PLACING RACE IN A HISTORICAL AND POLITICAL CONTEXT

Blacks first held political office in the United States during Reconstruction, being elected or appointed to most levels and types of state and federal offices. In 1870, for example, Mississippian Hiram Revels became the first black man to serve in the U.S. Senate, succeeding Jefferson Davis. Henry Hayne served as Secretary of State in South Carolina, and for 43 days in 1873 P. B. S. Pinchback served as acting governor of Louisiana's Reconstruction government, later winning election to the U.S. Senate (Pettigrew & Alston, 1988; Dynally, 1971). All told, approximately 800 African-American males were elected or appointed to office during this period, almost exclusively in the South. However, like most Reconstruction policies this trend of electoral inclusion was short-lived. The effectiveness or real power of black elected officials was minimal according to most scholars, and their tenure once the so-called "Black Codes" were enacted was brief.[3] After Reconstruction, black representation largely disappeared until after the Civil Rights movement of the mid-twentieth century. Between these two eras, the absence of black elected officials can largely be attributed to the institutionalization of racism, the small numbers of enfranchised African-Americans and overt white voter prejudice, though other electoral factors surely played a role in limiting black representation.

In contemporary American politics African-Americans have been elected to every type and level of political office, with the notable exception of president and vice-president. While black candidates have failed at four attempts to secure the presidency through a major party nomination (Congresswoman Shirley A. Chisholm in 1972, Reverend Jesse Jackson in 1984 and 1988 and Virginia Governor Douglas Wilder in 1992) they have made great strides in holding statewide and local offices. Potentially paving the way for more dramatic increases, some of the nation's most visible cities (e.g. Philadelphia, Los Angeles, New York, Washington, and Detroit) have elected African-Americans to municipal and county-level executive offices. The growth in the number of black elected officials – as much as 900% in 20 years[4] – is arguably significant and impressive, as are reported changes in attitudes of voters toward African American candidates. For example, Schuman et al. (1997) report that approximately 90% of voters say they would consider voting for a hypothetical African-American presidential candidate who had already secured their party's nomination.

Though significant, these gains appear a good deal less impressive when one considers that while African-Americans comprise approximately 11% of the national electorate, they hold less than 2% of the nation's 500,000 elected offices (JCPES, 1991; Stanley & Niemi, 1988). What accounts for this discrepancy? Undoubtedly, African-American candidates continue to face a number of electoral barriers that their white counterparts do not, including fragile voting coalitions and emphases on race from everyone from the media to their opponents to at times their own supporters. In addition, African-Americans are not always actively recruited by the major parties and are generally disadvantaged in raising campaign funds (Wilhite & Theilman, 1986). Furthermore, they must often contend with legislative redistricting plans that segregate black voters, and with certain election districts or states that impose more stringent restrictions on black politicians than on their white political competitors (Smothers, 1992; Pettigrew, 1972; Pettigrew & Alston, 1988). African American candidates are also often constrained by unreliable estimates of electoral support (Finkel, Guterbook & Borg, 1991; Clymer, 1989; Petigrew & Alston, 1988; Sussman, 1985; Bergholz, 1982).

Even if the existing structural barriers to black electoral success were eliminated, African-Americans seeking office at the national and statewide level or in majority white districts would still have to contend with one of the biggest barriers to elected office: the prejudicial attitudes of many white voters. In our estimation, some thirty-five years after the passage of the Civil Rights Act, the attitudinal biases of white voters still create a significant barrier to the election of African-Americans. Unfortunately, we still know very little about how black politicians are perceived and evaluated by the majority white national electorate, or how these attitudes affect voters' decision-making.

THE ABSENCE OF RACE IN EARLY MODELS OF CANDIDATE EVALUATION

Although there is a large and well-developed body of research on how voters evaluate candidates for office, this literature has assumed that white voters are evaluating white candidates for public office. Thus, while traditional vote models offer a general framework for understanding the voting behavior of white voters when assessing white candidates, they have little to offer to help explain how white voters' evaluate African American candidates. The absence of race and racial factors becomes evident when one looks at the development of scholarly interest in voting behavior.

Mainstream candidate evaluation research developed in the first part of the 20th century. The earliest approaches to understanding the determinants of candidate evaluation emphasized the role of socio-demographic factors. According to the Columbia Model (Lazarsfeld et al., 1940, 1948; Berelson et al., 1954) people ultimately cast their vote in accordance with the vote of "trusted others," defined as those from their own demographic groups. However, in a predominantly white and highly segregated society, the social and community context of voting largely excluded issues of race. In the 1950s and early 1960s, scholars in the Michigan tradition (Campbell, Gurin & Miller, 1954; Campbell, Converse, Miller & Stokes, 1960) began to add psychological determinants of voter decision-making to social and demographic ones. Again, however, these studies tended to ignore the role of race in their models.

More recent research has begun to consider the impact of candidates' biological characteristics on voters' assessments. For example, McDermott (1997) argues that in "low-information" elections a candidate's gender operates as an informational cue, leading voters to assume that a female candidate is more liberal than a male candidate of the same party would be.[5] Undoubtedly other candidate characteristics such as race also can and do serve as "cognitive shortcuts" in voters' evaluations. Research on this issue remains remarkably sparse, however, with many questions remaining unanswered.

For example, how does potential political information garnered from candidate race interact with other important vote cues such as partisanship and ideology. Does race become irrelevant? Does partisanship or ideology lose some or all of their impact? How does overt or subtle racism or racial stereotyping affect candidate evaluations? Extant research provides very little in the way of answers to these and related questions. In short, there currently is no reliable way to distinguish partisan or ideological voting from voting based on racial stereotyping or prejudice when considering white voters and non-white candidates.

We see several reasons for the neglect of black candidates in early voting research. First, there is the reality of our nation's history of exclusion rooted in racism and concomitant political oppression. As noted above, throughout much of our nation's history, black Americans have been effectively excluded from the polls and public office. Myriad factors excluded them from registering or voting, particularly in the South. These factors included *de jure* racism that either formally barred blacks from voting or produced a similar effect, economic barriers, extensive psychological warfare and substantial, even lethal physical harassment. In many states prior to the Voting Rights Act of 1965, registered blacks comprised less than 1% of the eligible electorate, but a considerably larger percentage in the population. In deep-south states like Alabama and Mississippi with some of the nation's largest concentration of African-American adults, official government acts and "unofficial" citizen actions ensured that blacks did not flock to the polls.[6] During this time virtually no black candidates sought public office. In fact, before the passage of the Voting Rights Act, less than 500 African-Americans held elective office nation wide. Thus, race of the candidate was not a source of variation for empirical research: it was a constant.

Second, we must acknowledge that our profession is not immune from the biases produced by individual prejudices and stereotypes as well as larger societal trends and forces. As noted previously, for several decades during the early development of social science models of voting, race was considered relatively insignificant. According to the Columbia school (Lazarsfeld et al., 1940, 1948; Berelson et al., 1954), vote choice could be adequately explained by socio-economic status, religious affiliation and place of residence (i.e. rural versus urban). Thus, while the Columbia researchers suggested that a person's social milieu provided the stimuli for making a vote choice, these stimuli did not directly include race. Moreover, "class" – the dominant paradigm of the day – may have been perceived as "including" race, due to the equating of African Americans with poverty and poverty with African Americans. Thomas Kuhn's (1986) admonition that truth is not always the criterion of scientific knowledge may well apply here.

Somewhat less obvious, but perhaps even more relevant, were the professional difficulties associated with studying race in the 1950s and early 1960s. As Robert Weissberg (1990) has observed, "It might be acceptable for middle class researchers to devote a career to, say, working class political movements or trade union politics; it is less acceptable to specialize in black politics" (1990, p. 10). Further, the "ideological minefield" of race encouraged political scientists to stick to well-developed models that were non-controversial and thus "risk free" because "the slightest misstep, or even appearance of misstep could mean the end of a career" (p. 9). Finally, the relatively few numbers of African Americans in the profession undoubtedly contributed to the under-studied and under-theorized role of race in American electoral behavior.

Regardless of the root causes, the relative absence of race in the development of mainstream research on voting has resulted in an important gap in our knowledge. And while in the 1980s a small literature on election "rules" emerged that focused on how at-large and staggered elections affected black electoral fortunes[7] this literature did not directly address the question of how white voters evaluated African-American candidates.

In more recent years social-cognitive models emerging out of the Michigan School have provided psychological depth to theories of vote choice in ways that have both indirect and direct implications for the study of race. In these models, voters are seen as becoming oriented to candidate information through the processes of categorizing and/or individuating. This research focuses on the specific cognitive mechanisms that underlie the formation of political judgments (for a review see Ottati & Wyer, 1981; Lau & Sears, 1986; Lodge & McGraw, 1995). Although prior work on the processes of vote assessments ignored candidates of color, the emphasis on the cognitive processing of candidate information stimulated an interest in studying candidate race as a social information "cue."

Scholarly interest in race as a voting cue paralleled the electoral advancement of black Americans. By the late 1970s approximately 1,470 blacks had been elected to political office, an increase most likely attributable to the enfranchisement of southern black voters and their powerful impact on the aspirations of black candidates in the region (Williams, 1990). Subsequent voter mobilization campaigns and court cases challenging the dilution of black votes also boosted the electoral prospects of African-American candidates.[8] As more blacks were elected to public office, social scientists began to focus their efforts on understanding the antecedents of white voters' evaluation of black politicians.

Besides the increase in African-American candidates and the de-institutionalization of racism, other factors triggered an increased interest in race as a voting cue in the 1970s, including a growing interest in liberal social issues, the social change resulting from the Civil Rights movement, the quest for black identity and the increase in black political scientists and black studies programs. While the role of race in elections is still arguably understudied and poorly understood, it is no longer ignored.

WHAT WE KNOW ABOUT CANDIDATE EVALUATIONS IN BIRACIAL ELECTIONS

In this section, we consider a range of studies on biracial elections and the evaluation of African American candidates. As we shall see, the existing literature is replete with measurement issues and methodological problems that have limited the development of this research.

Early Research and the Problem of Generalizability

The earliest empirical studies involving biracial elections tended to focus on the race of the voter as the key explanatory variable. Not surprisingly, researchers found that voters favor candidates of their own racial or ethnic group (Lorinskas et al., 1969: Hahn & Almy, 1971; Pettigrew, 1972; Murray & Ledlitz, 1978; Tate, 1993). In fact in some elections – primarily in the South – one's racial group affiliation was central to explaining individual vote choice.

Generalizations beyond these studies are difficult for two reasons, however. First, this research relied on individual case studies. Second, they focused primarily on three significant black candidates: Massachusetts Senator Edward Brooke, Mayor Tom Bradley of Los Angeles, and the Reverend Jesse Jackson. While providing many insights, the context-dependent and arguably unrepresentative nature of these elections limit the conclusions to be drawn from them. To be scientifically meaningful, research on biracial elections must result in a generalization or principle which is not limited to the immediate setting of the particular investigation (see Cook & Campbell, 1979). However, all political campaigns are bound by their historical context – particularly crucial where race is considered.

For example, the 1966 U.S. Senate race involving Edward Brooke (R) of Massachusetts occurred at a time when race was highly salient (in contrast with Jesse Jackson's candidacies in 1984 and 1988 when race was less overtly an issue). Federal orders to desegregate public schools and busing in Boston along with the racial rioting in cities like Watts kept race on the political front burner. Yet Brooke enjoyed high positive ratings in part because he took an extremely moderate stance on race during a time of increased black militancy. Brooke's partisanship – he was a liberal Republican in a Democratic-dominated state – also likely played a role in his popularity. Pettigrew (1976) stresses the importance of candidate image and other factors for African-American nominees in mediating and modifying the effects of [white's] racial attitudes on their voting (p. 22). As unusual as it was for a black to run as a Republican, Brooke's partisan affiliation alone would not likely have overturned racial stereotyping. However, Brooke "looked white" and so was possibly less likely to activate the black stereotype (Cutler, 1972).[9] In short, several interrelated and atypical factors appear to have offset the role of race in this case, giving Brooke a significant margin of victory (22%; see Becker & Heaton, 1967).

Thus, while early case studies helped researchers develop theory and generate hypotheses, differences in specific candidate images and racial contexts undermine their comparability and generalizability. Unfortunately, later accounts of campaigns involving African-American candidates such as the presidential bid of then Virginia Governor Douglas Wilder or the U.S. Senate bid by Harvey Gantt in North Carolina have been largely descriptive or anecdotal in nature.

While empirical analyses have suffered from a general lack of systematic data (especially at the national level) on white voter reactions to African-American candidates, over time a growing body of research on biracial elections has emerged using a more diverse array of methodologies including experiments, surveys, content analyses and case studies (e.g. Cole, 1976; Staples, 1982; Bullock, 1984: Sonenshein, 1990; Williams, 1990; Terkildsen, 1993; Sniderman et al., 1995; Reeves, 1997). From this research the crucial evaluative role of race has become more visible. What is clear is that to fully understand voters' decision-making in biracial elections one needs to include measures of specifically race-related attitudes and perceptions. It is precisely these race-related variables that distinguish models of candidate evaluation in biracial elections from the more traditional models.[10] Partisanship and ideology are two useful shortcuts habitually employed to evaluate white political candidates. However, with African-American candidates citizens appear to forego traditional voting considerations and rely instead on racial stereotypes and prejudice (e.g. Terkildsen, 1996; Reeves, 1997; Sears et al., 1987). For example, in 1984 Jesse Jackson was negatively evaluated by many white voters. This opposition resulted from explicitly race-based attitudes, outweighing the impact of more traditional vote cues such as partisan attachment (Sears et al., 1987). Jackson, unlike either Walter Mondale or Ronald Reagan was strongly associated with and evaluated in terms of race.

While existing research indicates that "race matters" in the evaluation of black candidates, measuring racial attitudes remains a difficult and unresolved issue. The earliest empirical studies of the relationship between racial attitudes and black candidate evaluations used attitudinal measures analogous to old-fashioned racism (Becker & Heaton, 1967). Historically it was easy to classify negative reactions to black politicians as motivated purely by biological racism. Many Americans believed in the racial inferiority of black Americans and freely expressed a desire to subordinate blacks through segregated public and private facilities, transportation and schools (Schuman et al., 1997). However, over time the number of survey respondents who express overtly racist opinions has declined significantly to about 15 to 20% of the population. Whether this decline represents a "true" shift in racial attitudes or a social acceptability bias that masks underlying attitudes is difficult to determine, however. As a result, researchers have attempted to tap racial attitudes in less direct ways. For example some have used "racial affect" (operationalized as how "warm" or "cold" an individual feels toward black Americans). But models using racial affect generally explain a relatively small part of the variance in white voters' evaluations of African American candidates. More recent studies treat racial stereotypes as the most immediate antecedent of white voters' evaluation of black candidates. But accurately measuring racial stereotypes has proven to be a difficult task for a variety of related reasons.

Measuring Racial Stereotypes and Their Impact on White Voters'
Evaluations of African American Candidates: The Problem of Sample Bias

The term "stereotype" was first used by psychiatrists at the end of the 19th century to describe what was considered a pathological condition. It did not mean a cognitive shortcut (Ashmore & Delo Boca, 1981) or a discriminatory response to certain outgroups (Bobo, 1988; Tajfel, 1982) as it does today. In 1922 the publication of Walter Lippmann's *Public Opinion* brought the term to the attention of social scientists. Lippmann posited that stereotypes serve to enhance individual perception and cognition of a "blooming and buzzing" world of confusion where direct hypothesis testing is not feasible (Ashmore & Del Boca, 1981). To Lippmann stereotypes were cognitive structures, "integral parts of the individual's personality that served to explain or rationalize his or her social standing" (Ashmore & Del Boca, 1979, p. 3).

Today, stereotypes generally refer to a "set of beliefs about the personal attributes of a group of people" (Ashmore & Del Boca, 1979, p. 61). They are accessible at the moment new social information is presented, whether or not the individual believes the stereotype to be true or is even aware that it has been activated (Gaertner & McLaughlin, 1983; Devine, 1989). Stereotypes may be cued from a visually prominent feature (e.g. race) which, in turn, acts as a schematic label when inter-personal judgments are generated (Ashmore & Del Boca, 1979; Fiske & Taylor, 1991). Thus, candidate race (i.e. skin color) acts as a physical "cue" in activating racial stereotypes and may also lead to more extreme racial judgments. More specifically, candidates with darker skin color may elicit harsher political evaluations, compared to candidates of lighter skin color.[11]

Social psychological research confirms the assignment of positive social traits to African-Americans with light or seemingly white skin and the ascription of negative traits to darker-skinned individuals both over time and in a variety of social settings: the family unit, the classroom, prospective marriage partners, and job enhancement (e.g. Richardson & Green, 1971; Powell-Hopson, 1962). That skin color "so notoriously unreliable as a determinant of individual qualities was and is so frequently used to decipher individual associations with 'inferior and superior social groups' is extremely paradoxical" (Lincoln, 1967, p. 127). Welcome to the world of race.

Incongruent or not, early in life people of all races develop value systems and behavior patterns based on skin color (Osgood, 1963; Lincoln, 1967; Isaacs, 1967). Given that white Americans typically hold negative stereotypes regarding blacks – that they are poor, lazy, irresponsible, aggressive, unintelligent, violence-prone, and superstitious (Devine, 1989; Bayton, 1941; Katz & Braly,

1933: Peffley & Hurwitz, 1996; Ashmore & Del Boca, 1979) – the impact of group stereotypes on political thinking about black politicians should be invariably negative. However, some studies show that neither candidate race nor racial prejudice influenced whites' evaluation of black candidates (e.g. Pettigrew, 1972, 1976; Hahn et al., 1976; Pettigrew & Allston, 1988; Citrin et al., 1990). In fact, one study (Colleau et al., 1990) finds evidence that black candidates are evaluated *more favorably* than are white candidates. Colleau and colleagues (1990) experimentally manipulated candidate race using a photograph of a white male and a black male, holding constant other candidate information. Using a composite scale of candidate traits and behaviors, white college students rated the black candidate more positively than his white counterpart.

Does this mean that being black is an asset for U.S. political candidates? In a nation characterized by deep-seated and enduring racial cleavages, probably not. More likely the use of a student sample may account for the findings in the Colleau et al. model. While there is no reason to expect differences among college students and adults in their level of knowledge about racial stereotypes or their basic cognitive processes, better-educated respondents may be more likely to view African-Americans as victims of a white society or past discrimination (Sniderman & Hagen, 1985) which may transfer into favoritism toward well-qualified blacks over comparable whites (Haas et al., 1991; McConahay, 1983). In short, college students may be more politically aware of race than the general population, and may have inflated their assessments and beliefs – either consciously or unconsciously to appear politically correct – of African-American candidates' positive traits and beliefs.

David Sears (1986) has gone so far as to question whether college student results are generalizable to adults, arguing that students tend to have an incomplete sense of self, un-crystalized socio-political attitudes, unusually strong cognitive skills, a strong need for peer approval, the tendency to comply with authority, unstable group relationships and little material self-interest in public affairs. Social psychologists have typically argued that the issue of the subject population is irrelevant because the phenomena under investigation are ubiquitous and universal. However, Sears lists many potential hazards of relying on such a narrow data base, including an erroneous description of the strength of the experimental relationship, mis-estimation and a limited range of independent values that do not map onto the value range found among the larger population. In short, the biases introduced by depending on one sub-population may reflect a genuine interaction of subject characteristics with the specific features of the research question being explored. We do not know whether general conclusions about the role of racial stereotypes in minority candidate evaluations based on student populations parallel those of adults in the real world, or are population-specific. Thus, research based on student samples may have critically underestimated the persistent impact of race on candidates of color.

The negative effects of racial stereotypes on candidate evaluations have likely been underestimated for other reasons besides the use of student samples. For example, researchers often fail to control for differences in racial intolerance among respondents (e.g. Colleau et al., 1990). As a result, there is the potential for mistakenly concluding that race is a less important factor than it may in fact be (i.e. accepting the null hypothesis when it is false). To offset the subject population bias that plagued previous experimental work, Terkildsen (1993) combined random sampling with experimental techniques. She used a localized random sample of jury pool members from the Kentucky court system (Jefferson County) to analyze white voters' evaluations of African-American candidates. The sampling frame included all residents who were licensed drivers and/or registered voters. In many ways the sample was more representative than the average independent survey research sample.[12]

Measuring Racial Stereotypes and Their Impact on White Voters' Evaluations of African American Candidates: The Problem of "Self Monitoring"

A larger, related problem in measuring racial stereotypes and determining their impact on white voters' assessments of non-white candidates results from the possibility that respondents provide socially acceptable responses to questions regarding racial attitudes, masking their true feelings. Research indicates that racial evaluations trigger impression management techniques in some individuals (Feldman & Hilterman, 1975; Sigall & Page, 1971; Gaertner & Dovidio, 1986). For instance, white subjects who indicated awareness of an experiment's racial intent rated African American job applicants more positively than did the unaware (Feldman & Hilterman, 1975).

To date only a handful of studies have investigated the possibility that white respondents "self-monitor" or regulate the reporting of their attitudes toward black candidates. In a study of Edward Brooke's Senate candidacy, Becker and Heaton (1976) used a "self-report" measure. They asked respondents if they knew of anyone who talked about voting for Brooke, but would not actually do so because of a belief that blacks should not be in the U.S. Senate. Twelve percent of their sample responded positively, providing evidence that at least some whites were aware of their acquaintances' self-monitoring behavior. Another study by Citrin et al. (1990) dismissed the notion that people regulate their race-related responses without formally testing it. The authors favored the explanation that contextual effects (e.g. candidate attributes, prior records and campaign strategies), rather than social desirability effects or candidate race in conjunction with voter racism defeated gubernatorial candidate Tom Bradley.

A concrete example of self-regulating behavior in this context can be found in the work of Terkildsen (1993) who examined the effect of self monitoring on white voters' evaluation of dark and light complexioned African-American candidates. Using direct measures of self-monitoring (for example, "I can look anyone in the eye and tell a lie," "When I am uncertain how to act in social situations I look to the behavior of others," and "My behavior is usually an expression of my true attitudes)", Terkildsen found that when candidate race is visually obvious (dark skin) racially-prejudiced voters who are high self-monitors reduced the expression of racial bias in their candidate evaluation to avoid perceived social hostility. In fact, self-monitoring completely eradicated and reversed the influence of racial prejudice on reported vote evaluations. However, when candidate race is less obvious (light skin), these same voters are more likely to use race in their evaluation.

Consequently, self-monitoring may explain the discordant findings of prior research, particularly the "reverse discrimination" effects found by Colleau et al. (1991), as well as a general lack of discrimination in real-world studies (Hahn et al., 1976; Pettigrew, 1976; Citrin et al., 1990). Importantly, it may also explain the divergence in public opinion polls and vote results in biracial contests in which white voters notoriously overestimate their level of vote support for African-American candidates in public opinion polls (Finkel et al., 1991; Clymer, 1989; Sussman, 1985; Balzar, 1982; Bergholz, 1982).

In conclusion, any attempt to accurately represent white voters' attitudes toward minority candidates in studies of U.S. contemporary society must include measures designed to tap self-regulating behavior.[13] Scholars must recognize that expressed racial attitudes do not necessarily equal behavior. Of course, to paraphrase Freud, "sometimes a cigar is just a cigar." That is, sometimes racially tolerant attitudes are just that – an unbiased view of African-Americans. It is precisely this uncertainty that makes developing reliable and valid measures of racial attitudes so difficult and yet so important.

Measuring Racial Stereotypes and Their Impact on White Voters'
Evaluations of African American Candidates: "Individuation versus
Categorization"

Another problem in the analysis of biracial elections has to do with the variability of individual candidate attributes. Unlike the previous problem of self-monitoring, which carries the risk of dismissing an existing race effect, individuation relates to the problem of explaining variation across candidates assessments. We know that whites who stereotype blacks as a group are less likely to vote for an African-American candidate than those who do not (Terkildsen, 1993; Williams, 1990). However, different political candidates may provide stronger or weaker fits to the "typical" black candidate stereotype. That is, the degree of fit may ultimately affect the strength of the group association and thus the magnitude of the race effect.

Research in social psychology indicates that once a group stereotype is activated, either by physical features or other information, the perceiver then tries to confirm the individual's fit with the group category. If the perceiver sees the individual and the category as analogous, the process ends. If, however, the initial fit is poor (i.e. the individual is not highly representative of her group), the perceiver may engage in a type of dual-processing – *individuating* – by developing either a group subtype or a subtype specific to the individual being evaluated (Brewer, 1988).[14] In other words, Brewer's model allows for two types of person-perception based on categorization or on individuation.[15] Huddy and Capelos (in press) question the "either or" nature of this dichotomy. Based on work by Kunda and colleagues (e.g. Kunda & Thagards, 1996: Kunda, Sinclair & Griffin, 1997), they argue that both individuation and stereotyping can occur simultaneously and that individuation does not completely remove the specter of stereotyping.[16]

Extending this line of reasoning, if the voter believes a black politician matches her beliefs about blacks as a social group, perhaps due to the candidate's personal background, physical features, electoral experience or other available information, then her initially activated group stereotypes will likely influence her evaluation of the candidate. If, however, the voter assesses the black candidate as different from blacks as a social group, she may cognitively set the stereotype aside and consider the politician's actual traits and issue positions. In other words, she will process idiosyncratic bits of information until she has formed a satisfactory "personalized" image of the candidate (data-driven processing).[17] Alternatively, following the "parallel processing" model, the voter may individuate the black politician as intelligent – a trait seen as atypical for blacks as a social group – yet also view the candidate along stereotypic lines as lazy or unmotivated. Furthermore, this view may be modified as additional candidate information is presented.

If individuation processes come into play, they may account for the success some African-American candidates enjoy in majority white districts. This assumes, however, that the evaluation is necessarily positive. What evidence supports this hypothesis? Social-psychological research indicates that when people make judgments about members of another group, an individual who appears to be unique from her group may be judged more positively than an identical member of the person's in-group (Linville & Jones, 1980; Locksley et al., 1982; Katz & Haas, 1988; Haas et al., 1991). Conversely, when an out-group member is perceived as typical of her group, subsequent judgments are usually just as extreme, but quite negative (Linville & Jones, 1980; Locksley et al., 1982; Katz & Haas, 1988).

Recent work by Callaghan, Swain and Terkildsen (2002) directly tested the significance of individuation processes for African-American politicians. A non-probability sample of Democratic voters residing in Nashville, Tennessee were exposed to a candidate who was or was not representative of stereotypic black politicians in terms of ideology, personal background and group affiliations. The black candidate who deviated from the group stereotype was favored over the more traditional African-American politician. Thus when presented with candidate information, voters activated the group stereotype and compared the available information with how well the candidate fit his racial group stereotype. For the "atypical" candidate, the cognitive fit was poor and required the formation of a person-based expectation ("data-driven" processing). But for the more stereotypic candidate, the group fit was confirmed and "theory-driven" processing took over. Thus, the propensity for dominant group members (i.e. whites) to make polarized judgments about politicians associated with an out-group label (i.e. black) suggests that *typicality* and *individuality* contribute to the willingness of white voters to support or reject African-American candidates in biracial elections.

But individuation processes do not explain all the variance in the model. Some African-Americans elected to federal-level office from majority white districts or states personify the black political stereotype: Democrat, liberal, with strong ties to the black community (e.g. Senator Carol Mosely-Braun from Illinois, Former U.S. Representative Alan Wheat from Missouri, and Former U.S. Representative Ronald Dellums from California, among others). Others, however, are almost diametrically opposite – Republican, conservative, with links to the corporate community (e.g. Senator Edward Brooke of Massachusetts, Former U.S. Representative Gary Franks of Connecticut and Former U.S. Representative J. C. Watts of Oklahoma). This suggests the presence of information processing techniques beyond those based on the candidate's correspondence with his or her group stereotype.

What else might modify the candidate categorization and individuation processes? One possibility is personal interactions with the candidate being judged. Candidate-voter interaction may be a key for shifting white voters' evaluation from group-related criteria to actual candidate criteria. Social psychologists have long recognized the potential benefits of inter-group interaction (Zajonc, 1968; Bornstein, 1989; Harrison, 1977) especially where racial attitudes are concerned (e.g. Cook & Selltiz, 1952; Deutsch & Collins, 1951). They assert that increased contact with members of other groups may enhance individuals' attitudes toward those groups. Bornstein (1989, p. 199) describes the process. First, an unfamiliar stimulus evokes multiple competing responses (e.g. curiosity, surprise, interest, and apprehension). Once the stimulus proves non-threatening, negative responses (e.g. fear, apprehension) weaken, while more positive responses (e.g. interest) are strengthened. Scholars do not agree, however, that mere exposure to a member of another racial group enhances a positive attitude; individuals may also need the positive reinforcement derived from pleasant social interaction. Of course, politicians have always seemed to understand this intuitively. Constituent service and a multitude of campaign events designed to "press the flesh" are regular campaign activities for savvy politicians. But for African-American candidates in particular the interaction with white voters may be a pre-condition for black electoral success.

Some evidence that meeting a black politician, rather than merely reading about him, alters a voter's propensity to stereotype and thus produces more favorable evaluations is found in the Callaghan et al. (2002) study. Participants were assigned to either 20 minutes of contact with a "real" candidate (former Representative Alan Wheat from Kansas) presented at a "meet and greet" event, or exposure to a series of printed brochures. Meeting the candidate produced more favorable evaluations for both the stereotypical and the atypical candidate than only reading about him, regardless of the negativity of voters' perceptions about blacks as a group. Voters apparently gained new information from their direct observations and interactions that disconfirmed the black candidate's fit with the group stereotype and created a need for sub-typing. Moreover, the effect due to candidate-voter contact was disproportionate, with the atypical black candidate benefiting more from interaction than the stereotypic politician. Conversely, the stereotypic African-American politician received the least favorable reception when subjects had no opportunity to personally meet the candidate. These findings suggest that race-based evaluations may be modified when an African-American candidate does not fit the traditional group profile, and when individuation – triggered through voter-candidate interaction – alters a voter's propensity to stereotype black candidates.

Inevitably, addressing one issue raises others. For example, how much do black candidates have to deviate from the group impression to override the group stereotype? Will the categorization process be the most accessible except for candidates who radically violate the black stereotype – i.e. by being ideologically conservative, highly successful, or extremely intelligent (a Colin Powell, for example)? Clearly, the processes underlying black candidate individuation warrant investigation. However, even given "atypical" candidate information (e.g. self-reliant, intelligent), it remains unclear whether individuation is a powerful or widespread enough process to produce substantial white support for black candidates. Some voters may ignore the disconfirming evidence, falling back on stereotypes to assess African American candidates. In short, a significant proportion of the white population may never vote for a black politician, even an "exemplary" one.[18]

CANDIDATE STEREOTYPES: FINE-TUNING THE MODEL

The studies described above have generally assumed that group stereotypes of African Americans serve as the basis for white voters' evaluations of African-American candidates. However, another prospect is equally plausible – that candidate stereotypes, albeit rooted in racial group stereotypes, are central to candidate assessments (see Terkildsen, 1993). That is, black *politicians* may be viewed as holding specific characteristics (e.g. personality traits, issue expertise, role-related behaviors) that adhere to the group trait, which directly or indirectly influence subsequent evaluations.

It is now generally agreed that stereotypes are composed of a variety of sub-elements, including group traits, beliefs about group behavior, physical features, and sometimes role-related behaviors (Katz & Braly, 1933; Ashmore & Del Boca, 1979; Deaux, 1984; Ashmore, Del Boca & Wohlers, 1986; Huddy & Terkildsen, 1993a, b). For example, research on gender stereotypes indicates that citizens view male and female candidates as each possessing a distinctive set of character traits, issue competencies, political beliefs and role-related behaviors (Koch, 2000; Huddy & Terkilsden, 1993, 1993b; Kahn, 1994; Kahn & Goldenberg, 1991; Leeper, 1991; Matland, 1994; Sapiro, 1982; Futron & Wyer, 1986). However, scholarly interest in gender stereotypes stands in marked contrast to the neglect of this concept in the black candidate literature. No studies have directly assessed the impact of candidate stereotypes on the evaluation of African American politicians. However, two studies are informative on this issue.

Moskowitz and Stroh (1994) found that racially intolerant voters judged a black candidate to be farther from their preferred issue positions than an identical white and made more negative evaluations about the African-American politician's personality. However, the authors used a composite measure of both group and candidate stereotypes, making it impossible to determine the precise influence of the latter (i.e. those specifically associated with the black *candidate* stereotype). Terkildsen (1996, 1997) measured candidate stereotypes directly and found that citizens use group stereotypes to infer candidate traits, related behaviors and political beliefs. Specifically, group stereotyping reduced the positive inferences white subjects made about the personality traits of the African American politician. The impact of race-related traits, role-related behaviors, and political beliefs significantly influenced black candidate evaluations and vote assessments.

But a more systematic analysis of this issue is needed. Specifically, two questions need to be addressed. First, "What is the exact content of African-American candidates stereotypes?" And second, "Precisely how and why do such stereotypes influence the evaluation of African-American candidates?" Trait-based judgments may allow white voters to perceive candidates of color as less politically qualified due to a mismatch on key personality attributes. That is, candidates of color, by virtue of their group association, may be perceived as occupationally unsuitable to hold higher office because competence and leadership are so pivotal in making political evaluations (Kinder, 1986; Wattenberg et al., 1986). If white voters perceive a mismatch between an African-American candidate and their categorization of the "ideal" politician (likely a white male) on personality trait dimensions that have been shown to be central to white candidate evaluations (Kinder, 1986; Rahn et al., 1990; Miller et al., 1986), then black contenders will be evaluated as less competent, negatively influencing vote judgments. However, the Kinder (1986) "presidential" trait dimensions (competency, leadership, empathy, and integrity) may be less relevant for black politicians. Instead, black candidate stereotypes should be more likely to include politically relevant adjectives linked to the race-related traits of African Americans, the specific typecasts about black political behavior and historical and contemporary information about black politics. Moreover, these dimensions may be the most salient to white voters' evaluative judgments.

For example, because of past and present black involvement in protest movements and the willingness of some blacks to use force to alter the political structure, black candidates may be viewed as more militant than their white counterparts and thus a power to be feared. If a particular voter associates African-Americans with "radical" or "militant" behaviors, she may infer that the candidate will engage in extreme behavior and hold issue positions that are extreme – i.e. outside the bounds of conventionality – regardless of the specific information available about the candidate's behavior. Similarly, particular categorizations may lead white voters to assume that African American politicians will engage in punitive behavior toward whites or favoritism towards blacks during their tenure in office.

Black politicians may also be assumed to possess other specific traits or expectations consistent with the group stereotype: fiscal irresponsibility, an inability to run government, or an eagerness to emphasize race-related policies and programs. Due to disproportionate media attention on real or perceived improprieties, African-American politicians may also be seen as "politicians-on-the-take." For instance, former Secretary of Agriculture and Mississippi Congressman Mike Espy's once transcendent political career was destroyed by a 30-count federal indictment over illegal gifts from companies regulated by the Department of Agriculture. Although Espy was found not guilty, investigations into every corner of his life ruined his career (see Whitaker, 1999). Similarly, allegations about Illinois Senator Carol Mosely-Braun's financial dealings helped end her first senate term and her candidacy for ambassador to New Zealand. Although accused of using campaign funds to buy designer clothing, jewelry and a stereo, the IRS was unable to verify the charges ("Mosely-Braun," 1999). Whether or not allegations such as these are more prevalent or covered differently when they involve black office holders or candidates, it seems clear that the media play an important role in both creating and reinforcing stereotypes (see Terkildsen & Damore, 1999).

On the political front, since most African-Americans are Democrats and liberals (Sigelman & Welch, 1991), this information may lead voters to make judgments about the issue positions advocated by specific candidates of color while ignoring their actual issues positions (Conover & Feldman, 1986). As a result, a black candidate is assumed to be liberal or a Democrat and thus assumed to support increased programs for minorities (much as women candidates are assumed to be Democrats and/or to hold more liberal positions, especially on social issues). Interpolating from the political ideology and partisanship of most African-Americans, voters may also stereotype particular black candidates as less concerned with or capable of handling business matters or the economy. Belief stereotypes may then inhibit voters from processing atypical ideological or partisan information when candidates of color hold moderate or conservative political convictions.

If white voters evaluate black candidates on the basis of specific personality traits or beliefs, and apply such trait schema consistently from election to election (Miller et al., 1986; Kinder 1986) then the influence of such factors may be as integral to any understanding of black candidate evaluations as more explicitly racial cues and stereotypes.

THE IMPACT OF CANDIDATE STEREOTYPES: AN EXPERIMENTAL APPLICATION

To explore the potential role of candidate stereotyping in biracial elections we conducted a simple laboratory experiment. Our subjects were 60 white undergraduate students from a major northeastern university (given our earlier discussion of the potential limits of generalizing from student samples, the results of this analysis should be taken with caution, though the likely impact of student bias would be to underestimate the strength of any evidence of racial stereotyping). Subjects were randomly assigned to one of four different experimental conditions in which candidate race and skin color was manipulated as a between-groups factor.[19] Subjects were presented with a photograph of a political candidate (a white male, a light-skinned black male, or a dark-skinned black male) or were assigned to an additional control condition where they were not exposed to a photograph of the candidate.[20]

Subjects viewed the candidate photograph via a computer program. The same photograph of an unfamiliar candidate from another state was used for all experimental manipulations. In order to control for the effects of physical attractiveness on global candidate evaluations, as well as to eliminate any possible confound between candidate skin color and physical attractiveness, the photographs used in the stimulus materials were professionally altered. A minimal transformation in the facial features of the experimental candidates were made by a professional consultant using a computer-assisted graphics design program. The stimulus materials were then loaded into the computer program.[21]

Following exposure to the candidate image, the subjects used a computer "mouse" to scroll through the candidate information, which included the candidate's political background, personal attributes, work habits and policy preferences, all excerpted from local newspapers and group-related publications (see Appendix A). The descriptions of the candidates were identical in every respect except for race. The candidate ("Roger Hiltman)" was described as the state treasurer of Oklahoma, a politically moderate to slightly conservative politician who was planning to run for governor. Hiltman, as we described him, favored the following issue positions: reducing acid rain, increasing funding for AIDS research, cutting taxes, extending the state's tax exemption laws to further benefit religious institutions, subsidizing low-income housing, and requiring stiffer jail sentences for repeat offenders. In terms of personal attributes, Hiltman was described as the self-reliant, well-educated son of working-class parents. He had political support from the Sierra Club International, the Oklahoma Medical Association, the Southern Baptist Association, and the Oklahoma Business Council. Hiltman was also endorsed by the *Oklahoma Sun Times*. The wealth of candidate information we supplied to participants (making it a "high-information" election) aimed at minimizing any potential effect of candidate race by giving subjects plenty of information on which to judge the candidate (see McDermott, 1997), but not so much as to overload subjects and trigger a race-based judgment (information overload can trigger heuristic processing – see note 16).

After reading the candidate information, subjects used the mouse to indicate their willingness to vote for Hiltman and to make a series of judgments about two aspects of the "black" candidate stereotype: personality traits and political behaviors. To determine the degree to which the trait components of racial stereotypes differentiate between black and white candidates and influence candidate evaluation, we exposed subjects to a battery of 18 traits, including stereotypical racial traits (e.g. unintelligent, angry, athletic, religious, unmotivated) and Kinder's (1986) presidential trait dimensions of competency, leadership, empathy, and integrity (e.g. hard-working, competent, decent, inspiring, charismatic). Subjects were also asked to infer the candidate's partisanship and ideology. Since most African-Americans run and win as Democrats, particularly in the South, and blacks as a group are strongly identified with the Democratic party and a liberal ideology, we would expect a differential effect of race on these dimensions. Additional belief inferences assessed the subjects' perceptions about Hiltman's activist nature (e.g. militant, radical). At the end of the study, subjects were presented with a series of racial attitude questions. See Appendix B for the complete set of measures and scale reliabilities.[22]

Table 1 presents the mean response to the trait and belief variables by each candidate condition. The table also presents the F-values associated with each item based on an Analysis of Variance (ANOVA). There are three points of comparison here. First, whether there is a main effect for candidate race. Second, whether the group means for the white and light skin candidates are significantly different from the black candidate condition. And third, whether the mean response for individuals exposed to a candidate race condition is significantly higher or lower than those who were exposed to the "control" candidate. Differences in group means are based on a contrast effects analysis. We adopt a less stringent 0.10 level of significance for the contrast effects due to sample size.

As Table 1 shows, the results for two of the presidential character variables (competence and leadership) follow the predicted "stereotypical" pattern. Although the effect of candidate race was not statistically significant, in both instances subjects rated the white and the control group candidates more favorably than either black candidate. For instance, when Hiltman was presented as a dark-skinned black, subjects made fewer positive inferences about his competence (–11%) and lowered their evaluation of his leadership ability by 3% compared to the white candidate. The impact of candidate race on judgments about the empathic nature of the candidate's personality was not statistically

Table 1. Candidate Stereotype Ratings by Candidate Race.

	Control (12)	White (16)	Light Skin Black (13)	Dark Skin Black (14)
CHARACTER TRAITS				
Presidential Traits				
DV 1: Competence	1.58	1.64	1.72	1.85
F-value: 0.824				
DV 2: Leadership	2.08	2.07	2.27	2.13
F-value: 0.615				
DV 3: Integrity	2.69	2.54	2.51	2.53
F-value: 1.938				
DV 4: Empathy	2.75	2.56	2.44*	2.48*
F-value: 1.468				
Racial Traits				
DV 5: Intelligence	1.67	1.88	1.77*	2.21*
F-value: 1.323				
DV 6: Motivation	1.50	1.63	1.88	1.93*
F-value: 0.955				
DV 7: Athletic Ability	3.00	2.94	3.00	2.86
F-value: 0.360				
DV 8: Religiosity	1.50	1.69+	1.62	1.38*
F-value: 0.982				
DV 9: Hostility	3.67	3.63	3.77	3.61
F-value: 0.243				
POLITICAL BEHAVIOR				
DV 10: Militancy Rating	3.25	3.38	3.23	3.14
F-value: 0.235				
DV 11: Corruptibility	2.83	2.66	2.77	2.50
F-value: 0.685				
DV 12: Fiscal Responsibility	1.33	1.44	1.31	1.29
F-value: 0.286				
DV 13: Radical/Extreme	2.55	2.73+	2.28	2.29
F-value: 1.779				
POLITICAL BELIEFS				
DV 14: Party Affiliation	2.92	3.31	2.77	2.67
F-value: 0.180				
DV 15: Ideology	3.83	3.81	3.46	3.29*
F-value: 1.324				

$*p < 0.05$; $+p < 0.10$. Analyses performed using a one-way analysis of variance (ANOVA). Entries are cell means for each condition: numbers in parentheses are cell's. Means with an asterisk are statistically different from the control group and means with a subscript are statistically different from the black candidate condition ($p < 0.10$) based on an ANOVA contrast analysis (separate variance estimates). Trait and behavior variables are coded 1"very well" to 4 "not very well." Party affiliation is coded 1 "strong Democrat" to 7 "strong Republican." Ideology is coded 1 "strong liberal" to 7 "strong conservative."

significant ($F = 1.468$, $p \leq 0.24$). However, the light and dark-skinned candidates were viewed as significantly more "empathic" than the white candidate (+12% and +10%, respectively). The impact of candidate race on the integrity trait was not discernible, although all candidates were viewed as more honest than the control group candidate. Based on these findings, African-American candidates appeared to fall short on two key personality characteristics attributed to the exemplary white politician – competence and leadership (see Kinder, 1986; Miller et al., 1986).

Looking at the "black" trait measures, when Hiltman was a dark-skinned "African-American" he was seen as less intelligent (–15%) and less motivated (–16%) than when he was "white" – two traits that are widely accepted components of the black stereotype. The light skinned African-American was also viewed as less motivated (–14%) but more intelligent (+5%) than the white candidate. Both African-American candidates differed from the control group on the intelligence trait but only the dark-skinned Hiltman differed on motivation. Candidate race did not significantly alter subjects' perception of his athletic ability and religiosity – two traits associated with the global black stereotype that may not be directly applicable to politics. However, the dark-skin candidate was seen as significantly more religious (+18%) than the white candidate ($M = 1.38$) ($p \leq 0.05$).

Furthermore, as Table 1 shows, three of the four behavioral expectations about Hiltman as a "black" candidate were "negative." Subjects rated the dark-skinned Hiltman as more "radical" ($M = 2.29$) than the white Hiltman ($M = 2.73$) (+16%). They also believed he was slightly more likely to resign his position because of a scandal and take illegal campaign money ($M = 2.50$) compared to the white Hiltman ($M = 2.66$) (+4%). Additionally, the dark-skinned Hiltman was seen as more "militant" ($M = 3.15$) than the white version ($M = 3.38$) (+7%). That the black Hiltman was perceived as more radical, militant, and extreme suggests that African-American political contenders are subject to stereotypic biases that are linked to the group stereotype. Importantly, the "black" trait and behavioral dimensions appear to be the most discriminating personality factors (largest mean differences between groups). Not surprisingly, the impact of being a light-skinned candidate, while generally following the direction of our hypothesis about the dark-skinned candidate, was less consistent in its effect across the trait and behavior measures (see note 21).

What about the control group? As we expected, most people assumed the candidate in the "no photo" condition was white – i.e. the candidate stereotyping measures were not differentiable as the contrast analyses show. This suggests that when a voter reads or hears about a candidate whose race is unidentified, she will assume the candidate is white and respond accordingly.

Finally, despite the identical policy positions and background of the black and white Hiltman, subjects viewed the black candidates along stereotyped lines – 14% more liberal for the dark-skinned black ($M = 3.29$, $p \le 0.05$) and 10% more liberal for the light-skinned candidate ($M = 3.46$, *ns*) compared to the control candidate ($M = 3.83$). Moreover, both black candidates were viewed as substantively more liberal than the white candidate ($M = 3.81$). Although subjects were not told whether Hiltman was a Republican or Democrat, they inferred that the black candidates' partisan preferences leaned more toward the Democratic party (for the dark-skinned black $M = 2.67$; for the light-skinned black $M = 2.77$), compared to the white candidate ($M = 3.31$), though these results are not statistically significant.

Altogether, these results provide some suggestive evidence that white voters see important differences between black and white candidates based solely on the candidate's race. Moreover, subjects associated the dark-skinned black candidate with the most negative traits and behaviors. If we assume that this subject population – students – has a greater tendency to inflate their positive beliefs about African-American candidates, then these findings may under-estimate the extent to which white stereotyping of black candidates occurs.

But are these dimensions the actual standards on which black candidates are judged? It is one thing to demonstrate that white voters possess stereotyped pre-conceptions of African-American candidates. It is another to show that these elements of character and behavioral expectations carry any weight in their candidate judgments. Is the evaluation of black candidates as a group based on the global black stereotypes? Or do racial traits and beliefs have a greater influence on judgments about candidates of color? Finally, how does the evaluative impact of racial traits compare to those of Kinder's (1986) personality dimensions?

In order to address these questions, we conducted a two-way Analysis of Variance with candidate evaluation as the dependent variable and "CANDI-DATE RACE X STEREOTYPING" as the interaction effects. We measured subjects' evaluation of the political candidates with a 10-point feeling thermo-meter scale ranging from "very negative" (1) to "very positive" (10). The independent variables are the same as those described in Table 1 except that we added a "group stereotype" measure composed of eighteen items in which subjects were asked to anchor black Americans as a group on a series of trait questions (see the Appendix B). A piecemeal strategy is necessary because of overall limitations in sample size.[23]

As Table 2 shows, the results regarding candidate stereotype paint an inter-esting picture. Although no one component is as strong as the "group" stereotype measure ($F = 4.079$, $p = 0.04$), the means are fairly consistent across measures

Table 2. Evaluative Impact of Candidate Stereotypes Controlling for Candidate.

	Control	White	Light Skin Black	Dark Skin Black
CHARACTER TRAITS				
Racial Traits				
Race X Intelligence				
F-value: 1.554				
High	8.50	7.67[a]	8.00	8.60
	(4)	(3)	(5)	(5)
Low	8.13	7.85	7.00*	7.17+
	(8)	(13)	(8)	(8)
Race X Motivation				
F-value: 2.760+				
High	7.42	7.31	8.45*	8.15+
	(7)	(8)	(7)	(6)
Low	6.00	6.00	6.00	5.00+
	(5)	(8)	(6)	(8)
Race X Religiosity				
F-value: 0.182				
High	8.75	7.67	8.17	7.88
	(6)	(5)	(5)	(8)
Low	8.50	7.47	7.50	7.33
	(6)	(11)	(8)	(5)
Race X Hostility				
F-value: 0.545				
High	7.75	7.71[a]	7.40	6.67*
	(4)	(8)	(5)	(5)
Low	8.00	7.89	8.22	7.60
	(8)	(8)	(8)	(9)
Presidential Traits				
Race X Competency				
F-value: 0.836				
High	8.50	8.20	9.10	8.15
	(3)	(8)	(6)	(5)
Low	8.67	6.80[a]	7.33	7.00
	(9)	(8)	(7)	(9)
Race X Leadership				
F-value: 1.709				
High	9.00	8.00*	8.80	8.25
	(6)	(6)	(5)	(10)
Low	8.25	7.38	6.67	6.73*
	(6)	(10)	(8)	(4)
Race X Empathy				
F-value: 3.174*				
High	8.67	7.57	8.00	8.22
	(8)	(12)	(8)	(9)
Low	8.50	7.33[a]	5.00*	5.00*
	(4)	(4)	(5)	(5)

Table 2. Continued.

	Control	White	Light Skin Black	Dark Skin Black
Race X Integrity				
F-value: 0.283				
High	8.63	7.56	7.56	8.00
	(9)	(9)	(8)	(9)
Low	8.33	8.00	8.50	7.80
	(3)	(7)	(5)	(5)
POLITICAL BEHAVIOR				
Race X Militancy				
F-value: 1.695				
High	8.43	7.91	7.00*	7.38*
	(4)	(7)	(5)	(5)
Low	8.00	7.33^a	8.25	8.67
	(8)	(9)	(8)	(9)
Race X Radical/Extreme				
F-value: 3.157*				
High	8.17^a	8.33^{a}*	7.67^a	6.17*
	(6)	(3)	(3)	(7)
Low	8.33	7.69	7.29	8.50*
	(6)	(13)	(10)	(7)
Race X Corruptibility				
F-value: 2.195$^+$				
High	8.75	7.73*	6.86*	7.22*
	(6)	(8)	(9)	(7)
Low	8.00	8.00	8.17	8.00
	(6)	(8)	(4)	(7)
Race X Fiscal Responsibility				
F-value: 0.854				
High	8.83	8.83	8.05	7.63*
	(8)	(9)	(8)	(9)
Low	8.00	8.62	8.00	8.00
	(4)	(7)	(5)	(5)
GROUP STEREOTYPES				
Race X Black Stereotype				
F-value: 4.079*				
High	7.59	8.40^a	7.67^a	6.67*
	(6)	(7)	(4)	(5)
Low	8.00	7.97	8.83*	9.00*
	(6)	(9)	(9)	(9)

*$p < 0.05$; $^+p < 0.10$. Analyses performed using analysis of variance (ANOVA). Entries are cell means for each condition; numbers in parentheses are cell Ns. Means with an asterisk are statistically different from the control group and means with a subscript are statistically different from the black candidate condition ($p < 0.10$) using ANOVA contrast analysis (separate variance estimates). The dependent variable is candidate evaluation coded 1 "unfavorable" to 10 "favorable."

and three of the interaction effects for the black candidate stereotype are statistically significant. For instance, the dark-skinned black with a low intelligence rating was evaluated 9% more negatively ($M = 7.17$) than the white candidate ($M = 7.82$), whereas the black candidate with a high intelligence rating was evaluated eleven% more positively ($M = 8.60$) than his white counterpart ($M = 7.67$) ($F = 1.544$, $p = 19$). Similarly, a low motivation rating produced a 17% more negative influence on the darker black's evaluation ($M = 5.0$) compared to the white candidate ($M = 6.0$), whereas a high motivation rating increased his evaluation by 10% ($M = 8.15$) over the white candidate ($M = 7.31$) ($F=2.760$, $p = 0.16$). As before, the results were more variable for the light-skinned black. For example, a high motivation rating produced a 14% increase in evaluation ($M = 8.45$) compared to the white candidate ($M = 7.31$). However, a low motivation rating did not alter his evaluation ($M = 6.00$ for both candidates). These results fit with the notion of "old fashioned" racism, with perceived intelligence as the key triggering variable.

Furthermore, as shown in Table 2, the most distinguishing pattern between candidate race and candidate stereotyping has to do with the candidate's political behavior. For instance, there is a statistically significant interaction between candidate race and subjects' expectations about the candidate's corruptibility ($F = 2.195$, $p = 0.10$) and his radical or extreme behavior ($F = 3.157$, $p = 0.03$). A third behavioral expectation, militancy, while following in the direction of our hypothesis, did not reach conventional levels of significance ($F = 2.35$, $p = 0.14$). In general, the mean differences in evaluation are largest for the dark-skinned candidate compared to the light-skinned candidate. However, comparisons between the black candidate and the control condition were more variable. Thus, almost across the board subjects relied more heavily on their racial traits attributions and belief inferences for the black candidate than for the white candidates.

By contrast, both candidates were affected by traditional personality trait dimensions. There is a statistically significant main effect for two of the Kinder trait variables (competency and leadership, data not shown) but no interaction for candidate race except for the empathy dimension ($F = 3.174$, $p < 0.04$). Thus, the "black" trait and beliefs dimensions are more central to the role of minority candidate evaluation than traditional presidential traits. Although the idea that people use the standard personality traits (e.g. competence, leadership) to evaluate politicians fits nicely with prior studies involving white candidates, the default value tends to be different for black political candidates.[24]

Of course, the interaction effects for the candidate stereotype measures are not very large. Still, in an electoral situation, the consistently negative influence of the racial trait and belief inferences indicates that white voters will be less likely to vote for African-American candidates and, in an election the difference between winning and losing can be small. These findings reinforce the already bleak picture for African-American candidates delineated by previous research – black politicians are perceived to possess more negative personality traits and work-related behaviors than white politicians. Even though subjects had access to the candidate's message, and could attend to it and process it at their leisure, they paid substantial attention to candidate race, concentrating on the negative personal attributes they associated with African-American candidates. The pernicious influence of racial prejudice and stereotypes appears to further dim the already limited electoral prospects of minority candidates.[25]

As further evidence in support of these conclusions, consider the following. Our Nashville, Tennessee study mentioned earlier asked participants the following open-ended question: "Please list everything that comes to mind about the candidate from the impressions you formed this evening." For the black politician 21% of the items were racial traits and beliefs (e.g. aggressive, religious, supports blacks, racist, discriminatory), whereas only 7% referred to the Kinder traits (e.g. honest, really cares, compassionate). For the white politician, 29% of the comments referred to the Kinder traits, while only 4% referred to racial traits.

Adding these findings to those of other studies reported on in this essay suggests that in a variety of populations (random and non-random samples; average adults, partisan adults, and college students), across regions (for example, New York, Tennessee, and Kentucky) and across time (1993–1998), the black candidate stereotype is prominent and politically influential.

CONCLUSIONS

While suggestive, the research presented in this essay leaves many questions unanswered. How much do specific traits and beliefs contribute to the total variance in candidate evaluations? Do racial traits and beliefs contribute uniquely to judgments about candidates of color, or are beliefs more important than traits? Are individual candidate and/or racial traits distinct in their impact, or might they cluster into specific dimensions? Which traits or beliefs are the primary or most immediate bases for formulating one's attitude toward a black candidate? Which have a direct or indirect effect? Under what conditions?

But the relationship between black candidate stereotypes and evaluation may be even more complicated than this. For example, a voter may infer that an African-American candidate endorses a given set of issue positions because she believes the candidate has certain personality traits (e.g. is militant) that combine to form her image. Alternately, the voter may infer the candidate's personal traits from issue positions. And it is plausible, based on prior research (Stroh, 1991; Conover & Feldman, 1989; Ottati et al., 1988; Feldman & Conover, 1983) that the voter's perception of her own reactions to the candidate may lead her to infer that the candidate has certain personality characteristics, issue positions or role-related behaviors that are consistent with these reactions. In other words the voter may project certain issue positions and behaviors onto candidates she likes and attribute unfavorable behaviors to disliked candidates. For example, prejudiced voters who are ideologically liberal may support particular domestic policies, but due to their dislike for African-American politicians, project what they believe to be unacceptable issue positions onto the candidate of color (e.g. lack of support for the domestic policy in question).[26]

Ultimately what is needed is a more fully integrated model that can address a wide range of candidate variations including those based on race. While presenting such a model is beyond the scope of this essay, we propose the following agenda. First, we need research that controls for the specific sub-dimensions of the black stereotype (e.g. ideology, group affiliations, personal background, role-related behaviors) along with other group and candidate stereotypes, thus allowing for more systematic evidence to assess whether and how evaluations of black politicians differ from that of whites. We have demonstrated that negative candidate stereotypes related to race have the potential to shape evaluations of black politicians. Yet work on the components of candidate stereotypes must be expanded to determine whether white voters use global black stereotypes, or separate subcategories, as they assess candidates of color and the precise nature of those domain-specific stereotypes.

Second, more research is needed on the reporting of political judgments, including the use of self-monitoring measures designed to capture impression management. Researchers must properly control for self-regulation in order to gauge the full impact of white prejudice. Without such controls, we cannot accurately portray the role of candidate race in biracial elections.

Of course, we can never fully know the full effects of race until we include minority voters (including but not limited to African Americans) in our analyses. Therefore, our third recommendation is to extend the empirical research on candidate race to include the candidate evaluations of other racial and ethnic groups. The coalitions built by black candidates between black, Hispanic, and sometimes Asian voters are crucial not only to maintaining their present electoral base, but to winning future elections. For example, Tom Bradley was elected mayor of Los Angeles in 1972 with the help of a coalition of white, Latino and black voters (Hahn et al., 1976). In the 1993 mayoral elections in New York City, Asian voters began to be key players. The near election of an Asian-American mayor in Los Angeles and the need of former New York City Mayor

David Dinkins to closely court the Asian vote also signal the beginning of a shift in the electoral significance of minority coalitions. While Asian-American voters are not a monolithic group, they tend to be ideologically more conservative and more Republican than most blacks and many Latinos. Based on the perceptions about the political beliefs of African-American candidates, Asian-Americans may be less willing to vote for candidates of color. Latinos may also be less inclined to vote for black candidates because of racial stereotypes, and African-American voters may penalize dark-skinned politicians, just as dark-skinned black children and adults face subtle discrimination. Research by Bobo and his colleagues (Bobo, 2001; Bobo & Massagli, 2001; Bobo & Johnson, 2000) suggests that the stereotypes of African Americans are generally the most consistent and harsh for all groups. In other words, there may well be a racial/ethnic hierarchy with black Americans (and perhaps black candidates) at the bottom.

Very little is known about minority voting preferences in part because national samples generally have not generated large enough numbers of non-whites to assess in any depth their political attitudes and behavior. For example, a national sample of 1500 respondents randomly selected by the National Election Studies typically includes about 170 blacks. While a few researchers such as Katherine Tate (1993) and Carol Swain (1993) have begun to utilize national samples with expanded black respondents, more work needs to be done. Our fourth recommendation is that national polls designed to describe and better understand voters' assessments of candidates over sample non-whites.

As the research reported on in this essay makes clear, understanding how race affects candidate evaluations requires also understanding how race interacts with other, more traditional election-related variables. We know, for example, that money matters in American election campaigns in various ways (e.g. Ferguson, 1995; Jacobson, 1997). However, we know much less about how money may differently affect non-white candidates or biracial elections. To better understand these relationships, we need to study races involving black and white candidates and compare them to the non-minority elections. Our fifth recommendation is that we more regularly and consciously consider the role of mainstream political science variables (e.g. incumbency, financial and political resources, name recognition) in creating a minority candidate's global image and in reinforcing or alleviating the impact of these images on minority candidates' prospects for electoral success.

In the next century whites will likely no longer represent a majority of the U.S. population, due to both immigration and differential birth rates. The result will be an increasingly racially and ethnically diverse society (e.g. Bobo, James, Johnson & Valenzuela, 2000). Inevitably, campaigns will become more diverse, with more Asians, Latinos and African Americans running for office, at times against members of their own ethnicity and at times against candidates that are ethnically different from themselves. Thus, the importance of better understanding how race and ethnicity affects candidate evaluations and ultimately the vote will also become increasingly important. Absent this, existing models that have largely ignored race will become decreasingly useful in explaining how voters come to their decisions. Thus, our sixth and most overarching recommendation is that the study of "race" not only be expanded, but that it also be better integrated into "mainstream" studies of electoral behavior. Social science research has much to gain from a complete understanding of biracial elections and candidate evaluation. Such research would help fill an important gap in our knowledge of regarding how voters assess minority candidates. It would help better understand how voters come to political judgement about candidates more broadly. It could play a role in identifying ways to increase the representation of minority citizens in elected office. And ultimately it could help us to confront the problems of race in contemporary American electoral politics.

NOTES

1. The term "white voters" tends to be used rather loosely in the social science literature. For the purposes of this essay, white voters refer to individuals of European ancestry, not all non-blacks.

2. More generally, self-monitoring refers to the phenomenon of using observation and self-control to guide individual behavior and attitudes in social situations. This well-documented theory in social psychology is applicable to a variety of populations in a myriad of situations in the social and political domain (Snyder, 1974, 1979; Jones & Baumeister, 1976; Synder & Cantor, 1980; Snyder & Campbell, 1982; Fiske & Taylor, 1991; Terkildsen, 1993).

3. In the late 1880s when the Supreme Court began restricting application of the 14th and 15th "Civil Rights" Amendments to the states, southern and midwestern legislatures took advantage of the nation's Constitutional void and passed a series of "Jim Crow" laws which legalized racial segregation and effectively eliminated blacks from voting and running for public office. In 1876, for example, the Supreme Court refused to extend the 15th Amendment, black male voting rights, to the states (*U.S. v. Reese* and *U.S. v. Cruikshank*). In 1883 by an 8–1 vote the Court declared the Civil Rights Act of 1875, a Congressional statute, unconstitutional. The Court reasoned that denying someone public accommodation could hardly be considered slavery (13th Amendment) or a "public action" by the states (14th Amendment); instead, it was a private action which was exempt from 14th Amendment coverage. However, the decision that sealed the legal coffin of black Americans was *Plessy v. Ferguson* (1896) in which the Supreme Court by an 8–1 vote held "separate, but equal" facilities did not violate the 14th Amendment.

4. Over the past twenty years the numbers of black officials elected at the municipal and county levels have increased 600% and 900% respectively. As of 1990 there were 313 African-American mayors. While the majority preside over small southern towns, 11% of black mayors govern cities with populations of 50,000 or more (JCPES, 1991).

5. Although women politicians are generally more liberal than their male counterparts, voters see them as even more liberal than their voting record suggests. Why? In part, because there have been more liberal women Democrats running for office than conservative women Republicans.

6. In the late 1940s the concentrated black vote in a few large cities in pivotal northern states became significant enough to influence close presidential elections. Harry Truman got the black vote due to his policy desegregating the army (Wilson, 1980; Moon, 1948). After Truman, however, the Democratic Party retreated from racial liberalism (Kinder & Sanders, 1996, p. 201). Thus, during this period, there was no variance in voting by race, though in some instances race played a role in municipal elections.

7. See, for example, Pillsbury (1995); Amy (1994); Still (1984); Karnig and Welch (1982); Bullock (1981); Davidson (1981).

8. Supreme Court challenges involved voting regulations that hindered or diluted the effects of minority voting, including at-large districts, multi-member legislative districts, and racial gerrymandering (see JCPES, 1991 for a complete history of the relevant cases).

9. An assessment of prominent blacks elected to high status offices in predominantly white electoral districts shows a penchant toward electing individuals with lighter skin color (e.g. David Dinkins, Hiltman Young, Douglas Wilder). Furthermore, survey research shows racial prejudice had a negative impact on Jesse Jackson, a well-known black candidate with a darker skin, but was almost non-existent in voters' evaluations of Tom Bradley, a black man with lighter skin tones (Citrin et al., 1990; Sears et al., 1987; Pettigrew, 1972, 1976; Hahn et al., 1976).

10. Of course, similar, but not identical, models work for white candidates when they link themselves or have been linked to race through racial issues (e.g. Kinder & Sanders, 1996; Callaghan, 1993, 2002; Sniderman, Swain & Elms, 1995; Sleeper, 1990).

11. Studies by black children of all ages from the mid-1940s to the late 1980s in both predominantly white and black societies reveal the importance of skin color as a social cue. In the famous "doll" study by Kenneth and Eleanor Clark (1950), white skin color was valued by children more than any other pigmentation, and darker shades of skin were associated with unfavorable traits like ugly, bad, dirty, and poor. Children also used skin color to infer job status and social class – whites were designated to managerial jobs and upper-class positions, while blacks were assigned to subservient tasks and given lower-class status. The Clark work is famous because of its relevance to the Supreme Court's *Brown v. The Board of Education* (1954) decision. Chief Justice Earl Warren cited it and other research as partial justification for the Court's decision that "separate but equal" schools are unconstitutional.

12. More than 60% of the adult population in Jefferson County was registered to vote. Moreover, adults not registered to vote were captured by the drivers' license or non-driver identification card lists maintained by the state (more than 90% of the adult population). Furthermore, since legal sanctions are imposed for failing to respond to jury service, the sample allowed access to respondents often hard to reach by telephone.

13. Some interview-related research methods do not necessitate controls for self-regulation. For example, focus groups may minimize self-regulatory behavior. A 1985

analysis conducted by Stanley Greenberg for the Democratic National Committee using focus groups of white, working-class voters in Macomb County, Michigan, showed that white voters were more than willing to express "a profound distaste for blacks" and race-related policies (see Edsall & Edsall, 1991, p. 182). The cohesive nature of the group was likely a significant factor in reducing self-monitoring and enhancing individual honesty. By the same token, group pressures to conform may have artificially inflated reported levels of intolerance.

14. This distinction between categorization and individuation is also referred to as theory-driven vs. data-driven processing (see Fiske & Taylor, 1991).

15. On dual processing models, see also Fiske & Neuberg,1990; Fiske & Pavelchak, 1986.

16. Using experimental data, Huddy and Capelos found that gender stereotypes do not completely disappear once a candidate is viewed as a distinct individual. Subjects were provided with information on a male or female candidate's competence and honesty, followed by a news story about the candidate's involvement in a scandal. While subjects individuated the candidate according to the initial profile, the scandal contradicted the honest candidate's profile, leading to further individuation. The scandal also evoked stereotypes of a typical politician as "crooked and "self-serving" that overlapped with gender stereotypes of male politicians as less honest than female politicians. The female candidate evaded some of this negativity because she did not fit the profile of a typical politician. This work implies that the processing model for African-American candidates may be more complicated than we have tested here.

17. The use of categorization versus individuation is dependent on many additional factors: amount and complexity of the information, time frame given for the evaluation, level of personal interaction in the future, perceived importance of the judgment, status differences, etc. (e.g. Bodenhausen & Lichtenstein, 1987; Pryor & Ostrom, 1981; Ostrom, Pryor & Simpson, 1981). Thus a one shot evaluation with high levels of information and low interest levels will in most voters produce category-based or category-dominated evaluations. This scenario would be analogous to the real world processing of many non-incumbent candidates.

18. The traditional NES question assessing racial voting behavior may shed some light on this issue: "Would you vote for a qualified black presidential candidate who has already secured your party's nomination?" While wildly hypothetical in a manner more extreme than even an experiment which uses a fictitious candidates, the question assumes: (1) a racially-atypical candidate (highly qualified); (2) a degree of voter-candidate compatibility (same party); and (3) the seal of approval of a majority of similar voters and the party hierarchy (party nominee). Responses to this question, not unlike tolerance attitudes (for example, "free speech)", are truncated at the extreme end of the scale with a super majority of white support. But issues of social desirability and political reality soon come into play (see Terkildsen, 1997).

19. Five subjects who did identify their race as white were excluded from the analysis. Thus the sample size for this analysis was $N = 56$.

20. Since white candidates are the baseline by which non-white contenders are often judged, subjects assigned to the white candidate serve as a control group. However, we also included a "no photograph" condition in our experimental design to provide additional information about the "default" or "baseline" levels of candidate stereotyping, as well as subjects' assumptions about candidate race. When voters read about a

candidate in the newspaper, the candidate's race is not usually mentioned unless the candidate is non-white. However, most voters assume the candidate is white (see Terkildsen & Damore, 1999). Therefore, we hypothesize that subjects will assume our control candidate is white, and as a consequence, mentioning his race is superfluous – i.e. there should be no differences in subjects' assessment of the white and the control group candidate.

21. To check whether subjects misclassified the candidate's race, we asked subjects to identify our candidate's ethnicity. Subjects were told that race had become an important factor in the gubernatorial contest; that many voters had confused the candidate's ethnicity, so their assessment of his race would be most helpful. Five standard categories (African American, Asian, Hispanic, Native American, and White), as well as "Other" were provided. "Accuracy" rates were highest for the white candidate (93%) followed by the dark-skinned candidate (71%). Accuracy rates were lowest for the light-skinned candidate (40%); therefore, we report but do not underscore these findings. Finally, as we hypothesized (see note 20), most of the subjects in the control group thought the candidate was white (50%). While this analysis does not comment on subjects' awareness of the candidate's race during the study, it is possible to conclude from this manipulation check that when asked at the end of the experiment to make a deliberate judgment about the candidate's race, 82% were fairly accurate in their assessment of the white or dark-skinned candidate.

22. Before we can see whether candidate race actually produced distinct stereotypic judgments, we needed to insure that the subjects assigned randomly to the two experimental conditions were in fact comparable. Therefore, we performed a series of comparisons across a range of attitudinal and demographic variables (prejudice, ideology, partisanship and gender). None of the F-values were statistically significant. Further, to insure that candidate physical attractiveness did not covary with the candidate race manipulation we conducted additional tests. Overall the candidate was perceived by subjects as moderately attractive with no significant differences between the two photos. These results reassured us that the only feature that separated the two groups was the "race of the candidate" manipulation.

23. We caution the reader in making too much of the results in which the means for the contrasted cells are based on fewer than five cases, even though the mean changes reported may be statistically significant.

24. Racial traits and beliefs may also mediate the effects of race, in addition to moderating them, as shown in the reported interactions. In order to test this model, we must first establish a direct effect of candidate race on evaluation. However, candidate race had a limited effect on evaluation with the dark and light-skinned politician evaluated only slightly less positively ($M = 7.70$ and $M = 7.66$, respectively) than the white politician ($M = 7.81$) ($F = 0.794$, ns). Thus, this model is outside the scope of the present study, but we encourage such analyses in future research.

25. These results are consistent with the earlier adult population findings (see Terkildsen, 1997), the primary difference is that those results were more pronounced and more consistent, a fact that might be due to sample size, subject population, or experimental procedure.

26. Terkildsen (1996) examined one aspect of the projection hypothesis with mixed results. To control for potential projection effects, she created an issue agreement score. Projection effects occurred on some issues but not others.

ACKNOWLEDGMENT

This research was supported in part by a Joseph P. Healey Grant from the University of Massachusetts, Boston.

REFERENCES

Amy, D. J. (1993) *Real Choices/New Voices: The Case for Proportional Representation Elections in the United States*. New York: Columbia University Press.

Ashmore, R. D., & Del Boca, F. K. (1979). Sex Stereotypes and Implicit Personality Theory: Toward a Cognitive-Social Psychological Conceptualization. *Sex Roles, 5*, 219–245.

Ashmore, R., Del Boca, F. K., & Wohlers, A. (1986). Gender Stereotypes. In: R. Ashmore & F. Del Boca (Eds), *The Social Psychology of Female-Male Relations* (pp. 50–63). New York: Academic Press.

Bayton, J. A. (1941). The Racial Stereotypes of Negro College Students. *Journal of Abnormal and Social Psychology, 36*, 97–102.

Becker, J. F., & Heaton, Jr, E. E. (1967). The Election of Senator Edward Brooke. *Public Opinion Quarterly, 31*, 346–358.

Berelson, B. R., Lazarsfeld, P. F., & McPhee, W. N. (1954). *Voting*. Chicago: Unersity of Chicago Press.

Bergholz, R. (1982). Anti-Bradley Vote Seen as Key Election Factor. *Los Angeles Times*, 7 November.

Bobo, L. D. (1988). Group Conflict, Prejudice, and the Paradox of Contemporary Racial Attitudes. In: P. Katz & D. A. Taylor (Eds), *Eliminating Racism: Profiles in Controversy* (pp. 85–114). New York: Plenum.

Bobo, L. D. (2001). Racial Attitudes and Relations at the Close of Twentieth Century. In: N. J. Smelser, W. J. Wilson & F. N. Mitchell (Eds), *America Becoming: Racial Trends and their Consequences* (pp. 262–299). Washington, D.C.: National Academy Press.

Bobo, L. D., & Johnson, D. (2000). Racial Attitudes in a Prismatic Metropolis: Mapping Identity, Stereotypes, Competition, and Views on Affirmative Action. In: L. D. Bobo, M. L. Oliver, J. H. Johnson & A. Valenzuela (Eds), *Prismatic Metropolis: Inequality in Los Angeles* (pp. 81–166). New York: Russell Sage Foundation.

Bobo, L. D., & Massagli, M. (2001). Stereotyping and Urban Inequality. In: A. D. O'Connor, C. Tilly & L. D. Bobo (Eds), *Urban Inequality in the United States: Evidence from Four Cities* (pp. 89–162). New York: Russell Sage Foundation.

Bobo, L. D., Oliver, M. Johnson, J. H., & Valenzuela, A. (2000). Analyzing Inequality in Los Angeles. In: L. D. Bobo, M. L. Oliver, J. H. Johnson & A. Valenzuela (Eds), *Prismatic Metropolis: Inequality in Los Angeles* (pp. 3–50). New York: Russell Sage Foundation.

Bodenahuasen G., & Lichtenstein, M. (1987). Effects of Stereotypes on Decision-Making and Information Processing Strategies. *Journal of Personality and Social Psychology, 52*, 871–880.

Bornstein, R. (1989). Mere Exposure Effects with Outgroup Stimuli. In: D. MacKie & D. Hamilton (Eds), *Affect, Cognition, and Stereotyping: Interactive Processes in Group Perception* (pp. 195–212). Orlando, FL: Academic Press.

Brewer, M. (1988). A Dual Process Model of Impression Formation. In: T. S. Srull & R. S. Wyer (Eds), *Advances in Social Cognition: A Dual Process Model of Impression Formation*. Hillsdale, NJ: Erlbaum.

Bullock, C. (1984). Racial Crossover Voting and the Election of Black Officials. *Journal of Politics*, *46*, 238–251.

Callaghan, K. (1993). An Experimental Investigation of the Impact of Racial Code Words on Candidate Evaluation. Ph.D. diss., State University of New York at Stony Brook.

Callaghan, K. (2002). Racial Rhetoric and White Voter Response: An Experimental Investigation. Unpublished manuscript.

Callaghan, K., Swain, C., & Terkildsen, N. (2002). Up Close and Personal: How Candidate-Voter Interaction Alters Electoral Support for Black Politicians. Manuscript Prepared for Submission.

Campbell, A., Converse, P. Miller, W., & Stokes, D. (1960). *The American Voter*. New York: Wiley.

Campbell, A., Gurin, G., & Miller, W. E. (1954). *The Voter Decides*. Westport, CT: Greenwood.

Citrin, J., Green, D., & Sears, D. (1990). White Reactions to Black Candidates. *Public Opinion Quarterly*, *54*, 74–96.

Clark, K. B., & Clark, M. P. (1950). Emotional Factors in Racial Identification and Preference of Negro Children. *Journal of Negro Education*, *19*, 341–350.

Clymer, A. (1989). Election Day Shows What the Opinion Polls Can't Do. *New York Times*, 12 November.

Cole, L. A. (1976). *Blacks in Power: A Comparative Study of Black and White Elected Officials*. Princeton: Princeton University Press.

Colleau, S. M., Glynn, K., Lybrand, S., Merelman, R. M., Mohan, P., & Wall. J. E. (1990). Symbolic Racism in Candidate Evaluation: An Experiment. *Political Behavior*, *12*, 385–402.

Conover, P., & Feldman, S. (1986). The Role of Inference in the Perception of Political Candidates. In: R. Lau & D. O. Sears (Eds), *Political Cognition* (pp. 127–158). Hillsdale, NJ: Erlbaum.

Conover, P., & Feldman, S. (1989). Candidate Perception in an Ambiguous World: Campaigns, Cues and Inference Processes. *American Journal of Political Science*, *33*, 912–940.

Cook, T. D., & Campbell, D. T. (1979). *Quasi-Experimentation: Design and Analysis Issues for Field Settings*. Boston: Houghton Mifflin.

Cook, S. W., & Selltiz, C. (1952). *Contact and Intergroup Attitudes: Some Theoretical Considerations*. New York: Research Center for Human Relations.

Cutler, J. H. (1972). *Ed Brooke: Biography of a Senator*. Indianapolis, IN: Bobbs-Merrill.

Deutsch, M., & Collins, M. (1951). *Interracial Housing: A Psychological Evaluation of a Social Experiment*. Minneapolis: University of Minnesota Press.

Deaux, K. (1984). From Individual Differences to Social Categories: Analysis of a Decade's Research on Gender. *American Psychologist*, *30*, 105–116.

Devine, P. G. (1989). Stereotypes and Prejudice: Their Automatic and Controlled Components. *Journal of Personality and Social Psychology*, *56*, 5–18.

Downs, A. (1957). *An Economic Theory of Democracy*. New York: Harper and Row.

Dynally, M. (1971). *The Black Politician: His Struggle for Power*. Belmont, CA: Duxbury.

Edds, M. (1990). *Claiming the Dream: The Victorious Campaign of Douglas Wilder of Virginia*. Chapel Hill, NC: Algonquin Books.

Edsall, T. B., & Edsall, M. D. (1991). *Chain Reaction: The Impact of Race, Rights and Taxes on American Politics*. New York: W. W. Norton.

Feldman, J. M., & Hilterman, R. J. (1975). Stereotype Attribution Revisited: The Role of Stimulus Characteristics, Racial Attitudes and Cognitive Differentiation. *Journal of Personality and Social Psychology*, *31*, 1177–1188.

Feldman, S., & Conover, P. (1983). Candidates, Issues and Voters: The Role of Inference in Political Perception. *Journal of Politics*, *45*, 810–839.

Ferguson, T. (1995). *Golden Rule: The Investment Theory of Party Competition and the Logic of Money-Driven Political Systems*. Chicago, IL: University of Chicago Press.

Finkel, S. K., Guterbock, T. M., & Borg, M. J. (1991). Race of Interviewer Effects in a Pre-election Poll. *Public Opinion Quarterly, 55*, 313–330.

Fiske, S. T., & Neuberg, S. L. (1990). A Continuum of Impression Formation, from Category-Based to Individuating Processes: Influences of Information and Motivation on Attention and Interpretation. In: M. P. Zanna (Ed.), *Advances in Experimental Social Psychology* (Vol. 23). New York: Academic Press.

Fiske, S. T., & Pavelchak, M. A. (1986). Category-based Versus Piecemeal-based Affective Responses: Developments in Schema Triggered Affect. In: R. M. Sorrentino & E. T. Higgins (Eds), *Handbook of Motivation and Cognition: Foundations of Social Behavior*. New York: Guilford Press.

Fiske, S. T., & Taylor, S. E. (1991). *Social Cognition*. New York: McGraw-Hill.

Futron, G. C., & Wyer, R. S. (1986). The Effects of Traits and Gender Stereotypes on Occupational Suitability Judgments and the Recall of Judgment-Relevant Information. *Journal of Experimental Social Psychology, 22*, 475–503.

Gaertner, S. L., & Dovido, J. F. (1996). The Averse Form of Racism. In: J. F. Dovidio & S. L. Faertner (Eds), *Prejudice, Discrimination, and Racism* (pp. 61–90). Orlando, FL: Academic Press.

Gaertner, S. L., & McLaughlin, J. P. (1983). Racial Stereotypes: Associations and Ascriptions of Positive and Negative Characteristics. *Social Psychology Quarterly, 46*, 23–30.

Haas, G. R., Katz, I. Rizzo, N. Bailey, J., & Eisenstadt, D. (1991). Cross-racial Appraisal as Related to Attitude Ambivalence and Cognitive Complexity. *Personality and Social Psychology Bulletin, 17*, 83–92.

Hahn Hahn, H., & Almy, T. (1971). Ethnic Voting and Racial Issues: Voting in Los Angeles. *Western Political Science Quarterly, 24*, 719–730.

Hahn, H., Klingman, D., & Pachon, H. (1976). Cleavages, Coalitions, and the Black Candidate: The Los Angeles Mayoral Elections of 1969 and 1973. *Western Political Quarterly, 29*, 507–520.

Harrison, A. A. (1977). Mere Exposure. In: L. Berkowitz (Ed.), *Advances in Experimental Social Psychology* (pp. 39–48). New York: Academic Press.

Huddy, L., & Capelos, T. (In press).The Impact of Gender Stereotypes on Voters' Assessment of Women Candidates. In: V. Ottati, R. Tindale, D. O'Connell, J. Edwards, E. Posavac, Y. Suarez-Balcazar, L. Heath & F. Bryant (Eds), *Social Psychological Applications to Social Issues: Developments in Political Psychology* (Vol. 5).

Huddy, L., & Terkildsen, N. (1993a). Gender Stereotypes and the Perception of Male and Female Candidates. *American Journal of Political Science, 37*, 119–147.

Huddy, L., & Terkildsen, N. (1993b). The Consequences of Gender Stereotypes for Women Candidates at Different Levels and Types of Office. *Political Research Quarterly, 46*(3), 503–525.

Jacobson, G. C. (1997). *The Politics of Congressional Elections*. New York: Longman.

Joint Center for Political and Economic Studies (1991). *Black Elected Officials: A National Roster 1990*. Washington, D.C.: Joint Center for Political and Economic Studies Press.

Jones, D. R. (1991). *Racism as a Factor in the 1989 Gubernatorial Election of Doug Wilder*. Lewiston, New York: Edwin Mellen Press.

Jones, E. E., & Baumeister, R. F. (1976). The Self-Monitor Looks at the Ingratiator. *Journal of Personality, 44*, 654–674.

Kahn, K. (1994). An Experimental Examination of Sex Stereotypes and Press Patterns in Statewide Campaigns. *American Journal of Political Science, 38*, 162–195.

Kahn, K., & Goldenberg, E. (1994). Women Candidates in the News: An Examination of Gender Differences in U.S. Senate Campaign Coverage. *Public Opinion Quarterly, 55,* 180–199.

Karnig, A., & Welch, S. (1982). Electoral Structure and Black Representation on City Councils. *Social Science Quarterly, 63,* 99–114.

Katz, D., & Braly, K. W. (1965). Verbal Stereotypes and Racial Prejudice. In: H. Proshansky & B. Seldenberg (Eds), *Basic Studies in Social Psychology.* New York: Holt, Rinehart and Winston.

Katz, I., & Hass, R. G. (1988). Racial Ambivalence and American Value Conflict: Correlational and Priming Studies of Dual Cognitive Structures. *Journal of Personality and Social Psychology, 55,* 893–905.

Kinder, D. (1986). Presidential Character Revisited. In: R. Lau & D. Sears (Eds), *Political Cognition.* Hillsdale, NJ: Erlbaum.

Koch, J. W. (2000). Do Citizens Apply Gender Stereotypes to Infer Candidates' Ideological Orientations? *The Journal of Politics, 62,* 414–429.

Kuhn, T. (1986). *The Structure of Scientific Revolutions.* Chicago: University of Chicago Press.

Lau, R. R., & Sears. D. O. (1986). Social Cognition and Political Cognition: The Past, the Present, and the Future. In: R. Lau & D. O. Sears (Eds), *Political Cognition* (pp. 347–366). Hillsdale, NJ: Erlbaum.

Lazarsfeld, P., Berelson, B., & Gaudet, H. (1940). *The People's Choice.* New York: Duell, Sloan and Pearce.

Leeper, M. S. (1991). The Impact of Prejudice on Female Candidates: An Experimental Look at Voter Inference. *American Politics Quarterly, 19,* 248–261.

Linville, P., & Jones, E. (1980). Polarized Appraisals of Out-Group Members. *Journal of Personality and Social Psychology, 5,* 689–703.

Lippman, W. (1922). *Public Opinion.* New York: Free Press.

Locksley, A., Hepburn, C., & Ortiz, V. (1982). Social Stereotypes and Judgments of Individuals: An Instance in the Base Rate Failure. *Journal of Experimental Social Psychology, 18,* 23–42.

Lodge, M., & McGraw, K. (1995). *Political Judgment: Structure and Process.* Ann Arbor: University of Michigan Press.

Lorinskas, R. A., Hawkins, B. W., & Edwards, S. (1969). The Persistence of Ethnic Voting in Rural and Urban Areas: Results From the Controlled Election Method. *Social Science Quarterly, 49,* 891–899.

McDermott, M. (1997). Voting Cues in Low-Information Elections: Candidate Gender as a Social Information Variable in Contemporary United States Elections. *American Journal of Political Science, 41,* 270–283.

Miller, A. Wattenberg, M., & Malanchuk, O. (1986). Schematic Assessments of Presidential Candidates. *American Political Science Review, 80,* 356–371.

Moon, H. L. (1948). *The Balance of Power: The Negro Vote.* Garden City, NY: Doubleday.

Moskowitz, D., & Stroh, P. (1994). Psychological Sources of Electoral Racism. *Political Psychology, 15,* 307–330.

Mosely-Braun Just Unfit (1999, October 22). *The Boston Herald,* p. A22.

Murray, R., & Vedlitz, A. (1978). Racial Voting Patterns in the South: An Analysis of Major Elections from 1960 to 1977 in Fe Cities. *Annals, 439,* 29–39.

Ostrom, T. M. Pryor, J. B., & Simpson, D. D.(1981). The Organization of Social Information. In: E. T. Higgins, C. P. Herman & M. P. Zanna (Eds), *Social Cognition: The Ontario Symposium* (Vol. 1). Hillsdale, NJ: Erlbaum.

Ottati, V., Fishbein, M., & Middlestadt, S. (1988). Determinants of Voters' Beliefs About the Candidate's Stands on the Issues: The Role of Evaluate Bias Heuristics and the Candidate's Expressed Message. *Journal of Personality and Social Psychology, 55*, 517–529.

Ottati, V., & Wyer, R. S. (1991). The Cognitive Mediators of Political Information Processing. In: J. A. Ferejohn & J. H. Kuklinski (Eds), *Information and Democratic Process* (pp. 186–216). Urbana, IL: University of Illinois Press.

Peffley, M., & Shields, T. (1996). White's Stereotypes of African Americans and their Impact on Contemporary Political Attitudes. In: M. Delli Carpini, L. Huddy & R. Shapiro (Eds), *Research in Micropolitics: Rethinking Rationality* (Vol. 5, pp. 179–212). Greenwich, CT: JAI Press.

Pettigrew, T. (1972). When a Black Candidate Runs for Mayor: Race and Voting Behavior. In: H. Hahn (Ed.), *People and Politics in Urban Society.* Beverly Hills, CA: Sage Publications.

Pettigrew, T. (1976). Black Mayoral Campaigns. *Urban Governance and Minorities.* New York: Praeger.

Pettigrew, T., & Alston, D. (1988). *Tom Bradley's Campaigns for Governor: The Dilemma of Race and Political Strategies.* Washington, D.C.: Joint Center for Political Studies.

Pillsbury, G. (1995). Problems with Winner-Take-All Voting for the At-Large Seats in the Boston City Council. Unpublished manuscript.

Powell-Hopson, D., & Hopson, D. S. (1988). Implications of Doll Color Preferences Among Black Preschool Children and White Preschool Children. *The Journal of Black Psychology, 14*, 57–63.

Pryor, J. B., & Ostrom, T. M. (1981). The Cognitive Organization of Social Information: A Converging-operations Approach. *Journal of Personality and Social Psychology, 41*, 628–641.

Rahn, W., Aldrich, J. H., Borgida, E., & Sullan, J. L. (1990). A Social Cognitive Model of Candidate Appraisal. In: J. A. Ferejohn & J. H. Kuklinski (Eds), *Information and Democratic Processes* (pp. 136–159). Urbana, IL: University of Illinois Press.

Reeves, K. (1997). *Voting Hopes or Fears.* New York: Oxford University Press.

Richardson, S. A., & Emerson, P. (1970). Race and Physical Handicap in Children's Preference. *Human Relations, 23*, 31–36.

Richardson, S. A., & Green, A. (1971). When is Black Beautiful? Colored and White Children's Reactions to Skin Color. *British Journal of Educational Psychology, 41*, 62–69.

Sapiro, V. (1982). If U.S. Senator Baker Were a Women: An Experimental Study of Candidate Images. *Political Psychology, 3*, 61–68.

Schuman, H., Steeh, C., Bobo, L., & Krysan, M. (1997). *Racial Attitudes in America: Trends and Interpretations.* Cambridge, MA: Harvard University Press.

Sears, David O. (1986). College Sophomores in the Laboratory: Influence of a Narrow Data Base on Social Psychology's View of Human Nature. *Journal of Personality and Social Psychology, 51*, 515–530.

Sears, D., Citrin, J., & Kosterman, R. (1987). Jesse Jackson and the Southern White Electorate in 1984. In: L. A. Moreland, R. Steed & R. Baker (Eds), *Blacks and Southern Politics.* New York: Praeger.

Sigall, H., & Page, R. (1971). Current Stereotypes: A Little Fading, A Little Faking. *Journal of Personality and Social Psychology, 18*, 247–255.

Sigelman, L., & Welch, S. (1991). *Black Americans' Views of Racial Inequality: The Dream Deferred.* New York: Cambridge University Press.

Sleeper, J. (1990). *The Closet of Strangers: Liberalism and the Politics of Race in New York.* New York: W. W. Norton and Co.

Smothers, R. (1992). In South Carolina: A Tale of Campaign Trickery. *New York Times*, April 15.

Sniderman, P. M., & Hagen, M. (1985). *Race and Inequality: A Study in American Values*. Chatham, NJ: Chatham House Publishers.

Sniderman, P., Swain, C., & Elms, L. (1995). The Dynamics of a Senate Campaign: Incumbency, Ideology, and Race. Paper presented at the American Political Science Association Meeting, Chicago, IL.

Snyder, M. (1974). Self-Monitoring of Expressive Behavior. *Journal of Personality and Social Psychology*, *30*, 526–537.

Snyder, M. (1979). Self-Monitoring Process. In: L. Berkowitz (Ed.), *Advances in Experimental Social Psychology*. New York: Academic Press.

Snyder, M., & Campbell, B. H. (1982). Self-Monitoring: The Self in Action. In: J. Suls (Ed.), *Psychological Perspectives of the Self*. Hillsdale, NJ: Erlbaum.

Snyder, M., & Cantor, N. (1980). Thinking About Ourselves and Others: Self-Monitoring and Social Knowledge. *Journal of Personality and Social Psychology*, *39*, 222–234

Sonenshein, R. (1990). Can Black Candidates Win Statewide Elections. *Political Science Quarterly*, *105*, 219–241.

Stanley, H. W., & Niemi, R. (1988). *Vital Statistics on American Politics* (4th ed.). Washington, D.C.: Congressional Quarterly Press.

Staples, R. (1982). Tom Bradley's Defeat: The Impact of Racial Symbols on Political Campaigns. *Black Scholar*, *13*, 37–46.

Still, E. (1984). Alternates to Single Member Districts. In: R. Davidson (Ed.), *Minority Vote Dilution* (pp. 249–267). Washington, D.C.: Howard University Press.

Stroh, P. (1991). Candidate Ambiguity and Voter Projections. Unpublished doctoral dissertation. State Unersity of New York at Stony Brook.

Sussman, B. (1985). Hidden Racial Attitudes Distorted Virginia Polls. *Washington Post*, 28, November.

Swain, C. (1993). *Black Faces, Black Interests: The Representation of African Americans in Congress*. Cambridge: Harvard University Press.

Swain, C. (1997). Women and Blacks in Congress: 1870–1996. In: L. Dodd & B. Oppenheimer (Eds), *Congress Reconsidered*. Washington, D.C.: CQ Press.

Tajfel, H. (1982) Social Psychology of Integroup Relations. *Annual Review of Psychology*, *33*, 1–39.

Tate, K. (1993). *From Protest to Politics: The New Black Voters in American Elections*. Cambridge: Harvard University Press.

Terkildsen, N. (1993). When White Voters Evaluate Black Candidates: The Processing Implications of Candidate Skin Color, Prejudice and Self-Monitoring. *American Journal of Political Science*, *37*, 1032–1053.

Terkildsen, N. (1996). Race, Ideology, and Voter Evaluations. Unpublished doctoral dissertation. State University of New York at Stony Brook.

Terkildsen, N. (1997). The Determinants of Black Candidate Evaluation: The Moderating Effect of Domain-Specific Stereotypes. Unpublished manuscript.

Terkildsen, N., & Damore, D. F. (1999). The Dynamics of Racialized Media Coverage in Congressional Elections. *The Journal of Politics*, *61*, 680–699.

Weissberg, R. (1991). The "Politics" of the Study of Race. Paper presented at the Midwest Political Science Association Meeting, Chicago, IL.

Whitaker C. (1999, April). Mike Espy Bruised But Unbowed. *Ebony*, 22–24.

Williams, L. (1990). White/Black Perceptions of the Electability of Black Political Candidates. *National Political Science Review*, *2*, 45–64.

Wilson, W. J. (1980). *The Declining Significance of Race*. Chicago: University of Chicago Press.
Yancey, D. (1990). *When Hell Froze Over: The Story of Doug Wilder: A Black Politician's Rise to Power in the South*. Dallas, TX: Taylor Publishing Co.
Zajonc, R. B. (1968). Attitudinal Effects of Mere Exposure. *Journal of Personality and Social Psychology Monograph Supplement*, 9, 2–27.

APPENDIX A

Stimulus Materials

(1) STATE TREASURER ANNOUNCES TAX CUT

Oklahoma City-State treasurer Roger Hiltman unveiled plans today to cut Oklahoma's capital gains tax by more than 30%. In a move sure to please oil and natural gas companies, Hiltman stated that "a cut in the capital gains tax is exactly what Oklahoma needs to ensure a competitive economic base and future business growth in both the natural resource and service sectors."

While the proposed tax cuts would temporarily reduce Oklahoma's revenues by $20 million to $25 million during fiscal year 1992, Hiltman and his staff project that by 1994, the relocation of new businesses and the expansion of current business and industry would add an estimated $40 million to $50 million annually to state revenues. Hiltman's proposal has gained early support from the State Business Council and local Chambers of Commerce, Oklahoma City Chamber included.

Cynthia Bouzet, *The Oklahoma Sun Times*, 1990

(2) "Thanks to Roger Hiltman's lobbying efforts, legislation to reduce state levels of acid rain is now an effective environmental reality in Oklahoma. In two years of enforcement, statewide levels of acid rain have dropped by 18%. Officials in Tulsa and environs, one of the worst polluters in the state, have also reported a significant decline in air pollution levels. Roger Hiltman has helped secure our children's environmental future."

Sierra Club International, 1987

(3) "We heartily endorse Roger Hiltman's energies to increase state funding for AIDS research. His compassion has saved countless lives in the struggle against AIDS the disease and AIDS the stigma."

Oklahoma American Medical Association, 1989

(4) "Mr. Hiltman's efforts to extend current tax exemption laws to further benefit Oklahoma churches is both visionary and prudent government. While we recognize the importance of separating church and state powers, as a religious, non-profit institution we are also highly aware of the dependent nature of our relationship on state government. The extension of state tax exemption laws is one effort toward equalizing those inequities . . . ."

Southern Baptist Association Newsletter, 1988

(5) **ROGER HILTMAN POTENTIAL GUBERNATORIAL CANDIDATE**
Oklahoma City-State treasurer Roger Hiltman hinted today that he may run for governor in 1992. At a news conference announcing his proposed plan to cut capital gains taxes by a third,

Hiltman was quoted as saying, "because the people deserve the best representation possible, it is time to explore the possibility of future races." When pressed Hiltman refused to mention the governorship specifically but said he wouldn't "rule out any potential races at this point."

Randolph Young, a Hiltman campaign manager and close friend, did acknowledge that the 1992 gubernatorial race is high, if not first, on Hiltman's list of activities for the future. Young also indicated that Hiltman's 1986 campaign committee for state treasurer held a strategy meeting over the weekend . . . .

Hiltman, the son of second-generation working-class immigrants, graduated from the University of Oklahoma in the top 25% of his class. The state treasurer financed his degree by working full-time. After graduating from Emory University Law School Roger Hiltman started his own law practice. Mr. Hiltman began his political career in 1979 with a tough campaign for the state senate in which he struggled to unseat incumbent Senator John Ulrich. Hiltman, who had to run a low-cost campaign financed mostly from small contributions and his own savings, barely defeated Ulrich . . . . During the 1985 state treasurer's race an editorial in this newspaper called Hiltman "an articulate leader to guide Oklahoma's financial future."

Jack Booth, *The Oklahoma Sun Times*, 1990

(6) "Someone must devise a solution, . . . the increase in statewide crime due to repeat offenders is at an all time high . . . Six months ago we challenged state politicians to draft effective legislation to eliminate the statewide crime wave due to repeat criminals. Less than one week later, Roger Hiltman spoke

up. Mr. Hiltman's timely proposal to enact legislation requiring stiffer jail sentences for repeat offenders has caught the eye of both the state legislature and the voters. Here's hoping Mr. Hiltman continues to represent the interests of Oklahoma for some time to come."

Editorial, *Oklahoma Free Gazette*, 1990

(7) Roger Hiltman is a rare politician . . . one of his legislate priorities, "affordable, government-subsidized housing for low income families," is exactly what the political climate of Oklahoma demands.

Editorial, *Tulsa Daily News*, 1990

APPENDIX B

Measures

A. Character Traits
Kinder's research on presidential character (e.g. Kinder, 1986) has shown that individual voters appear to base their appraisal of presidential candidates on four key personality characteristics: *competency, leadership, integrity and empathy*. We adopted these measures here. The competence factor included the traits experienced, hard-working, and intelligent, while inspiring, strong, and "commands respect" constituted the leadership dimension. The empathy dimension included the traits decent, compassionate, and "really cares." All alphas exceeded 0.72. Respondents were also exposed to a battery of traits, including stereotypical racial traits. The "black" trait dimension included intelligence, athletic ability, religiosity, hostility and motivation (alpha = 0.46). Given the low alpha, we abandoned the scale and treated the "black" traits individually. Subjects were asked how well each trait fit the candidate using a four-point ordinal scale ranging from 1 extremely well" to 4 "not well at all." Responses were averaged for the subset of questions in each trait dimension.

B. Political Belief and Behavioral Inferences.
Respondents were asked to infer the partisanship and ideology of the candidate using the standard seven-point NES measures (PID: 1 to 7) Ideology 1 to 7. Subjects' perceptions about the candidate's activist nature were also assessed. We asked how likely the candidate would be to advocate *radical or extreme* methods to achieve his policy goals. Three items were averaged to form a

"militancy" rating: (alpha $= 0.79$). A third belief inference assessed the candidate's potential *corruptibility* once in office. Subjects were asked how likely Hiltman was to "accept illegal campaign contributions," "take illegal money from special interests" and "resign his position because of a scandal" (alpha $= 0.81$). Finally, a fourth belief inference assessed subjects' perceptions about the candidate's *fiscal responsibility* (single-item question).

C. Racial Stereotypes

Racial stereotypes were measured via a five-item scale taken from the General Social Survey. Respondents were asked to rate black Americans as a group on a series of five-point scales with the end points labeled intelligent-unintelligent, hard working-lazy, violent-not violent, patriotic-unpatriotic, prefers to be self-supporting-prefers to live off welfare (alpha $= 0.86$). Extensive testing corroborates the reliability of this scale.

LIBERAL-CONSERVATIVE THINKING IN THE AMERICAN ELECTORATE

William G. Jacoby

Thirty-five years ago, Philip E. Converse stated that "mass belief systems do not surrender easily to empirical analysis" (1964, p. 206). Political scientists have apparently taken this warning to heart, as evidenced by the frustration, complaints, and attempts to redefine the topic that have appeared in the subsequent literature. For example, in an epistemological critique of belief systems research, Bennett (1977) argued that ". . . the field is moving toward increasing disarray" (p. 473). And, Smith (1980) charged that some of the central variables in the study of belief system structure constitute "false measures of ideological sophistication." Published exchanges among researchers working in this field have occasionally exhibited levels of impatience and petulance that are not usually encountered in scholarly professional journals (e.g. Pierce & Rose, 1974; Converse, 1974; Nie & Rabjohn, 1979; Sullivan, Piereson, Marcus & Feldman, 1979; Bishop, Tuchfarber, Oldendick & Bennett 1979; Judd & Milburn, 1980; Converse, 1980). The study of mass belief systems has been characterized as a "cottage industry" (e.g. Sharp & Lodge, 1985) and Luskin (1987, 1990) has repeatedly stated that the field is not really the study of citizen ideology per se, but rather an ongoing investigation into "political sophistication."

Such self-doubt and recrimination has led some scholars to throw up their hands and proclaim "Enough already about ideology!" (Kinder, 1982). Much the same message seems to permeate some of the recent literature on political cognition and information processing (Lau & Sears, 1986). To paraphrase a comment made to me by a prominent political psychologist: "Stop wasting our time searching for something that doesn't tell us anything about public opinion

Political Decision Making, Deliberation and Participation, Volume 6, pages 97–147.
© 2002 Published by Elsevier Science Ltd.
ISBN: 0-7623-0227-5

(presumably, this person was referring to ideology); let's move on to figure out precisely how citizens *do* think about politics!"

The problem, as I see it, is that the preceding judgments and recommendations are either arguably wrong, excessively narrow in focus, or premature. And, many of the earlier critiques of this field were somewhat misplaced in their attacks. I will try to present a different perspective: Within the overall endeavor to understand public opinion, the study of mass-level ideology is alive, well, and making useful progress in understanding how ordinary people use politically-relevant abstractions to look at and think about the political world. The purpose of this essay is to describe the current state of this important subfield.

The subject matter subsumed under the heading of "mass belief systems" is vast; indeed, it touches on virtually every aspect of public opinion and political behavior. Therefore, in order to enable a manageable treatment of the subject matter, this essay will focus on a somewhat narrower component: The extent to which American citizens use the liberal-conservative continuum to organize their political ideas.[1]

There are certainly other avenues that could be pursued, but this one has several points to commend it. First, there is practicality: Liberal-conservative terms provide a simple (albeit far-reaching) principle for organizing the diverse stimuli that exist within the political world. At the same time, they enable a relatively clear delineation of the area and concepts under investigation. Second, there is empirical veracity: Despite ongoing concerns about the public's ability to engage in ideological thinking, the fact remains that liberal-conservative self-placements comprise an extremely useful and frequently-used variable in substantive analyses. Ideological identifications seem to be one of the most important influences on a variety of phenomena, including voting choices, issue attitudes, and political participation. Third, and perhaps most important, the liberal-conservative continuum has a *political* importance that is not shared by alternative forms of belief system organization. Stated simply, political elites view the world this way and, as a result, American political conflict is organized along these lines. Shifting the research focus elsewhere would, therefore, evoke V. O. Key's earlier concerns about taking the politics out of the study of political behavior (Key & Munger, 1959).

The remainder of this essay addresses three very general topics: First, I will examine the resurgence of research on mass-level ideology that occurred from the late 1970s through the early 1990s. This is particularly interesting because a topic that seemed to be settled (i.e. Americans do not think in liberal-conservative terms) rather suddenly became the focus of a number of important and widely cited studies (i.e. how do ideological self-placements affect other beliefs, attitudes, and behavior?). Second, I will consider several conceptual refinements and shifts in research focus that have contributed directly to progress in theoretical understandings of liberal-conservative thinking within the American electorate. This work is useful because it delineates the boundaries of the relevant subject matter and also establishes the validity of several critical variables within the field. And third, I will survey the current state of knowledge about ideological reasoning within the general public. A systematic consideration of recent work will show that there is, in fact, a broad consensual understanding about the ways that liberal-conservative ideas impinge on other aspects of mass orientations. The essay will conclude with a brief consideration of some likely productive paths for future research in this field. As we will see, there remains a great deal to be learned about the nature, sources, and consequences of ideological thinking within American public opinion.

THE "RISE" OF MASS-LEVEL IDEOLOGY IN POLITICAL RESEARCH

While doubts about the prevalence of liberal-conservative thinking were addressed in some of the earliest empirical analyses of electoral behavior (e.g. Berelson, Lazarsfeld & McPhee, 1954), the modern scholarly debates about mass-level ideology really stem from the discussions in *The American Voter* (Campbell, Converse, Miller & Stokes, 1960) and the subsequent articles by Philip E. Converse (1964, 1970). These works retain an immediate relevance to current scholarship, despite the rather lengthy time period since their initial appearances. There is little need for me to summarize the basic lines of reasoning laid out in these seminal studies, since many others have already done so in perfectly acceptable ways (e.g. Kinder, 1983; Niemi & Weisberg, 1993). Furthermore, the originals are still easily obtained and widely read.

Most early explanations and models of individual voting behavior did not explicitly incorporate ideology as an explanatory variable (e.g. Goldberg, 1966; Jackson, 1975; Schulman & Pomper, 1975; Hartwig, Jenkins & Temchin, 1980; Asher, 1983). This omission was probably due to two different (though undoubtedly related) factors. First, *The American Voter*'s conclusions about the lack of ideological awareness within the electorate seemed compelling: Why complicate an empirical model with a variable that was already "known" to have no effect? Second, the predominant data source for research on mass political behavior – the Center for Political Studies' Biennial National Election Studies – did not include an item asking survey respondents their own ideological positions. Again, why take up precious time in an already-lengthy interview schedule asking about a political orientation that means little, if anything, to most people?

Thus, there were both theoretical and practical reasons for avoiding a systematic consideration of liberal-conservative influences on mass political attitudes and behavior.

This situation changed markedly, beginning in the late 1960s. The ground was probably broken by the 1968 Comparative State Elections Project (CSEP), an ambitious multiple-investigator survey of both the national public and several state electorates. CSEP was conceived as an alternative approach to voting behavior from the so-called "Michigan school" embodied in the National Election Studies (Prothro, 1973). Among many other innovations, the CSEP interview schedule asked respondents about their ideological self-placements, using a branching question similar in format to the traditional party identification item from the NES.[2] The resultant variable was a seven-point scale, with ideological gradations ranging from "strong conservative" at one end, to "strong liberal" at the other extreme.

The CSEP data were reported in a widely cited and influential paper that was, ironically, never published (Kovenock & Beardsley, 1970). But the results from this analysis seem to have provided the impetus for including an ideological self-placement scale in the National Election Studies. Accordingly, such a variable has been included in every NES administration from 1972 onward. The question format differs from that used in the CSEP study. Instead of the branching approach, the NES interview schedule employs a "graphical scale" to elicit ideological identifications. That is, respondents are handed a card showing a line segment with seven labeled and numbered points (from 1 for "extremely liberal" to 7 for "extremely conservative"). Then, they are asked to place themselves and several other political figures (usually, the major party presidential candidates and the two parties) along the scale.[3]

Such liberal-conservative identification questions seem to provide fairly detailed information about survey respondents positions – as well as their perceptions of party and candidate positions –   along a single summary dimension of political conflict. However, important questions remain about the degree to which this item really taps *ideological* reasoning within the mass public. For one thing, many of the NES respondents (typically, about one-fourth) fail to locate themselves along the liberal-conservative continuum, stating that they "haven't thought much about this."[4] And a sizable proportion of those that do place themselves (typically, one-third) select the neutral midpoint of the dimension.[5] In both cases, the survey respondents are explicitly refusing to employ fairly standard liberal-conservative abstractions in order to structure their political orientations. And this finding, in turn, appears to confirm earlier interpretations about the limited extent of ideological reasoning within the mass public.

More generally, respondents' placements along the seven-point ideology scale are completely subjective; there is absolutely no attempt to specify the "correct" political views associated with the liberal or conservative positions. Of course, this separation between ideological labels and their substantive implications is entirely intentional. But, it does raise questions about the quality and exact meaning of the responses to the ideology question.

There is quite a bit of empirical evidence to suggest that such concerns are justified. For example, Free and Cantril's widely-read study of public opinion during the 1960s found such widespread inconsistency between ideological identifications and policy preferences (e.g. self-professed conservatives who nevertheless strongly supported an activist national government) that they repeatedly referred to the "schizoid" tendencies of the American public (Free & Cantril, 1967). More recent findings continue to reveal similar marked discontinuities between ideological labels and issue positions, although a somewhat less shrill interpretation – public ambivalence toward government – has been suggested as the explanation (Cantril & Cantril, 1999). In a similar vein, many people seem to have difficulty using an ideological dimension to locate parties and candidates: For example, they place the Democratic Party at the same position, or to the right of the Republican Party along the liberal-conservative dimension, despite seemingly clearcut evidence that the opposite ordering is considerably more accurate (e.g. Levitin & Miller, 1979; Jacoby, 1988, 1995).

Thus, the inclusion of a liberal-conservative identification item in the NES – the major data source within the field of mass political behavior – is not enough, in itself, to assess the presence and/or scope of ideological thinking within the American public. Instead, it is necessary to link subjective ideological self-placements with more "objective" – or, at least, systematic – consequences, in terms of subsequent political beliefs, attitudes, and behavior. That is precisely the direction that has been taken in the literature on mass-level ideology since the 1970s. Let us consider how liberal-conservative orientations have become an increasingly important component in empirical analyses of voting behavior, public opinion, and political participation, respectively.

Liberal-Conservative Ideology and Voting Behavior

The CSEP ideology variable was probably influential within the research community precisely because it *was* correlated with individual voting choices in 1968 (albeit somewhat weakly). Similarly, the timing of the new NES liberal-conservative scale was particularly fortuitous, given the salience of ideological themes in the 1972 presidential election. Republicans successfully linked the

Democratic candidate, George McGovern, to "acid, amnesty, and abortion," thereby generating the specter of left-wing extremism (presumably in comparison to the moderate, pragmatic approach taken by the Nixon administration). The result was a serious fracture within the majority party, as conservative Democrats joined Republicans in opposition to the McGovern candidacy. In this manner, liberal-conservative ideology overwhelmed partisan identification as the predominant influence on citizens' electoral decisions and raised the possibility of major changes – even a realignment – within the party system (Miller, Miller, Raine & Brown, 1976). While these interpretations were hotly disputed (Popkin, Gorman, Philips & Smith, 1976; RePass, 1976; Steeper & Teeter, 1976), the basic evidence was clear in showing that ideological considerations are related to voting behavior within the mass public.

Subsequent work has both replicated and elaborated upon the preceding interpretation. For example, Holm and Robinson (1978) questioned the notion that individual ideology and policy attitudes are largely synonymous to each other (e.g. Nie, Verba & Petrocik, 1979). They argue instead that liberal-conservative self-placement helps define a person's own political identity and therefore functions in a manner similar to party identification as an influence on subsequent behavior. To this end, Holm and Robinson show that personal ideological orientations affect individual voting choices, even after the effects of issues and partisanship are explicitly taken into account.

Levitin and Miller (1979) also examine the impact of individual ideological sentiments, although their final conclusions are a bit more circumspect. After verifying that liberal-conservative identifications are, indeed, closely related to candidate choice, they look more closely at the nature of the "connections" among the various psychological orientations manifested within the mass public. They argue that the connections between general ideology, other political perceptions, and attitudes on specific public policies are subject to "considerable slippage." Therefore, Levitin and Miller conclude liberal-conservative ideology is important for understanding individual political behavior, but that many people employ this psychological orientation in markedly "non-ideological" ways.

Ideology now seems to be regarded as a central variable in the study of voting behavior (Dalton & Wattenberg, 1993); perhaps not a member of "the iron triangle (party identification, issues, and candidate evaluations)," but certainly close to that in importance. In terms of its theoretical location, vis-à-vis other factors, ideology is usually placed relatively distant from the ultimate voting decision, preceding even party identification in certain cases (Page & Jones, 1979). As such, it exerts both indirect and direct influences on electoral choice (e.g. Howell 1985; Miller & Shanks, 1996). And, it has been included routinely in empirical models of presidential voting behavior from the 1980s (e.g. Miller & Shanks, 1982) through the 1990s (e.g. Alvarez & Nagler, 1995, 1998).

Liberal-Conservative Ideology and Public Opinion on Political Issues

It is, perhaps, ironic that early research efforts stressed the inconsistencies between individual liberal-conservative identifications and citizens' preferences on specific policy matters (e.g. Free & Cantril, 1967), because the current scholarly consensus holds that ideological orientations serve as an important influence on the formation of issue attitudes. This basic finding has been demonstrated repeatedly, across a wide variety of topical areas (e.g. Fleishman, 1986b). These include not only traditional socioeconomic concerns like guaranteed jobs, national health insurance, government spending, and the entire idea of "big government" (Sears, Lau, Tyler & Allen, 1980; Bennett & Bennett, 1990; Jacoby, 1994), but also social issues like women's rights (Sears, Huddy & Schaffer, 1986), foreign affairs controversies like the Vietnam war (Lau, Brown & Sears, 1978), racial conflicts like school busing (Sears, Hensler & Speer, 1979), modern technological problems like responses to the energy crises of the 1970s (Sears, Tyler, Citrin & Kinder 1978), and the emotion-laden appeals surrounding the backlash against property taxes in the early 1980s (Sears & Citrin, 1985). Indeed, it is somewhat striking just how easily new issues can be fitted into the liberal-conservative framework. For example, emerging political conflicts like race/civil rights and nuclear power have conformed to, rather than supplanted, traditional ideological distinctions (e.g. Kuklinski, Metlay & Kay, 1982; Carmines & Stimson, 1989; Gamson & Modigliani, 1989).

A general explanation for ideology's pervasive impact on issue attitudes can be found in symbolic politics theory (e.g. Sears Lau, Tyler & Allen, 1980; Sears, 1993). This holds that liberal-conservative identifications constitute a symbolic predisposition for most citizens – that is, a stable, affective outlook which originates during the childhood socialization process and then persists, largely unchanged, into adult political life (Sears, 1983). The connection between general ideological positions and specific issue attitudes depends upon the fact that virtually all political issues are defined in highly symbolic terms (e.g. Edelman, 1964). The predominant symbols of American political culture (e.g. freedom, liberty, equal opportunity, etc.) comprise a highly salient element of the political environment confronting the mass public (Bennett, 1980) and they have been remarkably stable over time (Devine, 1972; McClosky & Zaller, 1984). So, it is easy for people to adopt those issue positions on which the symbolic content matches their own symbolic predispositions – e.g. liberal-conservative self-placements.

In this manner, ideology operates on a nearly emotional level, triggering habitual responses to stimuli in the political environment. Symbolic politics theory thus provides a parsimonious explanation for the existence of an ideological bias within American public opinion. Also, it does so without requiring that individual citizens' belief systems are organized along detailed liberal-conservative lines.

Liberal-Conservative Ideology and Political Participation

Although there has been relatively little research conducted on the topic, a connection does seem to exist between liberal-conservative orientations and political participation. For example, Verba and Nie (1972) show that stronger ideological inclinations correspond to higher levels of political activity, particularly among self-identified conservatives (also see Maddox & Lilie, 1984). Similarly, Palfrey and Poole (1987) show that citizens who adopt an ideological position for themselves – whether liberal or conservative – are far more likely to vote than those who take the moderate or middle-of-the-road position.

While the connection between ideology and participation is relatively clear-cut, the reasons for its existence remain the subject of some disagreement. One explanation hinges on socioeconomic status differences between conservatives and the rest of the electorate (Verba & Nie, 1972). But other analysts point out that external influences, such as the ideological positions of the candidates, account for differential voter turnout rates across liberals and conservatives (e.g. Beck & Jennings, 1979; Finkel & Trevor, 1986).

The predominant explanation is based upon the rationality of political participation. Specifically, a well-developed personal ideology should clarify the benefits that an individual receives from his/her activity and thereby helps to overcome the inherent costs of political participation (e.g. Downs, 1957; Neuman, 1986). While this perspective could account for the ideology-participation correlation, there is another, fundamentally different perspective that works just as well. This is based upon the idea that political activity, in itself, promotes greater clarity in ideological thinking simply through more detailed exposure to the realities of American politics (e.g. Converse, 1964; Bennett, 1975). Leighley (1991) uses a non-recursive causal model to show that there is empirical support for both of these arguments. That is, sophisticated ideological thinking promotes individual political participation, while certain kinds of participation (particularly campaign work and activities aimed at solving national problems) encourage a more ideological view of parties and candidates.

For present purposes, the exact structure of the connection between ideological thinking and political participation is probably less important than the fact that such a linkage exists in the first place. Stated simply, ideologically-oriented individuals are more likely than others to be politically active. Of course, this means that the messages which "get through" to political elites will undoubtedly have a more polarized content, since the views of moderates and other non-ideological citizens are not fully represented. Thus, the influence of self-professed liberals and conservatives is probably "magnified" beyond those individuals who eschew such personal identifications precisely because they are more likely to take explicit action in order to communicate their opinions to policy-makers.

Assessing the Rise of Research on Mass-Level Ideology

Liberal-conservative thinking is now definitely considered a legitimate and interesting focus for research in the field of mass political behavior. From one perspective, this scholarly consensus appears to be perfectly reasonable, given the content of contemporary American political rhetoric: Media accounts routinely cover such topics as the Democrats' apparent retreat from their traditionally liberal issue stands, the influence of the conservative wing within the Republican party, and so on. Ideological themes are just not hard to find in current American politics.

From another perspective, however, the scholarly attention to the liberal-conservative continuum is also somewhat surprising, given that most political scientists continue to believe in the "ideological innocence" of the electorate (e.g. Kinder & Sears, 1985; Luttbeg & Gant, 1985; Smith, 1989). A cynical explanation for this apparent inconsistency might hold that the recent flurry of activity with respect to ideology is simply the result of "opportunism." That is, once a new variable appears in the NES interview schedule (i.e. the seven-point liberal-conservative identification scale), it becomes grist for the scholarly mill. The result is a veritable "cottage industry" of studies examining ideological reasoning within the mass public.

Fortunately, the preceding type of skepticism is largely unfounded. The new research on mass ideology (i.e. that which has been conducted since the early 1980s) has been very successful at explicating the ways that the liberal-conservative continuum impinges on citizens' political beliefs, attitudes, and behavior. There has been a great deal of work in the area; results from different studies have been consistent and mutually supportive; and there appears to be a cumulation of knowledge with respect to ideological thinking in the mass public.

But the preceding optimistic interpretation raises a further question: How did this productive line of research and apparent scholarly consensus emerge from a field that, in earlier years, seemed to represent either a "dead end" or a veritable morass of conflicting findings and interpretations? I believe that this evolution is largely due to three factors: Differentiation of concepts; refinement of a central variable; and a major shift in the focus of attention. Let us consider each of these, in turn.

PROGRESS THROUGH DIFFERENTIATION

The initial forays into the world of mass belief systems – *The American Voter* and "The Nature of Belief Systems in Mass Publics" – actually stimulated further research into a number of topics that do not necessarily involve *liberal-conservative ideology* per se. These include voter rationality; issue voting; attitude stability; adherence to fundamental democratic principles; and citizen competence.[6] Recognition of the differences among these constructs is precisely where a great deal of progress has been made in the field. Through careful refinement and distillation of the subject content, scholars have distinguished concepts that are *related* to, but *different* from the question of ideological reasoning. Let us examine several of these ideas, and consider how they have been "pared off" from the concept of ideology, itself. Specifically, I will consider intercorrelations among issue attitudes, individual differences in belief system organization, and attitude stability in order to show that they are all conceptually distinct from ideology as that term is being used in this essay – to denote the organization of political beliefs, attitudes, and behavior along liberal-conservative lines.

Intercorrelations Among Issue Attitudes

The discussion about ideology in *The American Voter* begins with the empirical observation that citizens' attitudes on foreign policy are almost completely unrelated to their stands on domestic issues. Campbell et al. (1960) argue that such a finding could not occur if mass belief systems are consistent with or "constrained by" a set of overarching organizational principles. Converse (1964) continued this line of reasoning by showing that intercorrelations among survey responses to issue questions become larger as one moves upward through strata of increasing sophistication within the electorate. He also provided a more concrete standard for evaluating attitudinal constraint by demonstrating that even the most sophisticated citizens exhibit far lower attitude intercorrelations than do political elites (defined as candidates in congressional elections).

Subsequent analysts picked up where Campbell, Converse, and their colleagues left off, making "attitude constraint" one of the most prevalent topics in the study of mass-level ideology. And, constraint was almost always operationalized in terms of correlations among issue questions on public opinion surveys. The substantive conclusions based upon this kind of evidence varied quite a bit, depending upon the study. On the one hand, increases in issue consistency – usually defined as the magnitudes of the correlation coefficients – over time were interpreted by some researchers as evidence of heightened ideological awareness within the American electorate (Pomper, 1972; Nie & Anderson, 1974; Nie, Verba & Petrocik, 1979). Other scholars were more circumspect, pointing out that the interrelationships remained quite modest, both in absolute terms (Margolis, 1977) and in comparison to the opinions of political elites (Bishop & Frankovic, 1981). I take no stand on this matter; my intention here is merely to point out that correlations among issue attitudes played an important role in the research on mass ideology.

Despite the longstanding prominence and continuing importance of the constraint concept in the scholarly debates on ideological thinking, empirical analyses based upon intercorrelations of survey issue questions have now largely disappeared from the research literature. What happened to create such a marked shift in focus? I suspect that there are several causal factors at work here. One is conceptual in nature: Recent scholars have recognized that "constraint" involves the dependence of specific issue attitudes on more general, underlying, principles; specifically, the degree to which attitudes are consistent with the liberal-conservative continuum (e.g. Jacoby, 1991b; Miller & Shanks, 1996). Of course, this is *not* a new idea; Converse articulated precisely this position in "The Nature of Belief Systems in Mass Publics." Nevertheless, such an interpretation implies that the empirical intercorrelations among issue responses are actually spurious and due to their common dependence on the same organizational dimension. As such, these correlations are not particularly interesting in themselves. Stated simply, attitude constraint and interattitude correlations are just not the same thing.

A second, but related, factor involves more practical concerns: Intercorrelations have always been easy to calculate, and they bypass some of the thornier problems of data availability and coding that plagued early belief system research (particularly, those involving the levels of conceptualization and liberal-conservative identifications). As analysts have addressed these problems (i.e. produced new measures of ideological thinking), they have simply removed the need to rely upon indirect indicators of belief system structure like correlations among survey responses to issue questions.

Other factors in the decreasing reliance on intercorrelations among survey items are methodological in nature. Perhaps most telling, several analysts have demonstrated convincingly that the apparent increase in ideological constraint which occurred in the mid-1960s was due almost entirely to changes in the survey items that were used to elicit issue attitudes from respondents (e.g. Bishop, Tuchfarber & Oldendick, 1978; Brunk, 1978; Sullivan, Piereson & Marcus, 1978). Seemingly innocuous variations in question wording (e.g. questions that pose both sides of an issue, rather than merely asking respondents to agree/disagree with a single stated position) have major effects on the degree of consistency in responses across separate issues. Thus, much of the available evidence is simply untrustworthy.

Another methodological critique focuses on the use of correlation coefficients to measure attitudinal constraint. Barton and Parsons (1977) and Wykoff (1980) both point out that doing so involves a sort of ecological inference problem. Correlation is inherently a characteristic of an aggregate body (e.g. the electorate, or some stratum within it). But attitudinal constraint is a characteristic on an individual's belief system. These researchers argue that high levels of *individual*-level constraint could easily be accompanied by only modest correlations between issue variables. Once again, the evidence used to demonstrate the absence or presence of belief system structure is suspect, for technical reasons.

And finally, the use of attitudinal consistency – regardless how it is measured – has been questioned as an indicator of liberal-conservative thinking in the first place. The empirical evidence shows that attitude consistency levels are not very strongly related to other measures of ideological awareness or political sophistication (e.g. Converse, 1975; Wray, 1979; Wykoff, 1987). From a somewhat different perspective, Peffley and Hurwitz (1985) argue that attitudinal consistency can be derived from relatively discrete core values, rather than individual reliance on a general, ideological evaluative dimension. Apparently, people can make "connections" among separate issue attitudes without appealing to overarching abstractions for guidance. In that case, the notion of ideology-based attitudinal constraint becomes irrelevant to understanding the ways that people develop and organize their reactions to political issues.

I do not assert that any of the preceding critiques are "right" or "wrong." In fact, the state of knowledge about attitudinal constraint remains somewhat ambiguous. For example, the question-wording studies seem to provide incontrovertible evidence *against* significant increases in ideological awareness during the 1960s. But, this line of work does not address the fact that other measures, which are not dependent upon the wording of the survey issue questions (primarily the levels of conceptualization), also signal increases in ideological awareness during the same time period. Similarly, there is strong evidence that individual-level measures of attitudinal constraint (i.e. those *not* based upon intercorrelations among issue responses) are closely related to a person's own degree of attentiveness to the liberal-conservative continuum (e.g. Sharp & Lodge, 1985; Jacoby, 1991b). And one could argue that the existence of mid-level core values, like those suggested by Peffley and Hurwitz, merely echo Converse's original point about the "morselization" of political ideas that exists throughout much of American public opinion. Regardless of these alternative interpretations, there does seem to be ample evidence that attitudinal consistency should be regarded as a topic that is conceptually and empirically distinct from an individual's propensity to employ liberal-conservative concepts in his/her political orientations.

Complexity, Individual Differences and Dimensionality in Political Thinking

The mainstream research on mass-level ideology has always been somewhat vulnerable to the charge that researchers are imposing their own ideas about what constitutes a sufficiently well-organized belief system. Even a brief perusal of the relevant literature seems to suggest that this is, indeed, the case: The liberal-conservative continuum stands apart from other psychological principles as the cognitive organizational system "of choice." It is the standard against which relatively unsophisticated strata of the general public are compared. It also seems to be a hallmark of political orientations among the most attentive and active members of the American electorate.

There are two major reasons for this strong focus on liberal-conservative thinking, as opposed to other potential foundations for ideology that could exist within the mass public, such as class polarization (e.g. Jackman & Jackman, 1983; Shingles, 1989) or racially-motivated thinking (Aberbach & Walker, 1970; Allen, Dawson & Brown, 1989). First, as I have already mentioned (and will discuss further, below), elites clearly think about politics and society in these terms. This, alone, gives liberal-conservative ideology a privileged status, relative to other systems for belief system organization. Second, the authors of *The American Voter* are very clear in stating that they sought *any* kind of broad, capping abstractions that citizens might use to structure their opinions; but, the liberal-conservative continuum was the only one to emerge, out of several thousand interviews. Thus, the scholarly focus on this particular "brand" of ideology can be justified on both political and empirical grounds.

But does this focus imply that people who do *not* look at the world through a liberal-conservative lens are necessarily irrational and/or incapable of dealing effectively with the "buzzing, blooming confusion" of the political world? The answer to this question has to be a clear and resounding "Of course not!"

Even the major protagonists in the predominant view of mass belief systems have always stated that there are various sources available for the development of individual-level attitudinal structures. Some of these exist in the external environment – the "social sources of attitudinal constraint." This, of course, is where the liberal-conservative continuum lies, by virtue of its widespread usage and consensual understanding among active political elites and informed commentators. But, other foundations for organizing citizen political orientations exist largely within the heads of the individuals, themselves – the "psychological sources of attitudinal constraint." And, since these latter sources are, inherently, rather atomistic in nature it is only to be expected that they vary considerably from one person to the next.

Scholarly attention to the more individualized forms of mass political thinking has resulted in a long, productive, and ongoing field of research. In fact, the work has proceeded in several different, but related, directions. Some analysts have used in-depth interviews to probe the details of individual belief systems (e.g. Lane, 1962; Lamb, 1974; Gamson, 1992). This investigative strategy reveals that people often maintain detailed, but personalized, views about the nature of modern society, the workings of government, and their own roles within the political system. The quality of the reasoning and the scope of the thinking can often be questioned; however, the content of these idiosyncratic belief systems does seem to be quite functional for the individuals who possess them.

In a similar vein, Rosenberg (1988) argues that the traditional focus in mass belief systems research fundamentally mis-specifies the nature of ideological reasoning. Rather than thinking about ideology as a way of summarizing a broad array of phenomena, he argues that it should be viewed in terms of the ways that citizens develop mental constructs to deal with the world around them. Rosenberg suggests that an approach based upon Piagetan cognitive psychology, while incapable of providing the parsimony supplied by the liberal-conservative continuum, nevertheless provides a much more revealing and relatively accurate picture of citizens' conceptual understandings about politics and social phenomena.

Still another line of work focuses on the dimensionality of mass belief systems. Here, again, the authors of *The American Voter* started the process, by showing that citizens' issue attitudes did not conform to a unidimensional pattern, even though the content of the contemporary political rhetoric suggested that they should. This finding was, in turn, taken as evidence for the public's relatively poor grasp of political events and issues. Subsequent researchers seem to have interpreted these results in a markedly simpler manner: Basically, ideological thinking requires unidimensional structuring of issue attitudes.

While the preceding interpretation could be easily dismissed as a straw man (since neither Campbell et al. nor Converse ever made this argument), it has still provided the foundation for a number of influential studies that have appeared over the years. For example, Luttbeg (1968) examined public opinion on local political issues and found highly multidimensional attitude structures; in fact, political elites required *more* dimensions to account for their opinions than did members of the mass public. This, of course, is precisely the opposite of what *should* occur if political involvement leads to greater reliance upon a unidimensional evaluative standard like the liberal-conservative continuum.

Dimensionality is also an integral component of studies that examine the roles of core values (Feldman, 1988) or domain-specific constraint sources (Peffley & Hurwitz, 1985) in public opinion. Basically, the argument is that people generally possess several different values simultaneously, and that they think about political issues in terms of their substantive content. Both of these features work to prevent opinions from collapsing onto a single general evaluative dimension (liberal-conservative or otherwise). The problems and concerns that are involved in one segment of public policy (say, foreign relations) are often fundamentally different from those activated by other issues (say, civil rights). There is simply no reason to expect any particular common ground between them.

The concept of individual differences supplements the focus on multi-dimensionality in work by Marcus, Tabb and Sullivan (1974) and Conover and Feldman (1984). These authors take quite different approaches, but they reach quite similar conclusions: There are not only multiple evaluative dimensions underlying mass political orientations; there is a also great deal of variability from one person to the next in the degree to which individuals rely upon the respective dimensions to structure their own beliefs and attitudes.

The literature summarized above makes a fairly compelling case that many complex and widely divergent belief systems exist within the mass public. But, what does this tell us about liberal-conservative thinking? From my perspective, the answer is "not much." For one thing, there are methodological responses to some of these arguments: Dimensionality is a very slippery idea in itself, depending much more on the analytic approach and the researcher's subjective interpretations than on any truly "objective" criteria (Weisberg, 1974; Jacoby, 1991a; van Schuur & Kiers, 1994).

Another possible objection is more conceptual in nature: Research in cognitive psychology suggests that sophistication and involvement in some area of endeavor lead to greater complexity in thinking about that subject (Tetlock, 1983a, b, 1984). If this is the case, then the "connection" between liberal-conservative thinking and the existence of a single simplifying dimension breaks down. But there is some evidence to the contrary: Several studies have shown that citizens who are attentive to ideological themes are, indeed, precisely those whose issue attitudes are aligned most closely along a single evaluative dimension (e.g. Stimson, 1975; Jacoby, 1991b).

So, just as was the case with attitude constraint, the research on complexity and dimensionality in mass political thinking seems to lead in several directions at once. But it does seem clear that this is just not the same thing as ideology in public opinion. Clarifying the conceptual distinctions between the two general lines of work is a useful step for progress in both directions.

Attitude Stability

The topic of temporal stability in issue attitudes represents another battle-ground in the debate over mass ideology that was once extremely active but now stands virtually silent. Converse's initial observations on this matter are simple and straightforward: Even if people organize their political belief systems along lines that do not conform to scholarly expectations, reliance upon *any* meaningful psychological structuring principles – consensual or idiosyncratic, unidimensional or multidimensional – should provide relatively stable "viewing perspectives" with respect to major questions of public policy. This would, in turn, be manifested as high temporal stability, possibly accompanied by some *systematic* change, in citizens' issue attitudes (Converse, 1964, 1970, 1975).

The empirical evidence provides a very different picture. Continuity correlations (mostly calculated from panel study data collected in 1956–1960 and 1972–1976) for most issues are uniformly very low, except on those few matters that arouse particularly strident, emotional responses (e.g. race in the 1950s and moral issues in the 1970s). The coefficient values are not only quite pallid in absolute terms. They are also dwarfed by the much higher stability that does seem to exist in other political orientations, such as party identification and candidate evaluations (Converse, 1970; Converse & Markus, 1979).[7]

These low correlations do not appear to reflect reasonable individual responses to external changes in the content of the political environment. The latter would imply systematic patterns of movement across issue positions. But, the empirical array of attitudes over time conforms to a very different structure, composed of two distinct segments of people: (1) A set of individuals with perfectly stable issue attitudes; and (2) a set of individuals whose positions change randomly over time. The size of the first subset varies from one issue to the next (generally, getting larger as the substantive content of the issue becomes more laden with emotional symbolism, and less focused on socioeconomic conflict). But regardless of the policy question, there always appears to be a significant number of people who have no meaningful personal preferences about alternative courses of governmental action – in short, they possess "non-attitudes" on the issue. And, again, this simply cannot happen if citizens use personal ideologies to orient themselves with respect to the political world.

While researchers have very occasionally demonstrated that it is *possible* to obtain quite high levels of temporal stability in individual responses to issue questions (Brown, 1970), the empirical evidence is clear-cut enough that the basic existence of widespread, random, turnover in mass opinion has never been seriously questioned. Critics of the "non-attitudes" interpretation have focused instead on exactly how the low continuity correlations should be interpreted. Achen (1975) and others (e.g. Pierce & Rose, 1974; Judd & Milburn, 1980; Krosnick, 1991) argue that the survey items used to elicit issue attitudes are extremely unreliable; these problematic questions generate a sizable amount of random "noise" variability, which masks the actual underlying stability that does exist in issue attitudes. So, the "fault" lies with the survey questions rather than with the survey respondents.

But the latter interpretation does not resolve the issue, either. The unreliability surely exists, but it could just as easily be due to non-crystallized attitudes among the survey respondents as to vague issue statements and response alternatives in the survey questions. The data employed in the analyses cited above simply provide no way to disentangle these two distinctly different possibilities.

The overall problem of attributing response instability to respondents or to questions was addressed by Norpoth and Lodge (1985), who took the rather obvious, but nevertheless largely unprecedented, step of stratifying a set of experimental subjects according to levels of political sophistication, and collecting panel data on their issue attitudes. The empirical results indicate that the "blame" must be spread around in both directions: Survey questions on political issues invariably contain non-negligible amounts of random measurement error. Still, sophisticated respondents exhibit more stable issue attitudes than do non-sophisticated respondents.

Interestingly, the findings from this latter study appear to have largely settled the matter: Some work continues to be carried out on stability and reliability in survey issue questions (e.g. Krosnick, 1991; Krosnick & Berent, 1993). And, the prevalence of weakly held opinions on public policy – basically, non-attitudes – comprises a central component in an influential current theory about the general dynamics of public opinion (Zaller, 1992). But, the question of attitude stability has seldom been raised in recent analyses of mass ideology.

PROGRESS THROUGH REFINEMENT OF A CENTRAL IDEA

In the previous section, I argued that progress has been achieved through the differentiation of certain concepts that are related to, but different from, ideology itself. That is, the study of mass-level ideology has benefited from a more detailed delineation of the material that really is part of this topic and that which is not. But this, alone, cannot provide significant new insights about the ways the public employs liberal-conservative ideas in their political thinking. Therefore, it is very fortunate that some important work has also been aimed at strengthening the methodological, theoretical, and empirical underpinnings of a central variable in this field: The levels of conceptualization.

The origins of this variable are well-known: In order to determine how people organized their political thinking, the authors of *The American Voter* examined open-ended survey responses to a lengthy series of questions about the major political parties and presidential candidates. The content and organization of each individual's full set of responses was used to assign that person to one of several categories. These categories were developed in an inductive manner, based upon the themes and ideas that were actually articulated by the survey respondents.

The Original Levels of Conceptualization Variable

Somewhat surprisingly, only four rather broad categories were required to subsume virtually all of the comments expressed by the several thousand interviewees. The categories are labeled as follows: *Ideologue* – contains individuals who employ broad, abstract evaluative dimensions to organize beliefs and attitudes; *Group Benefits* – containing people who evaluate political stimuli in terms of their impact on prominent reference groups; *Nature of the Times* – involving broad, but vague, judgments about the ways that contemporary political actors affect the overall tenor of society; and *No Issue Content* – comprising people whose evaluations of parties and candidates are completely devoid of any substantive policy concerns whatsoever. Thus, the public's political conceptualizations conform to several distinct modal patterns – an important finding, in itself.[8]

At the same time, the varying conceptions of the political world could be ordered quite readily, with respect to the scope of content and degree of abstraction involved in each type of thinking. So, people classified in the "highest" conceptual category – ideologues – are able to use the liberal-conservative continuum as a general judgmental "yardstick" for evaluating virtually all of the stimuli that arise in the political world. Citizens who think about politics in terms of group benefits also have access to a broad evaluative standard, so long as political events and personalities are connected in some manner to the reference group. Individuals who think in terms of the goodness or badness of the times exhibited relatively limited judgments with little perceived connection between distinct political stimuli. And finally, those whose comments contain no issue content exhibit little wherewithal for addressing any of the substantive aspects of contemporary politics. So, the qualitative differences in the organization of political belief systems apparently reflect citizens' overall abilities to grasp the nature of political phenomena and their substantive understanding of public policy issues. Hence, the genesis of the term, *levels* of *conceptualization*.

The levels of conceptualization are definitely one of the central components to the general analysis presented in *The American Voter*. The number of people whose comments about parties and candidates placed them into the highest level was extremely small (about 11%). Therefore, the levels of conceptualization comprise a central piece of evidence underlying the original assertion that American citizens are "innocent of ideology" (Kinder & Sears, 1985).

Surrogate Variables and Replication

The levels' importance was recognized immediately, but initial attempts at further analyses were severely hampered by the nature of the variable itself. Stated simply, the general research community did not have ready access to the contents of the original, open-ended survey protocols, which are required to construct the levels of conceptualization in the same manner as was carried out in *The American Voter*. And data availability questions aside, the systematic content analysis required to place the full set of survey respondents into the respective levels is a difficult, time-consuming, and daunting task in itself.

For the preceding reasons, most of the early replication studies relied upon "surrogate" levels of conceptualization variables, constructed from the pre-coded content categories (often simply called the "Master Codes") for responses to the open-ended candidate/party like/dislike questions, which are supplied in the Appendices to the various National Election Study codebooks. In other words, researchers do not typically have access to the verbatim interview transcripts; instead, it is only possible to determine whether NES respondents made comments that fall into particular categories, such as (Likes candidate X because he is) "more liberal than most Democrats," (Dislikes Party/Candidate Y because it/he) "favors civil rights," or (Likes Party Z because) "prosperity/'the times'/general conditions are better under them." Of course, this strategy cannot be used to replicate precisely the original levels. Nevertheless, the Master Code categories are very extensive; they do provide quite a bit of detail about the content of respondents' feelings toward the parties and candidates. Accordingly, surrogate measures constructed from these coded comments provided a very reasonable course of action, given that no other alternative was readily available.

Several different surrogate versions of the levels of conceptualization appeared in the research literature during the 1960s and 1970s. For example, both Field and Anderson (1969) and Coveyou and Piereson (1977) created three-category versions of the levels. In both cases: "Explicit ideologues" were defined as people who used specific liberal-conservative terminology to describe their feelings about political parties and presidential candidates; "Implicit ideologues" discussed policies and issues in ideological terms, without using explicit liberal-conservative language; and "Non-ideologues" exhibited no awareness of ideology whatsoever in their comments. Nie, Verba and Petrocik (1979) used the NES Master Codes to create a six-category version of the conceptual levels. Very briefly, they are defined as follows: *Ideologues* (responses contain liberal-conservative themes as well as references to issues and social groups); *Near Ideologues* (references to ideological themes, without elaboration); *Issue Reference* (responses mention specific social problems or political issues); *Group Reference* (focus on benefits or disadvantages to particular social groups); *Party Reference* (vague statements about political parties); and *Apolitical* (various non-political responses). Along with the surrogate measures based upon the Master Codes, there were also two relatively precise replications of the levels in 1964 (Pierce, 1969, 1968) and (Klingemann, 1973, 1979), based upon the more difficult strategy of coding the open-ended responses to the survey questions.

The analyses that employed these measures generated a number of interesting results. First, the prevalence of ideological terminology within citizens' responses to parties and candidates varies significantly over time. Second, the "targets" of ideological thinking vary, with parties more consistently the "carriers of ideology" than candidates. And third, the ability to express spontaneous liberal-conservative comments about parties and candidates is a quite different phenomenon relative to affective reactions toward ideological groups, or specific knowledge about ideology (e.g. the parties' ideological positions, specific issue stands, and so on).

While occasional applications of the surrogate measures appeared in the 1980s (e.g. Jacoby, 1986), their usage has become largely unnecessary. This is due entirely to the massive coding effort initially undertaken by Hagner and Pierce, with extensions by Knight (Hagner, Pierce & Knight, 1989) and Jacoby (in progress). These researchers obtained access to the original National Election Study interview protocols, and replicated the original levels of conceptualization (that is, based upon the actual respondent comments rather than the pre-coded categories) for every presidential year from 1956 through 1988 (work is currently underway to extend the data series to 1992).

The importance of the Hagner-Pierce et al. replication effort stems from its ability to overcome the weaknesses inherent in the surrogate levels of conceptualization measures. The latter are simply incapable of addressing the presence or absence of psychological organizational mechanisms in the ways that people express their affective responses to political parties and presidential candidates. This is problematic because the *structure* of a person's open-ended comments is just as critical as the exact *words* he/she employs. In the absence of further information about internal context of the verbal responses, the surrogate variables could misrepresent the true degree of ideological thinking in serious, but unpredictable, ways. They could overestimate ideological awareness among people who use words like "liberal" or "conservative" simply because they heard them mentioned in the mass media. Alternatively, tabulation of the Master Codes could easily miss important, but subtle, aspects of political thinking, thereby underestimating ideological awareness in the mass public.

While the protocol-based replications do not completely eliminate the possibility of mistaken attributions concerning individual ideological thinking, they certainly do reduce the likelihood of this problem, along with the severity of its effects when (and if) it does occur. Access to the verbatim transcripts of the interviews allows the coder to follow the respondent's line of reasoning more closely. Themes that span several discrete comments will be apparent; they would almost certainly be missed in the Master Codes. At the same time, isolated appearances of particular terms will be more easily identifiable; confused and incomplete utterances of ideological words will probably not be mistaken for actual ideological thinking. Thus, the availability of the Hagner-Pierce et al. levels of conceptualization variable across a wide time span makes an important – indeed, critical – contribution to the infrastructure of research on mass-level ideology.

Criticism of the Levels

Even though they have been employed in some of the most prominent analyses conducted within the field of mass political behavior, the levels of conceptualization have not been universally accepted by scholars. Some of the criticisms are aimed at the empirical characteristics of the variable. Several researchers have questioned whether the levels are fully ordered with respect to political sophistication (e.g. Lau, 1986; Luskin, 1987): For example, do reactions based upon "the nature of the times" imply a more developed grasp of political ideas than judgments about candidate personalities and other idiosyncratic points? Others have questioned the degree of differentiation across the different levels: Some analysts argue that the ideologue and group benefits levels are very similar, since both involve broad standards for evaluating political phenomena (e.g. Converse, 1975; Miller & Levitin, 1977). Others hold that the major distinction occurs between the "highest" level (ideologues) and the other three, since the former involves an abstract judgmental dimension while the others do not (Jacoby, 1991b).

The preceding concerns about the levels of conceptualization are relatively minor. Over the years, the most vocal critic of this variable has been Eric R. A. N. Smith (1980, 1981, 1989), whose work has provided a rallying point for those who disagree with the predominant line of research on mass-level ideology. Smith argues that the levels of conceptualization can be questioned on methodological, conceptual, and theoretical grounds.

The methodological critique is based primarily upon the amount of temporal change that occurs in the levels. The line of reasoning is straightforward: The levels of conceptualization are supposed to capture variability in the fundamental principles that people employ to organize their political thinking. Cognitive organization is a central component of an individual's basic orientations toward the political world. Therefore, it should be regarded as a relatively permanent psychological characteristic. In operational terms, the themes and ideas that people use to structure their opinions toward parties and candidates should be very stable over time. However, the individual citizens' locations within levels of conceptualization exhibit quite a bit of temporal change over two- and four-year time periods. Smith argues that the amount of turnover is so great that the levels can only be regarded as hopelessly unreliable measures of political sophistication.

The conceptual objections follow directly from the preceding conclusion: If the levels are unreliable, it necessarily implies that they are "contaminated" by variability that is unrelated to the phenomenon the variable is intended to measure (ideological thinking, in this case). But where does this extraneous variation come from? Smith argues that the levels are merely picking up superficial responses to the content of recent political rhetoric, rather than the fundamental structural abstractions underlying individual political evaluations. To the extent that the levels do pick up meaningful variability across individuals, it is inextricably correlated with political sophistication (which is better operationalized by other means). So, the levels of conceptualization are not measuring the phenomena that they are intended to measure – in other words, they are invalid.

Smith goes on to question whether the levels of conceptualization even exist in the first place. He contends that this variable was constructed in an ad hoc manner, with no foundation whatsoever in psychological theory. And he states that there is no serious evidence that people engage in different modes of political thinking. Smith argues that the levels of conceptualization should be abandoned as an analytic construct: "Unless someone presents new support for the levels, we should conclude that their existence is an interesting but unproven hypothesis (1989, p. 83)."

Responses and a Resolution (Hopefully!)

Smith's critical stance with respect to the levels of conceptualization is widely cited in the research literature. However, empirical analyses that employ the levels have continued unabated; in fact, the sheer number of studies that incorporate the levels of conceptualization has almost certainly *increased* since the publication of Smith's work. Part of the reason for this ongoing attention is that Smith's challenge has been answered: There certainly *is* a great deal of "new support for the levels;" that is, empirical findings which clearly demonstrate the presence of significant qualitative differences in the ways that people organize their political thinking and behavior – variability that corresponds very closely to the categories inherent in the levels of conceptualization. This work will be discussed in greater detail below.

At the same time, Smith's various criticisms of the levels have been refuted directly by other researchers. For example, Cassel (1984) demonstrates that the levels of conceptualization show reliabilities that are fully comparable to those of the variables employed to measure many other prominent political attitudes. Furthermore, both Cassel and Abramson (1981) point out that, contrary to Smith's conclusions, the levels are almost perfectly stable once measurement error is taken into account. Thus, the levels of conceptualization's measurement characteristics stand up to close scrutiny, so long as we employ the same standards that are routinely applied to other variables in the field of mass political behavior.

The validity issues have been addressed in a number of different ways. Hagner and Pierce (1982) immediately established the criterion validity of the protocol-based variable (i.e. the version of the levels used most frequently since they were made available in the early 1980s) by showing that the levels covary in predictable ways with many different measures of political involvement and participation. But, Jacoby (1988, 1995) has also shown that the levels are not mere surrogates for political sophistication; the conceptual levels do account for significant variations in the degree of mass-level ideological thinking, even after other indices of political awareness (e.g. education, interest, overt participation, etc.) are taken into account. Knight (1990) and Hagner and Pierce (1991) both show that the proportion of ideologues (i.e. people in the "highest" level of conceptualization) does not covary directly with the ideological content of presidential campaign rhetoric. Smith's charge that the levels only tap superficial responses is not supported empirically. Thus, the validity of the levels of conceptualization seems to be established quite firmly.

Smith's questions about the levels of conceptualization's theoretical status also seem to be without merit. In fact, the psychological underpinnings of the levels suffer more from an embarrassment of riches than a dearth of theoretical foundation. The basic notion of variability in modes of political thinking is an idea that is widely-accepted in the scholarly community, even among those researchers who reject (e.g. Marcus, Tabb & Sullivan, 1974) or avoid (e.g. Conover & Feldman, 1984) the levels of conceptualization in their analyses. But what do these individual differences tell us about the psychology underlying American public opinion? It is on this point that there exists some divergence of scholarly orientations.

From one perspective, Lau (1986) points out that the levels of conceptualization are grounded in attitude theory. They index the cognitive structures that people use to establish their affective reactions toward political stimuli (i.e. attitudes). In this capacity, the levels of conceptualization are fully within the theoretical traditions established by Rosenberg (1956) and Fishbein (1963). From a different perspective, Jacoby (1988) has argued that the levels of conceptualization are fully consistent with information-processing models of political behavior; in effect, they determine *which* cognitive economy schemes people will employ to organize their reactions to incoming information about political stimuli (e.g. Hymes, 1986; Smith & Lerner, 1986; Fazio & Williams, 1986). Thus, there are at least two different theoretical traditions that could subsume the levels of conceptualization quite easily. Accordingly, it is specious to argue that the latter comprise an "atheoretical" idea, constructed entirely anew by the authors of *The American Voter*.

It is perhaps ironic that, while Smith's fundamental criticisms are easy to answer, the more limited questions about the ordinal nature of the levels remain somewhat problematic. In fact, virtually all of the recent research does suggest that the levels of conceptualization may *not* be fully ordered in the manner they were originally hypothesized to be. The most serious problem concerns the two "interior" levels. In other words, ideologues are clearly the most sophisticated people, while those individuals in the "no issue content" level are least sophisticated. However, on a wide variety of criteria, there seems to be virtually no difference between those who think about politics in terms of group benefits, and those who focus on the nature of the times (e.g. Hagner & Pierce, 1982). It might be better to regard the levels of conceptualization as a variable comprised of three, rather than four, ordered categories.

So where does all of this leave the levels of conceptualization as an analytic construct? I would argue that, regardless of the original intentions about this variable, the levels are best viewed as *qualitative* distinctions in individual perspectives, rather than a *quantitative* gauge of a person's ability to understand the various aspects of the political world. It is absolutely critical to recognize that the levels measure the presence of ideological thinking, rather than the more general concept of political sophistication (e.g. Lau & Erber, 1985; Lau, 1986; Jacoby, 1995). As such, the "levels" are probably most appropriately viewed as a dichotomy: The important distinction lies between the ideologue level and the other three, regardless of any variability in modes of thinking that may exist among the latter (Jacoby, 1988). From this perspective, questions about the psychological nature of the levels are a bit superfluous: Regardless whether they promote attitude formation or cognitive organization, their *political* ramifications are the same: The levels of conceptualization can be used to identify those people who seem to make active use of ideological concepts in their political orientations. And this is precisely where the variable's importance lies: Overall, the levels have had a profound, positive impact on mass-level ideology research, by enabling analysts to distinguish between those citizens who *do* think in liberal-conservative terms, and those who do not.

PROGRESS THROUGH A CHANGE IN FOCUS

Another source of progress in the study of ideological thinking can be addressed very succinctly: There has been a major shift in the focus of the work within this field. Much of the early research on mass belief systems was concerned with what Luskin (1987) called "the distributional question." That is, *how many* people think about politics in liberal-conservative terms? More recent analyses have emphasized a different question: *What impact* does the liberal-conservative continuum have on subsequent political beliefs, attitudes, and behaviors?

Many of the classic studies viewed the structure of mass belief systems as an end in itself. The importance of ideological thinking, or at least the reliance on broad organizational principles for political attitudes, was taken for granted. So the prevalence of liberal-conservative thinking and ideological awareness was regarded as a dependent variable in many analyses. Virtually all of the empirical studies conducted through the 1960s and 1970s stressed the ways that changing external conditions affected the distribution of individuals across the levels of conceptualization, the degree to which people could recognize differences between liberals and conservatives, the degree of polarization manifested in ideological attitudes, and so on.

The precise analytic results and the interpretations imposed upon them varied from one study to the next. But, even in the time periods that supposedly manifested heightened ideological awareness within the American electorate, the individuals who explicitly viewed the world along liberal-conservative lines always remained a limited subset of the general public. So, many of the scholarly exchanges on this topic are reminiscent of a "glass half-full versus glass half-empty" quandary.

The preceding state of affairs did not go unnoticed. Bennett (1977) provided a general Kuhnian critique of the belief systems literature, pointing to several "central breakdowns in knowledge." Shortly thereafter, Kinder's frustration over the ongoing, but largely repetitive, arguments resulted in his "Enough already about ideology!" proclamation (1982). Along similar lines, Hamill and Lodge (1986) urged that researchers should move away from ". . . an emphasis on frequencies (i.e. who is and who isn't an ideologue) . . ." and move toward an alternative stance which emphasizes ". . . the cognitive and behavioral consequences . . . (of political information processing)." These critical views were largely intended to move subsequent work *away* from a focus on ideological questions. For example, Kinder's (1983) essay in *Political Science: The State of the Discipline* had exactly this objective and it provided detailed suggestions for several alternative perspectives on public opinion.

The various criticisms certainly did have a pronounced effect, but one that was quite different from their original intentions: Recent and current research continues to regard mass-level ideology as a central concept. But now, the predominant view incorporates phenomena like political conceptualization and reliance on ideological symbols as *independent* variables. Rather than simply taking the liberal-conservative continuum's importance for granted, modern empirical analyses are working to demonstrate that it actually is relevant for understanding citizens' views of politics. This ongoing line of work has been extremely successful: It has produced a sizable array of important findings, which I will discuss in detail below. Indeed, it is probably fair to say that individual ideological orientations comprise one of the most important elements in the interactive relationship between the mass public and the political world.

THE CURRENT STATE OF KNOWLEDGE ON MASS-LEVEL IDEOLOGY

While the current research on ideology has approached the topic from several different directions, there is one general conclusion that seems to permeate almost all of the work that has been carried out: It is impossible to make broad statements about the ideological level of the American electorate (e.g. "citizens became more conservative in the late 1970s and early 1980s") because there is too much internal variability to permit any such simple characterizations and/or generalizations. Instead, it is more accurate to say that for some people, ideology is *everything*; for others, liberal-conservative ideas are effectively *not* a component of their political thinking at all. The distinguishing factor is the person's level of conceptualization, or more broadly, his/her degree of political sophistication. Thus, conceptualization and/or sophistication facilitate the linkage between *subjective* ideology (i.e. liberal-conservative self-placement) and *objective* ideology (i.e. structuring orientations toward the political world along liberal-conservative lines). Once the critical importance of this mediating factor is recognized, the subsequent empirical findings and theoretical interpretations become almost transparent: Within the subset of the public that is attentive to ideological concepts, the liberal-conservative continuum has pervasive effects on a variety of phenomena.

Beliefs about Party and Candidate Issue Positions

An ideological dimension provides a convenient mechanism for citizens to structure their beliefs about political parties, candidates and issues. This is important for the obvious reason that people must have information about elites' issue positions, in order to make informed, rational choices about them. The problem is that information can be difficult and costly to obtain. The liberal-conservative continuum can facilitate information processing for citizens by providing straightforward cues about political actors' stands on particular issues. This has been demonstrated empirically, in a number of different contexts.

People who are attentive to ideological concepts are more likely to identify candidate and party issue positions than those who do not view the world in liberal-conservative terms (e.g. Wright & Niemi, 1985; Hamill, Lodge & Blake, 1985; Granberg & Brown, 1992). Such issue placements are, of course, a necessary precondition to *any* kind of issue-based political decision making. But, ideological influence on political cognition goes further than this. Reliance on the liberal-conservative dimension also promotes relatively *accurate* perceptions of candidate and party issue stands; that is, ideological thinkers tend to place Democratic stimuli (i.e. the party and its candidates) to the left of Republican stimuli on specific issues (e.g. Levitin & Miller, 1979; Sharp & Lodge, 1985; Jacoby, 1988). Feldman and Conover (1983; Conover, 1981; Conover & Feldman, 1986) explicate the nature of the underlying psychological processes, emphasizing that personal ideology provides a basis for inferring the initially-unknown issue stands of parties and candidates.

Thus, liberal-conservative ideology has a number of important cognitive consequences for the content of American public opinion. It helps individuals act as "cognitive misers," dealing efficiently and easily with the informational demands of political decision making and opinion formation. People can "fill in the gaps" within their belief systems and make reasonable judgments about the issue stands of parties and candidates. But, again, these "advantages" of ideological thinking only exist for those who actively rely upon the liberal-conservative continuum as an organizational mechanism underlying their thinking (e.g. Hamill & Lodge, 1986). And such individuals comprise but a subset of the general public (e.g. Luttbeg & Gant, 1985).

Issue Attitudes

As discussed earlier, a long line of research has shown that liberal-conservative self-placements are related to issue attitudes within the mass public. But, it is critically important to recognize a caveat to this general conclusion: There are sizable individual differences in the impact of ideological identifications on citizens' issue attitudes. People vary in their personal ideological positions, and this variability should lead to different stands on specific issues. The "translation process" from ideology to issue is not uniform throughout the electorate. Instead, some people rely heavily on ideology to guide their policy orientations while many others do not.

Once again, this basic finding has been replicated in a number of different settings. For example, Kuklinski, Metlay and Kay (1982) show that ideology affects attitudes toward nuclear power, but only among relatively sophisticated strata of the public. This finding is particularly interesting because the issue involved is new, and therefore, lacks the traditional associations to liberal and conservative positions. Sniderman, Brody and Kuklinski (1984) and Sniderman, Hagen, Tetlock and Brady (1991) demonstrate the varying impact of ideology on attitudes toward racial equality. They argue that individuals develop opinions by reasoning from general premises to specific conclusions. While there are many different kinds of generalities that could lie at the beginning of these reasoning chains, liberal-conservative self-placements occupy an increasingly prominent position as one moves upward through educational strata within the mass public.

Jacoby (1991b) also examines the relationship between ideological identification and a broad variety of issue attitudes. But, his study differs from the others by explicitly comparing two separate sources of liberal-conservative thinking: Education and political conceptualization. Both of these variables have a mediating effect on the degree to which ideological identifications impinge on issue attitudes. Of the two, however, the impact of conceptualization – and specifically, an individual's location within the "ideologue" level of conceptualization – has the stronger effect.

Along with ideological influences on specific issue attitudes, political sophistication and conceptualization also affects the degree of coherence and structure *across* separate attitudes. For example, Hamill, Lodge and Blake (1985) show that attitude consistency is particularly strong among those people who maintain relatively strong affective feelings toward ideological groups. Similarly, Sharp and Lodge (1985) report that there is a positive relationship between political sophistication and the degree of attitudinal constraint. And finally, Jacoby (1991b) finds that ideological consistency in issue positions increases with education and conceptualization.

The basic thrust of the research on ideological self-placement and issue attitudes is clear-cut: The impact of the liberal-conservative continuum on citizens' policy orientations is, itself, dependent upon the degree to which individuals are attentive to ideological concepts and symbols. A large segment of the public simply does not think about politics in ideological terms; therefore, their issue judgments tend to be based upon criteria that are either specific to each particular issue (e.g. attitude toward technology in the case of nuclear power or feelings about the sources of discrimination in the case of racial equality) or grounded in longstanding, and easily visible partisan ties (i.e. party identification). On the other hand, ideologues (defined rather loosely, as anyone who thinks about politics in ideological terms) have ready access to a general, abstract judgmental standard which can be applied to just about any political issue, regardless of the substantive controversy that is involved. Hence, their policy orientations tend to be relatively coherent, predictable, and consistent.

Candidate Evaluation and Voting Choice

Given the clarity of the evidence presented so far, it should come as no surprise that ideological influences on citizens' candidate choices also vary according to levels of ideological awareness. Indeed, general evaluations of presidential candidates and subsequent voting decisions might be viewed as relatively simple culminations of prior political cognitions and issue attitudes; in that case, individual differences in ideological voting would follow as mere consequences of the psychological processes already discussed. But, the impact of liberal-conservative ideology extends beyond this and has important implications for the interpretation of American elections.

For one thing, ideology affects the composition of the basic "perceptual maps" that citizens bring to bear on their voting decisions. Of course, there is a wide range of criteria that could be employed to evaluate presidential candidates. While the effectiveness and rationality of the different judgmental standards is subject to some debate (Miller, Wattenberg & Malanchuk 1986), there can be little doubt that ideology remains unparalleled in its ability to "distill" separate political concerns into a single overarching orientation. And yet, only the most sophisticated strata within the electorate employ the liberal-conservative continuum as a prominent organizational principle within the cognitive structures that they maintain with respect to political candidates (Jacoby, 1986). MacDonald and Rabinowitz (1993) make a similar point, by demonstrating that the *nature* of ideological influence varies within the general public: Most citizens incorporate ideological information in a directional manner (i.e. "the stronger a candidate's ideological inclination in my direction, the better"), but relatively sophisticated people exhibit proximity-like judgments (i.e. "the closer a candidates' ideological stand is to my own, the better").

This "ideological stratification" of candidate evaluations has tangible and important behavioral consequences. For example, the consistency between liberal-conservative identification and voting choice increases markedly across levels of cognitive sophistication (e.g. Stimson, 1975). Also, this configuration of conditional effects exists even after other potentially spurious factors – like party identification, specific issue attitudes, and candidate personality assessments – are taken into account (Knight, 1985). These individual differences in ideological voting appear to be a fairly regular component of American political behavior: The same general pattern has occurred in presidential elections from the 1970s (Stimson, 1975) through the 1980s (Knight, 1985; Lyons & Scheb, 1992), and into the 1990s (Knight & Lewis, 1996; Knight & Erikson, 1997).

There has also been some research conducted on the cognitive psychology of ideological voting. This work has helped to clarify the structural linkages between liberal-conservative identification and candidate choice. Specifically, Rahn, Aldrich, Borgida and Sullivan (1990) show that ideological influence on perceptions of candidates' personal qualities and evaluations of their general competence varies by level of political sophistication. Of course, these kinds of assessments subsequently feed into more general evaluative judgments about the candidates and on into voting choice itself. Thus, individual differences are most pronounced among the indirect paths from ideology to electoral choice, with sophisticated citizens more likely to make the necessary connections (i.e. "I am a conservative and based upon this stand, I believe Ronald Reagan has more suitable qualities for the Presidency than his competitors; therefore, I like him best and vote accordingly"). On the other hand, the more direct route, straight from individual ideology to affect (i.e. "I am a conservative and so is

Ronald Reagan, therefore I like him and vote accordingly"), operates at fairly constant strength throughout the electorate, regardless of individual sophistication levels.

In fact, this distinction between the cognitive and affective consequences of ideology for voting behavior helps resolve a potential contradiction in the research literature. Some of the studies cited earlier in this essay seem to suggest that liberal-conservative identifications are a *general* influence on electoral choice (e.g. Holm & Robinson, 1978) while the work covered in this section emphasizes the sophistication-based limitations on mass-level ideological thinking. What seems to be happening is that many people are using ideological symbols in "non-ideological ways" to guide their voting choices. That is, they make connections between candidates and issue positions along the liberal-conservative continuum that are "wrong," by objective standards. Nevertheless, they can still crystallize feelings of loyalty, empathy, and hostility toward particular candidates and thereby supply an ideological component to American elections. This also occurs even though only a small minority of the public really uses the liberal-conservative continuum to organize their general outlooks on the political world.

Formal Models

Along with the empirical studies that have been discussed so far, there has also been some important research carried out on formal models of ideology. This work generally seeks to embed ideological reasoning within the spatial theory of voting. Such an undertaking is particularly interesting because positive political theories are often held up as "competitors" to the psychological conceptions of political behavior (e.g. Enelow & Hinich, 1984).

Ideology plays a critical role in Anthony Downs' seminal economic theory of democracy (1957). For individual citizens, party ideologies eliminate the need to become informed on every new issue that arises within the political system; thus, they cut information costs and facilitate rational political action. From the perspective of the parties themselves, ideology encourages moderation in political rhetoric, because party leaders want to amass enough electoral support to win elections. In addition, ideologies promote regularity in policy-making, because parties must articulate consistent ideologies (consistency both in terms of their internal components, and in the regularity of their appeals over time) in order to maintain credibility with voters.

Downs' conception of ideology has been very influential. But subsequent developments in the area of spatial models moved in a somewhat different direction, by assuming that candidates/parties can change their policy positions as needed in their efforts to maximize voter support, and also that voters are fully informed about elite positions, as well as their own issue stands. This view, of course, stands at odds with virtually all of the empirical work on American elections and political behavior. Furthermore, Downs has recently been criticized for being "vague and confused" about the precise connection between individual issues and general ideology (Hinich & Munger, 1992).

More recent spatial models have attempted to address these concerns by incorporating valence-type, non-policy criteria into preference functions (Enelow & Hinich, 1982b) and by positing the existence of more general predictive dimensions underlying the specific policy axes of the space within which candidates and parties compete (Hinich & Pollard, 1981; Enelow & Hinich, 1982a). For present purposes, the most important results from this kind of work are contained within the spatial theory of ideology proposed by Hinich and Munger (1994). Basically, they argue that ideology functions as a sort of "translation device" for making systematic predictions about elites' stands on specific policy issues. A somewhat simplified version of this theory can be expressed in an equation like the following:

$$\Omega_{\theta i} = \Pi_\theta V + e_i \tag{1}$$

In Eq. (1), $\Omega_{\theta i}$ is a vector containing individual i's expectation about candidate θ's positions on a set of issues; Π_θ is candidate θ's position along an underlying ideological dimension; V is the vector of coefficients that "translate" from the single ideological position, Π_θ, to the positions on each of the issues contained in $\Omega_{\theta i}$; and e_i is the error involved when individual i makes this translation for him/herself. The expected issue positions generated by Eq. 1 are employed to determine i's expected utility for candidate θ, that is, $U_i(\theta)$, as follows:

$$U_i(\theta) = -(\Omega_{\theta i} - X_i)^2 \tag{2}$$

In Eq. (2), X_i is a vector of i's ideal points with respect to the same issues on which candidate θ is evaluated (i.e. those contained in $\Omega_{\theta i}$). The negative sign on the right-hand side of the equation shows that utility decreases as the distance between i and θ increases, and vice versa.

Hinich and Munger view ideology as a "reduced dimensional space" for predicting many distinct issue positions on the basis of the candidates' locations along a single continuum. But this sounds suspiciously like the role assigned to ideological abstractions in virtually all of the information-processing models of political perception. Furthermore, there is nothing that prevents individual citizens from employing a similar translation process for developing their own issue stands (i.e. the X_i values) on the basis of a personal ideological position (presumably represented by a term like Π_i) in a process analogous to that depicted in Eq. (1). And the variance of the error term in Eq. (1), e_i, could be functionally related to i's level of political sophistication (i.e. higher sophistication is correlated with smaller error variance). In this manner, individual differences in ideological thinking can also be incorporated into the translation process.

Thus, Hinich and Munger's spatial theory of ideology is nicely consistent with virtually all of the empirical work on mass belief systems and liberal-conservative thinking in the American electorate! This conclusion is important not only because it unites two different epistemological approaches to political behavior that are often viewed as complete opposites to each other. Instead, the fundamental consistency between the formal and empirical models of ideology provides a *rational* basis for liberal-conservative thinking; it is a succinct and manageable way for citizens to make reasonable, utility-maximizing choices among the alternatives that are available to them.

Environmental Effects on Individual Differences?

Some critics have charged that the prevalence of ideological thinking within the mass public is quite fluid over time, and largely a function of the content of current political rhetoric (e.g. Smith, 1989). In other words, if candidates and the media present issues in liberal-conservative terms, then the public will respond by incorporating ideological themes into their own opinions – basically, "mimicking" the content of the messages they receive. If this is the case, then ideology loses much of its theoretical importance for understanding mass political behavior; instead, it merely becomes a set of abstract symbols, amenable to manipulation by elites, for purposes of optimizing their own positions and power within the political system.

However, the preceding "salience hypothesis" does *not* provide an accurate portrayal of ideological thinking within the American electorate. The evidence on this point is quite strong, and covers nearly the entire range of ways that ideology impinges on citizens' political orientations. For example, consider ideological identification. While there are some recognizable patterns over time in the public's mean self-placement along the liberal-conservative continuum, this variability seems to track governmental policy activities in a rational manner (Stimson, 1999). The distribution of mass-level ideological identifications is clearly not a function of the specific content of campaign themes and political rhetoric (Fleishman, 1986a; Robinson & Fleishman, 1988).

The results are somewhat different when we move to political perceptions. Finkel and Norpoth (1984) show that mass beliefs about the 1980 presidential candidates' ideological positions crystallized over the course of the campaign.

But, this appears to be more an instance of "real" campaign-related political learning (e.g. Gelman & King, 1993) rather than shallow responses to superficial media messages. This interpretation is also supported by Finkel's later work (1989), which shows that changes in ideological orientations are more likely to occur among the most attentive, educated strata of the electorate. Hence, campaign-based ideological polarization does not, in any way, negate the importance of ideology, itself, for understanding public opinion and political behavior.

To the extent that the external environment has *any* other impact on the degree of liberal-conservative thinking within the mass public, it appears to be confined to relatively superficial and shallow phenomena. And, it takes a particularly overt effort – such as George Bush's use of "the L-word" in 1988 – to bring about even these minimal effects (Jacoby, 1995). In contrast, the proportion of citizens who conceptualize politics in ideological terms, and the segment of the public that actively employs the liberal-conservative continuum to structure their own issue stands and candidate preferences seem to be almost completely impervious to the content of the specific appeals that are aimed at them by the parties, candidates, and media (Knight, 1990; Hagner & Pierce, 1991; Jacoby, 1995).

The situation with respect to voting behavior is particularly interesting: As mentioned earlier, the overall correlation between liberal-conservative identification and candidate choice does vary from one election to the next, suggesting a possible environmental effect on ideological thinking. But, there are several distinct "paths" by which ideological self-placements can be "connected" to voting decisions. Lyons and Scheb (1992) show that the "direct route" – the one in which liberal and conservative labels serve as simple cues for choice – has a stronger effect in an ideologically-charged electoral environment (i.e. 1988). On the other hand, the "indirect route," through issue attitudes and perceptions of the candidates, exhibits a fairly stable, ongoing influence, across several different electoral contexts with different levels of ideological fervor in the predominant rhetoric.

Assessment of Individual Differences in Ideological Thinking

These findings suggest the difficulties inherent in determining the "impact of ideology" in American political behavior. The problem in doing so is that ideological terms can be employed in markedly different ways – some are "easier" and hence more accessible to citizens, while others are "more difficult" and therefore restricted to only the most sophisticated subset of the electorate (Jacoby, 1995).

For example, terms like "liberal" and "conservative" can serve as straightforward symbols to generate feelings of empathy, loyalty, or hostility throughout the general public (e.g. Conover & Feldman, 1981). This kind of rhetoric has been more prevalent in some election campaigns (e.g. 1972, 1980 and 1988) than in others (e.g. 1976, 1984) and when this occurs, it creates a fairly clear and widespread ideological bias in voting behavior. However, the connections tend to be relatively shallow, involving primarily affective feelings about the candidates.

The willingness to apply ideological abstractions to specific issue positions, to candidate stands, and to voting choice remains confined within a fairly small subset of the electorate. Within this stratum of citizens, ideological structuring of political orientations and behavior seems to be a fairly stable phenomenon over time (although, of course, the specific issues and candidates change). Thus, the "ideological complexion" of the mass public is characterized by pronounced individual differences. There is just no way around this fact. Any analyses that ignore this kind of variability will almost certainly misrepresent the distribution of ideological thinking in and influences on American public opinion and political behavior.

THE POLITICAL RELEVANCE OF INDIVIDUAL DIFFERENCES

One possible response to the findings described above is that public opinion research should move on to other topics besides ideology, since most people just do not conceptualize politics in ideological terms. However, it is quite easy to counter such a critical perspective: Individual differences in liberal-conservative thinking have *political* relevance, because policy controversies and elite orientations are usually organized along precisely those lines (e.g. Quinn & Shapiro, 1991).

Consider the nature of the issue environment confronting the mass public – that is, the various policy positions which are used to characterize different stands in political controversies, and around which public opinion crystallizes. This environment comprises a set of stimuli that are drawn predominantly from the socioeconomic issues that have dominated American political rhetoric since the New Deal era (i.e. questions about social welfare, and governmental responsibility for helping needy subgroups within society), and these kinds of concerns are precisely those that most clearly define the differences between liberal and conservative positions (e.g. McClosky & Zaller, 1984). So-called "lifestyle" or "social" issues (e.g. abortion, school prayer, and so on) have a more limited and transitory impact on political cleavages in American society (Geer, 1992).

Moreover, studies of the underlying structure in mass political perception show that citizens think about most, but not all, issues in unidimensional, bipolar terms. Specifically, beliefs about the conflicting positions on socioeconomic issues can be represented as points varying along a single continuum, with liberal stands at one end (e.g. government should provide services, help minorities, guarantee employment, etc.) and conservative issue positions at the other (e.g. government should cut spending and all people should work to get ahead on their own). In contrast, the lifestyle and social issues exhibit no such common underlying structure (Jacoby, 1990, 1996).[9] Thus, empirical evidence suggests that the dominant components of issue conflict in American politics exhibit a high degree of ideological polarization. This is particularly striking because mass perceptions of issues were neither constrained to promote unidimensional structures nor explicitly linked to the liberal-conservative continuum.

At the same time, political elites definitely orient their political thinking and behavior along ideological lines. This has been demonstrated in a number of different ways, across a variety of different settings. For example, congressional candidates exhibit high levels of constraint and unidimensional structuring in their issue attitudes (Converse, 1964). Similarly, roll call votes in state legislatures and in the U.S. Congress routinely divide members in ways that reflect a liberal-conservative ordering of the alternatives (Entman, 1983; Poole & Daniels, 1985; Poole & Rosenthal, 1997). Also, interest groups' evaluations of Senators are clearly structured according to a unidimensional ideological continuum (Poole, 1981).

Moving to a somewhat different set of political elites, delegates to the national party conventions are much more attuned to the meaning and relevance of ideological symbols than are "ordinary" citizens (e.g. McClosky, Hoffman & O'Hara 1960). Convention delegates also exhibit more extreme ideological orientations than the public at large (Miller, 1988). And once again, delegates' opinions about issues and candidates are much more highly constrained than even the most sophisticated members of the general public (Jennings, 1992).

Throughout most of American history, it has been possible to identify liberal and conservative positions within the predominant political cleavages of the times (e.g. Hartz, 1955; Rossiter, 1962; Hofstadter, 1972). Contrary to some predictions that the United States has reached "the end of ideology" (Bell, 1965), there is some evidence that ideological polarization is actually increasing in American politics (Poole & Rosenthal, 1984; Paddock, 1992; Fleisher & Bond, 1996; McCarty, Poole & Rosenthal, 1997; Jacobs & Shapiro, 2000). Even supposedly non-partisan institutions like the federal bureaucracy and the U.S. Supreme Court frequently exhibit unmistakably ideological divisions in their decisions (e.g. Downs, 1967; Segal & Spaeth, 1993).

The ideological content of *elite* political action is vitally important for present purposes because political scientists are increasingly recognizing that public opinion does not exist in a vacuum. Instead, it results from a complex set of interactions between individual citizens and the external environment. The structure of the political stimuli and the content of the messages which are presented to the mass public will have an effect on the ways that people react to the political world. And of course, there is also influence in the opposite direction, as well: The structure of citizen demands should influence the activities of political elites. In either case, elite-mass communication and substantive representation is almost certainly enhanced among the more ideologically-attuned sectors of the American electorate. There is also likely to be a sort of "acceleration effect" on this relationship, because ideologues are more participatory than other citizens (e.g. Poole & Palfrey, 1987; Leighley, 1991). For these reasons, it is important to understand how ideologues – or at least, those people who are particularly attentive to liberal-conservative ideas – react to the political world, even though they only comprise a minority of the overall American electorate.

CONCLUSION: POSSIBLE DIRECTIONS FOR FUTURE RESEARCH

If nothing else, the content of this essay should demonstrate that an enormous amount of work has been carried out on the topic of mass-level ideology. Researchers have investigated many different aspects of the sources, nature, and consequences of liberal-conservative thinking in the American electorate. However, it is also important to emphasize that the subject matter has not been exhausted: There are several possible avenues of investigation that, if pursued, should generate useful contributions to scholarly theories and understandings of this phenomena.

Conceptual Definitions and Empirical Measurement

It is imperative that political scientists continue to refine the definitions and improve the measurement of concepts that have already been identified as important within this subfield. For example, questions remain about the measurement characteristics of the levels of conceptualization: Specifically, how well-ordered are the categories in this variable? Is it necessary and/or useful to distinguish between the "middle" levels? Do the levels represent mutually exclusive types of thinking?

At the same time, the measurement of political attitudes is an ongoing concern that has direct implications for the study of ideological thinking. The fundamental – and still, apparently, unresolved – questions revolve around measurement error: Is the apparent complexity of individual political orientations simply due to the poor quality of our empirical measurements? Is measurement error in issue attitudes a function of the survey questions or of the respondents' psychological characteristics? Does the variance of measurement error covary with individual attentiveness to ideological concepts?

Perhaps the most general conceptual/measurement question involves the very nature of ideological thinking: Is this the same thing as political sophistication? Some researchers have argued that they are, indeed, interchangeable ideas (Luskin, 1987, 1990), while others maintain that they are conceptually distinct from each other (Jacoby, 1995). Do all sophisticated people view the world through an "ideological lens"? Can relatively unsophisticated citizens employ liberal-conservative terms in meaningful ways?

The Nature of Ideological Identification

With all the attention that has been devoted to the impact of ideology, it may be somewhat surprising that there are still some fairly serious theoretical ambiguities about the basic nature of liberal-conservative self-placements. Ideological identification has been variously described as a symbolic politics orientation (e.g. Sears & Citrin, 1985), a reference group attachment (e.g. Conover & Feldman, 1981), and an information-processing schema (Jacoby, 1991b). These three interpretations are all plausible mechanisms through which liberal-conservative self-placements could influence political beliefs and attitudes. However, they do have varying substantive implications, so it is important to determine which one is the most accurate description of the public's ideological orientations.

A focus on the basic nature of ideological identification raises several important, difficult, questions: If liberal-conservative self-placements represent symbolic orientations or reference group attachments, then why is their impact largely limited to a fairly small subset of the electorate? Alternatively, if ideology is a schema that is only "available" to sophisticated citizens, then how does this account for the ideological patterns of attitudes and behavior that nevertheless exist (albeit weakly) among the less sophisticated strata of the public?

One unified answer to these questions has been provided by Sniderman, Brody and Tetlock (1991), who argue that liberal-conservative identification is a decision-making heuristic that operates in different ways for different people (also see Sanders, 1989). But, this raises further interesting questions about how the impact of ideology changes (if it does) under different types of heuristic reasoning; for example, does an *affective* ideological response have the same potency and scope as a *cognitive* ideological orientation? This is a central question, that must be addressed in future research on the political psychology of mass-level ideological thinking.

Consider a related question that has gone virtually unrecognized: Is liberal-conservative identification truly an *ideology* in the first place? And is this the same thing as saying that it is a structuring principle for other beliefs, attitudes and behavior? Most definitions of the term "ideology" emphasize its role as a comprehensive world view – a conception of the ideal society, along with the means of achieving it (e.g. Downs, 1957; Hinich & Munger, 1994). However, there has been virtually no empirical work that has attempted to discern whether ideological identifications operate in this capacity within the mass public.

The Scope of Liberal-Conservative Influence

The importance of ideology stems largely from the potential pervasiveness of its effects. The liberal-conservative continuum is an abstract judgmental standard that can be applied to virtually all political stimuli, regardless of their substantive nature or content. But, most of the research in this field has proceeded on a relatively piecemeal basis, examining separately the impact of ideology on issue attitudes, candidate choice, political beliefs, and so on. It would be extremely useful to unify the results from these different efforts and produce a comprehensive "catalogue" of liberal-conservative effects on public opinion and political behavior. Such an effort would not only be helpful for subsequent researchers; it would also clarify the degree of theoretical progress that has already occurred in scholarly efforts to understand mass ideology.

But, there are many aspects of ideological thinking that still need to be investigated: Does ideology produce effects that are discernibly different from other structuring mechanisms, such as party identification? Are there "boundaries" or limits to liberal-conservative influence? Do liberal and conservative self-identifications produce "symmetrically opposed" results in citizens' political orientations? Or are there *qualitative* differences in the implications of these conflicting ideological positions? In other words, do liberals and conservatives see the world in fundamentally different ways, rather than merely taking on positions at the opposing poles of various issue dimensions?[10] This is a key question for understanding how ideological abstractions interact with other political orientations.

Finally, it would be useful to explicate more fully the relationship between macro- and micro-level manifestations of citizen ideology. A prominent line of recent research holds that the general "contours" of mass opinion – including the relative prevalence of liberals versus conservatives within the public – provide critical information to guide political elites in their policy-making activities (Stimson, MacKuen & Erikson, 1995; Stimson, 1999). But, how does this view coexist with the pervasive evidence that most people have limited capacities for explicit ideological reasoning? Some analysts (e.g. Page & Shapiro, 1992; Stimson, 1999) contend that the aggregation process, itself, is sufficient to control for the effects of "noise" (e.g. non-attitudes, inconsistent policy preferences, measurement error, etc.). Others argue that aggregation is not a neutral process; instead, it results in a biased representation of citizen preferences (Kuklinski & Quirk, 2000). Also, regardless which of these views is correct, there is likely to be at least some degree of endogeneity in the system (Jacobs & Shapiro, 2000). That is, the prevalence of ideological symbols in the external environment will influence the extent of liberal-conservative thinking at the individual level; simultaneously, the degree to which citizens exhibit ideo-logically-oriented opinions will affect the subsequent salience of liberal and conservative symbols within contemporary political rhetoric. It will be extremely difficult to disentangle the various connections between these individual- and aggregate-level phenomena (Erikson, MacKuen & Stimson, 2002). Nevertheless, doing so will comprise an important step along the path toward understanding sources, nature, role, and impact of citizen ideology within the American political system.

All of the topics raised in this concluding section have received some, but not enough, attention in the research literature. The general point to be drawn from this discussion should be obvious: There is plenty more to be learned about the sources, nature, and consequences of liberal-conservative thinking within the American mass public. Rather than adhering to the frustrated cry of "Enough already about ideology!", I agree wholeheartedly with Stimson's recent comment that "Ideology won't go away. It's too important" (1999, p. 67).

NOTES

1. The coverage in this essay will be limited to studies of liberal-conservative thinking within the *American* electorate. Comparative research on mass-level ideologies is discussed in Budge, Crewe and Farlie (1976), Barnes and Kaase (1979), Inglehart (1990), and Dalton (1996), among many other sources.

2. In the CSEP interview schedule, respondents were first asked, "Now when it comes to politics in general, do you usually think of yourself as a conservative, as a liberal, as middle-of-the-road, or don't you think of yourself along liberal or conservative lines?

Respondents who stated that they did not think of themselves in ideological terms (i.e. they selected the last option in the question) were then asked "If you *had* to think of yourself along these lines, would you think of yourself as a conservative, as a liberal, or middle-of-the-road when it comes to politics?" Respondents who called themselves conservatives or liberals on either of these two questions were next asked "Would you call yourself a strong conservative (liberal) or a not very strong conservative (liberal)?" Middle-of-the-road respondents (on either of the first two questions) were asked "Well, do you think of yourself as closer to conservatives or closer to liberals?" Details about measuring ideology with the CSEP data are discussed in Beardsley (1973).

3. The NES question is worded as follows: "We hear a lot of talk these days about liberals and conservatives. Here is a 7-point scale on which the political views that people might hold are arranged from extremely liberal to extremely conservative. Where would you place yourself on this scale, or haven't you thought much about this?" Respondents are then handed a card with the following labels:

(1) Extremely Liberal
(2) Liberal
(3) Slightly Liberal
(4) Moderate; Middle of the Road
(5) Slightly Conservative
(6) Conservative
(7) Extremely Conservative

This is the standard ideology question which has been included in the Biennial NES surveys since 1972. In 1984, the NES also measured ideological self-placements using a series of branching questions similar to the standard party identification battery. Haltom (1990) provides a systematic comparison of the two question formats.

4. The percentage who say that they "haven't thought much about this" varies from 21.73% in 1996 to 33.42% in 1980. The mean percentage giving this response (from 1972 through 1996) is 26.61%.

5. The percentage of respondents who place themselves along the scale at the "moderate; middle of the road" position varies from 30.25% in 1996 to 37.72% in 1976. The mean percentage giving this response (from 1972 through 1996) is 33.15%.

6. Prior to about 1980, published literature reviews moved almost seamlessly across these different topics, without differentiating very clearly between most of them. For some prominent examples of this phenomenon, see Kessel (1972), Cobb (1973), or Bennett (1977).

7. According to Converse and Markus (1979), the mean two-year continuity correlation for issues in the 1950s is about 0.40. The mean two-year continuity correlation for non-morality issues in the 1970s is about 0.42. In contrast, the mean two-year continuity correlations for morality issues and candidate evaluations (both in the 1970s) are 0.66 and 0.60, respectively. The mean two-year continuity correlations for party identification are even higher, 0.84 in the 1950s and 0.81 in the 1970s. Interestingly, the four-year continuity correlation for liberal-conservative self-placements (the only value reported by Converse and Markus) falls in between these extremes, at 0.56.

8. *The American Voter* actually "subdivided" several of the levels into more specific categories. The highest level was divided into "ideology" and "near ideology" categories. The group benefits level was divided into "perception of conflict," "single-group interest,"

and "shallow group benefit responses." Also, the lowest level was divided into "party orientation," "candidate orientation," "no content," and "unclassified" categories. These finer distinctions have not been included in recent analyses that have used the levels of conceptualization.

9. These studies employ scaling methodologies which try to discern the structure of citizen perceptions without "contamination" from a researcher's prior expectations about the nature of any such structure.

10. A related, but different (from my perspective, at least) topic involves the dimensionality of liberal-conservative self-placements. Conover and Feldman (1981) argued that ideological identifications were "non-dimensional" in the sense that a liberal attachment is not necessarily the opposite of a conservative placement, and vice versa. However, current scholarly consensus does not seem to support this idea: Once response biases and measurement errors are taken into account, liberal and conservative identifications do appear to be opposing psychological orientations (Knight 1984; Green 1988).

ACKNOWLEDGMENTS

Special thanks go to Saundra K. Schneider; this paper could not have been completed without her help. Valerie A. Sulfaro provided invaluable research assistance during the early stages of the project. I would also like to thank Leonie Huddy and Robert Y. Shapiro for their comments and suggestions.

REFERENCES

Abramson, P. R. (1981). Comment on Smith. *American Political Science Review, 75,* 146–149.

Allen, R. L., Dawson, M. C., & Brown, R. (1989). A Schema-Based Approach to Modeling an African-American Racial Belief System. *American Political Science Review, 83,* 421–442.

Alvarez, R. M., & Nagler, J. (1995). Economics, Issues, and the Perot Candidacy: Voter Choice in the 1992 Presidential Election. *American Journal of Political Science, 39,* 714–744.

Alvarez, R. M., & Nagler, J. (1998). Economics, Entitlements, and Social Issues: Voter Choice in the 1996 Presidential Election. *American Journal of Political Science, 42,* 1349–1363.

Asher, H. B. (1983). Voting Behavior Research in the 1980s: An Examination of Some Old and New Problem Areas. In: A. W. Finifter (Ed.), *Political Science: The State of the Discipline.* Washington, D.C.: American Political Science Association.

Barnes, S. H., & Kaase, M. (1979). *Political Action: Mass Participation in Five Western Democracies.* Beverly Hills, CA: Sage.

Barton, A. H., & Parsons, R. W. (1977). Measuring Belief System Structure. *Public Opinion Quarterly, 41,* 159–180.

Beardsley, P. L. (1973). The Methodology of Electoral Analysis: Models and Measurement. In: D. M. Kovenock, J. W. Prothro & Associates (Eds), *Explaining the Vote: Presidential Choices in the Nation and the States, 1968. Part 1: The Theoretical Approach.* Chapel Hill, NC: Institute for Research in Social Science.

Beck, P. A., & Jennings, M. K. (1979). Political Periods and Political Participation. *American Political Science Review, 73,* 737–750.

Bell, D. (1965). *The End of Ideology: On the Exhaustion of Political Ideas in the Fifties* (Revised Edition). New York: Free Press.

Bennett, L. L., & Bennett, S. E. (1990). *Living with Leviathan: Americans Coming to Terms with Big Government*. Lawrence, KS: University Press of Kansas.

Bennett, W. L. (1975). *The Political Mind and the Political Environment*. Lexington, MA: D. C. Heath.

Bennett, W. L. (1977). The Growth of Knowledge in Mass Belief Systems: An Epistemological Critique. *American Journal of Political Science, 21*, 465–500.

Berelson, B. R., Lazarsfeld, P. F., & McPhee, W. N. (1954). *Voting*. Chicago: University of Chicago Press.

Bishop, G. H., & Frankovic, K. A. (1981). Ideological Consensus and Constraint Among Party Leaders and Followers in the 1978 Election. *Micropolitics, 1*, 87–111.

Bishop, G. F., Tuchfarber, A. J., & Oldendick, R. W. (1978). Change in the Structure of American Political Attitudes: The Nagging Question of Question Wording. *American Journal of Political Science, 22*, 250–269.

Bishop, G. F., Tuchfarber, A. J., Oldendick, R. W., & Bennett, S. E. (1979). Questions About Question Wording: A Joinder to Revisiting Mass Belief Systems Revisited. *American Journal of Political Science, 23*, 187–192.

Brown, S. R. (1970). Consistency and the Persistence of Ideology: Some Experimental Results. *Public Opinion Quarterly, 34*, 60–68.

Brunk, G. G. (1978). The 1964 Attitude Consistency Leap Reconsidered. *Political Methodology, 5*, 347–360.

Budge, I. Crewe, I., & Farlie, D. (Eds) (1976). *Party Identification and Beyond*. New York: Wiley.

Campbell, A., Converse, P. E., Miller, W. E., & Stokes, D. E. (1960). *The American Voter*. Chicago: University of Chicago Press.

Cantril, A. H., & Cantril, S. D. (1999). *Reading Mixed Signals: Ambivalence in American Public Opinion about Government*. Washington, D.C.: Woodrow Wilson Center Press.

Carmines, E. G., & Stimson, J. A. (1989). *Issue Evolution: Race and the Transformation of American Politics*. Princeton, NJ: Princeton University Press.

Cassel, C. A. (1984). Issues in Measurement: The 'Levels of Conceptualization' Index of Ideological Sophistication. *American Journal of Political Science, 28*, 418–429.

Cobb, R. W. (1973). The Belief Systems Perspective: An Assessment of a Framework. *Journal of Politics, 35*, 121–153.

Conover, P. J. (1981). Political Cues and the Perception of Candidates. *American Politics Quarterly, 9*, 427–448.

Conover, P. J., & Feldman, S. (1981). The Origins and Meaning of Liberal-Conservative Self-Identification. *American Journal of Political Science, 25*, 617–645.

Conover, P. J., & Feldman, S. (1984). How People Organize the Political World: A Schematic Model. *American Journal of Political Science, 28*, 95–126.

Conover, P. J., & Feldman, S. (1986). The Role of Inference in the Perception of Political Candidates. In: R. R. Lau & D. O. Sears (Eds), *Political Cognition*. Hillsdale, NJ: Lawrence Erlbaum.

Converse, P. E. (1964). The Nature of Belief Systems in Mass Publics. In: D. E. Apter (Ed.), *Ideology and Discontent*. New York: Free Press.

Converse, P. E. (1970). Attitudes and Non-attitudes: Continuation of a Dialogue. In: E. R. Tufte (Ed), *The Quantitative Analysis of Social Problems*. Reading, MA: Addison-Wesley.

Converse, P. E. (1974). Comment: The Status of Non-attitudes. *American Political Science Review, 68*, 650–660.

Converse, P. E. (1975). Public Opinion and Voting Behavior. In: F. I. Greenstein & N. W. Polsby (Eds), *Handbook of Political Science*. Reading, MA: Addison-Wesley.

Converse, P. E. (1980). Comment: Rejoinder to Judd and Milburn. *American Sociological Review*, *45*, 644–646.

Converse, P. E., & Markus, G. B. (1979). Plus ça Change . . .': The New CPS Election Study Panel. *American Political Science Review*, *73*, 2–49.

Coveyou, M. R. and Piereson, J. (1977). Ideological Perceptions and Political Judgement: Some Problems of Concept and Measurement. *Political Methodology*, *4*, 77–102.

Dalton, R. J. (1996). *Citizen Politics: Public Opinion and Political Parties in Advanced Industrial Democracies* (2nd ed.). Chatham, NJ: Chatham House.

Dalton, R. J., & Wattenberg, M. P. (1993). The Not So Simple Act of Voting. In: A. W. Finifter (Ed.), *Political Science: The State of the Discipline II*. Washington, D. C.: American Political Science Association.

Devine, D. J. (1972). *The Political Culture of the United States*. Boston: Little, Brown.

Downs, A. (1957). *An Economic Theory of Democracy*. New York: Harper and Row.

Downs, A. (1967). *Inside Bureaucracy*. Boston: Little, Brown.

Edelman, M. (1964). *The Symbolic Uses of Politics*. Urbana, IL: University of Illinois Press.

Enelow, J., & Hinich, M. (1982a). Ideology, Issues, and the Spatial Theory of Elections. *American Political Science Review*, *76*, 493–501.

Enelow, J., & Hinich, M. (1982b). Non-spatial Candidate Characteristics and Electoral Competition. *Journal of Politics*, *44*, 115–130.

Enelow, J., & Hinich, M. (1984). *The Spatial Theory of Voting*. New York: Cambridge University Press.

Entman, R. M. (1983). The Impact of Ideology on Legislative Behavior and Public Policy in the States. *Journal of Politics*, *45*, 163–182.

Erikson, R. S., MacKuen, M., & Stimson, J. A. (2002). *The Macro Polity*. Cambridge, U.K.: Cambridge University Press.

Fazio, R. H., & Williams, C. J. (1986). Attitude Accessibility as a Moderator of the Attitude-Perception and Attitude-Behavior Relations: An Investigation of the 1984 Presidential Election. *Journal of Personality and Social Psychology*, *51*, 505–514.

Feldman, S. (1988). Structure and Consistency in Public Opinion: The Role of Core Beliefs and Values. *American Journal of Political Science*, *32*, 416–440.

Feldman, S., & Conover, P. J. (1983). Candidates, Issues, and Voters: The Role of Inference in Political Perception. *Journal of Politics*, *45*, 810–839.

Field, J. O., & Anderson, R. E. (1969). Ideology in the Public's Conceptualization of the 1964 Election. *Public Opinion Quarterly*, *33*, 380–398.

Finkel, S. E. (1989). Effects of the 1980 and 1984 Campaigns on Mass Ideological Orientations: Testing the Salience Hypothesis. *Western Political Quarterly*, *42*, 325–346.

Finkel, S. E., & Norpoth, H. (1984). Candidates and Issues in the 1980 Campaign: The Ideological Connection. *Political Behavior*, *6*, 61–78.

Finkel, S. E., & Trevor, G. (1986). Reassessing Ideological Bias in Campaign Participation. *Political Behavior*, *8*, 374–390.

Fishbein, M. (1963). An Investigation of the Relationships Between Beliefs About an Object and Attitudes Toward that Object. *Human Relations*, *16*, 233–239.

Fleisher, R., & Bond, J. R. (1996). The President in a More Partisan Legislative Arena. *Political Research Quarterly*, *49*, 729–748.

Fleishman, J. A. (1986a). Trends in Self-Identified Ideology from 1972 to 1982: No Support for the Salience Hypothesis. *American Journal of Political Science*, *30*, 517–541.

Fleishman, J. A. (1986b). Types of Political Attitude Structure: Results of a Cluster Analysis. *Public Opinion Quarterly*, *50*, 371–386.

Free, L. A., & Cantril, H. (1967). *The Political Beliefs of Americans*. New Brunswick, NJ: Rutgers University Press.

Gamson, W. A. (1992). *Talking Politics*. New York: Cambridge University Press.

Gamson, W. A., & Modigliani, A. (1989). Media Discourse and Public Opinion in Nuclear Power: A Constructionist Approach. *American Journal of Sociology, 95*, 1–37.

Geer, J. (1992). New Deal Issues and the American Electorate, 1952–1998. *Political Behavior, 14*, 45–66.

Gelman, A., & King, G. (1993). Why are American Presidential Election Campaign Polls So Variable When Votes Are So Predictable? *British Journal of Political Science, 23*, 409–451.

Goldberg, A. S. (1966). Discerning a Causal Pattern Among Data on Voting Behavior. *American Political Science Review*, 60, 913–922.

Granberg, D., & Brown, T. A. (1992). The Perception of Ideological Distance. *Western Political Quarterly, 45*, 727–750.

Green, D. P. (1988). On the Dimensionality of Public Sentiment toward Partisan and Ideological Groups. *American Journal of Political Science, 32*, 758–780.

Hagner, P. R., & Pierce, J. C. (1982). Correlative Characteristics of the Levels of Conceptualization in the American Public: 1956–1976. *Journal of Politics, 44*, 779–807.

Hagner, P. R., & Pierce, J. C. (1991). Liberal is a Four Letter Word: Campaign Rhetoric and the Measurement of Political Conceptualization. Paper presented at the 1991 Annual Meetings of the Midwest Political Science Association.

Hagner, P. R., Pierce, J. C., & Knight, K. (1989). *Content Coding of Level of Political Conceptualization, 1956–1988 (United States)*. ICPSR 8151 (4th ed.). Ann Arbor, MI: Inter-University Consortium for Political and Social Research.

Haltom, W. (1990). Liberal-Conservative Continua: A Comparison of Alternative Measures. *Western Political Quarterly, 43*, 387–402.

Hamill, R., & Lodge, M. (1986). Cognitive Consequences of Political Sophistication. In: R. R. Lau & D. O. Sears (Eds), *Political Cognition*. Hillsdale, NJ: Lawrence Erlbaum.

Hamill, R. Lodge, M., & Blake, F. (1985). The Breadth, Depth, and Utility of Class, Partisan, and Ideological Schemata. *American Journal of Political Science, 29*, 850–870.

Hartwig, F., Jenkins, W. R., and Temchin, E. M. (1980). Variability in Electoral Behavior: The 1960, 1968, and 1976 Elections. *American Journal of Political Science* 24: 553–558.

Hartz, L. (1955). *The Liberal Tradition in America*. New York: Harcourt, Brace.

Hinich, M. J., & Munger, M. C. (1992). A Spatial Theory of Ideology. *Journal of Theoretical Politics, 4*, 5–30.

Hinich, M. J. and Munger, M. C. (1994). *Ideology and the Theory of Political Choice*. Ann Arbor, MI: University of Michigan Press.

Hinich, M. J., & Pollard, W. (1981). A New Approach to the Spatial Theory of Electoral Competition. *American Journal of Political Science, 25*, 323–341.

Hofstadter, R. (1972). *The American Political Tradition*. New York: New Vintage Edition.

Holm, J. D., & Robinson, J. P. (1978). Ideological Identification and the American Voter. *Public Opinion Quarterly, 42*, 235–246.

Hymes, R. (1986). Political Attitudes as Social Categories: A New Look at Selective Memory. *Journal of Personality and Social Psychology, 51*, 233–241.

Howell, S. E. (1985). Chasing an Elusive Concept: Ideological Identifications and Candidate Choice. *Political Behavior, 7*, 325–334.

Inglehart, R. (1990). *Culture Shift in Advanced Industrial Society*. Princeton, NJ: Princeton University Press.

Jackman, M. R., & Jackman, R. W. (1983). *Class Awareness in the United States*. Berkeley, CA: University of California Press.

Jackson, J. E. (1975). Issues, Party Choices, and Presidential Votes. *American Journal of Political Science, 19*, 161–185.

Jacobs, L. R., & Shapiro, R. Y. (2000). *Politicians Don't Pander: Political Manipulation and the Loss of Democratic Responsiveness*. Chicago: University of Chicago Press.

Jacoby, W. G. (1986). Levels of Conceptualization and Reliance on the Liberal-Conservative Continuum. *Journal of Politics, 48*, 423–432.

Jacoby, W. G. (1988). The Sources of Liberal-Conservative Thinking: Education and Conceptualization. *Political Behavior, 10*, 316–332.

Jacoby, W. G. (1990). Variability in Issue Alternatives and American Public Opinion. *Journal of Politics, 52*, 579–606.

Jacoby, W. G. (1991a). *Data Theory and Dimensional Analysis*. Newbury Park, CA: Sage.

Jacoby, W. G. (1991b). Ideological Identification and Issue Attitudes. *American Journal of Political Science, 35*, 178–205.

Jacoby, W. G. (1994). Public Attitudes Toward Government Spending. *American Journal of Political Science, 38*, 336–361.

Jacoby, W. G. (1995). The Structure of Ideological Thinking in the American Electorate. *American Journal of Political Science, 39*, 314–335.

Jacoby, W. G. (1996). Testing the Effects of Paired Issue Statements on the Seven-Point Issue Scales. In: J. R. Freeman (Ed.), *Political Analysis, Volume 5: 1993–1994*. Ann Arbor, MI: University of Michigan Press.

Jennings, M. K. (1992). Ideology Among Mass Publics and Political Elites. *Public Opinion Quarterly, 56*, 419–441.

Judd, C. M., & Milburn, M. A. (1980). The Structure of Attitude Systems in the General Public: Comparisons of a Structural Equation Model. *American Sociological Review, 45*, 627–643.

Kessel, J. H. (1972). Comment: The Issues in Issue Voting. *American Political Science Review, 66*, 459–465.

Key, V. O., Jr., & Munger, F. (1959). Social Determinism and Electoral Decision: The Case of Indiana. In: E. Burdick & A. C. Brodbeck (Eds), *American Voting Behavior*. Glencoe, IL: Free Press.

Kinder, D. R. (1982). Enough Already About Ideology! The Many Bases of American Public Opinion. Paper presented at the 1982 Annual Meetings of the American Political Science Association.

Kinder, D. R. (1983). Diversity and Complexity in American Public Opinion. In: A. W. Finifter (Ed.), *Political Science: The State of the Discipline*. Washington, D. C.: American Political Science Association.

Kinder, D. R., & Sears, D. O. (1985). Public Opinion and Political Action. In: G. Lindsey & E. Aronson (Eds), *Handbook of Social Psychology* (3rd ed.). New York: Random House.

Klingemann, H. D. (1973). Dimensions of Political Belief Systems: 'Levels of Conceptualization' as a Variable. Some Results for USA and FRG 1968/69. *Comparative Political Studies, 5*, 93–106.

Klingemann, H. D. (1979). Measuring Ideological Conceptualizations. In: S. H. Barnes & M. Kaase (Eds), *Political Action: Mass Participation in Five Western Democracies*. Beverly Hills, CA: Sage.

Knight, K. (1984). The Dimensionality of Partisan and Ideological Affect: The Influence of Positivity. *American Politics Quarterly, 12*, 305–334.

Knight, K. (1985). Ideology in the 1980 Election: Ideological Sophistication Does Matter. *Journal of Politics*, *47*, 828–853.

Knight, K. (1990). Ideology and Public Opinion. *Micropolitics*, *3*, 59–82.

Knight, K., & Erikson, R. S. (1997). Ideology in the 1990s. In: B. Norrander & C. Wilcox (Eds), *Understanding Public Opinion*. Washington, D. C.: CQ Press.

Knight, K., & Lewis, C. V. (1996). Does Ideology Matter? In: B. Ginsberg & A. Stone (Eds), *Do Elections Matter?* (3rd ed.). Armonk, NY: M. E. Sharpe.

Kovenock, D. M., & Beardsley, P. L. (1970). Status, Party, Ideology, Issues, and Candidate Choice: A Preliminary, Theory-Relevant Analysis of the 1968 American Presidential Election. Paper presented at the 1970 Meeting of the International Political Science Association.

Krosnick, J. A. (1991). The Stability of Political Preferences: Comparisons of Symbolic and Non-symbolic Attitudes. *American Journal of Political Science*, *35*, 547–576.

Krosnick, J. A. and Berent, M. K. (1993). The Stability of Party Identification and Policy Preference: The Impact of Survey Question Format. *American Journal of Political Science*, *37*, 941–964.

Kuklinski, J. H., Metlay, D. S., & Kay, W. D. (1982). Citizen Knowledge and Choices on the Complex Issue of Nuclear Energy. *American Journal of Political Science*, *26*, 615–642.

Kuklinski, J. H., & Quirk, P. J. (2000). Reconsidering the Rational Public: Cognition, Heuristics, and Mass Opinion. In: A. Lupia, M. D. McCubbins & S. L. Popkin (Eds), *Elements of Reason: Cognition, Choice, and the Bounds of Rationality*. New York: Cambridge University Press.

Lamb, K. A. (1974). *As Orange Goes: Twelve California Families and the Future of American Politics*. New York: Norton.

Lane, R. E. (1962). *Political Ideology*. New York: Free Press.

Lau, R. R. (1986). Political Schemata, Candidate Evaluations, and Voting Behavior. In: R. R. Lau & D. O. Sears (Eds), *Political Cognition*. Hillsdale, NJ: Lawrence Erlbaum.

Lau, R. R, Brown, T. A., & Sears, D. O. (1978). Self-Interest and Civilians' Attitudes Toward the Vietnam War. *Public Opinion Quarterly*, *42*, 464–483.

Lau, R. R., & Erber, R. (1985). Political Sophistication: An Information-Processing Perspective. In: S. Kraus & R. M. Perloff (Eds), *Mass Media and Political Thought*. Beverly Hills, CA: Sage.

Lau, R. R., & Sears, D. O. (Eds). (1986) *Political Cognition*. Hillsdale, NJ: Lawrence Erlbaum.

Leighley, J. (1991) Participation as a Stimulus of Political Conceptualization. *Journal of Politics*, *53*, 198–211.

Levitin, T. E. and Miller, W. E. (1979). Ideological Interpretations of Presidential Elections. *American Political Science Review*, *73*, 751–771.

Luskin, R. C. (1987). Measuring Political Sophistication. *American Journal of Political Science*, *31*, 856–899.

Luskin, R. C. (1990). Explaining Political Sophistication. *Political Behavior*, *12*, 331–361.

Luttberg, N. R. (1968). The Structure of Beliefs Among Leaders and the Public. *Public Opinion Quarterly*, *32*, 398–410.

Luttbeg, N. R., & Gant, M. M. (1985). The Failure of Liberal-Conservative Ideology as a Cognitive Structure. *Public Opinion Quarterly*, *49*, 80–93.

Lyons, W., & Scheb, J. M., II. (1992). Ideology and Candidate Evaluations in the 1984 and 1988 Presidential Elections. *Journal of Politics*, *54*, 573–584.

MacDonald, S. E. and Rabinowitz, G. B. (1993). Ideology and Candidate Evaluation. *Public Choice*, *76*, 59–78.

Maddox, W. S., & Lilie, S. A. (1984). *Beyond Liberal and Conservative: Reassessing the Political Spectrum*. Washington, D. C.: Cato Institute.

Marcus, G., Tabb, D., & Sullivan, J. L. (1974). The Application of Individual Differences Scaling to the Measurement of Political Ideologies. *American Journal of Political Science, 18,* 405–420.

Margolis, M. (1977). From Confusion to Confusion: Issues and the American Voter (1956–1972). *American Political Science Review, 71,* 31–43.

McCarty, N. Poole, K., & Rosenthal, H. (1997). *Income Redistribution and the Realignment of American Politics.* Washington, D. C.: American Enterprise Institute.

McClosky, H., Hoffman, P. J., & O'Hara, R. (1960). Issue Conflict and Consensus Among Party Leaders and Followers. *American Political Science Review, 54,* 406–427.

McClosky, H., & Zaller, J. (1984). *The American Ethos: Political Attitudes Toward Capitalism and Democracy.* Cambridge, MA: Harvard University Press.

Miller, A. H., & Miller, W. E. (1976). Ideology in the 1972 Election – A Rejoinder. *American Political Science Review, 70,* 832–849.

Miller, A. H., Miller, W. E., Raine, A. S., & Brown, T. A.. (1976). A Majority Party in Disarray: Policy Polarization in the 1972 Election. *American Political Science Review, 70,* 753–778.

Miller, A. H., Wattenberg, M. P., & Malanchuk, O. (1986). Schematic Assessments of Presidential Candidates. *American Political Science Review, 80,* 521–540.

Miller, W. E. (1988). *Without Consent: Mass-Elite Linkages in Presidential Politics.* Lexington, KY: University of Kentucky Press.

Miller, W. E. and Shanks, J. M. (1982). Policy Directions and Presidential Leadership: Alternative Interpretations of the 1980 Presidential Election. *British Journal of Political Science, 12,* 299–356.

Miller, W. E., & Shanks, J. M. (1996). *The New American Voter.* Cambridge, MA: Harvard University Press.

Neuman, W. R. (1986). *The Paradox of Mass Politics.* Cambridge, MA: Harvard University Press.

Nie, N. H., & Anderson, K. (1974). Mass Belief Systems Revisited: Political Change and Attitude Structure. *Journal of Politics, 36,* 540–587.

Nie, N. H., & Rabjohn, J. N. (1979). Revisiting Mass Belief Systems Revisited: Or, Doing Research is Like Watching a Tennis Match. *American Journal of Political Science, 23,* 139–175.

Nie, N. H., Verba, S., & Petrocik, J. R. (1979). *The Changing American Voter* (enlarged ed.). Cambridge, MA: Harvard University Press.

Niemi, R. G., & Weisberg, H. F. (1993). *Classics in Voting Behavior.* Washington, D. C.: CQ Press.

Norpoth, H., & Lodge, M. (1985). The Differences Between Attitudes and Non-attitudes in the Mass Public: Just Measurements? *American Journal of Political Science, 29,* 291–307.

Paddock, J. (1992). Inter-Party Ideological Differences in Eleven State Parties: 1956–1980." *Western Political Quarterly, 45,* 751–760.

Page, B. I., & C. C. Jones. (1979). Reciprocal Effects of Policy Preferences, Party Loyalties, and the Vote. *American Political Science Review, 73,* 979–995.

Page, B. I., & Shapiro, R. Y. (1992). *The Rational Public: Fifty Years of Trends in Americans' Policy Preferences.* Chicago: University of Chicago Press.

Palfrey, T. R., & Poole, K. T. (1987). The Relationship Between Information, Ideology, and Voting Behavior. *American Journal of Political Science, 31,* 511–530.

Peffley, M. A. and Hurwitz, J. (1985). A Hierarchical Model of Attitude Constraint. *American Journal of Political Science, 29,* 871–890.

Pierce, J. C. (1970). Party Identification and the Changing Role of Ideology in American Politics. *Midwest Journal of Political Science, 14,* 25–42.

Pierce, J. C., & Rose, D. D. (1974) Non-attitudes and American Public Opinion: The Examination of a Thesis. *American Political Science Review, 68,* 626–649.

Pomper, G. R. (1972). From Confusion to Clarity: Issues and American Voters: 1956–1968. *American Political Science Review, 66*, 415–428.

Poole, K. T. (1981). Dimensions of Interest Group Evaluation of the U.S. Senate, 1969–1976. *American Journal of Political Science, 25*, 49–67.

Poole, K. T., & Daniels, R. S. (1985). Ideology, Party, and Voting in the U.S. Congress, 1959–80. *American Political Science Review, 79*, 373–399.

Poole, K. T., & Rosenthal, H. (1984). The Polarization of American Politics. *Journal of Politics, 46*, 1061–1079.

Poole, K. T. and Rosenthal, H. (1997) *Congress: A Political-Economic History of Roll Call Voting.* New York: Oxford University Press.

Popkin, S., Gorman, J. W., Phillips, C., & Smith, J. A. (1976). Comment: What Have You Done for Me Lately? Toward an Investment Theory of Issue Voting. *American Political Science Review, 70*, 779–805.

Prothro, J. W. (1973). Explaining the Vote. In: D. M. Kovenock, J. W. Prothro & Associates (Eds), *Explaining the Vote: Presidential Choices in the Nation and the States, 1968.* Chapel Hill, NC: Institute for Research in Social Science.

Quinn, D. P., & Shapiro, R. Y. (1991). Economic Growth Strategies: The Effects of Ideological Partisanship on Interest Rates and Business Taxation in the United States. *American Journal of Political Science, 35*, 656–685.

Rahn, W. M., Aldrich, J. H., Borgida, E., & Sullivan, J. L. (1990). A Social-Cognitive Model of Candidate Appraisal. In: J. Ferejohn & J. Kuklinski (Eds), *Information and Democratic Processes.* Urbana, IL: University of Illinois Press.

RePass, D. E. (1976). Comment: Political Methodologies in Disarray: Some Alternative Interpretations of the 1972 Election. *American Political Science Review, 70*, 814–831.

Robinson, J. P., & Fleishman, J. A. (1988). Report: Ideological Identification: Trends and Interpretations of the Liberal-Conservative Balance. *Public Opinion Quarterly, 52*, 134–145.

Rosenberg, M. J. (1953). Cognitive Structure and Attitudinal Affect. *Journal of Abnormal and Social Psychology, 53*, 367–372.

Rosenberg, S. W. (1988). *Reason, Ideology, and Politics.* Princeton, NJ: Princeton University Press.

Rossiter, C. (1962). *Conservatism in America: The Thankless Persuasion.* New York: Vintage Books.

Sanders, A. (1989). Ideological Symbols. *American Politics Quarterly, 17*, 2227–255.

Schulman, M. A., & Pomper, G. M. (1975). Variability in Electoral Behavior: Longitudinal Perspectives from Causal Modeling. *American Journal of Political Science, 19*, 1–18.

Sears, D. O. (1983). The Persistence of Early Political Predispositions. In: L. Wheeler & P. Shaver (Eds), *Review of Personality and Social Psychology* (Vol. 4). Beverly Hills, CA: Sage.

Sears, D. O. (1993). Symbolic Politics: A Socio-Psychological Theory. In: S. Iyengar & W. J. McGuire (Eds), *Explorations in Political Psychology.* Durham, NC: Duke University Press.

Sears, D. O., & Citrin, J. (1985). *Tax Revolt: Something for Nothing in California.* Cambridge, MA: Harvard University Press.

Sears, D. O., Hensler, C. P., & Speer, L. K. (1979). Whites' Opposition to 'Busing': Self-Interest or Symbolic Politics? *American Political Science Review, 73*, 369–384.

Sears, D. O., Huddy, L., & Schaffer, L. G. (1986). A Schematic Variant of Symbolic Politics Theory, as Applied to Racial and Gender Equality. In: R. R. Lau & D. O. Sears (Eds), *Political Cognition.* Hillsdale, NJ: Lawrence Erlbaum.

Sears, D. O., Lau, R. R., Tyler, T. R., & Allen, H. M., Jr. (1980). Self-Interest vs. Symbolic Politics in Policy Attitudes and Presidential Voting. *American Political Science Review, 74*, 670–684.

Sears, D. O., Tyler, T. R., Citrin, J., & Kinder, D. R. (1978). Political System Support and Public Response to the Energy Crisis. *American Journal of Political Science, 22,* 56–82.

Segal, J. A. and Spaeth, H. (1993). *The Supreme Court and the Attitudinal Model.* New York: Cambridge University Press.

Sharp, C. and Lodge, M. (1985). Partisan and Ideological Belief Systems: Do They Differ? *Political Behavior, 7,* 147–166.

Shingles, R. D. (1989). Class, Status, and Support for Government Aid to Disadvantaged Groups. *Journal of Politics, 51,* 933–962.

Smith, E. R. and Lerner, M. (1986). Development of Automatism of Social Judgments. *Journal of Personality and Social Psychology, 50,* 246–259.

Smith, E. R. A. N. (1980). The Levels of Conceptualization: False Measures of Ideological Sophistication. *American Political Science Review, 74,* 685–696.

Smith, E. R. A. N. (1981). Reply to Abramson and Nie, Verba, and Petrocik. *American Political Science Review, 75,* 152–155.

Smith, E. R. A. N. (1989). *The Unchanging American Voter.* Berkeley, CA: University of California Press.

Sniderman, P. M., Brody, R. A., & Kuklinski, J. H. (1984). Policy Reasoning and Political Values: The Problem of Racial Equality. *American Journal of Political Science, 28,* 75–94.

Sniderman, P. M., Brody, R. A., & Tetlock, P. E. (1991). *Reasoning and Choice: Explorations in Political Psychology.* New York: Cambridge University Press.

Sniderman, P. M., Hagen, M. G., Tetlock, P. E., & Brady, H. E. (1991). Reasoning Chains. In P. M. Sniderman, R. A. Brody & P. E. Tetlock (Eds), *Reasoning and Choice: Explorations in Political Psychology.* New York: Cambridge University Press.

Steeper, F. T., & Teeter, R. M. (1976). Comment on 'A Majority Party in Disarray'. *American Political Science Review, 70,* 806–813.

Stimson, J. A. (1975). Belief Systems: Constraint, Complexity, and the 1972 Election. *American Journal of Political Science, 19,* 393–417.

Stimson, J. A. (1999). *Public Opinion in America: Moods, Cycles, and Swings* (2nd ed.). Boulder, CO: Westview Press.

Stimson, J. A., MacKuen, M. B., & Erikson, R. S. (1995). Dynamic Representation. *American Political Science Review, 89,* 543–565.

Sullivan, J. L., Piereson, J. E., & Marcus, G. E. (1978). Ideological Constraint in the Mass Public: A Methodological Critique and Some New Findings. *American Journal of Political Science, 22,* 223–249.

Sullivan, J. L., Piereson, J. E., Marcus, G. E., & Feldman, S. (1979). The More Things Change, the More They Stay the Same. *American Journal of Political Science, 23,* 176–186.

Tetlock, P. E. (1983a). Accountability and Complexity of Thought. *Journal of Personality and Social Psychology, 45,* 74–83.

Tetlock, P. E. (1983b). Cognitive Style and Political Ideology. *Journal of Personality and Social Psychology, 45,* 118–126.

Tetlock, P. E. (1984). Cognitive Style and Political Belief Systems in the British House of Commons. *Journal of Personality and Social Psychology, 46,* 365–375.

van Schuur, W. H., & Kiers, H. A. L. (1994). Why Factor Analysis Often is the Incorrect Model for Analyzing Bipolar Concepts, and What Model to Use Instead. *Applied Psychological Measurement, 18,* 97–110.

Verba, S., & Nie, N. H. (1972). *Participation in America.* New York: Harper and Row.

Walker, J. L., & Aberbach, J. D. (1970). The Meaning of Black Power: A Comparison of White and Black Interpretations of a Political Slogan. *American Political Science Review, 64,* 367–388.

Weisberg, H. F. (1974). Dimensionland: An Excursion into Spaces. *American Journal of Political Science, 18*, 743–776.

Wray, J. H. (1979). Comment on Interpretation of Early Research into Mass Belief Systems. *Journal of Politics, 41*, 1173–1181.

Wright, J. R., & Niemi, R. G. (1983). Perceptions of Candidates' Issue Positions. *Political Behavior, 5*, 209–224.

Wyckoff, M. L. (1980). Belief System Constraint and Policy Voting: A Test of the Unidimensional Consistency Model. *Political Behavior, 2*, 115–146.

Wyckoff, M. L. (1987). Issues of Measuring Ideological Sophistication: Level of Conceptualization, Attitude Consistency, and Attitude Stability. *Political Behavior, 9*, 193–224.

Zaller, J. R. (1992). *The Nature and Origins of Mass Opinion*. New York: Cambridge University Press.

PART 2:
POLITICAL DELIBERATION

THE DELIBERATIVE CITIZEN: THEORY AND EVIDENCE

Tali Mendelberg

ABSTRACT

Should citizens be encouraged to deliberate about matters of politics? A review of several literatures about group discussion yields a mixed prognosis for citizen deliberation. Group discussion sometimes meets the expectations of deliberative theorists, other times falls short. Deliberators can, as theorists wish, conduct themselves with empathy for others, equality, and open-mindedness. But attempts to deliberate can also backfire. Social dynamics can often account for both discussions that appear deliberative and for those that clearly fail to meet deliberative criteria.

In the beginning was the group. This is the fundamental truth about human nature and politics, and neither modern nor contemporary political theory has yet come to terms with it (Alford, 1994, p. 1).

INTRODUCTION

Increasingly, scholars and practitioners of politics in modern industrial societies are advocating more opportunities for citizens to deliberate about matters of politics. A variety of recent developments, political and academic, have sparked this interest in democratic deliberation. There are growing calls for remedies to the high level of citizen alienation (Fishkin, 1997; Putnam, 2000). There is

Political Decision Making, Deliberation and Participation, Volume 6, pages 151–193.
Copyright © 2002 by Elsevier Science Ltd.
All rights of reproduction in any form reserved.
ISBN: 0-7623-0227-5

a resurgent interest in the study of political participation broadly conceived (Barber, 1984; Rosenstone & Hansen, 1993; Sapiro, 1999; Verba et al., 1995). There are more opportunities for citizens to participate in bureaucratic governance (Rossi, 1997). There are increasing calls for more civility in American political discourse (Sapiro, 1999). Finally, there is a shift in U.S. politics from what government does for citizens, to what citizens do for themselves. These developments have come hand in hand with a growing sense that democracies should build significant opportunities for citizen deliberation about politics.

Not everyone is taken with deliberative prescriptions to the ills of democracy. The more one fears that discussion enhances the influence of the powerful at the expense of the disadvantaged, the more inclined one is to turn a skeptical eye on deliberative solutions. And the more doubtful one is that citizens are competent to handle matters of politics, the less enthusiastic one tends to be about citizen deliberation.

Empirical research can help to adjudicate between the advocates and skeptics. Further, a review of relevant social science findings about deliberation can point out aspects of deliberation that advocates and skeptics each may be missing, or mishandling. It can point out new ways of thinking about an old and now resurgent approach to politics. And it can lead to a more hardheaded confrontation with the problems of deliberation, and generate ideas for their solution.

Even for those uninterested in the effects of deliberation in particular, the study of deliberation is valuable because it sheds light in a more general way on how language matters for politics. Without understanding how people communicate about politics we are left with an incomplete picture of how politics works. As Fischer and Forester note, "language does not simply mirror or picture the world but instead profoundly shapes our view of it in the first place" (1993, p. 1). In no case is this truer than in deliberation.

In this essay I examine the current state of knowledge about citizen deliberation.[1] My point of departure is the fact that many real-world deliberations take place in small groups. There is little systematic research on the nature and consequences of deliberation in real settings (but see Lindeman in this volume). However, when we recognize that these real-world settings are often small group discussions, we can glean useful evidence from social science research about how people communicate in small group situations.

Deliberation is not merely a utopian ideal; it is practiced already, and may become so more and more widely. It is time we understood what it is expected to do, what it is in reality, and what it could become. Doing so can help us better understand how citizens should, do, and could practice politics in a democracy.

THEORIES OF DELIBERATION

What is deliberation? There is no single definition on which all theorists of deliberation agree (Macedo, 1999).[2] Still, it is possible to distill a working definition. Many theorists emphasize that during true deliberation, people rely on reasons that speak to the needs or principles of everyone affected by the matter at hand (Gutmann & Thompson, 1996; Habermas, 1989; Rawls, 1996). The promise of deliberation is its ability to foster the egalitarian, reciprocal, reasonable and open-minded exchange of language. The consequences, according to these theories, are a more empathic view of the other – even others considered beneath oneself; a better-informed perspective on public problems; and a broader understanding of one's interests. In this way, deliberative democracy can serve the common good where models of democracy based on narrow self-interest and negotiation may fail (Mansbridge, 1991).

If it is appropriately empathic, egalitarian, open-minded, and reason-centered, deliberation is expected to produce a variety of positive democratic outcomes (Barber, 1984; Benhabib, 1996; Bickford, 1996; Bohman, 1996; Chambers, 1996; Cohen, 1989; Fishkin, 1997; Gutmann & Thompson, 1996; Mansbridge, 1983, 1996; Sunstein, 1993; Warren, 1992, 1996). Citizens will become more engaged and active in civic affairs (Barber, 1984). Tolerance for opposing points of view will increase (Gutmann & Thompson, 1996). Citizens will improve their understanding of their own preferences and be able to justify those preferences with better arguments (Chambers, 1996; Gutmann & Thompson, 1996). People in conflict will set aside their adversarial, win-lose approach and understand that their fate is linked with the fate of the other, that although their social identities conflict they "are tied to each other in a common recognition of their interdependence" (Chambers, 1996; Pearce & Littlejohn, 1997; Yankelovich, 1991). Faith in the democratic process will be enhanced as people who deliberate become empowered and feel that their government truly is "of the people" (Fishkin, 1997).[3] Political decisions will become more considered and informed by relevant reasons and evidence (Chambers, 1996). The community's social capital will increase as people bring deliberation to their civic activities (Fishkin, 1997; Putnam, 2000). The legitimacy of the constitutional order will grow because people have a say in and an understanding of that order (Chambers, 1996; Gutmann & Thompson, 1996).

To summarize, deliberation is expected to lead to empathy with the other and a broadened sense of people's own interests through an egalitarian, open-minded and reciprocal process of reasoned argumentation. Following from this result are other benefits: citizens are more enlightened about their own and others' needs and experiences, can better resolve deep conflict, are more engaged in politics, place their faith in the basic tenets of democracy, perceive their political system as legitimate, and lead a healthier civic life.

These expectations are not mere descriptions of an ideal. They are meant to encourage more people to deliberate more on more matters of politics (Bohman, 1996; Gutmann & Thompson, 1996; Habermas, 1996; Nino, 1996, p. 152). Despite thin or non-existent empirical evidence for the benefits that deliberative theorists expect, many theorists argue forcefully for more citizen deliberation even in situations of entrenched conflict, in part on the argument that the only alternative may be separation or violence (Chambers, 1996; Gutmann & Thompson, 1996).

But separation or violence is not the only alternative to more deliberation. A more pessimistic approach to deliberation reminds us that there are forms of discourse that are not deliberative and that could help people avoid violence or separation. Theorists concerned about the inequalities of power in deliberative situations argue that deliberation is inferior to other, viable alternatives that are more egalitarian (Sanders, 1997; Young, 1996).[4] For example, Jane Mansbridge, perhaps the most thorough observer of deliberation, tempers her enthusiasm for deliberation with important cautions. In situations of deep conflict, argues Mansbridge, consensual deliberation is not the method of choice. Rather, people in conflict should settle the question according to the principle of proportional representation (1983). People can find creative ways to live with each other that are not oriented toward reaching common understandings but are inspired by a bargaining model of interest accommodation. They may want to consider these alternatives to deliberation in light of the possible ill effects of deliberation. Not only is deliberation sometimes inegalitarian, but it may also lead to greater conflict (Larmore 1994). Thus, when we evaluate deliberation in reality, we should remember that it is not the only way for people to settle their differences peacefully, and that it may not always work to the good.

Despite the cautions of more pessimistic theorists and the thinness of evidence showing that deliberation in fact works as expected, a wide array of efforts has been launched to implement more opportunities for more people to deliberate. "At least in the course of time," John Rawls wrote in *A Theory of Justice,* "the effects of common deliberation seem bound to improve matters" (1971, p. 359). Rawls' view seems to dominate today, as a plethora of deliberative efforts are underway. Citizens have increasing opportunities to deliberate in a wide variety of settings: in juries, town meetings of various kinds, local, state and regional boards and commissions, hearings that solicit citizen testimonials, workplaces, civic groups, and activist groups (Crosby, 1995; Dienel & Renn, 1995; Eliasoph, 1998; Fishkin, 1997; Gastil, 1993; Gastil & Dillard, 1999; Hastie et al., 1983; Jennings, 1993; Luskin & Fishkin, 1998; Lynn & Kartez, 1995, 88; MacRae,

1993, pp. 310–311; Mansbridge, 1983; Merkle, 1996; Rossi, 1997; Shapiro, 1999; Vari, 1995; Williams & Matheny, 1995; Witte, 1980; Wright, 1992).[5]

WHAT WE CAN LEARN ABOUT DELIBERATION FROM SOCIAL SCIENCE RESEARCH ON SMALL GROUPS

These more formal efforts to promote citizen deliberation are the focus of my review. Because they have generated little systematic research, however, I turn to the social science literatures about small group discussion as a close simulation of what goes on in these public deliberations. I begin with social dilemmas, proceed to intergroup relations, and end with group polarization and minority influence.

Social Dilemmas

A thoroughly neglected area of research of great relevance for deliberation is the social dilemma. In a social dilemma, the pursuit of narrow self-interest, while rational for individuals, is irrational and harmful for the group. The group is better off if everyone cooperates for the greater good, but individuals are tempted to pursue their individual self-interest instead. An intriguing finding from the perspective of deliberation is that no circumstance increases cooperation in social dilemma experiments more dramatically than face-to-face communication (Ostrom, 1998, p. 7; see also Bornstein, 1992; Dawes et al., 1990). A meta-analysis of over 100 experiments found that face-to-face communication in social dilemma games raises cooperation by 40 to 45 percentage points (Sally, 1995).

For these results to inform deliberative theory, however, we need to know what goes on during communication. Perhaps some people use it to mislead other players. They may use cooperative communication as a "cheap signal," fooling others into cooperating while they defect in private. Reassuringly for deliberative theory, such is not the case. Talk in social dilemmas can serve several good deliberative purposes. First, members use talk to reveal their genuine commitment to cooperation and their trustworthiness and to discover others' (Bornstein & Rapoport, 1988; Kerr & Kaufman-Gilliland, 1994; Orbell et al., 1988). When talk leads individuals to perceive a consensus to cooperate, it becomes a powerful predictor of actual cooperation (Bouas & Komorita, 1996).[6] Second, talk can create a norm of group-interest in which individuals come to see their own self-interest as consonant with the self-interest of every other member of the group. This norm in turn causes individuals to act with the goal of maximizing the group's interest. Through discussion people change their identity to include the group in their self-concept. The group's interest comes to serve as a heuristic to self-interest (Dawes et al., 1990; Orbell et al., 1988). Each of these functions might give deliberative theory some hope.

A still more encouraging finding is that the more deliberative the discussion, the more cooperation it produces. Bouas and Komorita randomly assigned groups of women either to a discussion of their common dilemma (in order to create a consensus to cooperate on the dilemma) or to a discussion about an irrelevant but salient matter (in order to create a general group identity unrelated to the dilemma).[7] They found that only discussion about the dilemma enhanced cooperation. These results may offer some support to deliberative theory. If creating a group identity had been sufficient to create cooperation, then reason-based deliberation about the dilemma is not necessary to create cooperation. Reason-based deliberation would then lose its distinctive promise to help resolve conflict in a meaningful way. But if group identity is insufficient, and what is required is a discussion among people exchanging good reasons about the course of action optimal for the good of all, then we can conclude that deliberative theory is grounded in empirical reality.[8]

Making trouble for the empathy component of deliberative expectations is that even these seemingly deliberative functions of group discussion can ultimately be distilled into a self-interested motive. We do not know for sure whether discussion in social dilemmas serves to transform individuals from largely self-regarding to more other-regarding.[9] Future studies seeking specifically to understand the deliberative functions of communication should isolate the self-regarding and other-regarding facets of communication.

A more complex picture emerges when social dilemmas pit subgroups rather than individuals against each other. Here, communication can improve or worsen competition. Some studies reach pessimistic conclusions. One research team has found that while communication consistently enhances cooperation among individuals, it undermines cooperation among groups (Insko et al., 1993). Bornstein and colleagues reach a more sanguine conclusion. They examined an intergroup version of the prisoner's dilemma,[10] in which individual interest clashes with ingroup interest, which in turn clashes with superordinate group interest. They found that communication between the two competing groups enhances cooperation between them, at the expense of ingroup interest but consonant with individual interest, as deliberative theory would wish. But communication within each ingroup enhances cooperation among individuals within the ingroup and against the outgroup (Bornstein, 1992). These results call on deliberative theory to account for the complex reality of group conflict:

cooperation among individuals can be anti-cooperative – and thus undermine empathy – in situations of group conflict.

The argument that deliberation helps to resolve conflict over resources or power thus receives considerable support, but also disconfirmation. Deliberation among individuals seems to produce empathy to an extent beyond what theorists could have hoped. Further work is required to verify that the effect of discussion is in fact based on empathetic deliberation and not some other, non-empathetic form of communication. More work too is needed to understand what deliberation may do in the more complex situation of intergroup dilemmas.

Inter-Group Cooperation

Deliberative theory can also draw lessons from research on intergroup cooperation. According to classic studies in social psychology, under specific conditions, groups in conflict can make progress toward resolving their conflict and eliminating bias and discrimination against the other group (the "outgroup") (Allport, 1954; Brewer & Miller, 1984, 1996; Gaertner et al., 1990; Sherif et al., 1961). Discussion between antagonistic groups can play an important role in reducing intergroup conflict and bias. But the discussion may take on one of two very different natures: interdependence and deliberation. If beneficial discussion is driven primarily by interdependence and common fate – members' sense that the well being of their group depends on the well being of the other group – then there may not be much of a role for deliberation. On the other hand, if a common fate does not alone explain intergroup cooperation, perhaps deliberative interaction between groups can matter.

One ambitious effort to answer this question comes in a recent study by Samuel Gaertner et al. (1999) that varied common fate and discussion independently. They assembled students into small groups (homogenous in gender), each composed of three Republicans or three Democrats. First, the groups were assembled separately and taken through a series of steps designed to foster a subgroup identity as Democrats or Republicans. Then the opposing groups were brought together in pairs in a way that maintained the groups' separate partisan identities. The groups were asked to deliberate about how to most effectively reduce the federal budget deficit and required to specify which programs to cut and which taxes to increase. They were told that there was an objective, bipartisan best solution to the budget problem, and that the two out of five randomly selected solutions that best approximated it would win a cash prize (two rather than one winner to avoid a sense of competition). Then they were informed either that the two groups shared a chance of winning by working together (common fate), or that their chances of winning were independent of the other group (independent fate). Each group was also instructed to interact fully, interact partially, or not interact. Groups that interacted fully were instructed to engage in free discussion and to reach consensus. Groups instructed not to interact sat in the same room but discussed the task only within each group. In partial interaction, groups discussed separately but then their members took turns reporting their group's solution to the other group. In the partial and no interaction conditions with common fate the experimenter informed the groups that their respective solutions would be combined through averaging.

Gaertner et al. found that interaction is somewhat more important than common fate in reducing intergroup bias. Furthermore, the more interaction the more intergroup bias declined, with full interaction causing the greatest decline and no interaction the least. However, partial interaction had almost as big an effect as full interaction. Disappointingly for deliberative expectations, discussion among individual group members with the goal of reaching a consensus is nearly as effective as the simple exchange of information about the group's fixed preferences.

Still more troubling for deliberative expectations are findings from situations when the groups are not equal in the number of members, as is often the case in reality. Recent evidence from laboratory and field studies suggests that when groups are highly mismatched in members, bringing them together for a joint interaction may actually exacerbate conflict and bias (Bettencourt & Dorr, 1998; Miller & Davidson-Podgorny, 1987). When a group finds itself in a numerical minority, its distinctive group identity tends to become more salient, making intergroup cooperation more difficult (Bettencourt & Dorr, 1998).

The intergroup relations literature has only recently turned its attention to the question of intergroup deliberation. But already it appears that while deliberation can work for the good, it is not alone, and it may be highly contingent. Groups engaged in consensual discussion do show markedly less conflict and bias toward each other. But this result obtains nearly as well with non-deliberative interaction. If groups achieve the same reduction in bias by signaling preferences as by exchanging reasons, we have reason to doubt the distinctive desirability of deliberative communication. Moreover, while the evidence on this point is meager, there is reason to believe that the good effects of communication among equally matched groups may backfire in the more common case of unequal groups.

Group Polarization

A body of research that both challenges and supports deliberative theory is *group polarization*. Put simply, group polarization is the finding that discussion tends to amplify the strength of a majority opinion (Moscovici & Zavalloni, 1969; Myers & Lamm, 1976). If the group starts out inclined toward one alternative, it emerges from the discussion with a strengthened commitment to that alternative. For example, simulated juries' punitive awards in personal injury cases show a dramatic polarization effect in which juries' inclination to punish severely or leniently increases considerably with deliberation (Schkade et al., 2000). Many other examples outside the jury situation show a pattern of polarization.

This robust finding has been explained most often by two very different mechanisms, one social, the other informational. One offers pessimistic implications for deliberative theory, the other hope. The pessimistic social mechanism is normative influence. Group polarization may be driven by *social comparison*, the attempt to present oneself to others in a positive light. Group members strive to be perceived as at least as good as, if not better than, average on some desirable dimension. The desirable dimension is associated with the task at hand. During discussion most people find out that in fact they do not exceed the average, and many shift in an attempt to catch up to the average.

A more general formulation of this hypothesis states that normative pressure shifts individuals in the direction of the group's norm, whatever that may be. The majority preference or perspective has more weight simply because it is the more popular (Noelle-Neumann, 1984). All it takes to change minds is to expose people to the central tendency of the group's opinion (the "mere-exposure" effect) (Baron & Roper, 1976; Blascovich et al., 1975; Isenberg, 1986; Myers, 1978; Myers et al., 1980). Even if individuals disagree with the central tendency, they comply, going along with it at least in public. For example, in simulated jury deliberation in which a small numerical minority disagrees with the majority, the minority often capitulates to the majority even when it continues to disagree with it in private (Davis et al., 1977, 1988, 1989; Penrod & Hastie, 1980).

This normative influence explanation implies that the most influential side in a conflict may not be the side with the best arguments, contrary to deliberative expectations. Rather, it is the side that is most influential socially (Turner, 1991, Chap. 4). In other words, discussion affects people's decision making not through the exchange of reasons but by setting the social norms of the overall group. Social muscle, not persuasive argumentation, carries the day.

A much more deliberative hypothesis exists, however. According to Burnstein, Vinokur and colleagues, groups polarize not because of social motivations but because deliberators in the majority can offer more novel and valid arguments for their side (Burnstein et al., 1973; Burnstein & Vinokur, 1977; Vinokur & Burnstein, 1978). Groups move in the direction suggested by the most novel and valid arguments, whatever that direction may be. It is only an artifact that groups polarize in the direction favored by the initial majority. The majority is simply more likely to offer novel arguments. If the balance of novel and valid arguments were skewed toward the minority, the group would move in its direction instead. In its emphasis on rational argumentation and its attempt to rule out any social motivation, this theory of persuasive arguments harmonizes quite well with deliberative theory. Certainly it comes much closer than do explanations that emphasize social pressures.

The evidence suggests that each model – the social and the informational – captures an important part of the reality.[11] When the situation affords no opportunity for argumentation, only social forces can explain group polarization. By the same token, group polarization in situations with little opportunity for social comparison can only be the result of argumentation (Isenberg, 1986). More often than not, both processes seem to go on simultaneously. It may be that persuasive arguments generate bigger effects, although meta-analytic comparisons of effect size have been rather fragile (Isenberg, 1986, e.g. note 15). In what may be the best head-to-head test of the two explanations, Vinokur and Burnstein (1978) explored what happens to opinions on various public issues when two conflicting groups of equal size are assembled into one overarching collective and exposed to arguments from the other side's perspective. In accordance with their persuasive arguments theory, they predicted that each group would be persuaded by the novel arguments offered by the other, and depolarize away from its own average and toward the other. Social comparison theory by contrast predicts a polarization of the groups away from each other and in the direction of each group's mean, as each member compares herself to others in her original group and attempts to show her credentials as a good member of that group. The results largely (though not thoroughly) vindicated persuasive arguments theory, as the groups depolarized to a considerable extent.

However, as Isenberg points out (1986), persuasive arguments theory did poorly on the most value-laden of the opinion items: those on capital punishment. Persuasive arguments theory appears to be least accurate on matters that center on values, and most accurate on matters that depend on facts (Laughlin & Earley, 1982). Kaplan and Miller's experimental results underscore this conclusion. In their study's mock jury awards, the more objective, factual, and intellective task of setting uncontroversial compensation damages was driven largely by information exchange, while the much less objective and more value-laden task of setting punitive damages was driven largely by normative influence (Kaplan & Miller, 1987).

The lessons for deliberation about politics are several, but I highlight two here. Most clearly, the more the discussion takes up questions of truth and fact, and the less it deals with values, the more isolated it becomes from the social pressures that deliberative theory would regard with alarm, and the more rational and argument-driven it becomes, as deliberative theory would like. On matters of value, opportunities for deliberation are likely to turn anti-deliberative. And even if they manage to turn argument-centered, they are unlikely to change minds. Advocates of deliberation would do well to promote deliberation on issues of fact but to advance alternatives to deliberation on issues of value.

Less obvious but equally important is the implication for severe conflict. When deliberation deals with an issue that has long generated deep conflict, it is unlikely that many novel arguments will be aired. And if novel and valid arguments are aired, they are not likely to persuade many people. Under circumstances of severe conflict, an argument-centered discussion is unlikely to change any minds.

THE INFLUENCE OF THE MINORITY VS. THE POWER OF THE MAJORITY

One of the hopes of deliberation advocates is that with good deliberation, sheer advantage of power will not overwhelm the ability of people to communicate their perspectives effectively. Deliberativists would worry a great deal if it turned out that the majority always wins, and that none of its minds had changed. Persuasive arguments theory provides some hope in this regard, as the last section showed. But there is a more general question here: do powerful groups ever listen to relatively disadvantaged groups? This question is of some urgency since deliberative theory rests not only on empathy and reason but also on equality. Reassuring on this score is the work on minority influence. While early studies suggested that conformity pressures guaranteed that minorities almost never have an effective say, over the past several decades, Serge Moscovici and his colleagues have argued to the contrary. Not only do minorities have a chance to influence; they can influence people in a way that majorities cannot (Moscovici, 1976, 1980).

If theories of minority influence are correct, when a minority succeeds in voicing its view, it may set in motion the kind of productive conflict for which deliberative advocates hope. The group's norms are a crucial mediating factor here. When the norm accents the need to reduce or control conflict and disagreement, communication becomes a conduit for social pressures to conform to the majority. In these circumstances, people often go along, at least in public, for the sake of the majority's approval (the familiar process of *social comparison*), often without any change in understanding (*compliance*) (Moscovici, 1980, 1985). But when the group's norm highlights the value of originality, the innovative are the influential (Moscovici, 1985). In these situations, those who offer the new, unique view of reality and succeed in challenging the majority's accepted perspective are those who are most valued. They succeed through a process of *validation* in which the majority critically evaluates the new arguments against the evidence. Because this change is driven by arguments and evidence, it tends to be long lasting and private rather than temporary and public (*conversion*).

This theory of minority influence has a basis in evidence. Several studies suggest that a numerical minority arguing against a majority may not succeed in changing the vote of the majority, but it can prompt the majority to think about new alternatives and from different perspectives, something the majority fails to do to the minority (Nemeth, 1986; Nemeth & Kwan, 1985; Nemeth & Wachtler, 1983; Turner, 1991). Minorities in fact seem to enhance a majority's information search and processing (Nemeth & Mayseless, 1987; Nemeth & Rogers, 1996), although perhaps only when the minority offers a view unusual for that minority (Wood et al., 1994, p. 337). The minority can prod members of the majority to ask themselves why the minority thinks as it does – in other words, through its arguments it can force the majority to become more empathetic. In a phrase that could easily have been authored by deliberative theorists, Moscovici argues that the majority then tries "to see what the minority saw, to understand what it understood" (Moscovici, 1980, p. 215). The minority in effect presents a "conflict of perceptions" and prompts the other side to try to reconcile its perception of reality with the minority's perception. This kind of thinking eventually leads people to understand a perspective different from their own, prompting private conversion.

Minority influence scholars argue that minority influence tends to be not only private but indirect, often affecting opinions related to the main issue rather than views about the main issue itself (Moscovici, 1980, 1985; Mugny et al., 1991). Although minorities are believed to influence majorities when norms emphasize original thought, minorities are nevertheless often stigmatized socially, which explains why members of the majority who are persuaded attempt to hide their conversion from public view. The simultaneous ability of minorities to influence and their continued stigmatization seems to be a paradox in the theory, and more recent treatments of minority influence demonstrate the need for separate estimates of the impact of stigmatization and conflict of opinion, which are too often confounded (Wood et al., 1994). Still, meta-analytic findings support the hypothesis that minorities are better at influencing indirect than direct opinions on the issue at hand (Wood et al., 1994).[12] In fact, minorities do seem to influence private indirect opinion more than majorities (Wood et al., 1994).

Of further relevance to deliberation is that a minority can only have an effective say if its members are consistent with each other (Moscovici, 1980, 1985; Wood et al., 1994, p. 334). That may be because consistency indicates certainty (Maass & Clark, 1984). While the minority must project certainty, some scholars find that it must also avoid the perception of dogmatism (Maass & Clark, 1984). Perhaps because it avoids the perception of dogmatism, consistency with a late moderate compromise may increase minority influence (Turner, 1991, Chap. 4). However, some scholars emphasize that the more rigid and less compromising the minority, the more it succeeds at indirect influence even as it loses direct influence (Moscovici, 1980). Perhaps these conflicting findings might revolve around the group's task; groups that must reach a decision may tend to steamroll over inflexible minorities, while groups charged only with discussion for its own sake may be much more amenable to giving an inflexible minority a full hearing (Smith et al., 1996, p. 147).

Also crucial to the minority's success is that its view appears to be grounded in objective fact and a more accurate rendition of the truth (Moscovici, 1985). Perhaps that explains why minorities are much more influential on perceptions of reality than on matters of subjective opinion (Wood et al., 1994, p. 333).

These findings all seem to support the view that minorities can engage the majority in a genuine deliberative enterprise that entails a real exchange of information-rich arguments and an open-minded process of persuasion. But there is also room for an interpretation that emphasizes a more socially driven, less deliberatively desirable process. These results can be interpreted to mean that a unanimous minority succeeds when it can set the overall group's norm about what is right (Turner, 1991, Chap. 4).[13] The late-compromising minority effect may mean that a minority only succeeds when it avoids the perception that it is socially divisive. Several findings support this interpretation. First, minorities that act consistently with fundamental majority norms are more effective than those that seem to violate the basic norms of the overall group (Bray et al., 1982; Nemeth et al., 1974; Nemeth & Brilmayer, 1987; Moscovici & Mugny, 1983, p. 59; Turner, 1991, pp. 93–94). Second, consistency may work best for a minority when the group norms are unclear (Moscovici, 1985). Third, minorities are more influential in groups whose members share a strong and widespread identification with the overarching group (Turner, 1991; Turner et al., 1987). Fourth, a numerical minority whose members belong to a salient social outgroup loses all influence on the majority (David & Turner, 1996). Fifth, a minority belonging to the ingroup succeeds better than either an outgroup minority or an ingroup majority in getting the audience to approve, process and recall the message, and to approve the source (Alvaro & Crano, 1996). Sixth, minorities have more influence (always on private views) when they deliver their views in absentia rather than in small face-to-face groups (Moscovici, 1980; Wood et al., 1994, p. 333). All these findings make it likely that the minority's credibility rests at least in part on its social appeal.[14]

Even if a minority uses arguments to influence the majority, the arguments may do their work in a non-deliberative way. The work of Kameda and colleagues suggests that just because a discussion is centered on arguments, this does not mean it is solid on deliberative grounds. The trait of "cognitive centrality" influences discussion in a way that makes trouble for deliberative theory (Kameda et al., 1997). Cognitively central people are individuals who hold a larger-than-average number of arguments in common with other members. Kameda and colleagues assembled three-person groups and instructed them to discuss a criminal case and decide by consensus whether the defendant should receive the death penalty. They found that people who were the most cognitively central had the largest influence over the group's decision – regardless of their competence or the quality of their arguments. In a second experiment, the investigators simulated a citizens' advisory board charged with making parole decisions, and manipulated participants' cognitive centrality, assigning every "treated" participant to be in a numerical minority in the group. They found that decisions were much more driven by the people randomly assigned to be cognitively central to their group than by people assigned to be cognitively peripheral. In fact, unlike their peripheral counterparts, cognitively central members single-handedly converted the initially quite skeptical majority in their group two-thirds of the time (Kameda et al., 1997, pp. 304–305). The people they converted were quite confident in their changed opinion.

These findings indicate clearly that people whose arguments overlap considerably with those of other deliberators have a disproportionate influence over the deliberation and its outcome. This may pose trouble for deliberative expectations to the extent that, as Kameda and colleagues argue, people rely on a "cognitive centrality heuristic." This heuristic leads people to assume that individuals who know more well known arguments are expert, while people who know many arguments unknown by others are incompetent. In that case, social influence, and not the deliberative quality of the information and arguments, is the driving mechanism. Numerical minorities who are cognitively peripheral and who may have a great deal to contribute stand little chance of being heard precisely because they are offering unfamiliar arguments.

The literature on minority influence provides some hope to deliberative advocates. Perspectives lacking in social advantages such as the power of numbers can nevertheless be effectively voiced in reason-based discussion. In fact, the lack of social advantage may even serve as an asset in deliberation, prodding people to consider the matter from a novel perspective and leading to more indirect, private persuasion. Questions remain, however, about the extent to which these encouraging findings are driven by deliberatively undesirable social pressures and motives. Particularly troubling are the findings on cognitive centrality.[15]

ANALYTICAL LEVERS

The previous section attempted to provide an overview of several literatures relevant to group deliberation. I now take a more analytical pass at the research on group discussion. In this section I tackle relevant social science literatures not in their own terms, but with questions and concepts that are rooted in deliberative theory.

Who Deliberates? The Pros and Cons of Inequality

One of the central themes in the criticism of deliberation is that inequality pervades it. Critics worry in particular about the damage that long-term inequalities based on class or status, gender and race cause during deliberation (Mansbridge, 1983; Sanders, 1997; Young, 1996). Does the relevant research reinforce or quiet these worries?

As with any mode of participation, people do in fact deliberate at highly unequal rates. Typically, in a jury of twelve, three members contribute over half of the statements (Strodtbeck et al., 1957), and over 20% of jurors are virtually silent (Hastie et al., 1983, pp. 28, 92). Studies of juries find that higher-status jury members (those with more prestigious occupations, more income, more education, etc.) tend to speak more, to offer more suggestions, and to be perceived as more accurate in their judgments (Hastie et al., 1983; Strodtbeck et al., 1957). The impact of status cannot be accounted for by accuracy. Status does not make people more accurate, simply more talkative (Hastie et al., 1983, 153). At least until the 1980s, women participated less frequently in jury deliberations, and their statements tended to convey agreement and solidarity more often than men's (James, 1959; Nemeth et al., 1976; Strodtbeck & Mann, 1956; Strodtbeck et al., 1957). Women tend to have less influence than men do in group interactions (Ridgeway, 1981). When a capital jury trial involves an African American defendant and a white plaintiff, African American jurors are more alienated from the decision making than white jurors: they report less participation in deliberation, less influence over other jurors, and less satisfaction with the process (Bowers et al., 2001).

Education in particular is likely to cause inequalities in deliberation, as it does in other forms of political participation (Verba et al., 1995). In one sense, that is a good kind of inequality for deliberative democracy to have. According to Nie, Junn and Stehlik-Barry, education makes people "democratically enlightened", that is, gives them cognitive tools to recognize that the interests of the community should sometimes override their own narrower self-interest, and that those with different views should be tolerated (1996). The well educated also have more sophisticated reasoning skills. Overall, then, education probably makes for more empathic deliberators (at least in the minimal sense of tolerance) and for more cognitively competent deliberators.

But educational inequalities are also troubling for the egalitarian requirement of deliberative theorists. People with little education are not only more likely to lack access to occupations where reasoning and public speaking skills develop. They also lack access to the pool of cultural arguments about public issues available to people in these occupations and in institutions of higher education (Nie et al., 1996). Class thus advantages the well educated not only by smoothing the path to participation, but also by giving them the means to influence deliberation. The well educated are more likely to show up to deliberate, and once there, can present both deliberatively good and socially legitimate arguments. The structural inequalities in society can thus undermine deliberation both through the ability to deliberate well and the ability to influence through social mechanisms not sanctioned by deliberativists.

This inequality is particularly troubling when we consider the possibility that the perspectives of the well educated differ from those of others. Education is strongly associated with a more prosperous class position. Class comes with a set of perspectives and interests of its own. Since the highly educated participate more, their particular class interests and perspectives are likely to be better represented during discussion (James, 1959; Mansbridge, 1983; Strodtbeck et al., 1957).[16]

There are also cognitive differences associated with – but not equivalent to – education that make some people better deliberators than others. People vary in their "need for cognition", defined as the motivation to think in depth about the essential merits of a message (Cacioppo & Petty, 1982). Need for cognition is correlated with intelligence and education, but has effects independent of them. It is more specific to people's tendency to think hard and at length about a challenging message or task (Cacioppo et al., 1996). Shestowsky, Wegener and Fabrigar (1998) conducted mock-jury discussions among dyads and found that people high in need for cognition had more influence over a discussion partner, in part because they were able to generate more arguments to support their pre-existing views. Not only did they generate more arguments, but they specifically generated more valid arguments, as deliberative theorists would like. On the down side, however, people high in need for cognition have stronger attitudes (Petty et al., 1995), and are therefore more resistant than others to arguments that contradict their views. So while they may be effective speakers, and listen for appropriate types of evidence and logic (Cacioppo et al., 1996) – all attributes reassuring to deliberative theorists – they may fail on the criterion of being too resistant to change even when confronted with meritorious arguments (Shestowsky et al., 1998).

One possible reform that might address this deficiency is to prompt the majority who are low in need for cognition to adopt the practices of people high in cognition. When people with low need for cognition feel the pressure of time, they behave more like good deliberators – they seek out more relevant information about the arguments they hear, and make better use of it (Verplanken, 1993). If people can be prompted to adopt the positive aspects of need for cognition without the negative resistance to arguments, there is hope that by structuring the situation (for example, introducing more time pressures), many people can become better deliberators overall.[17]

Inequalities matter in a different way too. When citizens deliberate with elites, as they do in hearings and advisory committees, inequalities of information and expertise come into play in a pronounced fashion. Elites almost always have vastly more access to information, to the concrete resources needed to gather and make effective use of information, and to expertise in how to use and present information. Research in psychology has documented that among the most important determinants of individuals' influence over the group's decision-making process is others' perception of the person as more expert or competent in the task at hand (Bottger, 1984; Kirchler & Davis, 1986; Ridgeway, 1981, 1987). Anecdotal accounts from real-world deliberations echo the worry about citizens' information disadvantage (Eliasoph, 1998, p. 166; Lynn & Kartez 1995, p. 87; MacRae, 1993, pp. 310–311). The vast gap between elite and citizen expertise is likely to make elites far more influential than citizens in any deliberative exercise that involves both. For deliberation to avoid the pitfalls of the knowledge gap, the gap must be narrowed considerably before any deliberation takes place. An obvious remedy would be for citizens to gain access, resources, and training in the use of relevant information.

Reason vs. Emotion

Deliberative theorists tend to emphasize the requirement that deliberation be based on reasons and principles. Some critics, however, have offered a far more expansive view of deliberation. Democratic discussion, they note, should be a mixture of reason and emotion. Furthermore, there may be no good way of distinguishing among them in any case (Mansbridge, 1999). As Eliasoph notes, some deliberative theorists seem to view deliberators as "brains engaged in calm, rational debate" instead of people with "tastes, passions, manners" (1998, p. 12). The problem with reason is that, as one communications scholar put it,

> Persuasive use of language does not so much appeal to reason but to the recipient's expectations and emotions. As its purpose is not so much to inform as to make people believe, and in the end to act upon their beliefs, he/she who sounds like one of us is the one we most easily trust (Sornig, 1989, p. 109).

Not only may emotion be at least as effective as reason in a discussion, reason can serve as an excuse for emotion. Reasonable discourse can serve as a means of justifying pre-existing, emotionally charged preferences. In general, people who feel strongly about a position offer more arguments for it and against the opposite view than people who don't much care (Howard-Pitney et al., 1986). In a literature known as *motivated reasoning,* social and cognitive psychologists have documented the variety of innovative ways that people who are strongly committed to a predetermined view find to interpret evidence to support their view. This bias occurs at every step of information processing, from setting goals, to gathering and evaluating evidence from the outside or from memory, to constructing inferences and judgments (Taber et al., 2001). People not only fail to attend to evidence that disconfirms their view, but they readily accept evidence as valid if it agrees with their view while questioning and ultimately rejecting the validity of information that challenges it (Ditto & Lopez, 1992; Wyer & Frey, 1983).

For example, perceptions of what is fair, of particular interest to deliberative theory, are highly susceptible to prior beliefs (Vallone et al., 1985). A series of behavioral economics studies conducted by Camerer and Loewenstein (1993) found that people agree in their perceptions of fairness only when they do not yet know what their interests are. Giving bargainers more information (about each other's costs, benefits and preferences) tends to interfere with their ability to reach a mutually satisfactory agreement because it enhances each bargainer's perception that the agreement is unfair to him or her.

Similar findings come from a very different research tradition on political information. In an influential study by Lord, Ross and Lepper (1979), people with strong positions about capital punishment were provided with two scientific pieces of research on the deterrent impact of capital punishment. The investigators found that the research did not challenge prior beliefs but rather provided a means by which subjects could reinforce their priors. It was the prior sentiment that drove the final opinion, but people worked hard to couch their views in the language of rationality and reason provided to them in the research reports. In addition, after using these scientific arguments to bolster their pre-existing views, participants became even more strongly committed to their prior positions.[18]

According to Bodenhausen and Macrae (1998, p. 23), people are susceptible to motivated reasoning both because of self-presentation concerns – the desire to appear good and reasonable to others – and through genuine self-deception, in which they fool themselves into thinking that they have been fair and even-handed. The latter motivation may be particularly insidious and makes considerable trouble for the deliberative expectation that people are rational enough to correct their biases when confronted with appropriate evidence.

These biases of individuals tend to be amplified by groups. Groups, especially if they are homogenous, are much more prone than individuals to search for information that confirms their preliminary preference (Schulz-Hardt et al., 2000). One group mechanism that exacerbates the individual tendency to search for confirming evidence is the group's ability to heighten individuals' "defense motivation" – the feeling that once one has made a decision, one should commit to it. Homogenous groups also work by increasing members' confidence; when a group agrees on what to do, the members are much more confident in that decision than they would be if making the same decision individually or when the group fails to agree (Schulz-Hardt et al., 2000). Heterogeneous groups are much less susceptible to these group biases.[19]

The use of reasoned argument to reinforce prior sentiment is a widespread phenomenon that poses a significant challenge to deliberative expectations. Motivated reasoning has considerable power to interfere with the motivation that deliberative theory cherishes – the motivation to be open-minded, even-handed and fair. Deliberators can hardly pursue truth and justice if they view everything in favor of their priors through rose-tinted glasses and everything against it through dark ones.

Still, the foregoing discussion in some ways rests on a questionable assumption behind much deliberative theorizing: that emotion is a negative force, to be supplanted by reason as much as possible (Mansbridge, 1999). A great deal of contemporary research in psychology cautions us not to view affect with such suspicion. When people's feelings and reasons diverge, often the feelings, not the reasons, "give a truer indication of our inclinations" (Marcus et al., 1995, p. 63). Emotional states such as anxiety alert people to the need to attend – and give more weight – to new information (Marcus et al., 2000; Marcus & Mackuen, 2001). Without these emotions, Marcus and his colleagues have argued, people would learn too little and rely on unthinking habit too much. True, people easily misattribute their affective states (Clore & Isbell, 2001; Schwarz & Clore, 1983). For example, citizens are likely to misattribute the enthusiasm they feel for a speaker to the content of the speech rather than the speaker's happy facial expressions even when it is actually the latter that affects them more (Masters, 2001). Nevertheless, affect is not merely a source of biased interference. Rather, it is an irreplaceable element of authentic self-expression. It prompts people to re-evaluate the status quo and plan new courses of action. Emotions provide a way to learn and grow.

Moreover, emotion not only helps people with their self-management tasks, but may be necessary for the full empathy that deliberativists wish to see. Bell distinguishes between the cognitive empathy on which many deliberative theorists focus and affective empathy. A person with cognitive empathy takes "the perspective of another person, and in so doing strives to see the world from the other's point of view." A person with affective empathy "experiences the emotions of another; he or she feels the other's experiences" (Bell, 1987, p. 204). Deliberative theory places the learning, growth and empathy that can come from group discussion at a premium. It must thus make a place for a more complex view of what emotions can do, not just against but for good deliberation (Marcus forthcoming).

The Nature of Language

The problem of motivated reasoning raises questions not only about the role of emotion in a process meant to highlight reason, but also about the role of language in a process meant to revolve around argument. On the whole, deliberative theory takes the nature of language to be unproblematic (Mendelberg & Oleske, 2000). But critics have argued that disadvantaged groups are also disadvantaged when it comes to language (Mendelberg & Oleske, 2000; Sanders, 1997; Young, 1996). Social psychologists have recently shed light on the ways people use language in group situations. Much of these findings reinforce the worries of critics of deliberation.

In a series of thought-provoking articles, Anne Maass and her colleagues have documented a consistent bias in the way people use language in group situations. The bias is not so much in the content of what people say as in the way they say it. The *linguistic intergroup bias* (LIB) is people's tendency: (1) to use *abstract* terms to describe their in-group's *positive* actions and their out-group's *negative* behaviors, and (2) to use *concrete* terms to describe the in-group's *negative* and the out-group's *positive* behaviors (Maass et al., 1989; Maass & Arcuri, 1996). The LIB rests on a set of categories that can be ranked from concrete to abstract. The most concrete category has "descriptive action verbs" ("A kicks B"). A somewhat more abstract category is "interpretive action verbs" ("A hurts B"). Still more abstract are state verbs ("A hates B"). The most abstract are adjectives ("A is aggressive"). The more abstract the speech, the more information the speaker provides about the subject of the sentence

("A") rather than its object ("B"). In addition, the more abstract the talks, the stronger the speaker's suggestion that the action is likely to recur in another time or place. As Maass, Ceccarelli and Rudin note, "abstract descriptions imply that the behavior represents a stable and enduring property of the actor" (1996, p. 513). As they deliberate, people can thus convey a great deal of meaning about their own group or others' simply by emphasizing abstract or concrete terms in their speech.

In a variety of situations and in several languages, LIB researchers found that people do seem prone to call attention, in this subtle and indirect way, to their own group at the expense of the other. They use the LIB to imply that their group's positive and the outgroup's negative qualities are inherent while their group's negative and the outgroup's positive characteristics are accidental or temporary and caused by circumstance. The LIB tends to spike up when the group feels threatened or enters a situation of conflict with another. For example, the LIB in Italian media coverage of the conflict with Iraq was much more pronounced during the Persian Gulf War than just afterward (Maass et al., 1994). The LIB appears to elevate both personal and group self-esteem, which suggests that people use linguistic forms and patterns to make themselves feel superior (Maass et al., 1996). The LIB may also undermine feelings of attraction and closeness that can develop during discussion, and thus may undermine affective empathy (Rubini & Kruglanski, 1996).

It seems, then, that in situations of conflict, deliberators may use the forms of language as a linguistic weapon. Rather than bringing people to common understandings and allowing them to express mutual respect, language can heighten estrangement and the sense that one's identity is being derogated. In fact, we have seen already how this happens with the content of language. The phenomenon of motivated reasoning suggests that people find a wide variety of seemingly justified words to convey negative impressions of people with whom they disagree. But the LIB suggests that language can be used to heighten conflict in still more subtle and indirect ways. Deliberators can use the format and not just the content of speech to undermine good deliberation.

Whether or not people do so consciously and with full intent is an open question. Webster, Kruglanski and Pattison suggest that speakers change levels of abstraction without knowing it (1997, p. 1130). If so, deliberative expectations are in for a very rough ride. Deliberators may not only transform discussion from a process of reason and empathy into a weapon of superiority; they may not be aware of doing so. People are unlikely to abandon their biased language forms if they are unaware of them. Or, more sanguinely, people may be able to move from language as a weapon to language as a bridge, but only if they are taught to do so. Who would do this teaching and how is unclear.

On the positive side of the equation are findings that people *can* use language to create a sense of common identity and facilitate cooperation. Speech acts that may contribute to an atmosphere of common identity include using the other's first name to convey solidarity, and using the first person plural ("we") to create a sense of shared identity (Sornig, 1989; see also Dawes et al., 1990). These forms of address are "very likely to create [an] atmosphere and feeling of shared situational assessment, natural understanding, and common destiny" (Sornig, 1989, p. 104). But to put these findings in perspective, creating a sense of group identity and cohesiveness does not necessarily serve the basic egalitarianism that deliberative theorists require in a democratic society. In fact, in Sornig's study the feelings of affinity and closeness were put to the service of greater ethnocentrism toward excluded outgroups (see also Mendelberg & Oleske, 2000).

The work of Giles and colleagues on *"speech accommodation theory"* sharpens the point that language may serve either deliberative or anti-deliberative aims. Giles and colleagues suggest that people have stereotypical notions of how social groups use language and that these notions are activated when people of different social identities come together for a discussion (Giles et al., 1987). The result is often a shift in the subtle ways that people use language – the length of pauses, the rate of speech, accent, dialect, and more. People either speak less like the other group than they usually do ("divergence"), or more like the other group than they usually do ("convergence"). People *converge* toward the outgroup's pattern most often when the outgroup has a higher status. For example, low-class speakers adopt high-class patterns of speech in order to project a competent image (Thakerar et al., 1982).[20] Speakers *diverge* from the outgroup's speech patterns when they seek to reinforce the distinctiveness of their own group's identity, often under conditions that highlight differences between groups or create competition between them (Hogg, 1985; Thakerar et al., 1982). When deliberators' social identity is threatened by an outgroup, they are likely to react by using language in a purposeful – if not always conscious – attempt to reinforce the social boundaries between themselves and others. When social identity is not under threat and there is little motivation to maintain group boundaries, the patterns of language can actively bring people together across lines of difference. In these circumstances, people often converge, and the result is that speakers are perceived as more friendly, cooperative, effective, and warm (Giles et al., 1987, p. 19).

The lesson for deliberation is that language can become a tool either for establishing common ground or for reinforcing conflict. If people's interests or social identity are threatened by the deliberation, conflict becomes more likely and deliberation may do more harm than good. If the deliberation is structured to minimize threats to interests and identities, then deliberation may create common ground in part by affording the opportunity for people's language patterns to converge on each other. Even in this case, however, the danger is that convergence comes disproportionately from disadvantaged groups' attempt to show that they are deserving of the benefits they seek, rather than a more mutual and egalitarian process in which each party decides to meet the other on the linguistic dimension.

Are Citizens Competent Enough to Deliberate?

It seems from the foregoing that many people are not cognitively skilled, justification easily replaces deliberation, reason is not easy to come by during deliberation, and people do not always use language in ways that are fully intentional and cooperative. The question becomes, are citizens capable of meeting the requirements of deliberation? The findings on deliberation jibe with the core finding of the public opinion literature of the past fifty years: the public has woefully inadequate levels of political information, its thinking about politics is incoherent, and it pays little attention to politics. Perhaps, then, citizens cannot deliberate adequately, and should not be expected to do so.

On the other hand, deliberation may go some ways toward remedying these deficits; at least, that is one important reason for introducing more deliberation (Fishkin, 1997). The eminent deliberative theorist Jürgen Habermas has detailed the potential for participatory democracy to transform individuals into better democratic citizens. According to Habermas, citizens may not start out with a clear and consistent set of political ideas; but deliberation facilitates their development by requiring that they provide reasons for their interests that others can accept (1996). Deliberation can thus motivate citizens to clarify their own interests and needs.

Do citizens become more competent after deliberating? Barabas's sophisticated study of a deliberative issues forum (2000), and Gastil and Dillard's analysis of such a forum (1999), suggest that certain types of people, in particular people who are less certain of their opinion going into the deliberation and people who know a great deal about the issue at hand, do change the way they consider the issues under discussion, and in deliberatively good ways. Somewhat unclear is whether these effects are caused specifically by deliberation itself rather than the associated information and attention that accompany it in these forums. And while useful, this research has not told us about empathy, reciprocity, or the use of arguments.

Another favorable answer comes from experimental research by Tetlock (1983, 1985) and Kruglanski and Freund (1983). These studies found that when people are told in advance that their judgments will become public, they are more likely to treat evidence objectively, and less likely to allow their reasoning to be biased. The mere anticipation of public deliberation may serve the function of democratic education. Accountability, believes Tetlock – as do the deliberative theorists Gutmann and Thompson (1996) – is at the heart of the matter. If people know that they will be held accountable for their judgments, they will expend more cognitive effort and give priority to the goal of accuracy over the goal of buttressing their prior beliefs (Tetlock & Kim, 1987).

However, deliberative motivation, which appears to be crucial for competence, seems to vary with an individual's status in the deliberating group. Levine and colleagues find that people's level of bias, and their motivation to acquire and process information, depend greatly on the number of supporters and opponents they expect to meet. If they expect to be in a small minority, they search for information that will support their view, and overlook information that contradicts it (Levine & Russo, 1995). But they also generate more thoughts against their position (Zdaniuk & Levine, 1996). In a situation of conflict, before they deliberate, people come prepared either to ignore opposing views (if they are in a large majority) or to listen to them in an active way (if they are in a small minority). Anticipating a public discussion by itself will not advance the educative function of deliberation.

Even if people are competent enough for deliberation, they may not want to deliberate – a problem not much anticipated by deliberativists. In part that is simply because many people may continue to show a distinct lack of interest in politics even with opportunities to deliberate. Many seem to dislike the conflict that comes with full-fledged deliberation in situations of disagreement (Hibbing & Theiss-Morse, 2001). In part too many people may have ideological and principled reasons for treating deliberation with suspicion (Eliasoph, 1998). In all, it seems that motivation to deliberate may be a key factor in fostering or retarding deliberative competence.

Are Several Heads Better Than One?

As does any demanding form of democratic participation, deliberation may prove a challenge to citizens. But don't deliberating groups at least offer an information advantage over individuals?[21] Deliberative theorists often take a "two heads are better than one" approach:

> The benefits from discussion lie in the fact that even representative legislators are limited in knowledge and the ability to reason. No one of them knows everything the others know, or can make all the same inferences that they can draw in concert. Discussion is a way of combining information and enlarging the range of arguments (Rawls, 1971, p. 359).

It turns out, however, that groups have predictable deficits when it comes to sharing information. "Groups," writes Stasser, "tend to talk about what all the members already know" (1992, p. 49). More than a dozen studies have documented the tendency of group members to discuss information they all know ("shared") more than information only one knows ("unshared") (Gigone & Hastie, 1993, 1997; Larson, Foster-Fishman & Franz, 1998; Larson et al., 1998; Stasser, 1992; Stasser & Titus, 1985; Stasser et al., 1989; Winquist and Larson, 1998; Wittenbaum et al., 1999). Not only is commonly held information discussed more often, it is discussed earlier, and repeated more often by leaders (Larson, Foster-Fishman & Franz 1998; Larson et al., 1998). Consequently, group decisions tend to be biased toward shared information at the expense of the information that each member is uniquely positioned to bring to the decision, even when the unshared information points to a much better alternative (what Stasser called the "hidden profile;" Larson et al., 1998; Stasser & Titus, 1985). Discussion mediates this bias (Kelly & Karau, 1999). When the discussion focuses on unshared information, the quality of the group decision increases significantly (Winquist & Larson, 1998).

This bias for shared information may be due to the simple reality of probability: the more people know a piece of information, the more chances it has to be mentioned by someone (Stasser & Titus, 1985). But more troubling for deliberative democracy, there is reason to suspect that the social processes of group dynamics are at work too.

In a well-known article, Stasser and Titus (1985) mimicked an election caucus by assembling undergraduates into groups of four. The groups were charged to decide on the best candidate for student president from a field of three fictional candidates. In each condition, the investigators arranged for Candidate A to be the best (based on a previous study). But each condition set up a different distribution of information to the participants. In the "shared" condition, all four members received identical information showing A to be best. In two "unshared" conditions, the same overall information was provided (showing that A was best), but it was divided up so that each member got only a fourth of the information favoring candidate A. The information that each member received thus contained more negative than positive information about A. The positive information differed across members so each member had unique information about A.[22] Thus, if the four members pooled their distinctive information during discussion, they would see that there was more net positive information about A than about the other candidates, and reach the correct conclusion that A was best (roughly with the same probability as the groups in the "shared" condition). But if they failed to share their distinctive information with each other, the balance of information during group discussion would reflect badly on A and the group would choose the wrong candidate.

And that is in fact what happened, despite the fact that the investigators warned the participants in advance that the information each received may be incomplete and that they may need to rely on information received by their fellows. In the shared condition, Candidate A was preferred by two-thirds of the people before discussion and by a huge 85% afterward. But in the unshared conditions, A was preferred by only a quarter of the people, and that percentage dropped slightly after discussion. Measures of information recall showed that discussion failed to prod people to recall the information that others lacked (that is, unshared information). Thus, discussion failed to bring out the unique perspective of each person and to promote better exchange of information of crucial importance to the group's decision. Stasser and Titus argued in part that motivated reasoning was at play here. Individuals erroneously conclude from their partial information profiles that the best is inferior, forget any information inconsistent with that conclusion, and allow their prior conclusion to bias the information they present during group discussion.

Wittenbaum, Hubbell and Zuckerman also underscore the notion that groups' information bias is caused in part by something more socially-driven than statistical chance: a cycle of "mutual enhancement" (1999). They argue that shared information appears more relevant and accurate to everyone, so that when a member mentions it, she is viewed as competent, and gets a positive response from the others. Not only that, but the listeners feel competent because someone has just articulated information they believe to be true. Providing shared information makes everyone feel more competent, which is why what everyone knows is reiterated over and over again at the expense of what only one person knows.

Regardless of what exactly goes on when individuals interact in groups, it is clear that the nature of the discussion matters. The extent to which the group focuses on correct information predicts with great accuracy the group's correct decision, which suggests that the discussion itself can create or attenuate the group's bias (Kelly & Karau, 1999). Some discussions can neutralize the bias of individuals (Gigone & Hastie, 1997; Kameda et al., 1997, p. 302). But when there is no objective standard of truth, as in most deliberations about public matters, the general rule is: when individuals begin the discussion with some sort of bias, the group tends to amplify that bias, not neutralize it (Kerr et al., 1996, pp. 699, 713–714).

This proposition holds not only when people bring different packages of information to the discussion. It holds too for a variety of other situations. For example, the work of Davis, MacCoun, Kerr, Stasser and others shows, with few exceptions, that juries are "more sensitive to proscribed information" than jurors. In general, jury deliberation tends to "amplify juror sins of commission" – the tendency to attend to misleading information (Kerr et al., 1996, p. 713).

Encouragingly, leadership may be a crucial moderating variable of groups' bias against pooling relevant information during discussion. Leaders of teams of physicians discussing medical cases are more likely to repeat relevant information than are other members, and they increase the rate at which they repeat "unshared" information (Larson et al., 1996). When leaders repeat information in this way, they focus members' attention and enhance their short-term memory for relevant unshared information, increasing the likelihood that it will be used in the group's decision.

The type of leadership style matters a great deal, however, and in a way that may trouble deliberativists. Larson, Foster-Fishman and Franz studied two leadership styles, "participative" and "directive." Participative leaders share power with subordinates, actively including as many views as possible, and muting one's own preferences until all views have been considered. Directive leaders place less emphasis on thorough and equal member participation, emphasize consensus, and seek agreement with their own preference. The study found that confederates trained as participative leaders generated more discussion of all types of information. But confederates trained to be directive leaders were more likely to repeat information, and especially the unshared information crucial to reaching an accurate decision. Directive leaders repeated their own unshared information, consonant with their leadership style, and perhaps because of their focus on consensus, they also repeated other members' unshared information once it was revealed (1998, p. 493). Not surprisingly, groups did best with a directive leader whose distinctive information was accurate. Overall, then, participative leadership styles, which may be more consonant with the ideals of egalitarian deliberation, tend to yield inferior decisions.

Overall, on the issues that matter in deliberative democracy, two heads are not better than one. Two heads can become better than one, but deliberative success requires a detailed understanding of the many and serious social pitfalls of groups' attempts to solve problems.

Formal Procedures: Unanimity vs. Majority Rule[23]

Deliberative theory often assumes that the group comes to a collective decision. But how should that decision be structured? Theorists do not provide strong expectations on this question. One perspective is exemplified by Dryzek, who argues that unanimity is best able to bring people to a common understanding of each other's perspective even when they disagree on basic assumptions (1990, p. 42). A second, opposing perspective is exemplified by Manin, who argues that majority rule is better than unanimity because it allows deliberation to fulfill its function in a more practical way (1987). Most people would agree with Manin: they tend to opt for majority rule, and may use it even when explicitly told to decide with unanimity (Davis et al., 1975).[24]

A third perspective comes from Mansbridge, who bases it on her extensive empirical observations (1983). She argues that in virtually all circumstances, a unanimous decision rule produces stronger social forces within a group. But in friendship groups, these forces need not mean that the minority is silenced, co-opted or brought to obedient conformity. By contrast, in groups lacking genuine ties of friendship, conformity often can mean silence, cooptation or alienation. Where inequalities are small, unanimous rule probably works well; where they are large, unanimous rule may exacerbate them. Thus according to Mansbridge, the effects of unanimous rule are complex and depend on other aspects of the situation.

The evidence we have from social psychology tends to confirm Mansbridge's conclusion. The impact of decision rules on outcomes is highly contingent.[25] Evidence on what decision rules do to people's satisfaction with the process is sparse, but the few studies that examined this matter found that people assigned to a unanimous rule mock jury were more satisfied than their majority rule counterparts that the deliberation was fair and complete (Kameda, 1991; Kaplan & Miller, 1987; Nemeth, 1977). Evidence is also sparse on the impact of decision rule on equal participation. In groups assigned an objective problem-solving task, majority rule may be better at neutralizing inequalities of influence within the group, though we do not know how robust this finding is (Falk, 1982; Falk & Falk, 1981).[26] Most studies agree that the stricter the rule (the more people have to agree), the longer the deliberation will last (Davis et al., 1997), and in some cases, the higher the chance of deadlock (Hastie et al., 1983, pp. 32, 60). The general consensus among researchers is that by itself, assigning majority vs. unanimous rule makes little consistent difference to the outcome (Hastie et al., 1983; Kameda, 1991; Miller, 1989; Nemeth, 1977; Davis et al., 1997 also found no impact on monetary awards in a civil liability mock trial).

But in interaction with other features of the situation, the decision rule can make a big difference both to the outcome and the process of deliberation. In a well-designed study, Kameda found that unanimous rule seems to create better conditions for deliberation than does majority rule (1991). In Kameda's study, some juries were instructed to deliberate in a closed-minded way by first staking out positions and then reviewing evidence in order to defend those positions (analogous to "verdict-driven" juries). Other juries were instructed to be open-minded by first sifting through evidence and then settling on a verdict (analogous to "evidence-driven" juries). In addition, some juries were instructed to decide unanimously and others by majority rule. Under majority rule, closed-minded juries produced numerous minorities who were less satisfied and discussions that were briefer than in open-minded juries. Unanimous rule, by contrast, neutralized the negative consequences of closed-mindedness. In other words, closed-mindedness can be overcome by unanimous rule but not by majority rule. Unanimous rule structures deliberation in such a way as to invite a more thorough hearing of minority views. Requiring unanimity is much like requiring people to make decisions with an open mind. It makes people more satisfied, and for good deliberative reasons. At least, this seems to be the case with a discrete choice (such as guilty or not guilty).

A study of continuous choice supports the notion that a unanimous decision rule matters a great deal but only in combination with other features of deliberation (Mendelberg & Karpowitz, 2000). When small face-to-face groups were asked to deliberate about how much of their earnings should be distributed to the worst off in the group (without knowing who would be the worst off), groups told to use unanimous rule – but not those told to decide by majority rule – polarized by gender. Only among unanimous groups, those composed of many women engaged in the most deliberative process and decided on the most egalitarian outcome, while groups composed mostly of men operated with a more conflictual, less cooperative style and generated inegalitarian outcomes. Majority rule groups did not polarize. Supporting these findings is a decision-rule study of women by Kaplan and Miller (1987). In this study, mock juries polarized from their pre-discussion preference (always for the plaintiff) in their punitive award decisions, but only under unanimous rule. Reassuring to deliberativists is that people not only shifted in their public decisions but in their private opinions too – the change was full and genuine, not merely for the purpose of public conformity (Kaplan & Miller, 1987, p. 309).

As Mansbridge might expect, under the right conditions, a unanimous decision rule appears to advantage the kind of discussion that deliberative theorists wish to promote. With favorable circumstances, unanimous rule creates deliberation that makes people more open-minded and willing to listen to minority views, resolving conflict properly and leaving deliberators feeling that everyone received a fair hearing.[27] While this finding may not hold in groups where pressures to conform are strong, nevertheless it provides reason for optimism about deliberation. Decision rules are easy to adopt or impose, and can make for much improved deliberation.

CONCLUSION: JUST WORDS?

Deliberation is more than mere words. Words do not only reflect underlying individual opinion. They shape power and strategy, conceptions of the possible and the impossible, of who should do what and why (Forester, 1993, p. 201). As Mansbridge puts it: "even the language people use as they reason together usually favors one way of seeing things and discourages others" (Mansbridge, 1991). One of the things that makes deliberation powerful is language.

Not only is deliberation about talk, it is about groups. An implicit but important theme in the research reviewed here is that because deliberation often takes place in groups, group forces matter a great deal. The dynamics of groups are often significantly social. Often, those forces work against the kind of conversation that deliberative advocates wish to see. Still, group forces can also be harnessed for more deliberative ends. In any case, deliberation must contend with the social model, whether to deepen its negative effects or harness its positive consequences.

Scholars in many areas of political science are putting their faith in the ability of the process of deliberation to produce valued ends, such as truth and fairness. But not everyone is sanguine about deliberation. In cases of deep conflict and other situations, people seeking to resolve conflict may be better off negotiating instead. Of course, it is better to get common understandings than not. But Mansbridge's point (1983) is that under some circumstances, the *attempt* to deliberate is likely to backfire, especially in cases of deep conflict. In these cases, rather than attempt to deliberate, fail, and exacerbate the conflict, people should negotiate a proportional division of resources or means to power (Mansbridge, 1990).[28]

Regardless of the merits of Mansbridge's specific proposal for negotiation, the point remains that deliberation should not be attempted under all circumstances as a cost-free solution to costly problems, nor should it be rejected wholesale. Deliberation is a policy intervention. As is true for any policy intervention, deliberation should be attempted only after careful analysis, design, and testing.

The research reviewed here sounds a cautionary note about deliberation. When groups engage in discussion, we cannot count on them to generate empathy and diminish narrow self-interest, to afford equal opportunities for participation and influence even to the powerless, to approach the discussion with a mind open to change, and to be influenced not by social pressures, unthinking commitments to social identities, or power, but by the exchange of relevant and sound reasons.

But more than anything, the point to emerge from existing research is that the conditions of deliberation can matter a great deal to its success. Sometimes deliberation succeeds and might encourage people to deliberate more, more of the time. Deliberation seems to work particularly well on matters of objective truth, especially when unanimous rule is imposed or with an authoritative leader who can overcome group biases.[29] Other times, deliberation is likely to fail. This outcome is especially likely when strong social pressures or identities exist, conflict is deep, and the matter at hand centers on values rather than facts.

But still a third implication comes out of the very contingency of deliberation. This alternative is for Advocates and skeptics alike should become more aware of the problems of deliberation. Then we can hope to create the conditions that allow deliberation to succeed. The role of empirical evidence in theories of deliberation should not be limited to arguments over whether a few successful deliberative exercises count as evidence for or against deliberation. Systematic empirical research can show the various dimensions of success and the means of achieving them.

NOTES.

1. By necessity my focus is on the United States. Negotiation, international relations, foreign policy, representative assemblies, and other forms of elite behavior are beyond the scope of this article.

2. An operational definition of an argument can be found in Sornig (1989): an assertion followed by justification and/or evidence.

3. "Deliberation that accords respect to all participants and rests outcomes on reasons and points of view that stand up under questioning generates outcomes that even opponents can respect," argues Mansbridge (1991).

4. Sapiro's historical review of the concept of civility comes to a similar conclusion (Sapiro, 1999).

5. Exactly how many people participate in deliberative discussions is unknown, but the number is certainly non-trivial. During the course of a year roughly 2,700,000 citizens deliberate in juries alone (Hastie et al., 1983). While no one knows how much discussion of public matters goes on at meetings of voluntary organizations, 53% of the adult population reports attending meetings of voluntary organizations from time to time during the course of a year (Verba et al., 1995, pp. 62–63).

6. It can also be used by the players to clarify for themselves what is the optimal strategy for each individual, which is why experimenters should test understanding before discussion begins. Talk can also be used to ensure commitment to the cooperative strategy, but when there is no enforcement mechanism this function becomes purely normative, with no concrete instrumental value.

7. Or to a common fate condition without interaction but with interdependence, or to a control condition with neither interaction nor interdependence. The latter two conditions yielded the same result as the discussion of irrelevant issue.

8. These results, however, are qualified by gender – men's cooperation (not studied by Bouas & Komorita) does appear to fluctuate with group identity (Kramer & Brewer, 1984). The good news for deliberation, in this regard, may be limited to women (see also Mendelberg & Karpowitz, 2000).

9. Further compounding the problem is the possibility that people who choose to engage in deliberation are more other-regarding to begin with.

10. In a prisoner's dilemma players are better off defecting if the others will defect, but cooperating if the others cooperate.

11. Note, however, that little work has been done to analyze the content of discussion. Zuber, Crott and Werner (1992) provide an exception, albeit based only on German males, and they find no evidence at all for persuasive arguments theory. In addition, they point out that little work has been done to distinguish between discussion-induced change in individual attitudes vs. in group choice.

12. In addition, Turner points out that the theory contains a paradox. It predicts that people are less influenced by those they think are correct, and the greater the perceived correctness the less thinking goes on and the less influence (1991, p. 103).

13. Some scholars argue that this outcome is only likely if the majority is internally divided and its ingroup norms are weak (Turner, 1991, Chap. 4).

14. Not only social or normative processes are at work. Group interests, likely to undermine empathetic perspectives on the common good, are too. The minority whose voice is heard is the one that persuades the majority that it and the majority share interests in common. Numerical minorities perceived as arguing in their own self-interest have lower credibility (in Turner, 1991, p. 97; citing Maass & Clark, 1982; Maass & Clark, 1984; Maass et al., 1982; Turner, 1985; Turner et al., 1987, Chaps 3 & 6). Even when a numerical minority avoids self-interested language, if it argues for a position that is likely to benefit itself it will be perceived as self-interested.

15. Perhaps cognitive centrality can serve as a non-deliberative counter-balance to other, still more deleterious forms of social influence such as the tendency of majorities to dominate group discussions and outcomes.

16. Intelligence itself may have significant effects on inequality during deliberation. In one study that set up ongoing discussion groups of university students, those who by the last round of discussion tended to speak least were also those judged by their peers to be less intelligent and who in fact had the lowest IQ scores (Paulhaus & Morgan, 1997). Lower intelligence may thus lead people to speak less and to carry less weight with others when they do speak. This may not trouble deliberative theorists much, unless intelligence is correlated with longterm inequalities in society.

17. Ironically, time pressure is, in the view of some deliberative theorists, a strong negative force against a considered exchange of views (e.g. Chambers, 1996). A separate line of research reinforces doubts about the positive utility of time pressure. Webster, Kruglanski and Pattison found that people high in need for *closure* – "a desire to possess a definite answer on some topic, any definite answer as opposed to confusion and uncertainty" (1997, p. 1122) – tend to discuss matters in a more efficient, more task-oriented, less egalitarian, and more conformity-oriented way (De Grada et al., 1999). They tend to speak in terms that create feelings of distance that may undermine the ability of groups to achieve their goals (Webster et al., 1997; see also Rubini & Kruglanski, 1996). Groups exacerbate these individual tendencies. By contrast with low-closure groups, the discussions of high-closure groups tend to have more conformity pressures and inegalitarian participation (De Grada et al., 1999). If need for closure rises with time pressures, the result may be a less deliberative discussion.

18. These findings are not an artifact of the experimental method. Using large sample surveys and soliciting reports from people with whom survey respondents discussed important matters, Huckfeldt, Sprague and colleagues have found that the more respon-

dents' candidate preferences diverged from their discussants' the more respondents distorted their perception of the discussant's preference to resemble their own (Huckfeldt et al., 2000). See also Mendelberg & Oleske, 2000 for a non-experimental studies of motivated reasoning in a deliberative setting.

19. A group situation also heightens motivated reasoning through people's social identities. Pool et al. found that people are more likely to engage in motivated reasoning when an argument comes from a group highly relevant to their identity (either in a negative or a positive way) than a group irrelevant to their identity (Pool et al., 1998; Wood et al., 1994). The motivated reasoning took the more subtle form of re-interpreting the meaning of a claim to bring it closer to participants' own views (Pool et al., 1998, p. 973).

20. High-status speakers also converge, but primarily from the assumption that the outgroup is incapable of understanding "normal" speech (e.g. native speakers raise the volume when talking to new immigrants) (Giles et al., 1987).

21. Scholars writing about citizen participation in bureaucratic decision-making, for example, often assume that "participation enhances the likelihood that the agency will reach a correct decision and minimizes the probability of decision-making errors" (Rossi, 1997, pp. 186–187; see also Mashaw, 1985, pp. 102–103).

22. This is a simplified rendition of the two "unshared" conditions.

23. Another structural variable that matters is size, but it is beyond the scope of this review.

24. And especially women.

25. Complicating the conclusions are the different thresholds of majority rule in various studies.

26. Jury studies tentatively find that with unanimous rule the minority participates more actively (Hastie et al., 1983, p. 32).

27. In addition to rules of decision, deliberation may be governed by rules of discussion, *Robert's Rules of Order* being the classic example. However, field research suggests that formal rules may backfire in some situations (Susskind & Cruikshank, 1987).

28. Note, though, a strand of work by Susskind and Cruikshank (1987) arguing that negotiation need not be limited to an adversarial model and should be re-conceptualized as a deliberative enterprise.

29. Of course, resting a great deal on the shoulders of an authoritative leader carries its own set of difficult problems for deliberative democracy.

ACKNOWLEDGMENTS

I thank Paul Gerber and James McGhee for research assistance.

REFERENCES

Alford, C. F. (1994). *Group Psychology and Political Theory*. New Haven, Connecticut: Yale University Press.

Allport, G. W. (1954). *The Nature of Prejudice*. Cambridge: Addison-Wesley Publishing Company.

Alvaro, E. M., & Crano, W. D. (1996). Cognitive Responses to Minority- or Majority-Based Communications: Factors That Underlie Minority Influence. *British Journal of Social Psychology, 35*, 105–121.

Barabas, J. (2000). Uncertainty and ambivalence in deliberative opinion models: Citizens in the Americans Discuss Social Security Forum. Paper presented at the Annual Meeting of the Midwest Political Science Association, Chicago, IL.

Barber, B. (1984). *Strong Democracy: Participation Politics For A New Age*. Berkeley, CA: University of California Press.

Baron, R. S., & Roper, G. (1976). Reaffirmation of Social Comparison Views of Choice Shifts: Averaging and Extremity Effects in an Autokinetic Situation. *Journal of Personality and Social Psychology, 33*, 521–530.

Bell, R. (1987). Social involvement. In: J. McCroskey & J. Daly (Eds), *Personality and Interpersonal Communication*. Newbury Park, CA: Sage.

Benhabib, S. (1996). Toward a deliberative model of democratic legitimacy. In: S. Benhabib (Ed.), *Democracy and Difference: Contesting the Boundaries of the Political* (pp. 67–94). Princeton, NJ: Princeton University Press.

Bettencourt, B. A., & Dorr, N. (1998). Cooperative Interaction and Intergroup Bias: Effects of Numerical Representation and Cross-Cut Role Assignment. *Personality and Social Psychology Bulletin, 24*, 1276–1293.

Bickford, S. (1996). Beyond Friendship: Aristotle on Conflict, Deliberation, and Attention. *The Journal of Politics, 58*, 398–421.

Blascovich, J., Ginsburg, G. P., & Veach, T. L. (1975). A Pluralistic Explanation of Choice Shifts on The Risk Dimension. *Journal of Personality and Social Psychology, 31*, 422–429.

Bodenhausen, G. V., & Macrae, C. N. (1998). Stereotype activation and inhibition. In: R. S. Wyer (Ed.), *Stereotype Activation and Inhibition: Advances in Social Cognition*. Mahwah, NJ: Lawrence Earlbaum.

Bohman, J. (1996). *Public Deliberation*. Cambridge, MA: MIT Press.

Bornstein, G. (1992). The Free-Rider Problem in Intergroup Conflicts Over Step-Level and Continuous Public Goods. *Journal of Personality and Social Psychology, 62*, 597–606.

Bornstein, G., & Rapoport, A. (1988). Intergroup Competition for the Provision of Step-Level Public Goods: Effects of Preplay Communication. *European Journal of Social Psychology, 18*, 125–144.

Bottger, P. C. (1984). Expertise and Air Time as Bases of Actual and Perceived Influence in Problem-Solving Groups. *Journal of Applied of Psychology, 69*, 214–221.

Bouas, K. S., & Komorita, S. S. (1996). Group Discussion and Cooperation in Social Dilemmas. *Personality and Social Psychology Bulletin, 22*, 1144–1150.

Bowers, W. J., Steiner, B. D., & Sandys, M. (2001). Race, Crime, and the Constitution: Death Sentencing in Black and White: An Empirical Analysis Of The Role Of Jurors' Race And Jury Racial Composition. *University of Pennsylvania Journal of Constitutional Law, 3*, 171–274.

Bray, R. M., Johnson, D., & Chilstrom, J. T. (1982). Social Influence by Group Members with Minority Opinions: A Comparison of Hollander and Moscovici. *Journal of Personality and Social Psychology, 43*, 78–88.

Brewer, M. B., & Miller, N. (1984). Beyond the contact hypothesis: Theoretical perspectives on desegregation. In: N. Miller & M. B. Brewer (Eds), *Groups in Contact: The Psychology of Desegregation* (pp. 281–302). Orlando, FL: Academic Press.

Brewer, M. B., & Miller, N. (1996). *Intergroup Relations*. Buckingham, England: Open University Press.

Burnstein, E., & Vinokur, A. (1977). Persuasive Argumentation and Social Comparison as Determinants of Attitude Polarization. *Journal of Experimental and Social Psychology, 13*, 315–332.

Burnstein, E., Vinokur, A., & Trope, Y. (1973). Interpersonal Comparison Versus Persuasive Argumentation: A More Direct Test of Alternative Explanations For Group-Induced Shifts in Individual Choice. *Journal of Experimental and Social Psychology, 9*, 236–245.

Cacioppo, J. T., & Petty, R. E. (1982). The Need For Cognition. *Journal of Personality and Social Psychology, 42*, 116–31.

Cacioppo, J. T., Petty, R. E., Feinstein, J., & Jarvis, W. B. G. (1996). Dispositional Differences in Cognitive Motivation: The Life and Times of Individuals Varying in Need for Cognition. *Psychological Bulletin, 119*, 197–253.

Camerer, C. F., & Loewenstein, G. (1993). Information, fairness, and efficiency in bargaining. In: B. A. Mellers & J. Baron (Eds), *Psychological Perspectives on Justice: Theory and Applications.* Cambridge University Press.

Chambers, S. (1996). *Reasonable Democracy.* Ithaca: Cornell University Press.

Clore, G. L., & Isbell, L. M. (2001). Emotion as virtue and vice. In: J. H. Kuklinski (Ed.), *Citizens and Politics: Perspectives from Political Psychology.* Cambridge: Cambridge University.

Cohen, J. (1989). Deliberation and democratic legitimacy. In: A. Hamlin & P. Pettit (Eds), *The Good Polity: Normative Analysis Of The State.* Cambridge: Basil Blackwell.

Crosby, N. (1995). Citizens juries: One solution for difficult environmental questions. In: O. Renn, T. Webler & P. Wiedemann (Eds), *Fairness and Competence in Citizen Participation* (pp. 157–174). Dordrecht, Netherlands: Kluwer Publishers.

David, B., & Turner, J. C. (1996). Studies In Self-Categorization And Minority Conversion: Is Being A Member Of The Out-Group An Advantage? *British Journal of Social Psychology, 35*, 179–199.

Davis, J. H., Au, W. T., Hulbert, L., Chen, X., & Zarnoth, P. (1997). Effects of Group Size and Procedural Influence on Consensual Judgments of Quantity: The Example of Damage Awards and Mock Civil Juries. *Journal of Personality and Social Psychology, 73*, 703–718.

Davis, J. H., Bray, R. M., & Holt, R. W. (1977). The empirical study of decision processes in juries: A critical review. In: J. L. Tapp & F. J. Levine (Eds), *Law, Justice, and the Individual in Society.* New York: Holt, Rinehart and Winston.

Davis, J. H, Kameda, T., Parks, C., Stasson, M., & Zimmerman, S. (1989). Some Social Mechanics of Group Decision Making: The Distribution of Opinion, Polling Sequence, and Implications for Consensus. *Journal of Personality and Social Psychology, 57*, 1000–1012.

Davis, J. H., Kerr, N. L., Atkin, R. S., Holt, R., & Meek, D. (1975). The Decision Processes of 6- and 12-Person Mock Juries Assigned Unanimous and Two-Thirds Majority Rules. *Journal of Personality and Social Psychology, 32*, 1–14.

Davis, J. H., Stasson, M., Ono, K., & Zimmerman, S. (1988). Effects of Straw Polls on Group Decision-Making: Sequential Voting Pattern, Timing, and Local Majorities. *Journal of Personality and Social Psychology, 55*, 918–926.

Dawes, R. M., van de Kragt, A. J. C., & Orbell, J. M. (1990). Cooperation for the benefit of us: Not me, or my conscience. In: J. Mansbridge (Ed.), *Beyond Self-Interest* (pp. 97–110). Chicago, IL: The University of Chicago Press.

De Grada, E., Kruglanski, A. W., Mannetti L., & Pierro, A. (1999). Motivated Cognition and Group Interaction: Need for Closure Affects The Contents and Processes of Collective Negotiations. *Journal of Experimental Social Psychology, 35*, 346–365.

Dienel, P. C., & Renn, O. (1995). Planning cells: A gate to 'fractal' mediation. In: O. Renn, T. Webler & P. Wiedemann (Eds), *Fairness and Competence in Citizen Participation* (pp. 117–140). Dordrecht, The Netherlands: Kluwer publishers.

Ditto & Lopez (1992). Motivated Skepticism: Use of Differential Decision Criteria for Preferred and Non-preferred Conclusions. *Journal of Personality and Social Psychology, 63*, 568–584.

Dryzek, J. S. (1990). *Discursive Democracy: Politics, Policy, and Political Science.* Cambridge: Cambridge University Press.

Eliasoph, N. (1998). *Avoiding Politics: How Americans Produce Apathy in Everyday Life.* Cambridge, U.K: Cambridge University Press.

Falk, G. (1982). An Empirical Study Measuring Conflict in Problem-Solving Groups Which Are Assigned Different Decision Rules. *Human Relations, 35,* 1123–1138.

Falk, G., & Falk, S. (1981). The Impact of Decision Rules on The Distribution of Power in Problem-Solving Teams With Unequal Power. *Group and Organization Studies, 6,* 211–223.

Fischer, F., & Forester, J. (1993). Editors' introduction. In: F. Fischer & J. Forester (Eds), *The Argumentative Turn in Policy Analysis and Planning.* Durham: Duke University.

Fishkin, J. S. (1997). *The Voice of the People.* New Haven: Yale University Press.

Forester, J. (1993). Learning from practice stories: The priority of practical judgment. In: F. Fischer & J. Forester (Eds), *The Argumentative Turn in Policy Analysis and Planning.* Durham: Duke University.

Gaertner, S. L., Dovidio, J. F., Rust, M. C., Nier, J. A., Banker, B. S., Ward, C. M., Mottola, G. R., & Houlette, M. (1999). Reducing intergroup bias: Elements of intergroup cooperation. *Journal of Personality and Social Psychology, 76,* 388–402.

Gaertner, S. L., Mann, J. A., Dovidio, J. F., Murrell, A. J., & Pomare, M. (1990). How Does Cooperation Reduce Intergroup Bias? *Journal of Personality and Social Psychology, 59,* 692–704.

Gastil, J. (1993). *Democracy in Small Groups: Participation, Decision Making, and Communication.* Philadelphia PA: New Society.

Gastil, J., & Dillard, J. P. (1999). Increasing Political Sophistication Through Public Deliberation. *Political Communication, 16,* 3–23.

Gigone, D., & Hastie, R. (1993). The Common Knowledge Effect: Information Sharing and Group Judgment. *Journal of Personality and Social Psychology, 65,* 959–974.

Gigone, D., & Hastie, R. (1997). The Impact of Information on Small Group Choice. *Journal of Personality and Social Psychology, 72,* 132–140.

Giles, H., Mulac, A., Bradac, J., & Johnson, P. (1987). Speech Accommodation Theory: The First Decade and Beyond. *Communication Yearbook, 10,* 13–48.

Gutmann, A. & Thompson, D. (1996). *Democracy and Disagreement.* Cambridge, MA: Harvard University Press.

Habermas, J. (1989). *The Structural Transformation of The Public Sphere: An Inquiry Into a Category of Bourgeois Society,* trans. by T. Burger with the assistance of F. Lawrence. Cambridge, MA: MIT Press.

Habermas, J. (1996). *Between Facts and Norms: Contributions to a Discourse Theory of Law and Democracy.* Cambridge, MA: MIT Press.

Hastie, R., Penrod, S. D., & Pennington, N. (1983). *Inside the Jury.* Cambridge, MA: Harvard University Press.

Hibbing, J. R., & Theiss-Morse, E. (2001). Process Preferences and American Politics: What the People Want Government to Be. *American Political Science Review, 95,* 145–153.

Hogg, M. A. (1985). Masculine and Feminine Speech in Dyads and Groups: A Study of Speech Style and Gender Salience. *Journal of Language and Social Psychology, 4,* 99–112.

Howard-Pitney, B., Borgida, E., & Omoto, A. M. (1986). Personal Involvement: An Examination of Processing Differences. *Social Cognition, 4,* 39–57.

Huckfeldt, R., Sprague, J., & Levine, J. (2000). The Dynamics of Collective Deliberation in the 1996 Election: Campaign Effects on Accessibility, Certainty, and Accuracy. *American Political*

Insko, C. A., Schopler, J., Drigotas, S. M., Graetz, K. A., Kennedy, J., Cox, C., & Bornstein, G. (1993). The Role of Communication in Interindividual-Intergroup Discontinuity. *Journal of Conflict Resolution, 37*, 108–138.

Isenberg, D. J. (1986). Group Polarization: A Critical Review and Meta-Analysis. *Journal of Personality and Social Psychology, 50*, 1141–1151.

James, R. (1959). Status and Competence of Jurors. *The American Journal of Sociology, 64*, 563–570.

Jennings, B. (1993). Counsel and consensus: Norms of argument in health policy. In: F. Fischer & J. Forester (Eds), *The Argumentative Turn in Policy Analysis and Planning*. Durham: Duke University.

Kameda, T. (1991). Procedural Influence in Small-Group Decision Making: Deliberation Style and Assigned Decision Rule. *Journal of Personality and Social Psychology, 61*, 245–56.

Kameda, T., Ohtsubo, Y., & Takezawa, M. (1997). Centrality in Sociocognitive Networks and Social Influence: An Illustration in a Group Decision-Making Context. *Journal of Personality and Social Psychology, 73*, 296–309.

Kaplan, M. F., & Miller, C. E. (1987). Group Decision Making and Normative vs. Informational Influence: Effects of Type of Issue and Assigned Decision Rule. *Journal of Personality and Social Psychology, 53*, 306–313.

Kelly, J. R., & Karau, S. J. (1999). Group Decision Making: The Effects of Initial Preferences and Time Pressure. *Personality and Social Psychology Bulletin, 25*, 1342–1354.

Kerr, N. L., MacCoun, R. J., & Kramer, G. P. (1996). Bias in Judgment: Comparing Individuals and Groups. *Psychological Review, 103*, 687–719.

Kerr, N. L., & Kaufman-Gilliland, C. M. (1994). Communication, Commitment, and Cooperation in Social Dilemmas. *Journal of Personality and Social Psychology, 66*, 513–529.

Kirchler, E., & Davis, J. H. (1986). The Influence of Member Status Differences and Task Type on Group Consensus and Member Position Change. *Journal of Personality and Social Psychology, 51*, 83–91.

Kramer, R. M., & Brewer, M. B. (1984). Effects of Group Identity on Resource Use in Simulated Commons Dilemma. *Journal of Personality and Social Psychology, 46*, 1044–1057.

Kruglanski, A. W., & Freund, T. (1983). The Freezing and Unfreezing of Lay Inferences: Effects on Impressional Primacy, Ethnic Stereotyping, and Numerical Anchoring. *Journal of Experimental Social Psychology, 19*, 448–468.

Larmore, C. (1994). Pluralism and Reasonable Disagreement. In: C. Larmore (Ed.), *Morals of Modernity*. Cambridge: Cambridge University Press.

Larson, J. R., Foster-Fishman, P. G., & Franz, T. M. (1998). Leadership Style and The Discussion of Shared and Unshared Information in Decision-Making Groups. *Personality and Social Psychology Bulletin, 24*, 482–495.

Larson, J. R., Christensen, C., Franz, T. M., & Abbott, A. S. (1998). Diagnosing Groups: The Pooling, Management, and Impact of Shared and Unshared Case Information in Team-Based Medical Decision Making. *Journal of Personality and Social Psychology, 75*, 93–108.

Laughlin, P. R., & Earley, P. C. (1982). Social Combination Models, Persuasive Arguments Theory, Social Comparison Theory, and Choice Shift. *Journal of Personality and Social Psychology, 42*, 273–280.

Levine, J. M., & Russo, E. (1995). Impact of Anticipated Interaction on Information Acquisition. *Social Cognition, 13*, 293–317.

Lord, C., Ross, M., & Lepper, M. (1979). Biased Assimilation and Attitude Polarization: The Effects of Prior Theories on Subsequently Considered Evidence. *Journal of Personality and Social Psychology, 27*, 2098–2109.

Luskin, R. C., & Fishkin, J. (1998). Deliberative Polling, Public Opinion and Democracy: The Case the National Issues Convention. Paper presented at the American Association for Public Opinion Research Annual Meeting, Saint Louis, MO, May 14–17, 1998.

Lynn, F. M., & Kartez, J. D. (1995). The redemption of citizen advisory committees: A perspective from critical theory. In: O. Renn, T. Webler & P. Wiedemann (Eds), *Fairness and Competence in Citizen Participation*. Boston MA: Kluwer Academic.

Maass, A., & Arcuri, L. (1996). Language and stereotyping. In: C. N. Macrae, C. Stangor & M. Hewstone (Eds), *Stereotypes and Stereotyping* (pp. 193–226). New York: The Guilford Press.

Maass, A., Ceccarelli, R., & Rudin, S. (1996). Linguistic Intergroup Bias: Evidence for In-Group-Protective Motivation. *Journal of Personality and Social Psychology, 71*, 512–526.

Maass, A., & Clark R. D. (1982). Internalization versus Compliance: Differential Processes Underlying Minority Influence and Conformity. *European Journal of Social Psycology, 13*, 197–215.

Maass, A., Clark, R. D., & Haberkorn, G. (1982). The Effects of Differential Ascribed Category Membership and Norms on Minority Influence. *European Journal of Social Psychology, 12*, 89–104.

Maass, A., & Clark, R. D. III. (1984). Hidden Impact of Minorities: Fifteen Years of Minority Influence Research. *Psychological Bulletin, 95*, 428–450.

Maass, A., Corvino, G., & Arcuri, L. (1994). Linguistic Intergroup Bias and The Mass Media. *Revue de Psychologie Sociale, 1*, 31–34.

Maass, A., Salvi, D., Arcuri, L., & Semin, G. R. (1989). Language Use in Intergroup Contexts: The Linguistic Intergroup Bias. *Journal of Personality and Social Psychology, 57*, 981–993.

Macedo, S. (1999). Introduction. In: S. Macedo (Ed.), *Deliberative Politics: Essays on Democracy and Disagreement* (pp. 3–14). New York: Oxford University Press.

MacRae, D. (1993). Guidelines for policy discourse: Consensual vs. adversarial. In: F. Fischer & J. Forester (Eds), *The Argumentative Turn in Policy Analysis and Planning*. Durham: Duke University.

Manin, B. (1987). On Legitimacy and Political Deliberation. *Political Theory, 15*, 338–368.

Mansbridge, J. (1983). *Beyond Adversary Democracy*. Chicago, IL: University of Chicago Press.

Mansbridge, J. (1990). The rise and fall of self-interest in the explanation of political life. In: J. Mansbridge (Ed.), *Beyond Self-Interest*. Chicago: University of Chicago Press.

Mansbridge, J. (1991). Democracy, deliberation, and the experience of women. In: B. Murchland (Ed.), *Higher Education and the Practice of Democratic Politics*. Dayton, OH: Kettering Foundation.

Mansbridge, J. (1996). Using power/fighting power: The polity. In: S. Benhabib (Ed.), *Democracy and Difference: Contesting the Boundaries of the Political* (pp. 46–66). Princeton: Princeton University Press.

Mansbridge, J. (1999). In: S. Macedo (Ed.), *Deliberative politics: Essays on Democracy and Disagreement* (pp. 3–14). New York: Oxford University Press.

Marcus, G. E. (forthcoming). *The Sentimental Citizen: Emotion in Democratic Politics*. State College, PA: Penn State University Press.

Marcus, G. E., Sullivan, J. L., Theiss-Morse, E., & Wood, S. L. (1995). *With Malice Toward Some: How People Make Civil Liberties Judgments*. Cambridge: Cambridge University Press.

Marcus, G. E., Neuman, W. R., & MacKuen, M. (2000). *Affective Intelligence and Political Judgment*. Chicago: University of Chicago Press.

Marcus, G. E., & MacKuen, M. (2001). Emotion and politics: The dynamic functions of emotionality. In: J. H. Kuklinksi (Ed.), *Citizens and Politics: Perspectives from Political Psychology*. Cambridge: Cambridge University.

Mashaw, J. L. (1985). *Due Process in the Administrative State*. New Haven, CT: Yale University.

Masters, R. D. (2001). Cognitive neuroscience, emotion, and leadership. In: J. H. Kuklinski (Ed.), *Citizens and Politics: Perspectives from Political Psychology*. Cambridge: Cambridge University.

Mendelberg, T., & Oleske, J. (2000). Race and Public Deliberation. *Political Communication, 17*, 169–191.

Mendelberg, T., & Karpowitz, C. (2000). Deliberating about justice. Paper presented for the American Political Science Association Annual Meeting, Washington.

Merkle, D. M. (1996). Review: The National Issues Convention Deliberative Poll. *Public Opinion Quarterly, 60*, 588–619.

Miller, C. E. (1989). The social psychological effects of group decision rules. In: P. Paulus (Ed.), *Psychology of Group Influence* (pp. 327–355). Hillsdale, NJ: Erlbaum.

Miller, N., & Davidson-Podgorny, G. (1987). Theoretical Models of Intergroup Relations and The Use of Cooperative Teams as an Intervention for Desegregated Settings. *Review of Personality and Social Psychology, 9*, 41–67.

Moscovici, S. (1976). *Social Influence and Social Change*. New York: Academic Press.

Moscovici, S. (1980). Toward a Theory of Conversion Behavior. *Advances in Experimental Social Psychology, 13*, 209–239.

Moscovici, S. (1985). Innovation and minority influence. In: G. Lindzey & E. Aronson (Eds), *The Handbook of Social Psychology* (Vol. 2, pp. 347–412). New York: Random House.

Moscovici, S., & Mugny, G. (1983). Minority influence. In: P. B. Paulus (Ed.), *Basic Group Processes* (pp. 41–65). New York: Springer Verlag.

Moscovici, S., & Zavalloni, M. (1969). The Group as a Polarizer of Attitudes. *Journal of Personality and Social Psychology, 12*, 125–135.

Mugny, G., Sanchez-Mazas, M., Roux, P., & Perez, J. A. (1991). Independence and Interdependence of Group Judgments: Xenophobia and Minority Influence. *European Journal of Social Psychology, 21*, 213–223.

Myers, D. G. (1978). Polarizing Effects of Social Comparison. *Journal of Experimental Social Psychology 14*, 554–563.

Myers, D. G., & Lamm, H. (1976). The Group Polarization Phenomenon. *Psychological Bulletin, 83*, 602–662.

Myers, D. G., Bruggink, J. B., Kersting, R. C., & Schlosser, B. A. (1980). Does Learning Others' Opinions Change One's Opinion? *Personality and Social Psychology Bulletin, 6*, 253–260.

Nemeth, C. J. (1977). Interactions Between Jurors as a Function of Majority vs. Unanimity Decision Rules. *Journal of Applied Social Psychology, 7*, 38–56.

Nemeth, C. J. (1986). Differential Contributions of Majority and Minority Influence. *Psychological Review, 93*, 23–32.

Nemeth, C. J., & Brilmayer, A. G. (1987). Negotiation vs. Influence. *European Journal of Social Psychology, 17*, 45–56.

Nemeth, C. J., Endicott, J., & Wachtler, J. (1976). From The '50s to The '70s: Women in Jury Deliberations. *Sociometry, 39*, 293–304.

Nemeth, C. J., & Kwan, J. (1985). Originality of Word Associations as a Function of Majority and Minority Influence. *Social Psychology Quarterly, 48*, 277–282.

Nemeth, C. J., & Mayseless, O. (1987). *Enhancing Recall: The Contributions of Conflict, Minorities, and Consistency*. Berkeley, CA: University of California.

Nemeth, C. J., & Rogers, J. (1996). Dissent and the Search for Information. *British Journal of Social Psychology, 35,* 67–76.

Nemeth, C. J., Swedlund, M., & Kanki, B. (1974). Patterning of the Minority's Responses and Their Influence on the Majority. *European Journal of Social Psychology, 4,* 53–64.

Nemeth, C. J., & Wachtler, J. (1983). Creative Problem Solving as a Result of Majority vs. Minority Influence. *European Journal of Social Psychology, 13,* 45–55.

Nie, N. H., Junn, J., & Stehlik-Barry, K. (1996). *Education and Democratic Citizenship in America.* Chicago: University of Chicago Press.

Nino, C. S. (1996). *The Constitution of Deliberative Democracy.* New Haven, CT: Yale University Press.

Noelle-Neumann, E. (1984). *Spiral of Silence.* Chicago: University of Chicago Press.

Orbell, J. M., van de Kragt, A. J. C., & Dawes, R. M. (1988). Explaining Discussion-Induced Cooperation. *Journal of Personality and Social Psychology, 54,* 811–819.

Ostrom, E. (1998). A Behavioral Approach to the Rational Choice Theory of Collective Action. *American Political Science Review, 92,* 1–22

Paulhaus, D. L., & Morgan, K. L. (1997). Perceptions of Intelligence in Leaderless Groups: The Dynamic Effects of Shyness and Acquaintance. *Journal of Personality and Social Psychology, 72,* 581–591.

Pearce, W. B., & Littlejohn, S. W. (1997). *Moral Conflict: When Social Worlds Collide.* Thousand Oaks CA: Sage Publications.

Penrod, S., & Hastie, R. (1980). A Computer Simulation of Jury Decision Making. *Psychological Review, 87,* 133–159.

Petty, R. E., Haugtvedt, C. P., & Smith, S. M. (1995). Elaboration as a determinant of attitude strength: Creating attitudes that are persistent, resistant, and predictive of behavior. In: R. E. Petty & J. A. Krosnick (Eds), *Attitude Strength: Antecendents and Consequences* (pp. 93–130). Mahwah, NJ: Erlbaum.

Pool, G. J., Wood, W., & Leck, K. (1998). The Self-Esteem Motive in Social Influence: Agreement With Valued Majorities and Disagreement With Derogated Minorities. *Journal of Personality and Social Psychology, 75,* 967–975.

Putnam, R. D. (2000). *Bowling Alone: The Collapse and Revival of American Community.* New York: Simon and Schuster.

Rawls, J. (1971). *A Theory of Justice.* Cambridge, MA: Belknap Press of Harvard University Press.

Rawls, J. (1996). *Political Liberalism.* New York: Columbia University Press.

Ridgeway, C. L. (1981). Non-conformity, Competence, and Influence in Groups: A Test of Two Theories. *American Sociological Review, 46,* 333–347.

Ridgeway, C. L. (1987). Nonverbal Behavior, Dominance, and the Basis of Status in Task Groups. *American Sociological Review, 52,* 683–694.

Rosenstone, S. J., & Hansen, J. M. (1993). *Mobilization, Participation, and Democracy in America.* New York: Macmillan.

Rossi, J. (1997). Participation Run Amok: The Costs of Mass Participation for Deliberative Agency Decision Making. *Northwestern University Law Review, 92,* 173–249.

Rubini, M., & Kruglanski, A. W. (1997). Brief Encounters Ending in Estrangement: Motivated Language Use and Interpersonal Rapport in the Question-Answer Paradigm. *Journal of Personality and Social Psychology, 72,* 1047–1060.

Sally, D. (1995). Conversation and Cooperation in Social Dilemmas: A Meta-Analysis of Experiments From 1958 to 1992. *Rationality and Society, 7,* 58–92.

Sanders, L. M. (1997). Against Deliberation. *Political Theory, 25,* 347–376.

Sapiro, V. (1999). Considering Political Civility Historically: A Case Study of the United States. Prepared for delivery at the *Annual Meeting of the International Society for Political Psychology*, Amsterdam, The Netherlands.

Schkade, D., Sunstein, C. R., & Kahneman, D. (2000). Deliberating About Dollars: The Severity Shift. *Columbia Law Review, 100*(May), 1139–1175.

Schulz-Hardt, S., Frey, D., Luthgens, C., & Moscovici, S. (2000). Biased Information Search in Group Decision Making. *Journal of Personality and Social Psychology, 78*, 655–669.

Schwarz, N., & Clore, G. L. (1983). Mood, Misattribution, and Judgments of Well-Being: Informative and Directive Functions of Affective States. *Journal of Personality and Social Psychology, 45*, 513–523.

Shapiro, I. (1999). Enough of deliberation: Politics is about interests and power. In: S. Macedo (Ed.), *Deliberative Politics: Essays* on *Democracy and Disagreement* (pp. 28–38). New York: Oxford University Press.

Sherif, M., Harvey, O. J., White, B. J., Hood, W. R., & Sherif, C. W. (1961). *Intergroup Conflict and Cooperation: The Robbers Cave Experiment.* Norman, OK: University Book Exchange.

Shestowsky, D., Wegener, D. T., & Fabrigar, L. R. (1998). Need For Cognition and Interpersonal Influence: Individual Differences in Impact On Dyadic Decisions. *Journal of Personality and Social Psychology, 74*, 1317–1328.

Smith, C. M., Tindale, R. S., & Dugoni, B. L. (1996). Minority and Majority Influence in Freely Interacting Groups: Qualitative Versus Quantitative Differences. *British Journal of Social Psychology, 35*, 137–149.

Sornig, K. (1989). Some remarks on linguistic strategies of persuasion. In: R. Wodak (Ed.), *Language, Power, and Ideology: Studies in Political Discourse.* Philadelphia: J. Benjamins Pub. Co.

Stasser, G. (1992). Pooling of unshared information during group discussion. In: S. Worchel, W. Wood & J. A. Simpson (Eds), *Group Process and Productivity* (pp. 48–67). Newbury Park: Sage.

Stasser, G., Taylor, L. A., & Hanna, C. (1989). Information Sampling in Structured and Unstructured Discussions of 3-Person and 6-Person Groups. *Journal Personality and Social Psychology, 57*, 67–78.

Stasser, G., & Titus, W. (1985). Pooling Of Unshared Information in Group Decision Making: Biased Information Sampling During Discussion. *Journal of Personality and Social Psychology, 48*, 1467–1478.

Strodtbeck, F. L., James, R., & Hawkins, C. (1957). Social Status In Jury Deliberations. *American Sociological Review, 22*, 713–719.

Strodtbeck, F. L., & Mann, R. D. (1956). Sex Role Differentiation in Jury Deliberations. *Sociometry, 19*, 3–11.

Sunstein, C. (1993). *Democracy and the Problem of Free Speech.* New York: Free Press.

Susskind, L., & Cruikshank, J. (1987). *Breaking the Impasse: Consensual Approaches to Resolving Public Disputes.* New York: Basic Books.

Taber, C. S., Lodge, M., & Glathar, J. (2001). The motivated construction of political judgments. In: J. H. Kuklinksi (Ed.), *Citizens and Politics: Perspectives from Political Psychology.* Cambridge: Cambridge University.

Tetlock, P. E. (1983). Accountability and The Perseverance of First Impressions. *Social Psychology Quarterly, 4*, 285–292.

Tetlock, P. E. (1985). Accountability: A Social Check on The Fundamental Attribution Error. *Social Psychology Quarterly, 48*, 227–236.

Tetlock, P. E., & Kim, J. I. (1987). Accountability and Judgment Processes in a Personality Prediction

Thakerar, J. N., Giles, H., & Cheshire, J. (1982). Psychological and linguistic parameters of speech accomodation theory. In: C. Fraser & K. R. Scherer (Eds), *Advances in The Social Psychology of Language* (pp. 205–255). Cambridge, U.K.: Cambridge University Press.

Turner, J. C. (1985). Social categorization and the self-concept: A social cognitive theory of group behavior. In: E. G. Lawler (Ed.), *Advances in Group Processes* (pp. 77–122). Greenwich, CT: JAI Press.

Turner, J. C. (1991). *Social Influence.* Pacific Grove CA: Brooks/Cole Publishing Company.

Turner, J. C., Hogg, M. A., Oakes, P. J., Reicher, S. D., Wetherell, M. S. et al. (1987). *Rediscovering the Social Group: A Self-Categorization Theory.* Oxford: Basil Blackwell.

Vallone, R. P., Ross L., & Lepper, M. R. (1985). The Hostile Media Phenomenon: Biased Perception and Perceptions of Media Bias in Coverage of The Beirut Massacre. *Journal of Personality and Social Psychology, 49,* 577–585.

Vari, A. (1995). Citizens' advisory committee as a model for public participation: A multiple-criteria evaluation. In: O. Renn, T. Webler & P. Wiedemann (Eds), *Fairness and Competence in Citizen Participation* (pp. 157–174). Dordrecht, Netherlands: Kluwer Publishers.

Verba S., Schlozman, K. L., & Brady, H. E. (1995). *Voice and Equality: Civic Voluntarism in American Politics.* Cambridge, MA: Harvard University Press.

Verplanken, B. (1993). Need for Cognition and External Information Search: Responses to Time Pressure During Decision Making. *Journal of Research in Personality, 27,* 238–252.

Vinokur, A., & Burnstein, E. (1978). Depolarization of Attitudes in Groups. *Journal of Personality and Social Psychology, 36,* 872–885.

Warren, M. (1992). Democratic Theory and Self-Transformation. *American Political Science Review, 86,* 8–23.

Warren, M. (1996). Deliberative Democracy and Authority. *American Political Science Review, 90,* 46–60.

Webster, D. M., Kruglanski, A. W., & Pattison, D. A. (1997). Motivated Language Use in Intergroup Contexts: Need-For-Closure Effects on The Linguistic Intergroup Bias. *Journal of Personality and Social Psychology, 72,* 1122–1131.

Williams, B. A., & Matheny, A. R. (1995). *Democracy, Dialogue, and Environmental Disputes: The Contested Languages Of Social Regulation.* New Haven: Yale University.

Winquist, J. R., & Larson, J. R., Jr. (1998). Information Pooling: When It Impacts Group Decision Making. *Journal of Personality and Social Psychology, 74,* 371–377.

Witte, J. F. (1980). *Democracy, Authority, and Alienation in Work: Workers' Participation in an American Corporation.* Chicago: University of Chicago Press.

Wittenbaum, G. M., Hubbell, A. P., & Zuckerman, C. (1999). Mutual Enhancement: Toward an Understanding of The Collective Preference for Shared Information. *Journal of Personality and Social Psychology, 77,* 967–978.

Wood, W., Lundgren, S., Ouellette, J. A., Busceme, S., & Blackstone, T. (1994). Minority Influence: A Meta-Analytic Review of Social Influence Processes. *Psychological Bulletin, 115,* 323–345.

Wright, R. F. (1992). Why Not Administrative Grand Juries? *Administrative Law Review, 44,* 465–521.

Wyer, R. S., & Frey, D. (1983). The Effects of Feedback About Self and Others On The Recall and Judgments Of Feedback-Relevant Information. *Journal of Experimental Social Psychology, 19,* 540–559.

Yankelovich, D. (1991). *Coming to Public Judgment: Making Democracy Work in a Complex World.* Syracuse, NY: Syracuse University Press.

Young, I. (1996). Communication and the other: Beyond deliberative democracy. In S. Benhabib (Ed.), *Democracy and Difference: Contesting The Boundaries of The Political* (pp. 120–136). Princeton: Princeton University Press.

Zdaniuk, B., & Levine, J. M. (1996). Anticipated Interaction and Thought Generation: The Role of Faction Size. *British Journal of Social Psychology, 35*, 201–218.

Zuber, J. A., Crott, H. W., & Werner, J. (1992). Choice Shift and Group Polarization: An Analysis of The Status of Arguments and Social Decision Schemes. *Journal of Personality and Social Psychology, 62*, 50–61.

OPINION QUALITY AND POLICY PREFERENCES IN DELIBERATIVE RESEARCH

Mark Lindeman

What I want is to get done what the people desire to have done, and the question for me is how to find that out exactly.

Attributed to Abraham Lincoln (Crespi, 1989, p. 1).

If Lincoln were a contemporary American politician and made the statement above, many pundits would criticize him for pandering to the masses, governing with a finger to the winds of the opinion polls (here and elsewhere, I will let readers judge how far beyond the United States my arguments can be generalized). But many public opinion researchers would venture a different critique. Lincoln's goal, they would argue, is not so much irresponsible as chimerical. People's policy preferences are not merely uninformed, but largely *unformed*. Most Americans score poorly on simple tests of political knowledge – and many venture "opinions" on non-existent people or laws (Neuman, 1986, pp. 14–25; Delli Carpini & Keeter, 1996). People's policy "opinions" often vary sharply when questions are reworded (Rosenbaum, 1997; Goot, 1998). In fact, individuals' responses to *identical* questions often vary over time: at the limit, they resemble random noise (Converse, 1964, 1980; see also Zaller, 1992). Extrapolating "collective policy preferences" (Page & Shapiro, 1992, p. 15) from such data may seem like descrying the future from animal entrails. Differently put, if *vox populi, vox Dei*, then public opinion researchers incline toward reverent or irreverent agnosticism.

Political Decision Making, Deliberation and Participation, Volume 6, pages 195–221.
Copyright © 2002 by Elsevier Science Ltd.
All rights of reproduction in any form reserved.
ISBN: 0-7623-0227-5

Researchers' reticence about public preferences creates a paradoxical gap in political discourse. George Gallup and other early innovators had hoped that survey research would provide a reliable source of information by which to judge competing claims about public preferences (Gallup & Rae, 1940). Instead, most political survey research is variously designed to inform political tactics (Morris, 1998; see Jacobs & Shapiro, 2000); to assert public support for the sponsor's favored policies; to inform journalistic accounts pitched at a high level of generality; or to address academic issues that are orthogonal to Lincoln's question about popular preferences. Thus, despite the widespread perception of politicians' "slavish obedience" to public opinion (Toner, 2000), we have little reliable information about public preferences that could be obeyed. Indeed, we have no agreement on whether meaningful public preferences exist, or how they could be measured.

A growing number of researchers propose various forms of *deliberative research* to study citizens' considered political judgments. These researchers do not march under a common banner, but their work shares the goals of providing participants with access to relevant information and arguments about a policy issue, opportunity to deliberate on the issue, and a means to express their considered views about the issue. Thus, deliberative research addresses two conjoined problems: the low quality of prevailing public opinion, and the difficulty of measuring whatever "genuine underlying preference[s]" (Inglehart, 1990, p. 131) do exist. These efforts are subject to criticism on several grounds: that they fail to improve opinion quality; that they fail adequately to measure opinion quality; and/or that the apparent preferences they evoke have no normative legitimacy or political relevance.

This essay argues that deliberative research can complement traditional survey research to offer valid and valuable insights into public preferences. As the questions raised – and begged – in the preceding paragraph illustrate, the argument must traverse difficult definitional terrain and address the disparate concerns of several audiences. Quite obviously, deliberative research does not magically transform all political debates into technical problems, then conveniently solve them. However, I do conclude that deliberative research can be both intellectually rigorous and politically germane.

The essay proceeds as follows. First, because our relative ignorance about public preferences is rarely stated as a major problem of public opinion research, I sketch an argument that places it there. Next I define the scope of deliberative research and describe some of the diverse research methods. Then I discuss ways in which deliberation might affect (but not always improve) individual opinion, and how these various aspects might be operationalized in quality measures. Finally, I present some brief case studies of deliberative research addressing public preferences. These case studies illustrate how multiple methods can enhance – and complicate – our understanding of public opinion, and indicate possible directions for future research.

THE STAKES: ASSESSING DEMOCRATIC RESPONSIVENESS

If public preferences are unknowable, then we can no longer ask whether government does "what the people desire to have done," much less whether it should. At best we can trace whether public opinion and policy seem to change in the same direction (e.g. Page & Shapiro, 1983; Stimson et al., 1995). The Stimson et al. study concludes that shifts in public opinion do, in general, evoke changes in policy. However, the study has a little-noticed and troubling subtext. The study's data imply that Americans on average wanted government policy to become more liberal in every year from 1955 through 1990, and that overall policy was actually slightly more conservative in 1990 than in 1955. This result suggests that policy may be fundamentally *non-responsive* to public opinion despite their tendency to change in the same direction – *if* we take the public opinion measure at face value. Yet in much of the analysis this measure is rescaled, without explanation, to indicate that the public sometimes desires more liberal policy and sometimes desires more conservative policy – a result that many observers of American politics certainly would find plausible. The same authors more recently conclude that while "policy activity" has had a liberal slant at some times and a conservative slant at others, the actual "cumulative liberalism of federal policy" has grown over time (Erikson et al., 2001, p. 331); it is unclear whether this new interpretation resolves or deepens the riddle of policy responsiveness. Thus, Stimson et al.'s analysis exemplifies a common limitation of public opinion analysis generally: while their opinion measure offers interpretable variance, the measure itself resists substantive interpretation.

Monroe (1998) presents one of the few systematic attempts to study the substantive agreement between what (according to polls) people want the government to do and what the government actually does. Monroe reviews over 500 issues over the period 1980–1993, and concludes that overall, policy and opinion were "congruent" on 55% of the issues. It is hard to tell whether we should regard this rate as high or low. Certainly it is not extremely high – considering Monroe's dichotomous measures of policy and opinion, and the observed proportions of public *support* for policy change and *actual* policy change, we would expect about a 48% congruence rate if policymakers were indifferent to public opinion. In short, the literature is equivocal about both the content of public preferences and the extent of policy responsiveness.

Not only academic analysts are confused about public preferences. Former senator Warren Rudman has commented:

> If you can tell me how my constituents feel on a particular issue, I would be *delighted* to consider – unless I had *violent* objections to their decision – casting a vote on behalf of their view. I never knew what they thought! Does anybody? ... On 99.9% of the issues you don't know what your constituency thinks (Fried, 1997, p. 185).

If elected officials are as uncertain about public preferences as Rudman suggests, then Lincoln's ideal of doing "what the people desire to have done" is quixotic indeed. Granted, one rarely hears complaints that members of Congress know too *little* about public preferences. Yet across the range of legislation considered by Congress, publicly available survey data typically provide sparse and enigmatic substantive guidance however they are interpreted. Moreover, members of Congress may doubt that the results of national surveys reflect the views of their own constituencies.

For some observers, the question of democratic responsiveness seems ultimately not very important. Many stand in the representative-democratic mainstream summed up by Lippmann: "To support the Ins when things are going well; to support the Outs when they seem to be going badly, this, in spite of all that has been said about tweedledum and tweedledee, is the essence of popular government" (Lippmann, 1925, p. 126; Neuman, 1986, p. 187; Rose, 1989, p. 53; Zaller, 1992, p. 332). This ability to "vote out the Ins" provides some protection against tyranny, and some responsiveness to public preferences, without – it may be hoped – overtaxing people's limited political competence.

Yet even if we set aside normative concerns (Dahl, 1985), this view does not seem to tell the whole story about democratic politics. Most Americans, without considering themselves policy experts, apparently do believe that they have policy preferences. Most also believe that government should be responsive to majority preferences. Finally, many believe that government is not doing what the public wants. Does this criticism have any validity? What, if anything, *do* majorities want as public policy?

DELIBERATIVE RESEARCH

A small but growing group of researchers have conducted a varied array of *deliberative research* intended to complement (or, for some, to supplant) the evidence about public preferences available from conventional survey research. In their excellent review of deliberative research methods, Price and Neijens (1998) cite the search for "informed public opinion" as a common thread of this research (see also Yankelovich, 1996). Because "informed" has misleadingly narrow connotations of factual knowledge, I prefer to state that deliberative researchers seek to evoke and to study people's *considered judgments*. James Fishkin (1994) has defined considered judgments as "the conclusions [i.e. policy preferences] people would reach if they were better informed, and had a better opportunity to think through the issues." Yankelovich (1991) emphasizes that considered judgment implies not raw knowledge (useful though this may be), but a willingness to accept the likely costs and risks of one policy as opposed to another.

What puts the deliberation in deliberative research? Although deliberative researchers have no consensual definition of "deliberation" (nor of considered judgment), my own definition embraces diverse forms of deliberative research: Deliberation is a cognitive process in which individuals form, alter, or reinforce their opinions as they weigh evidence and arguments from various points of view. (As should become clear, I do not mean that this process is narrowly rational.) Adolf Gundersen's definition is in much the same spirit: "Democratic deliberation occurs anytime a citizen either actively justifies her views (even to herself) or defends them against a challenge (even from herself). The more demanding the audience, the more powerful the challenge, the better the resulting deliberation" (Gundersen, 1995, p. 199).

While this definition of "deliberation" carries less normative freight than those that include concepts of the "common good" or "general interest" (e.g. Bohman, 1996, p. 5), and does not insist on a distinctive group process, my own approach assumes that most people take the common good – not just their own – into account in their political deliberations. Further, I argue that people can consider the common good by themselves, not only with other people. Surveys need not reinforce an "individualistic" (Dryzek, 1991. p. 172) or "atomized" (Herbst, 1995, p. 101) conception of politics – even in survey settings, public-spirited deliberation is possible. I argue (following Page & Shapiro, 1992; Page, 1996) that collective deliberation involving ordinary people happens constantly. People necessarily draw on social processes and experiences in survey conversations as in other settings. They deliberate with other people in mind, even if not in the room.

A prime difficulty of evaluating deliberative research is its multiple and varied goals, ranging from improving the quality of individuals' opinions to achieving collective policy consensus or improving policy institutions (Price & Neijens, 1998). In this essay I emphasize just a few objectives. An overarching objective is to explore collective public policy preferences – not only those "considered judgments" that participants may develop, but the more inchoate preferences that people hold in daily life. That is, the outcome of artificial hothouse deliberation (as a critic might deride it) can enhance our understanding of "ordinary" public opinion. This enhancement depends on two narrower objectives: to evoke high-quality opinion, and to evaluate opinion quality. Although the evocation and measurement of "quality" are hardly straightforward technical problems, they are certainly more approachable than, say, transforming American political discourse.

Why focus on evoking and measuring quality? Many observers will agree that in principle, at least the considered judgments of citizens deserve careful attention in democratic policymaking. However, if these considered judgments can be induced only by subjecting a small group of participants to intensive (and expensive) deliberative exercises, they are unlikely to command much attention, no matter how forcefully these exercises' creators urge their "recommending force" (Fishkin, 1997). The question arises, do such considered judgments bear any resemblance to the somewhat pallid image of public opinion that emerges from conventional surveys? Even many advocates of deliberation conclude that the answer obviously is negative. In Benjamin Barber's words, public opinion polls "tap. . . the status of private prejudices. To take the public pulse means only to take the measure of aggregated impulse, to elicit undeliberated biases unmediated by reason or common deliberation" (Barber, 1993, p. 68). In my view, conventional survey results often reveal a great deal of "honesty and common sense" (Gallup & Rae, 1940, p. 287). But such assessments should be grounded in evidence about both the quality and the substance of the opinions we are evaluating. Deliberative research invites us to judge opinion quality by specific criteria instead of armchair assertions, and to examine whether and how improving opinion quality alters the shape of collective policy preferences.

DELIBERATIVE POLLING AND DELIBERATIVE FACILITATION

While there are numerous approaches to the study and application of deliberative democracy, most proponents fall into one of two camps. Some are *deliberative pollers* who favor large-sample designs with an emphasis on forced-choice surveys; others are *deliberative facilitators* who favor intensive discussions, usually in small groups. Certain criticisms are typically directed at each camp, sometimes by the other but more often by third parties. The most ambitious attempt to synthesize the two approaches, James Fishkin's National Issues Convention in 1996, predictably was criticized on both fronts. Here I briefly sketch these camps and criticisms, and argue that we cannot do without either approach.

At the limit, researchers in the "deliberative polling" camp see deliberation as a (sometimes) individual and relatively undemanding process. Thus, the

Americans Talk Issues Foundation's "deliberative telephone polls" (Kay, 1998) assume that when relevant facts and arguments are fairly presented, people *often* can come to considered judgments within a few minutes, in the course of the telephone interview. In partial contrast, Ted Becker and Christa Daryl Slaton's Televotes (Slaton, 1992) provide several days for deliberation, and encourage – but do not require – participants to discuss their views with other people. "Polling" methods can readily accommodate large numbers of participants, potentially enhancing their representativeness. Because the information they present is tightly scripted, they lend themselves to replication and experimentation. Common objections include that such methods offer almost no opportunity for reflection, especially on unfamiliar and immediately uncomfortable ideas; that political deliberation properly should entail that people talk with each other, not only with themselves; and that polls force participants to respond in language set for them by survey designers.

Deliberative facilitators often argue that the "common good" to be pursued by government is a social construct that must be continually redefined, and that people can think about complicated tradeoffs better together than they can individually (Mathews, 1994). Their methods can be thought of as efforts to approximate Habermas's "ideal speech situation" (Habermas, 1985; Yankelovich, 1991; Renn et al., 1995). In many Public Agenda Foundation studies (Doble, 1988; Doble & Johnson, 1990), participants led by an impartial moderator discuss a set of broad policy alternatives designed to highlight the key choices and tradeoffs in an issue area. In Citizens Juries (Crosby, 1995, 1996), typically both partisan and non-partisan experts offer testimony, and participants question these witnesses. Such methods can provide considerable depth of discussion, give participants chances to ask their own questions, and (in some cases) allow participants to formulate their considered preferences in their own words. Principal objections are that these methods cannot be generalized to the citizenry at large – because participants are probably not representative to begin with and become less so after being subjected to predictable and unpredictable influences – and that informational and social biases can loom even larger in these methods than in the polling methods.

The advantages and weaknesses of these two broad approaches are, in many respects, complementary. Unsurprisingly, practitioners of each approach tend to be skeptical of the other: what pollers see as rigor and replicability, facilitators see as superficiality; what facilitators see as depth and richness, pollers see as methodological slackness and capricious group dynamics. However, if our object is to evoke and to measure high-quality opinion, then both approaches have merit. Deliberative facilitators and deliberative pollers alike affirm that participants rise to the challenge of policy deliberation with enthusiasm and seriousness of purpose, and offer, in the main, reasonable views. While individual studies do face tradeoffs between richness and rigor, cumulatively these studies can complement each other (and other opinion research), as illustrated by the case studies toward the end of the chapter.

One difficulty in cumulating the results of deliberative research is deliberative studies' common propensity to confound many experimental influences (Price & Neijens, 1998). If, for instance, participants (1) are provided with written information, (2) gather in small groups to discuss their reactions, and then (3) meet with avowed policy experts to ask questions, there is no way of telling which element or combination of elements "really works," nor how variations in these three phases – e.g. a different facilitation model, or even a quirk of group dynamics, at phase 2 – would affect the results. Most deliberative researchers have, understandably, been more interested in doing all they can to enhance opinion quality than in isolating effects of changes in method. Unfortunately, these researchers often have paid scant attention to each other's work when planning their research and describing their results. It is probably unreasonable to expect a comprehensive theory of deliberative methods, but to treat every research model as *sui generis* needlessly undermines possibilities of cumulation. Bluntly put, if deliberative researchers function as isolated utopian sects, they must expect their work to be discounted accordingly.

ASPECTS OF QUALITY: HOW DELIBERATION CAN CHANGE MINDS (AND VOICES)

How might deliberation improve – or, in some cases, worsen – the "quality" of people's expressed policy opinions? Several mechanisms suggest themselves (I will discuss five), and each one implies possible design criteria for deliberative research. By the same token, these mechanisms imply different criteria or dimensions of opinion quality, and thus reveal a twofold definitional problem. First, no consensus exists on the relative importance of these various "quality" dimensions. Second, some dimensions are very difficult to define operationally, and hence to measure. Research can proceed fruitfully without consensus, but not so fruitfully without operational definitions.

Unfortunately, some deliberative studies employ no quality measures at all; participants' final opinions are treated as high-quality by assumption based on the presumed validity of the method. In other studies, quality is evaluated on plausible but ad hoc substantive grounds, such as after-the-fact assessment of whether preferences seem contradictory, or anecdotal evidence about the quality of discussion. These practices may be partly rooted in a reluctance to be seen as "grading" the participants in deliberation: who are we to "flunk the whole human race?" (Schattschneider, 1960, 1975, p. 132). However, skeptics are entitled to ask how we know whether putative considered judgments deserve to be taken seriously, and deliberative researchers should be prepared with good answers.

Here are some of the ways in which deliberation may affect various aspects of opinion quality:

(1) Altering people's factual basis for evaluation may enable people to draw more, or less, "correct" inferences from their core values to their policy preferences. For instance, in a 1995 survey, the average respondent overestimated the proportion of the U.S. budget devoted to foreign aid by a factor of fifteen; after they were supplied with the correct percentage (1% of the federal budget), the percentage who agreed that "too much is spent on foreign aid" dropped from 75% to 18% (Kull & Destler, 1999, pp. 123–127). Kuklinski et al. (1996a) found that when respondents were supplied with six basic facts about welfare, they were roughly 12 points less likely to support cuts in welfare programs than a control group that "guessed" the facts. However, the difference between people provided with the correct facts and another control group with no mention of the facts was insignificant (Kuklinski et al., 1996b). Apparently, the group that "guessed" the facts deliberated on misinformation and came to distinct (but not, presumably, improved) opinions.

Deliberative researchers typically attempt to provide participants with reasonably comprehensive and balanced information. Since we lack objective criteria of "comprehensive and balanced," most deliberative research employs procedural standards to ensure that experts with opposing views agree on the overall fairness of the information presented to participants. Researchers focus on requisite knowledge – facts that seem essential to underpin any considered judgment worthy of the name – rather than a broader inculcation of expert information. "Quiz-show knowledge" about politics, such as the measures used by Zaller (1992), Bartels (1996), or Althaus (1998), demonstrably is a correlate of competent political reasoning – but inculcating this knowledge (e.g. what William Rehnquist does for a living) will do little directly to promote better reasoning on any particular policy issue. Moreover, much expert knowledge is relatively tangential to the most important decisions in a policy domain. Yankelovich (1991, p. 162) cites the case of the hapless expert who began his remarks on crime policy by explaining the difference between "jail" and "prison." While this definitional point might trip up a respondent on a poorly designed survey question, no important policy decision hinges on it.

Much deliberative research has used knowledge measures sparingly if at all. Mindful that demonstrating people's ignorance tends to diminish their interest, deliberative researchers tend to adopt the role of avuncular tutors: "You'll pick this stuff up soon enough, nothing to it!" Pedagogical instincts aside, a de-emphasis of factual knowledge finds some warrant in on-line tally theories of political judgment: people's judgments may be based on many more facts than they are able to retrieve separately (e.g. Lodge, 1995). Other political heuristics contribute to people's ability to form plausible judgments in the absence of full information (Mondak, 1993). All this said, some level of ignorance or misinformation (as in the foreign aid example above) becomes difficult to reconcile with any plausible standard of considered judgment. Designs that measure requisite knowledge will yield more credible results than those that do not.

(2) In the course of deliberation, people may learn to interpret policy questions as policy questions. For instance, when General Social Survey (GSS) respondents are asked whether "we're spending too much ... [or] too little money" on various "problems" such as "improving and protecting the environment," we cannot tell how many people intend their responses to be interpreted as policy preferences. Since people are well aware that their remarks and survey responses are not translated directly into policy, they are free to indulge in phatic rather than reasoned replies. These "sociable" exclamations (Gamson, 1992) patently may not reflect the quality of their underlying opinions. When a focus group participant blurts, "I think first you shoot all the experts – anybody who's an economist and who has a Ph.D. or master's or something in economy [sic]" (Harwood Group, 1993, p. 20), one need not proclaim that she needs to deliberate more seriously on her proposal, or even that she is expressing a "private prejudice" (see also Yankelovich, 1996, pp. 4–5, on criminal justice issues). Systematic deliberation – apart from generating considered judgments – may cue people to *report* these judgments, to answer as if the answer mattered.

Unfortunately, many policy-related survey questions do *not* clearly ask actual policy questions, nor do they neatly measure policy-related values. Often survey designers appear to follow what I call the principle of *correlative confusion* – the view that policy-related questions should be as vague and unformed as the attitudes they presumably measure. The GSS "spending" battery mentioned above is one example: respondents are simply left to guess the meaning of "we're" (the federal government? all levels of government? citizens? all sectors of society?). Another classic example has been asked in National Election Studies since 1956: "This country would be better off if we just stayed home and did not concern ourselves with problems in other parts of the world." It is hard to say exactly what this question measures, but it surely is not a very informative measure of policy preferences.

Not only do questions like these not allow respondents to state coherent and meaningful preferences, but (as readers can confirm) they tend to punish thoughtfulness ("'Just stayed home'? What does that *mean*? . . . I bet you want to ask me another 60 questions just like that one, too. Yeesh."). Yet answers to these questions are routinely treated as errorless measures of "public opinion." This approach tacitly assumes that intelligible policy preferences do not exist or are not worth knowing: a defensible view, but I believe an unfortunate one. Of course more specifically framed questions do not dissolve the problems of opinion quality. Still, public opinion researchers should (and do) at least sometimes give respondents a fighting chance to make sense.

Here my claim about opinion quality and measurement is essentially a negative one: vague and ambiguous questions cannot evoke high-quality expressions of preference. Of course the inverse is not true: specific and pellucid questions can elicit low-quality answers. Also, if better and more engaging questions actually coax participants to think more clearly about politics, then deliberative researchers should note that the act of measurement has altered the characteristic they set out to measure, a result that is normatively desirable but methodologically inconvenient.

(3) Where people's core values and beliefs have ambivalent implications for the issue at hand, new (or freshly presented) arguments may lead people to use different evaluative criteria – that is, to think about the issue in a different way. This mechanism can be conceptualized as a priming or framing effect (Iyengar & Kinder, 1987, p. 63; Kinder & Sanders, 1990; Freedman, 1996) or a change in issue salience (Jones, 1994). For instance, if someone thinks of abortion as the morally suspect killing of innocents *and* as a personal decision for which government intervention is suspect, then emphasizing one argument or the other may influence the respondent's summary opinion of abortion even though the respondent is not newly persuaded of the argument itself. Or a new argument may persuade a respondent to introduce a new evaluative dimension, or to alter her evaluation in an existing dimension. Ideally, respondents should avoid the halo effect: the inclination to believe that a policy preferable in one dimension is preferable in all dimensions (Jervis, 1976, p. 137). They should not disregard a patently important dimension even if they choose to give more weight to another one.

Procedurally, because the choice of evaluative criteria is so important, most deliberative researchers conclude that participants should be exposed to a variety of arguably pertinent criteria, and then given opportunity to consider for themselves which should be given the most weight. Moreover, where alternative proposals vary on several dimensions, a deliberative setting can be structured to lead participants through various evaluative criteria systematically, thus easing the burden of information processing and allowing participants to focus on how to prioritize across the criteria (Neijens, 1987, esp. pp. 21–28).

Despite the obvious difficulties of evaluating other people's evaluative criteria, some reasonable standards present themselves. Neijens (1987) illustrates two in particular – net utility calculations and tests for halo effects – that I discuss further below, along with more ambitious examinations of consistency. However, insofar as a touchstone of considered judgment is willingness to accept consequences, simple tests may be most important. Yankelovich and Public Agenda often rely heavily on the use of "even-if" questions: for instance, circa 1988, does a respondent favor deep reductions in nuclear weaponry *even if* much greater spending on conventional weapons is required to maintain military balance? Such questions have obvious limitations: reasonable observers may disagree on the accuracy of the supposed consequence; accordingly, it may not be clear whether the respondent is accepting a consequence or denying it. With that caveat, "even-if" questions can be simple and effective ways of probing for blatant and pathological framing effects. For instance, one or two well constructed "even-if" questions should expose whether participants truly are gripped by the infamous "free lunch" or "something-for-nothing" syndrome (wanting more government spending without acknowledging that someone has to pay for it).

(4) Where respondents manifest deep ambivalence about how their core beliefs should be applied to a policy question, deliberation may enable them to move toward a stable resolution of this ambivalence. This stable resolution may entail a prioritizing of competing values in a particular policy context, or a new synthesis that reconciles them (e.g. Hochschild, 1993, pp. 192–193).

Procedurally, efforts to evoke considered judgment should probe apparent contradictions in people's expressed opinions. Inasmuch as arriving at a "new synthesis" spurred by these contradictions takes time and effort, some observers will conclude that deliberative polling techniques are fundamentally inadequate for this task. However, this verdict should be tempered: Kay (1998) shows how a series of deliberative polls can cumulatively explore and often resolve apparent contradictions in collective preferences.

The prevalence of "new syntheses" is not a compelling quality criterion in itself, but the ability to recognize contradictions and to move toward resolving them is. Two broad measurement approaches pertain here. First, researchers can test for outright contradictions in expressed preferences: i.e. stating inconsistent views on essentially identical policy issues and/or expressing support for logically incompatible positions. Second, researchers can measure the integrative complexity of people's expressed policy positions (cf. Suedfeld et al., 1992; Conway et al., 1999). One simple approach is to ask participants to state arguments for and against a policy proposal (see Zaller, 1992, p. 61). Further comments on measuring the consistency of opinion appear below.

(5) Deliberation may help to "create new selves and new interests" (Mansbridge, 1993, p. 96). Beyond accepting new arguments or forming new syntheses, people may adopt new social roles and identities: "organizer in the community," "environmentalist," "mediator between factions," "pro-life activist," "Perot supporter," "PTA leader," "born-again Christian," and so forth. These new roles often entail behavioral covenants, explicitly with others or tacitly with oneself (Mathews, 1994; Moscovici & Doise, 1994). Joint covenants, whether explicitly "political" or not, may greatly influence politics. Such covenants are much more likely to emerge in group settings than in deliberative polls. It is also possible that group settings encourage participants to set aside enemy stereotypes and apparent conflicts of interest (Warren, 1996, p. 255) – indeed, this result may be regarded as a possible danger (Amy, 1987). Group settings may encourage people to act more "public-spirited" than they do in other circumstances; like other effects we have discussed, this one can be seen as a distortion or a collateral benefit.

Procedurally, most deliberative studies attempt to emphasize common interests, although few if any attempt to instruct participants in the virtue of highmindedness. Most aspects of "new selves and new interests" go beyond my purposes in this essay, although it would be worthwhile to know how participation in various deliberative research may influence later political and social participation. Here I focus on a narrower issue: do participants' preferences tend to be polarized along lines of group identity, personal interest, or ideological commitment – and does deliberation alter the degree of polarization (that is, the difference in group means)? These questions do not lend themselves to a straightforward quality measure: while observers might hope that deliberation would help people to resolve their differences in interest, we can also hope that it should enable people to *recognize* differences of which they were unaware (Mansbridge, 1993). The research of Delli Carpini and Keeter (1996) and Althaus (1998) indicates that, for instance, the differences between politically knowledgeable "liberals" and "conservatives" on policy issues often is much greater than that between their less knowledgeable counterparts. Lindeman (2000), canvassing results from several deliberative studies, finds that demographic and ideological polarization is usually modest prior to deliberation, and that deliberation has no consistent or large effect on polarization. Further, transcripts of small-group studies often support the conclusion that participants are applying common-interest norms (although by no means are their differences in interest and belief obliterated).

One aspect of group covenants deserves special attention: groups, unlike isolated individuals, can bargain and compromise. Although individuals can make good-faith efforts to consider others' interests and values, they can hardly anticipate every aspect of other people's preferences. In this respect, Barber's earlier-quoted statement that polls tap "private prejudices" has some truth. A group discussion is very likely to alter participants' perceptions of what range of outcomes would be fairest and/or most satisfactory to others, and the preferences they express may converge in consequence. It might be concluded that surveys can never yield any useful knowledge of "collective preferences," if that phrase denotes the policy that would emerge from group deliberations. But this problem is somewhat contrived. If the "collective preferences" of the United States Congress are any clearer than those of the U.S. public, it is only because Congress follows certain procedures to enact those "preferences" in law, while no procedures exist to enact public preferences. That said, if we wonder how the policy preferences expressed by individuals in polls may differ from the preferences that emerge from group processes, we may as well find out.

MEASURING CONSISTENCY IN POLITICAL OPINIONS

Some studies employ factor-based or correlational measures of internal opinion consistency. An early and important study in this genre, Stimson (1975), found that political "experts" had more organized opinions than novices, in the sense that one or two statistical factors accounted for a greater proportion of the variance in their opinions. Whereas Stimson conducted an exploratory factor analysis on practically every issue question in the 1972 National Election Study, later studies have posited scales a priori. Gastil's (1994) analysis of National Issues Forums uses correlational measures to operationalize "conceptual complexity" (a concept closely related to the earlier-cited concept of integrative complexity). Gastil groups conceptually related issue items into scales; he uses correlations between items within each of his scales as a measure of "schematic coherence," and correlations between the scales as measures of "schematic integration" or "schematic differentiation," depending on whether the expected correlation is positive or negative. More elaborate hierarchical models, in which specific policy positions derive from prior attitudes, beliefs, and values at multiple levels of generality (e.g. Hurwitz & Peffley, 1987), have rarely been applied in deliberative research.

Luskin (1987) has cogently described common pitfalls of efforts to transmute statistical correlations into measures of sophistication. Among their weaknesses, most such measures are collective, not individual; the analyses generally give no indication of how many people are responding at some given level of presumed sophistication. Because the measures typically are sensitive to changes in the questions asked and the response categories provided, they cannot be compared across studies. Moreover, in the absence of a comprehensive theory of right political thinking, we have no *logical* basis for saying what degree of correlation evinces collective (or individual) "sophistication" – as opposed to monomania. While we recognize that liberal beliefs tend to "go together" (Converse, 1964), most observers would be more appalled than impressed if a respondent managed to give "the liberal answer" on every single question in a survey.

Despite these caveats, correlational approaches can be compelling when used judiciously. An excellent example is Delli Carpini and Keeter's (1996) demonstration that issue positions better predict vote choices among people with high levels of political knowledge than among less knowledgeable respondents. Rational choice theory offers a simple rationale for treating this predictive power as a quality measure. Correlational measures built on explicit rationality arguments have some face validity as *collective* measures of considered judgment. Moreover, they may lend themselves to individual measures: for instance, scores based on outright contradictions in expressed opinion (as alluded to above), or whether an individual's responses to "narrow" policy issues can be used accurately to predict her position on a broader issue (as in Neijens, 1987, described below).

An under-utilized approach to measuring opinion quality *qua* consistency involves the strength of prestige and other framing effects. An example from an Americans Talk Issues deliberative telephone poll illustrates a prestige effect: a zero-toxic-discharge standard received 15 percentage points more support when it was said to be "recommended by environmental groups like Greenpeace and the National Wildlife Federation" (ATIF, 1992a, p. Q20), even after, by survey standards, an unusually long (84-word) exposotion of the arguments for and against the standard. A pair of 1997 polls on balanced budget amendments (Rosenbaum, 1997) illustrates a very subtle framing effect. A *New York Times*/CBS News survey in January 1997 asked, "Do you think requiring the Federal Government to balance the budget is the kind of issue you would like to change the Constitution for, or isn't balancing the budget that kind of issue?" 39% responded that it was that kind of issue, and 49% that it was not. A survey conducted by CBS News two weeks later asked, "Would you favor or oppose a balanced budget amendment to the Constitution that would require the Federal Government to balance its budget by the year 2002?" With this phrasing 76% said they would favor it, against only 17% opposed. Except for the mention of the year 2002, there is no tangible policy difference between the two questions, and no major event between the surveys can explain the seeming contradiction. Apparently, in responding to the first question, people focused on the seriousness of changing the Constitution; in responding to the second, people focused on the desirability of a balanced budget. High-quality opinion should be relatively unsusceptible to these prestige and framing effects, and this criterion can be readily tested in many deliberative polling formats.

QUALITY MEASURES: AN EXEMPLARY – AND CAUTIONARY – CASE STUDY

Neijens (1987) presents some of the best quality measures and experimental controls. In effect, the choice questionnaire designed by Neijens and colleagues during Holland's General Social Debate tested whether people's stated policy preferences were consonant with their stated expectations about the consequences of each policy – whether they appeared to act as utility-maximizers. The task was, in brief, to choose three out of six options for meeting energy demands (including conservation), as listed in Table 1 below. In the Choice Questionnaire, participants assigned point values to various possible advantages or disadvantages of each energy option, rating the importance of each as an advantage or disadvantage. Then they chose their three favored options (as reported in the "Choice Questionnaire" column of Table 1). A control group participated in a conventional public opinion survey in which they chose three energy sources (as reported in the "Control survey" column of Table 1). They then were given an information book on the consequences. In a subsequent reinterview, the control group assigned ratings to the consequences, just as the experimental group had, and then was asked again to choose their three favored sources (the "Control reinterview" results in Table 1). In each case, Neijens defined respondents' choices as consistent if they selected the three options to which they had given the highest ratings. Neijens reports:

> The quality of the choices in the public opinion survey was not very good. Only 37% of the respondents made a consistent choice, i.e. the majority of the respondents made a choice that does not agree with their own judgement [in the reinterview] of the consequences of the options. The quality of the choices made in the Choices Questionnaire is significantly better: 68% of the respondents made. . . a consistent choice (Neijens, 1987, 161).

Table 1. Policy preferences in the General Social Debate study. Percentage of respondents citing each option among their top three choices.

(see discussion in the text)

Option	Control survey	Control reinterview	Choice Questionnaire
Natural gas	77%	76%	75%
Oil	26%	17%	15%
Conservation	69%	81%	85%
Coal	29%	21%	15%
Nuclear power	12%	18%	19%
Wind energy	87%	88%	92%

Unlike many studies, this approach presents an explicit and theoretically defensible definition of quality in terms of consistency, although scholars uncomfortable with the concept of utility maximization of course will not be satisfied. It also offers some measure of individual respondents' rationality, as well as collective performance. The obvious limitation of this approach is that we cannot directly measure how rational people's assessments of consequences are.

A further useful quality test in Neijens (1987) is the examination of possible halo effects – i.e. tendencies to rate favored policies highly in every area, disregarding risks and tradeoffs. Neijens argues that correlations among judgments on each issue should be low: for instance, while most respondents might regard a particular energy source as both cheaper and cleaner than other sources, a respondent who rates the source as especially cheap should be no more likely to consider it especially clean. Neijens concludes that in fact such "halo effects" are generally weak in the Choice Questionnaire results.

Neijens says little about the policy substance of his research's results. The basic finding (see Table 1 for details) is that although some of the differences among these results would generally be considered substantively significant (and are statistically significant), the same three options are favored across the board. If the policy preferences themselves were our sole measure of "deliberation effects," we might conclude that deliberation made very little difference. A fairer conclusion seems to be that respondents' "considered judgments" in the aggregate reasonably resemble typical measures of uninformed opinion. Unless we have some compelling a priori grounds for saying that summary policy preferences *should change*, we cannot use aggregate changes in preference as a criterion of considered judgment or effective deliberation. (Regrettably, many discussions of the 1996 National Issues Convention have neglected this point.)

TAPPING THE POWER OF MULTIPLE METHODS

For the purposes of cumulating knowledge, deliberative research works best when multiple studies are conducted on a single theme. Here I briefly consider two case studies: health care reform, and environmental regulation.

Health Care Reform

Why was no health care reform enacted in 1994? Some analysts argue that public support for reform – for universal coverage in particular – "evaporated into thin air" when people confronted the costs (Yankelovich, 1996, p. 3; see also Yankelovich, 1994; Blendon, 1994; Brodie & Blendon, 1995). Other analysts, drawing on similar survey evidence, sharply disagree (Skocpol, 1996; Shapiro, Jacobs & Harvey, 1995). Many scholarly analyses have hinged on a single NES battery in which respondents placed themselves and key political actors on a seven-point scale, with a "government insurance plan" at one extreme, and "paid by individuals, and through private insurance" at the other. Although this measure provides more "interpretable variance" than the isolationism questions discussed earlier, the policy substance is similarly ambiguous. While informed respondents tended to place President Clinton near the "government insurance" end of the spectrum (and themselves near the middle), in fact the Clinton plan relied heavily on private insurance. We might conclude that these respondents were misinformed, or that they were trying to make the best of a bad scale. At any rate, we cannot infer much about their views on universal coverage.

Lindeman (1997) closely examines two deliberative studies of public health care preferences from the fall of 1993 – a Public Agenda study conducted in 13 cities around the country, and a national Citizens Jury of 24 citizens gathered in Washington, D.C. Here I synopsize the results: the American people in general apparently really did want universal health coverage.

In the Public Agenda study (Immerwahr & Johnson, 1994), as in every study I have seen, a large majority of respondents expressed support for the goal of universal coverage. But the Public Agenda participants did more than that. In both the preliminary and the final survey, about two thirds of respondents supported an employer mandate with government subsidies to small businesses – even after weighing projections of the jobs to be lost under such a mandate. Even larger majorities supported stiff taxes on cigarettes and alcohol in order to expand insurance coverage; the cigarette tax (an additional $1 per pack) was supported even by a plurality of smokers. It is unclear what greater evidence of "real" support could fairly be demanded.

In the Citizens Jury, something surprising happened – after four days of testimony on the pros and cons of the Clinton and Republican reform plans, jurors tentatively voted for Paul Wellstone's single-payer proposal. The lead Republican advocate, former representative Vin Weber, had argued: "The single payer proposal is an overt replacement of the existing system with a totally governmental system. . . . I believe in essence what the Clinton administration has proposed to us is as close as they could possibly get to a total governmental takeover of the health system." Having heard Wellstone's brief initial testimony, jurors invited him to testify twice more. At the end, at least 16 of the 24 indicated that they favored Wellstone's proposal; a total takeover of the *insurance* system sounded pretty good to them. However, jurors declined to recommend the Wellstone plan or any other plan formally. Instead, they voted *against* the Clinton plan, and unanimously voted that Congress should provide for universal, comprehensive coverage with "reasonable but limited access to medical technology." Certainly we cannot conclude from these results that single-payer was the considered preference of Americans at large – especially since a modest plurality of Public Agenda participants opposed it. Still, the results dramatically infirm arguments that public support for universal coverage evaporated at the mention of disadvantages.

In the Public Agenda study, possible advantages and disadvantages of single-payer were presented schematically; no reference was made to other countries. In the Citizens Jury, Paul Wellstone argued that single-payer had worked in Canada and other countries, while Vin Weber argued that health care costs had undermined other countries' economic performance. Wellstone evidently got the best of the debate, perhaps in part because jurors found him personally charming (this is clear from the transcripts), and because Weber's primary mandate was to refute Clinton, not Wellstone.

The detailed pre/post survey design of the Public Agenda study allows us to make some judgments about quality, although not to measure consistency as Neijens did. Following Gastil's (1994) example, many of the questions on the survey can be grouped into logically related scales. Correlations within each scale (as summarized by Cronbach's alpha) typically increased from pretest to posttest; correlations between logically related scales increased in magnitude, while correlations between logically unrelated scales did not change appreciably. Thus we can say that respondents as a group at least moved in the direction of recognizing connections between similar issues – while retaining the ability to differentiate among distinct issues.

The study also evoked some encouraging – but fragmentary – evidence about increases in requisite knowledge. Participants were asked whether the federal government spent more on "health care for older Americans" or "humanitarian aid to other countries." This was a tricky question, because neither figure was supplied in the discussion – and, as mentioned earlier, Americans notoriously overestimate the scope of humanitarian aid. Nonetheless, by the posttest, 44% correctly concluded that spending on health care for older Americans was greater, compared to just 16% in the pretest. A few other knowledge questions also showed improvement. However, the study was not well-designed for the purpose of evaluating whether, overall, respondents knew "enough" to form considered judgments.

Because the Public Agenda study was conducted in 13 cities, it provides some evidence about the strength of unpredictable group effects (Tindale, 1996). Broadly speaking, intergroup variations were statistically significant for many of the more controversial issues, but do not fundamentally alter the interpretation of collective preferences (see Lindeman, 1997 for details). Obviously this result does not imply that group effects are never very important – the Citizens Jury might be a counterexample – but it should temper some observers' suspicions that the results of small-group research are inherently ungeneralizable.

In the Citizens Jury study, we are largely limited to impressionistic evaluations of quality. After reading transcripts of the entire study, I believe that the quality of discussion was fairly high: jurors took their roles seriously and canvassed the likely consequences of various policies thoughtfully. Thus, while I am unable to assess individual jurors, I provisionally conclude that the quality of the jurors' unanimous conclusions is high.

However, Ned Crosby (1994) raises two specific, related concerns about the quality of the jurors' reasoning: that participants did not sufficiently appreciate the immensity of health care spending, and that in their eagerness to resist "rationing" health care, they did not recognize how hugely expensive it would be to offer unlimited experimental care to everyone who wanted it. In the latter case, the transcript does at least imply that many participants never came to terms with the logical implications of their views. (Note that the jurors' recommendations do *not* call for "unlimited experimental care." Crosby's concern is based on jurors' reactions to a hypothetical discussion about rationing early in the project.) To deny even very expensive and speculative, but potentially life-saving, medical care strikes many people as murderous. Yet in other contexts, people are not so reluctant to oppose much smaller and probably more effective investments. As Margolis (1996, p. 154) pungently argues in a different context, "A visitor from Mars, watching what we do, could only conclude that we do not mind trading off dollars for lives, we just do not want to be pushed into noticing it." I am unconvinced that this resistance to trading off lives affected the policy conclusions of the jurors, but the question is open.

Notice that these studies differ in at least three salient respects: the depth of the arguments, the amount of time given to consider them, and the manner presented (neutral moderator vs. advocates). These differences are not all intrinsic to the models. A follow-up study might emulate the Public Agenda model but focus on single-payer arguments in greater detail. Another study, in the Citizens Jury vein, might emphasize the testimony of neutral-by-role experts. Other studies might focus on the apparent irrationality of people's resistance to rationing. As these examples suggest, exploring the substance of public preferences on health care entails a rich and diverse research agenda. However, and crucially, the common view that disparages public support for health care reform receives so little support in these studies that no amount of methodological refinement seems likely to reverse the result.

CAFE Standards and Environmental Policy

One of the most criticized, but least examined, aspects of American public opinion is the putative American love affair with gas-guzzling cars. Undeniably cheap gasoline and low population densities have encouraged U.S. consumers to own larger cars and drive them more often than people in other similarly prosperous countries. Does this automotive passion allow any scope whatsoever for effective environmental regulation? Apparently it does. In the 1990 debate over the renewal of the Clean Air Act, the limited survey evidence indicated that large majorities of the public favored new CAFE standards that would require new cars to average 40 miles per gallon (mpg) by the year 2000. For instance, a 1990 poll for the Union of Concerned Scientists found that 75% of respondents would support a 40-mpg standard even if they "knew that a new car would cost the buyer $500 more" (Fried, 1997, p. 211). Fried describes how opponents of the new standards selectively mobilized the public, possibly misleading members of Congress as to the true distribution of public opinion. What members "really thought" about public opinion is somewhat beside the point. Certainly, if major pundits felt that Congress had thwarted the public will, they kept this conviction to themselves. After all, one or two poll results do not demonstrate a "mandate." Public opinion surveys obviously cannot provide reliable information on policy preferences if they provide almost *no* information on policy preferences.

Several deliberative studies replicate the finding of strong public support for strict CAFE standards. In a Public Agenda study on the greenhouse effect, 75% of participants supported a 40 mile per gallon standard for new cars by the year 2000, and 59% endorsed a 50 mpg standard, although warned (somewhat dubiously) that this would "sharply increase the price of new cars and decrease the performance of full-size cars and station wagons" (Doble & Johnson, 1990, pp. 27, 39). In a 1991 Americans Talk Issues Foundation deliberative poll, after considering five arguments for "doing something about automobile fuel economy" and four arguments against, again, 75% of respondents endorsed raising the standard to 40 mpg (ATIF, 1992b). Jointly, while these studies do not offer strong opinion quality measures, they do suggest that public support for higher CAFE standards circa 1990 was robust against counterarguments.

Superficially, these findings on CAFE standards seem to contradict other studies that show public resistance to even modest increases in gasoline and energy taxes. As Lindeman (2000) argues in detail, the resolution of this discrepancy lies in two directions.

First, public opposition to energy taxes is often overstated. Apart from the turned up only fifteen survey questions, between 1989 and mid-1998, on support for increases in gasoline or energy taxes with an environmental purpose more specific than energy conservation. Seven of these showed majority support for the tax increase, six showed majority opposition, and two had no majority position. Thus, in this case among others, "conventional" survey results tend not to support conventional wisdom about public preferences.

Second, closer questioning in these studies, as well as the small-scale survey and depth-interview research of Kempton et al. (1995, pp. 139–153), indicates that people make a reasoned distinction between tax increases and regulatory technology-forcing standards. Most respondents regard energy tax increases as regressive and ineffective in reducing consumption. Technology forcing is widely perceived as less regressive (since more affluent people are more likely to buy new cars), more desirable (trading money for convenience), and more efficient in reducing pollution than tax increases. In fact, many environmentalists come to similar conclusions (e.g. Hawken et al., 1999). Although public environmental reasoning is open to criticism – for instance, many people seem mistakenly convinced that greenhouse gases can somehow be filtered out of automotive exhausts – it is far "greener" than many observers realize.

Similarly, in the political debate on the Kyoto Protocol to reduce global greenhouse emissions, public preferences seem to be widely misunderstood or simply disregarded. Large public majorities in conventional and deliberative surveys (for instance, an unpublished 1998 Mellman/World Wildlife Fund study; Kay, 1998, pp. 137–145, 313–321; Krosnick et al., 2000) express apparently thoughtful support for the Kyoto Protocol and other stringent international environmental policies, consistent with the depth-interview results of Kempton et al. and Gundersen (1995). Some observers argue, quite speciously, that the popularity of sport utility vehicles (SUVs) implies public opposition to stringent regulation. Even if we were to suppose that most Americans owned SUVs (and were aware of their environmental impacts), it is unreasonable to treat small-scale individual actions as a touchstone of support for large-scale collective actions. (Imagine someone arguing circa 1980 that public support for a U.S. defense buildup was illusory because people were not spontaneously sending contributions to the Pentagon.) I suggest that most political commentators, rather than treat the disparity between public preferences and actual policy on these environmental issues as a puzzle or even a datum, either disregard public preferences or mentally "adjust" them to be more consistent with policy outcomes. Such mental adjustments appear common, as witness the myths of Ronald Reagan's popularity (King & Schudson, 1995) and public "new isolationism" (Kull & Destler, 1999).

CONCLUSIONS

Both these case studies assert strong public support for policy initiatives rejected by Congress. This outcome may not be unusual. Alan Kay (1998, p. 2) bluntly concludes that "people rightly perceive that the government is not doing what most citizens want" on a wide range of domestic and foreign policy issues. To be sure, skepticism is always warranted in weighing claims about the substance and quality of public preferences. I argue that as much as possible, and increasingly, such arguments should be engaged in deliberative frameworks. People should not be exhorted to greater civic-mindedness, in the hope that somehow their virtue will improve the working of the American system. Instead, they should be invited into rich policy discussions of many kinds at every opportunity. Public opinion researchers can pursue this agenda in many different ways, if we will risk being troubled by the results.

Variegated deliberative research could increase our ability to distinguish between core beliefs that are relatively insusceptible to change, and narrower opinions (or "non-opinions") that are more malleable. It may yield clearer knowledge of defects, as well as virtues, in ordinary people's political reasoning. It may shed light on the sources and trajectories of mass political debates. It may sharpen our thinking about the extent (or the meaning) of "democratic responsiveness" in American politics (cf. Jacobs & Shapiro, 2000). It could even provide guidance to policymakers who accept the normative or pragmatic desirability of "starting with the people" (Yankelovich & Harman, 1988), and to others who feel the urgency of continually reinventing democratic institutions. Even if the content of informed public opinion on major issues might be "merely of benefit to future historians" (Neijens, 1987, p. 14), it is of natural interest to public opinion researchers.

ACKNOWLEDGMENTS

Bob Shapiro, Leonie Huddy, Michael Delli Carpini, and Jill Edy offered extensive comments on precursors of this essay. Steve Farkas and the Public Agenda Foundation generously provided data from the health care study discussed herein. Ned Crosby and Alan Kay also provided access to their data and archives, as well as hospitality and thoughtful discussion of their research methods. Correspondence with John Gastil, Ted Becker, Heather Hurlburt, Jamil Shahin, and Martin Gilens has sharpened portions of my arguments. The remaining errors, fallacies and non sequiturs are solely my responsibility.

REFERENCES

Althaus, S. L. (1998). Information effects in collective preferences. *American Political Science Review, 92*, 545–558.

Amy, D. J. (1987). *The Politics of Environmental Mediation.* New York: Columbia University Press.

ATIF (Americans Talk Issues Foundation) (1992a). Survey No. 19: PIP-E II: The Economy, Energy, Security and the Environment. Washington and St. Augustine: Americans Talk Issues Foundation.

ATIF (Americans Talk Issues Foundation) (1992b). Survey No. 20: PIP-E III: The Economy, Energy, Security and the Environment. Washington and St. Augustine: Americans Talk Issues Foundation.

Barber, B. R. (1993). Reductionist Political Science and Democracy. In: G. E. Marcus & R. L. Hanson (Eds), *Reconsidering the Democratic Public* (pp. 65–72). University Park, PA: Penn State University Press.

Bartels, L. M. (1996). Uninformed Votes: Information Effects in Presidential Elections. *American Journal of Political Science, 40*, 194–230.

Blendon, R. (1994). The Gridlock Is Us. *New York Times*, May 22, p. E15.

Bohman, J. (1996). *Public Deliberation: Pluralism, Complexity, and Democracy.* Cambridge, MA: MIT Press.

Brodie, M., & Blendon, R. J. (1995). The Public's Contribution to Congressional Gridlock on Health Care Reform. *Journal of Health Politics, Policy and Law, 20*, 403–410.

Converse, P. E. (1964). The nature of belief systems in mass publics. In: D. E. Apter (Ed.), *Ideology and Discontent* (pp. 206–261). New York: Free Press.

Converse, P. E. (1980). Comment: Rejoinder to Judd and Milburn. *American Sociological Review, 45*, 644–646.

Conway, L., Suedfeld, P., & Tetlock, P. E. (1999). Integrative complexity and political decisions that lead to war or peace. In: R. Wagner & D. Christie (Eds), *Handbook of Peace Psychology.* Hillsdale, NJ: Earlbaum.

Crespi, I. (1989). *Public Opinion, Polls, and Democracy.* Boulder: Westview Press.

Crosby, N. (1994). Toward Major Uses of the Citizen Jury Process. Unpublished manuscript. Minneapolis: Jefferson Center for New Democratic Processes.

Crosby, N. (1995). Citizens Juries: One Solution for Difficult Environmental Questions. In: O. Renn, T. Webler & P. Wiedemann (Eds), *Fairness and Competence in Citizen Participation: Evaluating Models for Environmental Discourse* (pp. 157–174). Dordrecht and Boston: Kluwer Academic Publishers.

Crosby, N. (1996). Creating an Authentic Voice of the People. Prepared for presentation at the annual meeting of the Midwest Political Science Association, April 18–20, Chicago.

Dahl, R. (1985). *Controlling Nuclear Weapons: Demsocracy Versus Guardianship.* Syracuse, NY: Syracuse University Press.

Delli Carpini, M. X., & Keeter, S. (1996). *What Americans Know About Politics and Why It Matters.* New Haven: Yale University Press.

Doble, J. (1988). *U.S.-Soviet Relations in the Year 2010: Americans Look to the Future.* New York and Providence: Public Agenda Foundation and Center for Foreign Policy Development.

Doble, J., & Johnson, J. (1990). *Science and the Public: A Report in Three Volumes. Volume I: Searching for Common Ground on Issues Related to Science and Technology.* New York: Public Agenda Foundation.

Dryzek, J. (1991). *Discursive Democracy.* Cambridge: Cambridge University Press.

Erikson, R. S., MacKuen, M. B., & Stimson, J. A. (2001). *The Macro Polity.* Cambridge: Cambridge University Press.

Fishkin, J. S. (1994). Ideal citizens give a considered judgement. *The Independent*, (9 May), p. 8.

Fishkin, J. S. (1997). *The Voice of the People: Public Opinion and Democracy.* Revised edition. New Haven: Yale University Press.

Freedman, P. (1996). Framing the Abortion Debate. Paper presented at the annual meeting of the Midwest Political Science Association, Chicago, April 18–20.

Fried, A. (1997). *Muffled Echoes: Oliver North and the Politics of Public Opinion.* New York: Columbia University Press.

Gallup, G., & Rae, S. F. (1940). *The Pulse of Democracy: The Public-Opinion Poll and How It Works.* New York: Simon and Schuster.

Gamson, W. A. (1992). *Talking Politics.* New York and Cambridge: Cambridge University Press.

Gastil, J. (1994). *Democratic Citizenship and the National Issues Forums.* Unpublished doctoral dissertation, University of Wisconsin at Madison.

Goot, M. (1998). Australia's "Stolen Children": Which Poll Would a Poll-following Prime Minister Have Followed?" *International Journal of Public Opinion Research, 10*, 349–364.

Gundersen, A. G. (1995). *The Environmental Promise of Democratic Deliberation.* Madison: University of Wisconsin Press.

Habermas, J. (1985). *Reason and the Rationalization of Society*, Vol. 1 of *The Theory of Communicative Action.* T. McCarthy (Trans.). Boston: Beacon Press.

Harwood Group (1993). *Meaningful Chaos: How People Form Relationships with Public Concerns.* Dayton, OH: Kettering Foundation.

Hawken, P., Lovins, A., & Lovins, L. H. (1999). *Natural Capitalism: Creating the Next Industrial Revolution.* Boston: Little, Brown and Company.

Herbst, S. (1995). On the Disappearance of Groups: 19th- and Early 20th-Century Conceptions of Public Opinion. In: T. L. Glasser & C. T. Salmon (Eds), *Public Opinion and the Communication of Consent* (pp. 89–104). New York: Guilford Press.

Hochschild, J. L. (1993). Disjunction and Ambivalence in Citizens' Political Outlooks. In: G. E. Marcus & R. L. Hanson (Eds), *Reconsidering the Democratic Public* (pp. 187–210). University Park, PA: Penn State University Press.

Hurwitz, J., & Peffley, M. (1987). How Are Foreign Policy Attitudes Structured? A Hierarchical Model. *American Political Science Review, 81*, 1099–1120.

Immerwahr, J., & Johnson, J. (1994). *Second Opinions: Americans' Changing Views on Healthcare Reform.* New York: Public Agenda Foundation.

Inglehart, R. (1990). *Culture Shift in Advanced Industrial Society.* Princeton: Princeton University Press.

Iyengar, S., & Kinder, D. R. (1987). *News That Matters: Television and American Opinion.* Chicago: University of Chicago Press.

Jacobs, L. R., & Shapiro, R. Y. (2000). *Politicians Don't Pander: Political Manipulation and the Loss of Democratic Responsiveness.* Chicago: University of Chicago Press.

Jervis, R. (1976). *Perception and Misperception in International Politics.* Princeton, NJ: Princeton University Press.

Jones, B. D. (1994). *Reconceiving Decision Making in Democratic Politics: Attention, Choice, and Public Policy.* Chicago: University of Chicago Press.

Kay, A. F. (1998). *Locating Consensus for Democracy: A Ten-Year U.S. Experiment.* St. Augustine, Florida: Americans Talk Issues Foundation.

Kempton, W., Boster, J. S., & Hartley, J. A. (1995). *Environmental Values in American Culture.* Cambridge, MA: MIT Press.

Kinder, D. R., & Sanders, L. M. (1990). Mimicking Political Debate with Survey Questions: The Case of White Opinion on Affirmative Action for Blacks. *Social Cognition, 8*, 73–103.

King, E., & Schudson, M. (1995). The Press and the Illusion of Public Opinion: The Strange Case of Ronald Reagan's "Popularity." In: T. L. Glasser & C. T. Salmon (Eds), *Public Opinion and the Communication of Consent* (pp. 132–155). New York: Guilford Press.

Krosnick, J. A., Holbrook, A. L., & Visser, P. S. (2000). The impact of the Fall 1997 debate about global warming on American public opinion. *Public Understanding of Science, 9*, 239–260.

Kuklinski, J. H., Quirk, P. J., Schwieder, D., & Rich, R. F. (1996a). Misinformation and Public Opinion. Prepared for presentation at the annual meeting of the Midwest Political Science Association, April 18–20, Chicago.

Kuklinski, J. H., Quirk, P. J., Schwieder, D., & Rich, R. F. (1996b). Two Democratic Norms Meet Some Empirical Evidence. Prepared for presentation at the annual meeting of the American Political Science Association, San Francisco.

Kull, S., & Destler, I. M. (1999). *Misreading the Public: The Myth of a New Isolationism.* Washington, D.C.: Brookings Institution.

Lindeman, M. (1997). Public Preferences in Health Care: Evidence from Deliberative Studies. Prepared for presentation at the annual meeting of the Midwest Political Science Association, April 10–12, Chicago.

Lindeman, M. (2000). *Considered Judgment and Democratic Deliberation.* Unpublished doctoral dissertation, Department of Political Science, Columbia University.

Lippmann, W. (1925). *The Phantom Public.* New York: Harcourt Brace Publications.

Lodge, M. (1995). Toward a Procedural Model of Candidate Evaluation. In: M. Lodge & K. M. McGraw (Eds), *Political Judgment: Structure and Process* (pp. 111–139). Ann Arbor: University of Michigan Press.

Luskin, R. C. (1987). Measuring Political Sophistication. *American Journal of Political Science, 31*, 856–899.

Mansbridge, J. (1993). Self-Interest and Political Transformation. In: G. E. Marcus & R. L. Hanson (Eds), *Reconsidering the Democratic Public* (pp. 91–109). University Park, PA: Pennsylvania State University Press.

Margolis, H. (1996). *Dealing with Risk: Why the Public and the Experts Disagree on Environmental Issues.* Chicago: Chicago: University of Chicago Press.

Mathews, D. (1994). *Politics for People: Finding a Responsible Public Voice.* Urbana and Chicago: University of Illinois Press.

Mondak, J. J. (1993). Cognitive Heuristics, Heuristic Processing, and Efficiency in Political Decision Making. In: M. Delli Carpini, L. Huddy & R. Shapiro (Eds), *Research in Micropolitics* (Vol. 4, pp. 117–142). Greenwhich, CT: JAI Press.

Monroe, A. D. (1998). Public Opinion and Public Policy, 1980–1993. *Public Opinion Quarterly, 62*, 6–28.

Morris, D. (1998). *Behind the Oval Office: Getting Reelected Against All Odds.* Second edition. Los Angeles: Renaissance Books.

Moscovici, S., & Doise, W. (1994). *Conflict and Consensus: A General Theory of Collective Decisions.* W. D. Halls (Trans.). London & Thousand Oaks, CA: Sage Publications.

Neijens, P. (1987). *The Choice Questionnaire: Design and evaluation of an instrument for collecting informed opinions of a population.* Amsterdam: Free University Press.

Neuman, W. R. (1986). *The Paradox of Mass Politics: Knowledge and Opinion in the American Electorate.* Cambridge, MA: Harvard University Press.

Page, B. I. (1996). *Who Deliberates?: Mass Media in Modern Democracy.* Chicago: University of Chicago Press.

Page, B. I., & Shapiro, R. Y. (1983). Effects of Public Opinion on Policy. *American Political Science Review, 77*, 175–190.

Page, B. I., & Shapiro, R. Y. (1992). *The Rational Public: Fifty Years of Trends in Americans' Policy Preferences*. Chicago: University of Chicago Press.

Price, V., & Neijens, P. (1998). Deliberative Polls: Toward Improved Measures of "Informed" Public Opinion? *International Journal of Public Opinion Research, 10*, 145–176.

Renn, O., Webler, T., & Wiedemann, P. (1995). *Fairness and Competence in Citizen Participation: Evaluating Models for Environmental Discourse*. Dordrecht and Boston: Kluwer Academic Publishers.

Rose, R. (1989). *Ordinary People in Public Policy: A Behavioural Analysis*. London and Newbury Park: Sage Publications.

Rosenbaum, D. E. (1997). Deficit: Public Enemy No. 1, It's Not. *New York Times*, February 16, Section 4, pp. 1, 3.

Schattschneider, E. E. (1960/1975). *The Semisovereign People: A Realist's View of Democracy in America*. Hinsdale, IL: Dryden Press.

Shapiro, R. Y., Jacobs, L. R., & Harvey, L. K. (1995). Influences on Public Opinion Toward Health Care Policy. Prepared for presentation at the annual meeting of the Midwest Political Science Association, Chicago.

Skocpol, T. (1996). *Boomerang: Clinton's Health Security Effort and the Turn against Government in U.S. Politics*. New York: W. W. Norton & Company.

Slaton, C. D. (1992). *Televote: Expanding Citizen Participation in the Quantum Age*. New York: Praeger Publishers.

Stimson, J. A. (1975). Belief Systems: Constraint, Complexity, and the 1972 Election. *American Journal of Political Science, 19*, 393–417.

Stimson, J. A., MacKuen, M. B., & Erikson, R. S. (1995). Dynamic Representation. *American Political Science Review, 89*, 543–565.

Suedfeld, P., Tetlock, P. E., & Streufert, S. (1992). Conceptual/integrative complexity. In: C. Smith (Ed.), *Handbook of Thematic Content Analysis* (pp. 393–401). New York: Cambridge University Press.

Tindale, R. S. (1996). Groups are Unpredictably Transformed by Their Internal Dynamics. *The Public Perspective, 7*(1), 16–18.

Toner, R. (2000). The Right to Click. *New York Times Book Review*, February 27th, 7.

Warren, M. E. (1996). What Should We Expect From More Democracy?: Radically Democratic Responses to Politics. *Political Theory, 24*, 241–270.

World Wildlife Fund (1998). Global Warming Action Now: WWF's Public Opinion Poll. Unpublished report.

Yankelovich, D. (1991). *Coming to Public Judgment: Making Democracy Work in a Complex World*. Syracuse, NY: Syracuse University Press.

Yankelovich, D. (1994). What Polls Say – and What They Mean. *New York Times*, September 17, 23.

Yankelovich, D. (1996). A New Direction for Survey Research. *International Journal of Public Opinion Research, 8*, 1–9.

Yankelovich, D., & Harman, S. (1988). *Starting with the People*. New York: Houghton Mifflin.

Zaller, J. R. (1992). *The Nature and Origins of Mass Opinion*. Cambridge and New York: Cambridge University Press.

PART 3:
POLITICAL PARTICIPATION

CITIZENSHIP AND CIVIC ENGAGEMENT IN PUBLIC PROBLEM-SOLVING

Beth Haney, Eugene Borgida and James Farr

Political theorists and social scientists have long been interested in the significance and importance of civic participation. Active community engagement and participation have been hypothesized to have personal as well as community benefits (Boyte & Kari, 1996; Pateman, 1970; Thompson, 1970). Political activists report a variety of gratifications they receive from their work, including material gains such as career advancement, social gains such as the company they enjoy, civic gains such as fulfilling a sense of duty, and collective outcomes such as the opportunity to influence government policy (Verba, Schlozman & Brady, 1995). Other forms of civic engagement, like volunteering, have been found to be related to additional psychological functions and needs such as providing individuals with a way to express their values or to learn more about a particular social issue (e.g. Clary, Snyder, Ridge, Copeland, Stukas, Haugen & Miene, 1998; Omoto & Snyder, 2002). Further, volunteer activity has been associated with an increase in self-esteem (Yates & Youniss, 1996a) and with improved personal health outcomes (e.g. Andrews, 1990). With respect to community advantages, researchers have argued that the efficiency of a local government and the economic development of an area may be strongly influenced by the active engagement of the local citizenry in community affairs (Fukuyama, 1995; Putnam, 1993). In addition, as Putnam (1995a) has noted, researchers in fields as varied as health, education, urban poverty, and criminology have all concluded that communities benefit from an active citizenry.

Political Decision Making, Deliberation and Participation, Volume 6, pages 225–252.
Copyright © 2002 by Elsevier Science Ltd.
All rights of reproduction in any form reserved.
ISBN: 0-7623-0227-5

The many benefits of civic engagement have not been lost on those outside of academia. Structured efforts aimed at stimulating active citizen engagement in community affairs and public problem-solving have recently been initiated around the country, both within school settings (Rutter & Newman, 1989; Yates & Youniss, 1997) and outside of these more traditional citizenship education environments. Many of the programs have arisen independently and predominantly in response to local needs. Yet, there also has been a concerted nationwide effort to encourage citizens to become more involved in their communities. For example, in 1993, federal legislation created The Corporation for National Service, an organization dedicated to funding and supervising community efforts to engage the citizenry in local affairs. One of the Corporation's initiatives, AmeriCorps, has enrolled over 250,000 young people to get involved in hundreds of programs around the country since 1994. The 1997 President's Summit for America's Future, an event co-hosted by President Clinton and each of his living predecessors, celebrated the role of citizen engagement in both the public and private spheres of our society.

A common theme among each of the aforementioned programs and events is one of active involvement by citizens and a common goal of encouraging citizens to continue their involvement in their communities. As such, it is important to determine how much we know about the psychological processes through which individuals who get involved in civic opportunities are influenced and to understand the extent to which these processes can actually stimulate more civic participation by those individuals. The purpose of the current essay is to provide a selective and multidisciplinary review of research that addresses such questions. We begin by reviewing several past and current perspectives on citizenship and civic engagement. Next, we take a political psychological approach, introducing individual-level assumptions we believe are being made by participatory programs and reviewing research applicable to each assumption. In this context, we also discuss relevant findings from our own research that assesses the effects of an ongoing civic participation program.

PAST APPROACHES AND REVITALIZATION

The "return of the citizen" (Kymlicka & Norman, 1994) has been hailed in the literature of recent political theory. Spurred on by disheartening reports of voter apathy and assaults on the welfare state in the West to the world-historic revolutions in Eastern Europe and the former Soviet Union, political theorists are bearing witness to one of those "intermittent revivals" (Walzer, 1989, p. 211) of interest in citizenship that can be traced back through the French and American Revolutions to classical antiquity. We are being reminded that citizenship expresses the ancient aspiration of the members of political societies to participate meaningfully in the legislation or execution of the laws to which they must obey, as well as to enjoy securely the rights and privileges that protect their lives, liberty, and property. As such, historians of political thought have undertaken in-depth studies of the classical theorists of citizenship, especially Aristotle, Cicero, Machiavelli, and Rousseau. Likewise, communitarian critics of liberalism (Sullivan, 1986) have revived the ideology of "classical republicanism" (Ignatieff, 1995; Pocock, 1995; Skinner, 1992), calling for greater attention to civic virtue, public participation, or the good that is not already entailed by liberalism's own commitments to citizenship. A call for a "citizen politics" has accompanied the revival of the ideals of "the commonwealth" (Boyte, 1989), and feminists have disputed whether or not citizenship is connected to "mothering" or maternal practices (compare Dietz, 1985; Elshtain, 1981). Doubts have been raised, especially by cultural pluralists and theorists of identity (Young, 1990; Phillips, 1993; Benhabib, 1996), whether one can speak any longer, if ever one could, of a unitary culture of citizenship, given the great and abiding differences of individuals and groups in "civil society" (Walzer, 1995), and thus, some have argued that "multicultural citizenship" (Kymlicka, 1995), may be the only coherent conception of citizenship available for multi-nation states or for a trans-national world. This "explosion of interest in the concept of citizenship" by political theorists (Kymlicka & Norman, 1994, p. 352) shows no sign of abating any time soon, despite or perhaps because of the real distance that exists between the ideals and the realities of effective citizen participation in modern politics.

Political theorists, of course, are not unique in espying the return of the citizen. In fact, a renewed interest in the theory and practice of citizenship is shared widely by social scientists more generally and is the focus of several current debates in a variety of literatures.

The Social Capital Debate

One of the most recent ways of thinking about citizenship and civic participation is represented in the theory of *social capital*. Social capital, a concept originally developed by Coleman (1990), but most recently advanced by Putnam (e.g. 1995a, 2000) and others (e.g. see Mondak, 1998), refers to "features of social life – networks, norms, and trust – that enable participants to act together more effectively to pursue shared objectives" (Putnam, 1995b, pp. 664–665). The defining features of social capital include the amount of civic participation within a community and the relationship between participation and the amount of trust citizens have for one another. However, the significance of social capital is its purported influence on the surrounding community. For example, Putnam (1993) concludes from his twenty-year study of the history and government of the regional districts of Italy that a high amount of social capital within a community is positively associated with the efficiency of the local bureaucracy and with the economic development of the region. The implication is that communities at large benefit from high levels of social capital (cf. Berman, 1997).

Alternative empirical research examining some of the issues of social capital has employed an individual-level analysis and has offered insight about the relationships between the key social capital features and other relevant constructs. In an analysis of the General Social Survey (1972–1994), Brehm and Rahn (1997) found that individuals' confidence in government and its institutions is influenced by both the amount of the individuals' civic engagement and their trust in their fellow citizens. The researchers found a negative relationship between participation and confidence in government, but a positive relationship between interpersonal trust and confidence in government. Importantly, the latter relationship is much stronger than the former. Brehm and Rahn concluded that the relationship between social capital and attitudes toward the government is complicated.

Many critiques of the theory of social capital have appeared in the literature (e.g. Edwards & Foley, 1997; Jackman & Miller, 1996; Levi, 1996), but one of the most vigorous debates focuses on whether levels of social capital within American society have decreased recently. Putnam (1995a) argued that these levels have steadily declined over the past three decades and he supports the claim with statistics revealing decreased voter turnout; decreased involvement in community affairs; decreased attendance at religious services; and decreased membership in organizations as diverse as labor unions, the PTA, the League of Women Voters, the Red Cross, fraternal organizations, and bowling leagues. Finally, Putnam (1995b) noted that social trust, or trust in "most" other people, has decreased by approximately one third since 1972. His conclusion was that the prospects do not look good for America, given the importance of social capital in relation to the health of communities.

In response to the statistics presented by Putnam, the Roper Center (1996) gathered alternative statistics that indicate that the amount of civic engagement in America in fact has not decreased. Rather, membership in the PTA has been influenced by the number of school-aged children, and membership in the PTA by parents with children in the appropriate age-bracket has actually increased by 28% since 1982. Further, data reveal that although voter turnout has decreased recently, citizen activism in other forms of civic participation has not. Citizens were just as likely to report attending a political meeting or rally in 1987 as they were in 1967 (Verba, Schlozman & Brady, 1995). The Independent Sector, a coalition of charitable, educational, religious, health and social welfare organizations committed to strengthening democracy, found (1999) that 56% of Americans reported volunteering within the last year. Such data are inconsistent with Putnam's conclusions about America's declining social capital.

Related critiques contend that the types of civic engagement may be changing (Schudson, 1996; Skocpol, 1996). For example, Lemann (1996) argued that while enrollment in Little League baseball may be down, enrollment in youth soccer leagues has increased from 127,000 twenty years ago to 1.2 million ten years ago to 2.4 million more recently. Further, critics note that Putnam's data do not take into account the various grassroots political movements that have occurred within the last three decades (e.g. the civil rights movement, the feminist movement, the Christian Right movement, various militia movements), which, they argue, required some sort of active citizen participation (Minkoff, 1997; Schudson, 1996; Valelly, 1996).

Both sides of this debate have marshalled statistical evidence to support their reasoning, and thus the conclusions to be drawn are indeed debatable. However, the demonstrable changes in people's attitudes and beliefs are less disputable. As Putnam (1995b) noted, levels of interpersonal trust have declined – 54% of Americans agreed that most people can be trusted in 1964, while only 35% agreed that most people can be trusted in 1995 (Morin & Balz, 1996). Approximately 53% of college freshmen thought "keeping up-to-date with politics" was important in 1970, but only 29% held this belief in 1995 (American Council on Education and the Higher Education Research Institute at UCLA, 1996). Levels of citizens' political efficacy may be down too. According to NES data, in 1960, 73% of Americans disagreed with the statement, "People like me don't have a say in what the government does," but only 55% disagreed in 1988 (Rosenstone & Hanson, 1993). Thus, the purported decline in social capital may be valid, if in no other way than in the weakening of the beliefs and attitudes that represent America's social capital.

What is Missing from the Debate?

Of course, such debates are necessarily limited and thus cannot address the full range of issues associated with active citizen involvement in community affairs. For example, there has yet to be a concerted effort to comprehend the processes through which civic involvement can be stimulated and maintained. In our opinion, given the aforementioned importance of civic engagement for communities and individuals alike, understanding these processes is paramount, regardless of whether current levels of civic engagement are low in comparison to those of twenty years ago or not. Others concur (e.g. Youniss, McClellan & Yates, 1997), yet neither Putnam nor his critics sufficiently address how the goal of greater engagement may be realized. Putnam (1996) indicated that "public policy will be part of the answer" (p. 28), but he failed to explicate the kind of public policy he had in mind. He also implied that citizens themselves need to be part of the solution, but again, he failed to explain how. Importantly, understanding the processes through which levels of participation are positively influenced would help elucidate how policy makers, practitioners, and citizens themselves should proceed.

Researchers have historically turned to the role of education when thinking about such processes (see Ehman, 1980; and Ferguson, 1991 for reviews). And, to be fair, Putnam (1995b) examined the influence of education, along with a litany of other factors (e.g. economic hard times, suburbanization, the movement of women into the workforce, television), claiming that we must first ascertain the causes of the decline in social capital if we are to address it. In fact, Putnam concluded that education has a dramatic influence on civic engagement. Yet, after pointing out that educational levels have increased at the same time as civic engagement supposedly has decreased, and that the decline has occurred within every educational stratum, he essentially retreated from a focus on the potential of educational efforts. Moreover, his references to "civic education" per se are extremely rare and vague. In his analysis of his study of social capital in Italy, Putnam mentioned that important social norms are taught and maintained through socialization processes, "including civic education" (1993, p. 171), but the precise nature of these processes was not further developed.

Additional investigations of factors influencing civic and political participation echo the importance of formal education (e.g. Beck & Jennings, 1982; Brehm & Rahn, 1997; Milbrath & Goel, 1977; Nie, Junn & Stehlik-Barry, 1996; Rosenstone & Hanson, 1993; Verba & Nie, 1972; Wolfinger & Rosenstone, 1980). For example, Verba, Schlozman and Brady (1995) first divided the factors affecting participation into three broad categories – resources, psychological motivations, and institutional recruitment – and then presented an extensive analysis of the influence of education on each of these factors. They concluded that education has both a strong direct effect on participation as well as multiple indirect effects through its influence on income, opportunities to gain and develop necessary civic skills, political interest and knowledge, and increasing institutional involvement.

That education has consistently appeared as having such a strong influence on participation may lead one to assume that education is the simple answer to the question of how to encourage more involvement. However, as mentioned earlier, Putnam (1995b) noted that increases in education have paralleled decreases in civic engagement. In addition, the task of increasing educational levels may not necessarily be so simple, as years of educational reform demonstrate. Finally, simply arguing that we should improve citizens' education does not provide advice as to how these reforms should be made, or what specific effects they may have.

Perhaps a more efficacious strategy for understanding the processes through which greater civic engagement can be achieved is one that focuses on the role of specific interventions designed to encourage participation and/or to actively engage citizens in public problem-solving. As previously noted, many such participatory endeavors exist; not only can one consider conventional civics' classes, extracurricular activities, and school-sponsored community service programs, but also alternative efforts aimed at initiating and maintaining an active citizen movement. For example, programs like Boston's City Year provide opportunities and resources for diverse groups of young adults to work together to improve surrounding communities by building parks, renovating housing, organizing community clean-ups, or various other tasks. Public Allies, in Washington D.C., recruits individuals from under-privileged neighborhoods and teaches them organizational and leadership skills. Similar, but more established, programs include VISTA and the Jesuit Volunteer Corps.

However, for the most part, the primary goals of these programs are practical and concentrated on making a difference in the community, rather than on citizenship education and/or members' development. Evaluations of such programs usually focus on the effects on the community or on the recipients of the work, rather than on the participants themselves (cf. Gray, Ondaatje, Geschwind, Robyn & Klein, 1996).[1] Consequently, these evaluations fail to demonstrate how (and often whether) the programs influence their participants' orientations toward civic involvement and how the programs induce their participants to continue to participate in community affairs. Nonetheless, one might hypothesize that getting involved in these programs' efforts would have a favorable and prosocial effect on the participants. One approach to the analysis of such efforts is to examine various potentially relevant psychological assumptions associated with the effects on participants. We discuss this approach in the next section by drawing on different disciplinary bodies of empirical research.

A POLITICAL PSYCHOLOGY PERSPECTIVE ON CIVIC PARTICIPATION

From our perspective, by presuming that individuals' civic engagement has a positive effect on their future engagement, one implicitly makes assumptions about how the engagement influences important psychological constructs (i.e. beliefs and attitudes) and about how those constructs may be related to subsequent behaviors. Specifically, four assumptions that link individuals' involvement with their understandings of citizenship and their "civic selves" and that in turn connect these psychological constructs to the individuals' future involvement can be identified. Those assumptions are as follows:

- Individuals have conceptualizations of what it means to be a "citizen," or a member of a community. These conceptualizations can be linked to action, and an understanding of political efficacy may be implicit in them.
- It is possible to influence individuals' citizenship conceptualizations as well as the beliefs associated with those understandings. An effective means of accomplishing this may be to provide individuals with concrete opportunities to engage in public problem-solving activities.
- It is also possible that, by engaging in civic action, individuals alter their "civic selves," or their social identities as members of their communities.
- Ultimately, citizenship conceptualizations and a civic self may be linked to actual behavior in the form of civic engagement, which includes both political and non-political participation in the community.

In the remainder of this essay, we discuss each of the above assumptions, drawing upon theory and research from various disciplines (including political science, education, developmental psychology, and social psychology), to examine more closely the linkage between psychological processes and civic participation.

Citizenship Conceptualizations

Although much of the research on citizenship and participation differentiates classifications of citizenship based on political theory (see Ichilov, 1990), there is also research examining how citizens themselves understand the concept of a "citizen," especially that of a "good citizen." For example, some of the classical work in political science (e.g. Jennings & Niemi, 1974, 1981; Lane, 1965) attempted to document the role citizens think they and others should play within their own communities. Classic research also revealed that the orientations of individuals' citizenship conceptualizations can be active (e.g. political participation and assisting in community problem-solving) and/or passive (e.g. having rights and obeying laws) (Almond & Verba, 1963).

Recent research on individuals' citizenship conceptualizations and civic identities (Conover, 1995; Conover, Crewe & Searing, 1991, 1993; Conover, Leonard & Searing, 1993) continues to examine the active and passive dimensions within these understandings and suggests that cultural differences may exist (see also Ichilov & Nave, 1981). There also appears to be much variation within the American culture in terms of how involved individuals think citizens should be in politics and community affairs. For example, there may be normative, developmental changes in individuals' citizenship conceptualizations. In their study of children's political attitudes and beliefs, Hess and Torney (1967) found that young children (7–9 years old) are likely to understand a "good citizen" as equivalent to a "good person" (e.g. someone who helps others and obeys the laws), but that by their early teens, children are more likely to incorporate political participation into their conceptions of a "good citizen." Jennings and Niemi (1974) also found that 60% of a sample of high school seniors indicated that good citizens vote and/or pay attention to politics (see Shantz, 1972, as well). A more recent study conducted by Peter D. Hart Associates for People For the American Way (1989), however, revealed that only 12% of 15 to 24 year olds include voting and/or being involved in politics in their definition of a good citizen.[2]

In addition to normative differences in citizenship conceptualizations, individual differences may exist among American adults too. Using Q-sort methodology, Theiss-Morse (1993) found four distinct conceptualizations of the participatory responsibilities of citizens. The first of these, the *Representative Democracy*, represents a perspective advocating that citizen involvement be limited to voting and staying informed. The *Political Enthusiast* perspective submits that politics is pervasive and that citizens should use any and every means possible to get involved, while the *Pursued Interests* perspective is endorsed by individuals who think that informed citizens alone should be involved in the political process and that they should do this by supporting the activity of special interests groups. Finally, the *Indifferent* perspective agrees that citizens should vote and be informed, yet individuals who endorse this perspective are likely to feel some alienation from and apathy toward the political system. Thus, citizenship conceptualizations not only differ in terms of how active a citizen is expected to be in political affairs, but also in terms of which activities citizens are expected to perform.

Our first assumption also states that an understanding of political efficacy may be implicit in the conceptualizations citizens hold. As demonstrated in the Theiss-Morse (1993) research, people who endorse an Indifferent conceptualization are not as likely to believe that citizens have the power to effect real political change as are those who endorse a Political Enthusiast perspective. The concept of political efficacy, including both the belief that citizens have the ability to engage in political activities and the belief that those actions will actually be influential, has a long history within the study of political psychology and participation (e.g. Almond & Verba, 1963; Campbell, Converse, Miller & Stokes, 1960; Jennings & Niemi, 1974, 1981; Milbrath & Goel, 1977; Rosenstone & Hanson, 1993; Verba & Nie, 1972; Verba, Schlozman & Brady, 1995). In general, those with a greater sense of political efficacy are more likely to be involved in political and civic activities and thus should be more likely to endorse citizenship conceptualizations with participatory expectations.

In sum, the literature supports the assumption that individuals hold specific understandings of the role citizens should play in political and social affairs. Further, these conceptualizations can be examined in terms of several dimensions, including the degree to which people think citizens should be actively involved in addressing community affairs and the degree of efficacy citizens have in the political system. We now turn to an examination of whether such conceptualizations have been shown to be mutable.

Changing Citizenship Conceptualizations

The second assumption we identified asserts that it may be possible to influence individuals' citizenship conceptualizations as well as the beliefs associated with those understandings. Further, it states that an effective means of accomplishing this change may be to provide individuals with concrete opportunities to engage in public problem-solving activities. If we think of citizenship conceptualizations as schemas, or cognitive structures that embody the duties and rights of citizenship, then there is some empirical basis for believing that these conceptualizations can be influenced by interventions involving problem-solving and/or participation. Torney-Purta (1989, 1990) advocates thinking about political constructs in this way. For example, she found that after participating in the decision making of an international crisis simulation, adolescents are likely to develop more complex schemas of how the political and economic systems can address foreign policy (Torney-Purta, 1992). Leighley (1991) demonstrated that people who engage in campaign activities and problem-solving at a national level (e.g. by contacting a public official), acquire more abstract and developed understandings of the political system as assessed by their "political conceptualizations," a measure similar to political sophistication (Luskin, 1987) and political knowledge (Delli Carpini & Keeter, 1996). Research by Avery and colleagues (e.g. Avery, Bird, Johnstone, Sullivan & Thalhammer, 1992) has shown that exposure to a political tolerance curriculum that engages students in role-playing and simulations may result in more complex and abstract understandings of issues surrounding civil liberties. Likewise, a focus on civic participation and the role citizens can play in community problem solving may influence individuals' citizenship conceptualizations, especially if those individuals are given the opportunity to be involved in the decision making themselves.

However, in their reviews of research examining the influence of civics curricula on students' attitudes, beliefs, and behaviors, both Ehman (1980) and Ferguson (1991) conclude that traditional American civics and government courses do *not* appear to have a significant impact on political attitudes and beliefs, including how politically active students think citizens should be. Other findings suggest that the effects of school and civics curricula on political attitudes toward government are positive, but rather small and weak effects (Niemi & Junn, 1998, see Table 6.5). Perhaps this should not be surprising, as numerous researchers have concluded that traditional social science texts, courses, and teachers offer a very narrow and limited view of the citizen's role in society and the political system (e.g. Ichilov, 1990; Oliner, 1983; cf. Anderson, Avery, Smith & Sullivan, 1997). Nonetheless, other aspects of the schooling experience (i.e. participation in school government and/or other extracurricular activities, a non-traditional classroom climate and/or school culture) are often related to political beliefs and attitudes in positive ways (Ferguson, 1991; Niemi & Junn, 1998; Patrick & Hoge, 1991). For example, students who participated in a comprehensive student government program allowing for a great deal of student self-governance demonstrate greater gains in their knowledge about citizen duties than students who participated in a more traditional student government program (Borg, 1966). Similarly, Dillon and Grout (1976) found that students in open-classrooms (i.e. environments in which students help design the classroom structure) are less likely to feel politically alienated, although other researchers have not found significant effects for classroom climate (see Ehman, 1980).

It is also possible to examine how participation and involvement in community decision making apart from formal schooling and curricula, but within the political arena or within other structured environments, influences citizenship conceptualizations. For example, Hamilton and Fenzel (1988) found that adolescents who had participated in community service programs developed a greater understanding of the rest of society's responsibility to help those in need, especially if the youth were involved in projects that required greater responsibility and autonomy from adults (see Conrad & Hedin, 1982; Newmann & Rutter, 1983; Yates & Youniss, 1998 as well). In their panel study, Jennings and Niemi (1981) found that college graduates who had been involved with political protests were more likely than those who had not protested to emphasize active political involvement and to de-emphasize the passive, obedient role when describing a good citizen. Finkel (1985) demonstrated that voting and campaign activity may have positive effects on individuals' sense of external political efficacy, or the degree to which they believe that their actions will affect government policy and actions. In comparing employees in a democratic work environment to those in more traditional, authoritative work environments, Elden (1981) found that participation in workplace decision making may also have a positive influence on political efficacy.

Thus, there is support in the literature for the claim that participating in public problem solving, whether in the school, political arena, or workplace, may alter how citizens understand their responsibilities and abilities within the community. However, it should be noted that although some of the relevant studies are experimental research endeavors, many of them are correlational in nature. Thus, it is possible that many of the findings reflect a self-selection bias such that individuals who are already more participation-oriented than others are more likely to become involved in the "interventions" reviewed. In addition, there is some evidence that some of the curricula and participation opportunities may have a greater influence on individuals of some segments of society (i.e. the less advantaged; Finkel, 1985; Jennings, Langton & Niemi, 1974) more than others (see also Jones, 1974; Litt, 1963). Such differential effects should be important to consider when thinking about the influence of civic participation on individuals' conceptualizations of who citizens are and what they should do. The next section reviews research suggesting that individuals' civic identities, or their conceptualizations of themselves, may also be influenced by their active participation in the community.

The Emergence of Civic Selves

Our third assumption focuses on an additional potential intra-personal consequence of civic engagement; it maintains that by engaging in civic action, individuals may alter their "civic selves," or their social identities of themselves as members of their communities. Current psychological theory on the self acknowledges that there are many different dimensions of the self and that these dimensions can be found within individuals' self-schemas, or the cognitive representations individuals hold about who they are (Baumeister, 1998; Linville & Carlston, 1994; Markus, 1977). Self-schemas are believed to be primarily a result of past experiences and thus to represent previous aspects of the self, although they can also portray dimensions of the self that individuals want to realize in the future (Markus & Nurius, 1986).

Several different lines of research focus on individuals' *civic* selves, or on their self-schemas as members of communities and/or as civic beings. For example, Conover and Searing (Conover, 1995; Conover, Crewe & Searing, 1991, 1993; Conover, Leonard & Searing, 1993) found that individuals present unique depictions of themselves and their rights and responsibilities in relation to the community and that such self-understandings are, in part, culturally determined. Other researchers specifically focus on the self-concepts of individuals who have participated extensively in community involvement. For example, Hart and Fegley (1995; Hart, Yates, Fegley & Wilson, 1995) studied the self-schemas of "care exemplars," a group of adolescents who had exhibited an unusual amount of commitment to their surrounding social environments. According to the findings, such adolescents, as compared to a matched sample of adolescents who were not involved in community service, are more likely to attribute moral and caring personality traits to themselves. The researchers also found that there is greater congruency between the care exemplars' ideal selves (the kind of persons the adolescents would like to be) and their actual selves (the kind of persons the adolescents think they actually are), and that there is more continuity between care exemplars' past, present, and future selves. They concluded that the care exemplars differ from the matched sample predominantly in the way in which they incorporate moral dimensions into their self-concepts (see Teske, 1997). Importantly, these moral dimensions are usually civically oriented.

As psychological theory on the self (Bem, 1972; Linville & Carlston, 1994) would suggest, research demonstrates that participation in civic efforts may alter individuals' civic selves (cf. Finkel, 1985). First, individuals who participate in community affairs view themselves as having changed as a result of their civic involvement (Fendrich, 1993; Hamilton & Fenzel, 1988; McAdam, 1988). Further, studies that compare individuals' identities before and after participation opportunities also reveal increases in the degree to which those individuals include civically-oriented aspects in their self-understandings (e.g. Conrad & Hedin, 1982; Giles & Eyler, 1994; Newmann & Rutter, 1983). A recent study of university students participating in community affairs as part of their academic learning (Gray et al., 1996) found that participation positively influenced how committed students felt they were to serving the community and to engaging in community action programs. Similar findings emerged for the influence of participation on individuals' beliefs about their own leadership abilities and about their own understandings of community and national problems. Finally, within their emerging line of research, Yates and Youniss (Yates, 1998; Yates & Youniss, 1996a, b, 1997, 1998) have studied the effect of a mandatory service program on high school juniors' identity formation. They have found that after participating in the program, students are more likely to identify themselves in relation to others in society and/or in relation to their own role in effecting societal change. In sum, there is reason to believe that civic engagement may change individuals' self-schemas such that a "civic self" may begin to emerge and become more prominent in how people think about themselves.

Ideally, individuals who participate in civic efforts will be motivated to continue their engagement in community affairs long after their participation in any one program or experience is over (Fendrich & Lovoy, 1988; Flanagan et al., 1998; Hanks & Eckland, 1978; Hart, Atkins, & Ford, 1998; McAdam, 1989; Rosenthal et al., 1998; Yates & Youniss, 1998). The significance of self-schemas, then, is that they are assumed to be powerful determinants of future behavior (Cantor, Markus, Niedenthal & Nurius, 1986; Markus & Nurius, 1986). That is, it is believed that if individuals hold strong images of themselves as civic beings, then they will be more likely to behave in ways that are in line with this image (Hart, Yates, Fegley & Wilson, 1995). Thus, those with more well-defined civic selves should be more likely to actually engage, and to stay engaged, in civic behaviors. In the next section, we examine research relevant to the relationships between individuals' psychological constructs and their civic behaviors.

The Links Between Psychological Constructs and Behavior

Our fourth assumption states that citizenship conceptualizations and civic selves may be linked to actual behavior in the form of civic engagement, and that this engagement may include political and non-political participation, or prosocial behavior. Again, there is empirical research to support this linkage. For example, a recent study by Cole and Stewart (1996) revealed that there may be a positive relationship between having a strong sense of social responsibility, as assessed by one's sense of community and one's sense of personal political efficacy, and engaging in a wide range of political behaviors (see Funk, 1998 as well). Moreover, this relationship appears to be independent of one's sense of political identity. As noted earlier, Finkel (1985) provided evidence that participating in campaign activities and voting positively influence one's sense of external political efficacy, but he also demonstrated that this relationship is reciprocal, such that increases in external political efficacy result in a greater likelihood of engaging in these political behaviors. Other research indicates that the relationship between citizenship conceptualizations and political behavior may differ depending on the type of political behavior being considered. Rosenstone and Hanson (1993) found that stronger feelings of civic duty had a small impact on whether one voted, but no real influence on whether one worked on a political campaign, donated money to a political campaign, or tried to influence how another would vote. Interestingly, Theiss-Morse (1993) found a direct association between the type of citizenship conceptualization individuals endorsed and the type of political behavior in which they engaged. That is, citizens who endorsed a citizenship perspective that emphasized voting as the most important political behavior were indeed more likely to vote, whereas those who endorsed perspectives that were either indifferent to politics or that advocated alternative political behaviors were less likely to vote. Of the people who endorsed one of these latter two perspectives, those who were indifferent to politics were also less likely to engage in unconventional political behaviors such as joining in a protest or refusing to obey an unjust law. Yet those who advocated political behaviors other than voting were more likely to engage in these unconventional political behaviors. Such findings lend support to the idea that if it is possible to modify individuals' cognitions and attitudes about what being a citizen means, then it may also be possible to influence their civic behaviors.

A similar relationship is believed to exist between how individuals think of themselves as civic beings and their civic participation (Youniss, McClelland & Yates, 1997). As discussed earlier, there is psychological evidence that our self-schemas serve as important mediators of our behaviors (Cantor, Markus, Niedenthal & Nurius, 1986; Markus & Nurius, 1986). For example, well-defined self-schemas appear to guide individuals toward specific roles or social situations in which they are more likely to be able to verify those self-schemas (Niedenthal, Cantor & Kihlstrom, 1985; Setterlund & Niedenthal, 1993; Swann, 1983). Therefore, it may be that individuals with well-defined civic selves prefer social situations in which they have a greater opportunity to engage in civic affairs, thereby making such behaviors all the more likely. Other research provides more direct evidence that the extent to which individuals endorse positive social attributes or specific self-concepts positively influences the extent to which they will engage in a prosocial behavior related to those social attributes or self-concepts (e.g. Brown & Smart, 1991; Gorassini & Olson, 1995). In fact, Cole & Stewart (1996) found that one's political identity may be positively related to the number of political behaviors, both formal and informal, in which one engages. Finally, qualitative evidence documents that individuals who have a clear sense of themselves in relation to their community and society are more likely to be actively involved in the affairs of the community and society (e.g. Colby & Damon, 1995; Hart & Fegley, 1995; McAdam, 1988). Thus, it seems likely that if a participatory program is able to instill a well-defined civic self in its participants, it will also be able to affect the likelihood that those individuals will continue their civic engagement.

In sum, there is sufficient evidence to support each of the four hypotheses we identified as implicit in efforts aimed at influencing citizens' future civic behaviors by first encouraging them to engage actively in current civic affairs and discussions. In this context, we now present findings from our own research on a specific civic engagement program that generally pertain to the first three of these four hypotheses.

Involvement in Public Achievement: A Case Study

Public Achievement, designed by the Center for Democracy and Citizenship at the University of Minnesota's Hubert H. Humphrey Institute of Public Affairs in conjunction with the University's Political Science Department, is a youth and politics initiative that stresses active civic engagement for middle and high school students along with college undergraduates in selective schools in Minneapolis-St. Paul, Kansas City, Milwaukee, and elsewhere.[3] The program's primary goal is to encourage the younger students to get more involved in civic affairs by identifying problems in and around their schools and communities, and then working in small groups throughout the academic year to try to solve or clarify those problems. For example, students may try to initiate a curriculum to address sexual harassment in the hallway, plant trees in their neighborhoods, change their school uniform policy, raise money for new playground equipment, develop a plan to get after-school jobs, or organize a peace march at the state capitol building. *Public Achievement's* civic philosophy is one of public works. That is, by engaging in public problem-solving in the most immediate surroundings, citizens of all ages can begin to master the civic skills needed to continue their political involvement and, potentially, to take their newly developed problem-solving skills to different or broader political contexts.

The structure of *Public Achievement* is designed to be flexible and loose, depending upon school structure and community institutions. Throughout most of the academic year, the middle and high school students meet for approximately one hour each week in groups dedicated to the problem they have identified. In these meetings, the students report advances in their work, plan future directions, and discuss the implications of their efforts (both for themselves and for the community at large). But there are no formal requirements or set structures regarding how each student group's experience will unfold. University of Minnesota and other undergraduates, as well as some teachers, parents, and the program's staff, act as "coaches" for the youth, introducing the key concepts and helping develop the civic skills. However, it is the younger students themselves who must take all of the necessary steps to implement their public problem-solving ideas, from discussing the sexual harassment policy with the school principal, to presenting a suggested new uniform policy to school board members, to surveying parents for support of a new playground, to soliciting neighbors for after-school jobs, to calling the police to coordinate a planned peace march. Again, the emphasis of *Public Achievement* is on actual involvement in (rather than just discussion about) political and social issues. Because of this, it represented an opportunity to examine empirically some of the general hypothesized effects of citizen involvement discussed earlier. Below we present an overview of the findings from this investigation.

Assessing the Effects of Public Achievement

After identifying the aforementioned implicit assumptions of this type of effort, Haney and Borgida (1997) were particularly interested in the effect of *Public Achievement* on students' conceptualizations of the role of students in the school community, on their sense of political efficacy, and on their own civic self-concepts.[4] Thus, during the 1994–1995 and 1995–1996 academic years, Haney and Borgida assessed the civic attitudes and beliefs of 4th–8th graders in three Twin Cities schools that sponsored the *Public Achievement* program. Specifically, they administered a brief questionnaire to students in their classrooms at three different points each year – prior to the start of *Public Achievement* (September/October), at a midpoint (March), and after the program had ended (May). Based on the program's goals and rationales, Haney and Borgida predicted that involvement in the experiential civics program would have a direct, positive impact on each of several key psychological constructs (i.e. a citizenship conceptualization about active participation, a civic self-concept of being problem-solvers, a civic self-concept of being able to work well with others).

To assess the influence of continued involvement, analyses were conducted using repeated measures analyses of variance on each of the psychological constructs across the survey administrations.

In two of the schools, *Public Achievement* was not offered to all students. Therefore, participation in the program could be used as a dichotomous between-subjects variable for the analyses within these schools.[5] However, the students who participated in the program in these schools were also not the same during the two years of the research. Therefore, separate analyses need to be conducted for the 94–95 academic year and the 95–96 academic year within these schools (see Table 1 for the sample sizes).

The few significant results obtained in these analyses displayed effects opposite to the predictions – students participating in the program were actually *less* likely to endorse some of the psychological constructs (i.e. the active participation citizenship conceptualization, the civic self-concept of being problem-solvers, and the civic self-concept of being able to work well with others) as the year progressed, and as compared to students not participating

Table 1. Sample Sizes for the Two Participating Schools

		Participating in *Public Achievement*	Not Participating in *Public Achievement*
School A	94–95	13	15
	95–96	21	27
School B	94–95	26	22
	95–96	17	27

in the program. By the end of the second year, however, participating students in one school endorsed the citizenship conceptualization about active participation as much as they had in the beginning of the year.

In the third school, all students were expected to participate in *Public Achievement* during both years of the research. Thus, a comparison group was not available in this school, but it was possible to identify forty-eight students who were involved in the program both years and completed the survey at each of the six administrations across the two years. This afforded Haney & Borgida (1997) the opportunity to examine whether the program's effects may emerge beyond one year. Again, they predicted that the effects of the program would be positive and cumulative over the two years. And again, the majority of the statistically significant effects revealed that students participating in *Public Achievement* were actually less likely to endorse some of the psychological constructs (i.e. political efficacy in their school, political efficacy in their neighborhoods, a civic self-concept of being community-oriented) as their involvement in the program progressed. Nonetheless, the general trend for a last significant effect revealed a very different pattern. That is, students participating in *Public Achievement* were less likely at the end of the first year to endorse a civic self-concept of being able to work well with others, but were significantly *more* likely to endorse this self-concept as the second year progressed.

In conclusion, the findings reported in Haney and Borgida (1997) are suggestive that participation effects may emerge over time. But, rather than having a positive influence on students' citizenship conceptualizations, efficacy, and civic selves, participation in *Public Achievement* may actually decrease the likelihood that students will endorse these beliefs and attitudes, as least in the short-term. It is important to remember that working together to solve common problems or address social issues is hard work, requiring cooperation and persistence in the face of possible failure. Therefore, it is possible that the student-citizens in this program were simply acknowledging the difficulties and rigors associated with civic problem-solving. However, the results from the third school also suggest that with time, and as students gain some additional experience with public problem-solving, they may begin to show improvements on some of the key psychological dimensions. Importantly, one of these long-term effects may include a positive influence on their perceptions of their ability to work well with others, an effect participatory theory would predict (Thompson, 1970) and other research has also documented (e.g. Rutter & Newmann, 1989).

There are several important methodological constraints, however, that limit the strength of inference and generalizability of findings from the Haney & Borgida (1997) study of the *Public Achievement* program to other community service or experiential learning programs. Participants in the study of *Public Achievement*, for example, were not randomly assigned to the program or to a control group and therefore self-selection biases may have influenced the pattern of results. Similarly, the format of *Public Achievement*, which was developed in the absence of any guiding research design or methodology, was set up such that students who participated in the program attended all other classes with students who did not attend the program; hence, to some unknown extent, students in the comparison groups may have been informally exposed to information presented in the treatment groups. While exposure to the *Public Achievement* curriculum was only approximately one hour per week for participating students, this possible "contamination" nevertheless could serve to undermine further the strength of an already minimal programmatic treatment.

While these kinds of methodological concerns constrain the strength and scope of claims that can be made about *Public Achievement*, the strength of (positive or negative) effects associated with community service and experiential learning programs that have been evaluated with stronger research designs also tend to be small and inconsistent (Hamilton & Fenzel, 1988). In fact, "while scholars and professionals affirm the value of adolescents engaging in responsible activities in their communities, evaluators have often found it difficult to document the developmental benefits of participation in community service or other forms of experiential learning" (Hamilton & Fenzel, 1988, p. 66). There are several factors that may account for this difficulty (Hamilton & Fenzel, 1988). The experiences of younger students (e.g. those of middle school age), in particular, would be expected to vary considerably in programs like *Public Achievement*. Second, there may also be notable variability within treatment conditions such that student participants selectively focus on aspects of the treatment program that may not be central to the evaluative criteria used to assess programmatic success. Third, more general and enduring changes in, for example, self-esteem, efficacy, or social responsibility are unlikely as a function of typically minimal and specific treatment approaches (like *Public Achievement*).

A fourth reason why effects associated with programs like *Public Achievement* may be difficult to assess involves the kind of quantitative and qualitative measures typically included in studies of program effects. It may be the case, for example, that the survey-based measures used to assess the program's effects are either too specific or too global for the program under investigation. Specific beliefs about and attitudes toward *Public Achievement*, for example, were not assessed by Haney & Borgida (1997) who instead included measures to gauge the broader impact of the program on a range of beliefs and attitudes pertaining to civic participation. As with other programs, qualitative as well as quantitative measures also should be incorporated into research designs to assess as many different aspects of the treatment approach as possible. Haney & Borgida (1997), for example, reported anecdotal findings about impressive student-initiated projects generated by participation in *Public Achievement* that were simply not captured by quantitative measurement; but a systematic qualitative assessment of the program was beyond the scope of the research project. Finally, it is also important to include measures of participants' baseline civic skills and political knowledge (e.g. Delli Carpini & Keeter, 1996). Lack of civic skills in youth and adults, for example, may account for the low level of participation in some programs (Patrick & Hoge, 1991). Knowing whether the parents of student participants themselves are involved in community service is also important to assess; students whose parents are so involved and/or emphasize a social responsibility ethic are more likely to intend to be and to be involved in community service (Fitch, 1987; Flanagan, Bowes, Jonsson, Csapo & Sheblanova, 1998; Hart et al., 1995; Rosenthal, Fiering & Lewis, 1998).

In summary, the assessment of programs like *Public Achievement* requires a comprehensive (i.e. qualitative and quantitative) measurement approach and a commitment to a longitudinal research design that will enable investigators to examine the long-term as well as the short-term effects of community service programs (Youniss, McClellan & Yates, 1997).

CONCLUSIONS

The focus of this essay has been an examination of the psychological processes that may characterize individuals who are civically engaged. We suggest that an understanding of the processes through which civic involvement can be stimulated and maintained is an important but neglected aspect of the social capital debate that has dominated and continues to influence the ways in which political theorists and political psychologists think about citizenship and civic participation (e.g. Mondak, 1998). If the level of social capital has indeed been declining, then an understanding of these individual-level processes can contribute to designing educational and experiential programs that may stimulate and maintain civic engagement over time. On the other hand, if, as some have suggested, social capital in the United States has *not* been a steep decline, then an understanding of these processes may be necessary for a more complete understanding of how civic engagement can be maintained and potentially enhanced over time. We have suggested in this essay, in other words, that assumptions about civic involvement and conceptions of citizenship and civic selves may play an important role *either* in reviving civic participation *or* in maintaining involvement.

The evidence that we marshaled to examine these assumptions is illustrative rather than exhaustive. Citizenship conceptualizations indeed seem to be held by individuals and seem to vary in terms of how active citizens are expected to be and how diverse an array of activities they are expected to engage in. What seems to be clear is that embedded within these citizenship expectations are participatory tendencies that, if targeted appropriately, could be influenced by persuasion-based approaches. There also seems to be some support for the assumptions that these conceptualizations are malleable which in turn suggests again that there is the potential for programs like *Public Achievement* and other service learning programs to affect the nature and perhaps even the stability of these intra-individual conceptualizations.

But the identification and assessment of such effects, as suggested by Hamilton & Fenzel (1988) and others, depends in part on the substantive nature of the programmatic "treatment" involved, in part on whether the hypothesized effects are examined short-term (albeit, post-treatment), and in part on the sophistication of the measurement approach incorporated into the research design used to examine the target program. Self-selection may be quite a threat to validity in studies of programs like *Public Achievement* in that more highly motivated participants, those who may already be more committed to civic participation and community service, may be more likely to maintain and extend civic engagement over time. Self-selection and other methodological artifacts, therefore, must be addressed in order to more rigorously assess the extent to which civic selves mediate civic engagement. Moreover, these research designs should be developed and in place at the inception of each program (and preferably implemented by independent researchers).

Finally, any serious consideration of civic engagement over time must begin to address the question of the effects on actual behaviors, which were not examined in the research reported in the previous section of the essay. To what extent does changing civic self-concepts or inducing a sense of civic self contribute to our understanding of the processes associated with sustained civic participation? More importantly, by asking such questions, political psychologists may play an important role in determining whether and the ways in which programs like *Public Achievement* can be effective in initiating, sustaining, and enhancing the quality of civic engagement over time. In turn, insights into these questions may also shed light on the extent to which programs that promote public problem-solving may ultimately build social capital.

NOTES

1. However, evaluations of the "service learning movement," a related movement aimed at incorporating civic participation into education curricula, have attempted to document the impact of involvement on students' academic performance (e.g. Markus, Howard & King, 1993).

2. Haney, Burgess, Rahn, Sullivan and Snyder (1996) argue that more recent generations of youth, as compared to earlier generations, are, and may have good reason to be, more pessimistic about their current social and political circumstances. The weak endorsement for political participation by the current generation of youth may be part of the broader trend of decreasing social capital discussed earlier.

3. More description and analysis of Public Achievement may be found in Farr (1997) and in Boyte and Farr (1997).

4. Because Public Achievement considers children's role of being students in a school as equivalent to adults' roles of being "citizens in a community," questions assessing students' citizenship conceptualizations were framed in terms of the role of students in the school.

5. Descriptive analyses revealed that students from these schools differed systematically along several dimensions, including age and socioeconomic status. Thus, analyses were run separately for each school. Further, it should be noted that there was an issue of non-independence in the observations (see Kenny & Judd, 1986), in that students participated in groups of approximately ten during their public problem-solving efforts. However, because of the small sample sizes in each school, Haney and Borgida needed to use the individual as the unit of analysis, rather than the students' problem-solving groups. The extremely small sample sizes within each school also prevented a break down of the data by gender, age, and prior participation in Public Achievement.

REFERENCES

Almond, G., & Verba, S. (1963). *The Civic Culture: Political Attitudes and Democracy in Five Nations*. Boston: Little Brown and Co.

Anderson, C., Avery, P. G., Smith, E. S., & Sullivan, J. L. (1997). Divergent perspectives on citizenship education: A Q-method study and survey of social studies teachers. *American Education Research Journal, 34*, 333–364.

Andrews, H. F. (1990). Helping and health: The relationship between volunteer activity and health-related outcomes. *Advances, 7*, 25–34.

Avery, P. G., Bird, K., Johnstone, S., Sullivan, J. L., & Thalhammer, K. (1992). Exploring political tolerance with adolescents. *Theory and Research in Social Education, 20*, 386–420.

Baumeister, R. F. (1998). The Self. In: D. Gilbert, S. T. Fiske & G. Lindzey (Eds), *The Handbook of Social Psychology* (4th ed., Vol. 1, pp. 680–740). New York: Mcgraw-Hill.

Beck, P. A., & Jennings, M. K. (1982). Pathways to participation. *American Political Science Review, 76*, 94–108.

Bem, D. J. (1972). Self-perception theory. In: L. Berkowitz (Ed.), *Advances in Experimental Social Psychology* (Vol 6, pp. 1–62). New York: Academic Press.

Benhabib, S. (Ed.) (1996). *Democracy and difference: Contesting the boundaries of the political.* Princeton: Princeton University Press.

Berman, S. (1997). Civil society and political institutionalization. *American Behavioral Scientist, 40*, 562–574.

Borg, W. R. (1966). Student government and citizenship education. *Elementary School Journal, 67*, 154–160.

Boyte, H. C. (1989). *CommonWealth: A return to citizen politics.* New York: Free Press.

Boyte, H. C., & Kari, N. N. (1996). *Building America: The democratic promise of public work.* Philadelphia: Temple University Press.

Boyte, H. C., & Farr, J. (1997). The work of citizenship and the problem of service-learning. In: R. Battistoni & W. Hudson (Eds), *Experiencing Citizenship: Concepts and Models for Service-learning in Political Science* (pp. 35–48). Washington, D.C.: American Association for Higher Education.

Brehm, J., & Rahn, W. (1997). Individual level evidence for the causes and consequences of social capital. *American Journal of Political Science, 41*, 999–1023.

Brown, J. D., & Smart, S. A. (1991). The self and social conduct: Linking self-representations to prosocial behavior. *Journal of Personality and Social Psychology, 60*, 368–375.

Campbell, A., Converse, P. E., Miller, W. E., & Stokes, D. E. (1960). *The American voter.* New York: John Wiley & Sons.

Cantor, N., Markus, H., Niedenthal, P., & Nurius, P. (1986). On motivation and the self-concept. In: R. M. Sorrentino & E. T. Higgins (Eds), *The Handbook of Motivation and Cognition: Foundations of Social Behavior* (pp. 96–121). New York: The Guilford Press.

Clary, E. G., Snyder, M., Ridge, R. D., Copeland, J., Stukas, A. A., Haugen, J., & Miene, P. (1998). Understanding and assessing the motivations of volunteers: A functional approach. *Journal of Personality and Social Psychology, 74*, 1516–1530.

Colby, A., & Damon, W. (1995). The development of extraordinary moral commitment. In: M. Killen & D. Hart (Eds), *Morality in Everyday Life: Developmental Perspectives* (pp. 342–370). Oxford: Cambridge University Press.

Cole, E. R., & Stewart, A. J. (1996). Meanings of political participation among black and white women: Political identity and social responsibility. *Journal of Personality and Social Psychology, 71*, 130–140.

Coleman, J. S. (1990). *Foundations of social theory.* Cambridge, MA: Harvard University Press.

Conover, P. J. (1995). Citizen identities and conceptions of the self. *The Journal of Political Philosophy, 3*, 133–165.

Conover, P. J., Crewe, I. M., & Searing, D. D. (1991). The nature of citizenship in the United States and Great Britain: Empirical comments on theoretical themes. *Journal of Politics, 53*, 800–832.

Conover, P. J., Crewe, I., & Searing, D. D. (1993). Citizen identities in the liberal state. Paper prepared for the Annual Meetings of the American Political Science Association, September, 1993.

Conover, P. J., Leonard, S. T., & Searing, D. D. (1993) Duty is a four-letter word: Democratic citizenship in the liberal polity. In: R. Hansen, G. Marcus & J. L. Sullivan (Eds), *Reconsidering the Democratic Public* (pp. 147–171). State College, PA: Pennsylvania State University.

Conrad, D., & Hedin, D. (1982). The impact of experiential education on adolescent development: Youth participation and experiential education. *Child and Youth Services, 4,* 57–76.

Delli Carpini, M., & Keeter, S. (1996). *What Americans know and why it matters.* New Haven, CT: Yale University Press.

Dietz, M. G. (1985). Citizenship with a feminist face: The problem with maternal thinking. *Political Theory, 13,* 19–35.

Dillon, S. V., & Grout, J. A. (1976). Schools and alienation. *Elementary School Journal, 76,* 481–489.

Edwards, B., & Foley, M. W. (Eds) (1997). Social capital, civil society, and contemporary democracy. *American Behavioral Scientist, 40.*

Ehman, L. H. (1980). The American school in the political socialization process. *Review of Educational Research, 50,* 99–119.

Elden, J. M. (1981). Political efficacy at work: The connection between more autonomous forms of workplace organization and a more participatory politics. *American Political Science Review, 75,* 43–58.

Elshtain, J. B. (1981). *Public man, private woman: Women in social and political thought.* Princeton: Princeton University Press.

Farr, J. (1997). Political theory. In: R. Battistoni & W. Hudson (Eds), *Experiencing Citizenship: Concepts and Models for Service-learning in Political Science* (pp. 99–108). Washington, D.C.: American Association for Higher Education.

Fendrich, J. M. (1993). *Ideal citizens.* Albany: SUNY Press.

Fendrich, J. M., & Lovoy, K. L. (1988). Back to the future: Adult political behavior of former student activists. *American Sociological Review, 53,* 780–784.

Ferguson, P. (1991). Impacts on social and political participation. In: J. P. Shaver (Ed.), *Handbook of Research on Social Studies Teaching and Learning* (pp. 385–399). NY: MacMillan Publishing Company.

Finkel, S. E. (1985). Reciprocal effects of participation and political efficacy: A panel analysis. *American Journal of Political Science, 29,* 891–913.

Fitch, R. T. (1987). Characteristics and motivations of college students volunteering for community service. *Journal of College Student Personnel, 28,* 424–431.

Flanagan, C. A., Bowes, J. M., Jonsson, B., Csapo, B., & Sheblanova, E. (1998). Ties that bind: Correlates of adolescents' civic commitments in seven countries. *Journal of Social Issues, 54,* 457–476.

Fukuyama, F. (1995). *Trust: The social virtues and the creation of prosperity.* New York: The Free Press.

Funk, C. L. (1998). Practicing what we preach? The influence of societal interest value on civic engagement. *Political Psychology, 19,* 601–614.

Giles Jr., D. E., & Eyler, J. (1994). The impact of a college community service laboratory on students' personal, social, and cognitive outcomes. *Journal of Adolescence, 17,* 327–339.

Gorassini, D. R., & Olson, J. M. (1995). Does self-perception change exaplin the foot-in-the-door effect? *Journal of Personality and Social Psychology, 69,* 91–105.

Gray, M. J., Ondaatje, E. H., Geschwind, S. A., Robyn, A. E., & Klein, S. P. (1996). *Summary of findings, learn and serve America, higher education.* Santa Monica, CA.: RAND Institute.

Hamilton, S. F., & Fenzel, L. M. (1988). The impact of volunteer experience on adolescent social development: Evidence of program effects. *Journal of Adolescent Research, 3,* 65–80.

Haney, B., & Borgida, E. (1997). Public Achievement: A longitudinal study of a public problem-solving program. Unpublished data, University of Minnesota.

Haney, B., Burgess, D., Rahn, W., Snyder, M., & Sullivan, J. L. (1996). *A selected review of trends and influences of civic participation*. Report prepared for The Pew Charitable Trusts and Rock the Vote.

Hanks, M., & Eckland, B. K. (1978). Adult voluntary associations and adolescent socialization. *The Sociological Quarterly, 19*, 481–490.

Hart, D., Atkins, R., & Ford, D. (1998). Urban America as a context for the development of moral identity in adolescence. *Journal of Social Issues, 54*, 513–530.

Hart, D., & Fegley, S. (1995). Prosocial behavior and caring in adolescence: Relations to self-understanding and social judgment. *Child Development, 66*, 1346–1359.

Hart, D., Yates, M., Fegley, S., & Wilson, G. (1995). Moral commitment in inner-city adolescents. In: M. Killen & D. Hart (Eds), *Morality in Everyday Lives: Developmental Perspectives* (pp. 317–341). Cambridge: Cambridge University Press.

Hess, R. D., & Torney, J. (1967). *The development of political attitudes in children*. Chicago: Aldine Press.

Ichilov, O. (1990). Dimensions and role patterns of citizenship in democracy. In: O. Ichilov (Ed.), *Political Socialization, Citizenship Education, and Democracy* (pp. 11–24). New York: Tecahers College Press.

Ichilov, O., & Nave, N. (1981). "The good citizen" as viewed by Israeli adolesents. *Comparative Politics, 13*, 361–376.

Ignatieff, M. (1995). The myth of citizenship. In: R. Beiner (Ed.), *Theorizing Citizenship* (pp. 53–78) Albany: State University of New York Press.

Independent Sector (1999). *Giving and volunteering in the United States: Findings from a national survey*. Washington, D.C.: Author.

Jackman, R. W., & Miller, R. A. (1996). The poverty of political culture. *American Journal of Political Science, 40*, 697–716.

Jennings, M. K., Langton, K. P., & Niemi, R. G. (1974). Effects of the high school civics curriculum. In: M. K. Jennings & R. G. Niemi, *The Political Character of Adolescence: The Influence of Families and Schools* (pp. 69–75). Princeton, NJ: Princeton University Press.

Jennings, M. K., & Niemi, R. G. (1981). *Generations and politics: A study of young adults and their parents*. Princeton, NJ: Princeton University Press.

Jones, R. (1974). Student political involvement and attitude change. *Teaching Political Science, 2*, 256–274.

Kenny, D. A., & Judd, C. M. (1986). Consequences of violating the independence assumption in analysis of variance. *Psychological Bulletin, 99*, 422–431.

Kymlicka, W. (1995). *Multicultural citizenship: A liberal theory of minority rights*. Oxford: Oxford University Press.

Kymlicka, W., & Norman, W. (1994). Return of the citizen: A survey of recent work on citizenship theory, *Ethics, 104*, 352–381.

Lane, R. (1965). The tense citizen and the casual patriot: Role confusion in American politics. *Journal of Politics, 27*, 735–760.

Leighley, J. (1991). Participation as a stimulus of political conceptualization. *Journal of Politics, 53*, 198–211.

Lemann, N. (1996). Kicking in Groups. *The Atlantic Monthly, 277*, 22–26.

Levi, M. (1996). Social and unsocial capital: A review essay of Robert Putnam's *Making Democracy Work*. *Politics and Society, 24*, 45–55.

Linville, P. W., & Carlston, D. E. (1994). Social cognition of the self. In: P. G. Devine, D. L. Hamilton & T. M. Ostrom (Eds), *Social Cognition's Impact on Social Psychology* (pp. 143–193). New York: Academic Press.

Litt, E. A. (1963). Civics education, community norms, and political indoctrination. *American Sociological Review, 29,* 69–75.

Luskin, R. C. (1987). Measuring political sophistication. *American Journal of Political Science, 31,* 856–899.

Markus, G. B., Howard, J. P. F., & King, D. C. (1993). Integrating community service and classroom instruction enhances learning: Results from an experiment. *Educational Evaluation and Policy Analysis, 15,* 410–419.

Markus, H. (1977). Self-schemata and processing information about the self. *Journal of Personality and Social Psychology, 35,* 63–78.

Markus, H. & Nurius, P. (1986). Possible selves. *American Psychologist, 41,* 954–969.

McAdam, D. (1988). *Freedom Summer.* New York: Oxford University Press.

McAdam, D. (1989). The biographical consequences of activism. *American Sociological Review, 54,* 744–760.

Milbrath, L. W., & Goel, M. L. (1977). *Political participation: How and why people get involved in politics.* Chicago: Rand-McNally.

Minkoff, D. C. (1997). Producing social capital: National social movements and civil society. *American Behavioral Scientist, 40,* 606–619.

Mondak, J. J. (Ed.) (1998). *Special issue: Psychological approaches to social capital. Political Psychology, 19,* 433–637.

Morin, R., & Balz, D. (*Washington Post,* 1/28/96). Americans losing trust in each other and institutions.

Newmann, F. M., & Rutter, R. A. (1983). *The effects of high school community service programs on students' social development.* Madison, WI: Wisconsin Center for Education Research, University of Wisconsin.

Nie, N. H., Junn, J., & Stehlik-Barry, K. (1996). *Education and democratic citizenship in America.* Chicago: University of Chicago Press.

Niedenthal, P. M., Cantor, N., & Kihlstrom, J. F. (1985). Self to prototype matching: A strategy for social decision-making. *Journal of Personality and Social Psychology, 48,* 575–584.

Niemi, R. G., & Junn, J. (1998). *Civic education: What makes students learn.* New Haven: Yale University Press.

Oliner, P. (1983). Putting "community" into citizenship education: The need for prosociality. *Theory and Research in Social Education, 11,* 65–81.

Omoto, A. M., & Snyder, M. (2002). Considerations of community: The context and process of volunteerism. *American Behavioral Scientist, 45,* 846–868.

Pateman, C. (1970). *Participation and democratic theory.* Cambridge: Cambridge University Press.

Patrick, J. J., & Hoge, J. D. (1991). Teaching government, civics, and law. In: J. P. Shaver (Ed.), *Handbook of Research on Social Studies Teaching and Learning.* NY: MacMillan Publishing Company.

People for the American Way. (1989). *Democracy's next generation: American youths' attitudes on citizenship, government, and politics.* Washington, D.C.: Author.

Phillips, A. (1993). *Democracy and difference.* College Station: The Pennsylvania University Press.

Pocock, J. G. A. (1995). The ideal of citizenship since classical times. In: R. Beiner (Ed.), *Theorizing Citizenship* (pp. 29–52) Albany: State University of New York.

Putnam, R. D. (1993). *Making democracy work: Civic traditions in modern Italy,* Princeton, NJ: Princeton University Press.

Putnam, R. D. (1995a). Bowling alone: America's declining social capital. *Journal of Democracy, 6,* 65–78.

Putnam, R. D. (1995b). Tuning in, tuning out: The strange disappearance of social capital in America. *PS: Political Science and Politics, 28,* 664–683.

Putnam, R. D. (1996). Robert Putnam replies. *The American Prospect, 25*, 26–28.

Putnam, R. D. (2000). *Bowling alone: The collapse and revival of American community*. New York: Simon & Schuster.

Rosenstone, S. J., & Hanson, J. M. (1993). *Mobilization, participation, and democracy in America*. New York: MacMillan Publishing Company.

Rosenthal, S., Feiring, C., & Lewis, M. (1998). Political volunteering from late adolescence to young adulthood: Patterns and predictors. *Journal of Social Issues, 54*, 477–494.

Rutter R. A., & Newmann, F. M. (1989). The potential of community service to enhance civic responsibility. *Social Education, 53*, 371–374.

Sax, L. J., Astin, A. W., Korn, W. S., & Mahoney, K. M. (1996). *The American Freshman: National Norms for Fall 1996*. Los Angeles: Higher Education Research Institute, UCLA.

Schudson, M. (1996). What if civic life didn't die? *The American Prospect, 25*, 17–20.

Setterlund, M. B., & Niedenthal, P. M. (1993). "Who am I? Why am I here?": Self-esteem, self-clarity, and prototype matching. *Journal of Personality and Social Psychology, 65*, 769–780.

Shantz, E. (1972). Sideline citizens: The political education of high school students. In: B. G. Massialas (Ed.), *Political Youth, Traditional Schools: National and International Perspectives* (pp. 64–76). Englewood Cliffs, NJ: Prentice-Hall.

Skinner, Q. (1992). On justice, the common good, and the priority of liberty. In: C. Mouffe (Ed.), *Dimensions of Radical Democracy: Pluralism, Citizenship, and Community* (pp. 211–224). London: Routledge.

Skocpol, T. (1996). Unravelling from above. *The American Prospect, 25*, 20–25.

Sullivan, W. M. (1986). *Reconstructing public philosophy*. Berkeley: University of California Press.

Swann, W. B., Jr. (1983). Self-verification: Bringing social reality into harmony with the self. In: J. Suls & A. G. Greenwald (Eds), *Psychological Perspectives on the Self* (Vol. 2, pp. 33–66). Hillsdale, NJ: Erlbaum.

Teske, N. (1997). Beyond altruism: Identity-construction as moral motive in political explanation. *Political Psychology, 18*, 71–91.

The Roper Center (1996). *The public perspective: A Roper Center review of public opinion and polling*, Vol. 7. Storrs, CT: Author.

Theiss-Morse, E. (1993). Conceptualizations of good citizenship and political participation. *Political Behavior, 15*, 355–380.

Thompson, D. F. (1970). *The democratic citizen*. Carbondale: Southern Illinois University Press.

Torney-Purta, J. (1989). Political cognition and its restructuring in young people. *Human Development, 32*, 14–23.

Torney-Purta, J. (1990). From attitudes and knowledge to schemata: Expanding the outcomes of political socialization research. In: O. Ichilov (Ed.), *Political Socialization, Citizenship Education, and Democracy,* (pp. 98–115). New York: Teachers College Press.

Torney-Purta, J. (1992) Cognitive representations of the political system in adolescents: The continuum from pre-novice to expert. In: H. Haste & J. Torney-Purta (Eds), *The Development of Political Understanding: A New Perspective,* (pp. 11–25). San Francisco: Jossey-Bass.

Valelly, R. M. (1996). Couch-potato democracy? *The American Prospect, 25*, 25–26.

Verba, S., & Nie, N. H. (1972). *Participation in America: Political democracy and social equality*. New York: Harper & Row.

Verba, S., Schlozman, K. L., & Brady, H. (1995). *Voice and equality: Civic voluntarism in American politics*. Cambridge, MA: Harvard University Press.

Walzer, M. (1989). Citizenship. In: T. Ball, J. Farr & R. L. Hansen (Eds), *Political Innovation and Conceptual Change* (pp. 211–219). Cambridge: Cambridge University Press.

Walzer, M. (1995). The civil society argument. In: R. Beiner (Ed.), *Theorizing Citizenship* (pp. 153–174), Albany: State University of New York Press.

Wolfinger, R. E., & Rosenstone, S. J. (1980). *Who votes?* New Haven: Yale University Press.

Yates, M. (1998). Community service and political-moral discussions among adolescents: A study of a mandatory school-based program in the United States. In: M. Yates & J. Youniss (Eds), *Roots of Civic Identity: International Perspectives in Community Service and Activism in Youth* (pp. 16–31). New York: Cambridge University Press.

Yates, M., & Youniss, J. (1996a). A developmental perspective on community service in adolescence. *Social Development, 5,* 85–111.

Yates, M., & Youniss, J. (1996b). Community service and political-moral identity in adolescents. *Journal of Research on Adolescence, 6,* 271–284.

Yates, M., & Younis, J. (1997). *Community service and social responsibility in youth.* Chicago: University of Chicago Press.

Yates, M., & Younis, J. (1998). Community service and political identity development in adolescence. *Journal of Social Issues, 54,* 495–512.

Young, I. M. (1990). *Justice and the politics of difference.* Princeton: Princeton University Press.

Youniss, J., McClellan, J. A., & Yates, M. (1997). What we know about engendering civic identity. *American Behavioral Scientist, 40,* 620–631.

PARADIGMS OF MINORITY AND IMMIGRANT POLITICAL PARTICIPATION IN THE UNITED STATES

David K. Park and Carlos Vargas-Ramos

The 2000 presidential election saw the two major political parties and their candidates reach out to minorities with targeted appeals to vote for them. America's two largest cities, New York and Los Angeles, produced strong Latino candidates for mayor in 2001. They both ultimately failed in their attempt, but their campaigns left a greatly mobilized and energized minority electorate (mostly among Latinos and African Americans). These events may have signaled a shift in the political participation of minorities from what had been a languid involvement. This lethargy had been the subject of apparently solid theoretical explanations, some of which still prevail. In this essay we review the most recent literature on political participation among minority populations and the newest and fastest-growing immigrant groups in the United States: Latinos and Asian Americans. After a brief description of recent demographic developments, we provide an overview of the dominant paradigms on political participation, and how successfully they have explained minority and immigrant political participation. We examine alternative models of immigrant political participation, and then suggest areas of future research, in light of the success of the models in responding to the substantive questions raised about the current and the future participation of minorities and immigrants. Of particular interest are the factors that may promote the participation of minorities,

Political Decision Making, Deliberation and Participation, Volume 6, pages 253–293.
Copyright © 2002 by Elsevier Science Ltd.
All rights of reproduction in any form reserved.
ISBN: 0-7623-0227-5

due to the challenges that unequal participation in the population pose for normative democratic theory.

THE UNITED STATES' POPULATION, CIRCA 2000

The continued and rapid growth of the immigrant population in the United States[1] and the concomitant proportionate drop in the majority population has given a new urgency to the study of how the increasing ethnic and racial diversity in the country will affect social and political relations. In 1990, 80.3% of the U.S. population was white (74.5%, if limited to non-Hispanic whites). By 2000, this percentage had decreased to 75.1 (69.1% non-Hispanic white).[2] Across the largest states, where immigrant populations tend to settle, the proportions are even larger. In California, minorities are now the majority.[3] According to the latest census non-Latino whites' share of the California population dropped below 50% (Booth, 2000). The last time whites were not a majority in California was in 1860.

This population growth is not new, continuing a trend that dates back to the 1960s and that has accelerated since the 1970s after the 1965 Immigration and Naturalization Act. Also not new is the study of the political attributes, behavior and general incorporation into the political system of the groups that constitute this immigrant population. Ever since the American Civil War and Reconstruction, and increasingly since the dismantling of the segregation regime, scholars have examined the conditions surrounding the politics of immigrants. After a second wave of migration from Europe in the 1880s the surge and diversity in the foreign-born population prompted policy-makers and academics to champion what had already become a political and social goal – assimilation (Myrdal, 1962 [1944]; Roucek & Eisenberg, 1982). Where assimilation was not possible or desirable, the outcome became separation.[4]

Assimilation became the standard by which to understand the incorporation of Americans, new and old, into its social and political system. Those unable or unwilling to assimilate as well as those prevented from assimilating tended to coincide with racialized minorities. However, challenges to the dominant discourse that resulted from the failure of the assimilation paradigm to account for lack of full incorporation allowed for new theories and explanations (e.g. multiculturalism) (Glazer & Moynihan, 1963).

The burgeoning population has grown not only as a result of higher birth rates, but also through growing immigration. Thus, the analysis of the incorporation of immigrants and their descendents has to account not only for "ethnicity," as with earlier immigrants, but also for "race," a distinct albeit related social and analytical concept.[5] Moreover, the traditional dichotomous paradigm of white-black that had been used to explain social, political and economic race/ethnic relations in the United States has proven limited in addressing inter-racial and intra-racial relations, and is being revisited in efforts to account for differences attributable to the country's multi-ethnic and multi-racial make-up (Alex-Assensoh & Hanks, 2000). Relations beyond more than two particular racial groups – extended to Latino and Asian American groups – need to be taken into consideration in order to accurately describe and explain political dynamics across the different regions of the country, especially in the largest urban centers. It may make sense to study differences in the voting patterns, the level of trust or the amount of contacts with elected officials between African Americans and whites in Alabama or South Carolina, but certainly this is not enough when the geographical setting of the analysis is San Francisco or Hartford, CT, New York or California, or the Southwest or the Northeast.

Moreover, African Americans, Native Americans, Asian Americans and Latinos are not evenly distributed throughout the country. Their patterns of settlement as groups have been influenced by historical and structural circumstances. The analysis of their behavior has therefore tended to be fractured geographically as well. Most research on Asian Americans has concentrated on California, where their numbers are greater, and to a much lesser extent in some mid-Atlantic states. Studies of Latinos have tended to focus alternatively on the Southwest, the Northeast or Florida. For Native Americans, the focus has been in the even more fractured Indian country, which extends through vast but relatively sparsely populated expanses of the Dakotas, Arizona, New Mexico, Montana, Idaho and Oklahoma, or more insular settlements in the Southeast, the Great Lakes region and New York. African Americans, traditionally the largest and most salient minority, have had a wider area of settlement, but still reside substantially in the South, southern New England and the mid-Atlantic states, the Midwest and California.

Another factor to consider as immigrants continue to arrive in the United States is that they are confronted not only with a majority population that tends to be different from them in race and ethnicity, but also with members of their own ethnicity and/or race who are native born, non-immigrant populations. This creates new dynamics, not only with respect to the majority population but also among the different population groups and subgroups that constitute the minority. For instance, there are likely both commonalities and differences between a second-generation Cuban American and a Peruvian recently arrived in Union City, NJ, or between a second-generation Japanese American and a Korean American who may have lived in Los Angeles for fifteen years. Commonalities may be also weak and even non-existent between Chinese and

Indian subcontinent immigrants living in Queens, NY. Even within the same ethnic group, differing historical experiences may give way to tenuous relations between, for example, an East Indian immigrant recently departed from Bangalore and a third-generation Guyanese who lives in the same neighborhood in Brooklyn, NY.

Lumping together individuals or groups who fall within a wide racial or ethnic category may also lessen the nuances of interactions that transpire between different racial or ethnic groups. For instance, in discussing African American-Latino relations in New York City, generalizations may be made in terms of inter-group competition that may vary in degree and substance when the Latino group is Puerto Rican as opposed to Mexican (Falcón, 1988). Significant differences may also emerge when the geographic location shifts to south Florida and the Latino group in question is Cuban American (Harris, 1994). There is also the inter-generational conflict that may arise within the same racial and even ethnic group. A third-generation Chinese American from San Francisco may share little material interests with an undocumented immigrant from Fujian province recently arrived in the city.

MINORITY POLITICAL PARTICIPATION: THE STATE OF KNOWLEDGE

What do we know about the political participation of African Americans, American Indians, Asian Americans and Latinos in the United States? How do their rates of participation compare to that of the majority white population? What are the similarities and differences in participation among members of minority groups?

Following Conway (1991) we take political participation to be activities used by members of a polity to "attempt to influence the structure of government, the selection of government authorities or the policies of the government" (pp. 4–5). Furthermore, we circumscribe the scope of political participation in this review to activities that take place within the parameters of a legal or constitutional framework.

Due to the relatively small populations, and hence the relatively small number of respondents in most survey samples, of Latino and Asian American groups in the past, there has been a dearth of systematic and representative research. When these studies are available, the data provided tend to focus on voting exclusively, with studies focusing on other forms of electoral and non-electoral participation being sparse. Research focusing explicitly on minority participation tends to be small community-based studies or larger studies in the West and Southwest (examining Latino and Asian Americans). There has been little research in other parts of the U.S., especially in the relatively diverse Northeast. Furthermore, there has been little large-scale research of this sort, with the exception of the Latino National Political Survey (LNPS). Nonetheless, there are data that give us an indication of where minority participation stands today.

National turnout rates figures for the November 1996 elections show that 58.4% of citizens voted (Casper & Bass, 1998). The breakdown along racial/ethnic lines was as follows: non-Hispanic whites (60.7%), non-Hispanic blacks (53%), non-Hispanic Asian and Pacific Islanders (45%) and Latinos (44.3%).[6] We can see that Asian and Pacific Islanders and Latinos turned out at rates of more than 15 percentage points lower than whites and about 8 percentage points lower than non-Hispanic blacks. The turnout rate was more than 7% lower for blacks than for whites. As a percentage of their numbers in the voting-age population as a whole, 59.6% of whites and 50.9% of blacks voted, but only 25.7% of the total Asian and Pacific Islanders and 26.9% of the Latinos.

Survey results from a large national sample conducted in 1989–1990 (the Citizen Participation Study) showed that 34% of Americans had contacted an elected official during the previous 12 months, with 37% of non-Hispanic whites having done so compared to 24% of African Americans and 14% of Latinos (Verba et al, 1995). Twenty-four percent of Americans had contributed at least $250 to a political campaign, including 25% of whites, 22% of African Americans and 11% of Latinos. Eight percent of the population had worked in a political campaign, with 8% of whites, 12% of African Americans and 7% of Latinos having done so. Six percent had engaged in some form of protest over an issue (5% of whites, 9% of African Americans and 4% of Latinos). And 17% had been involved in informal communal activity (17% of whites, 19% of African Americans and 12% of Latinos). As with voting, these figures allow us to discern a pattern where, by and large, whites are more active in politics than minorities and Latinos and Asian Americans tend to have significantly lower rates of activity.

In a 1986 study of registered voters in California, Asian Americans lagged far behind the 72% of Californians who were registered voters (Nakanishi, 1986). Only 43% of the state's eligible Japanese Americans were registered and the figures are sharply lower for Chinese (35.5%), Filipinos (27.0%), Koreans (13%), Asian Indians (16.7%), and Vietnamese (4.1%). What explains these differences?

THEORETICAL FRAMEWORKS

Explanations offered to account for the political participation of the population and differential patterns within it have relied on socio-demographic characteristics of individuals and groups, such as age, gender, race, ethnicity, educational attainment, income level and/or occupation; psychological and cultural aspects, such as attitudes and orientations; and, political and legal structures and institutions, such as the party system, movement politics or discriminatory legal obstacles (Conway, 1991). Several theoretical frameworks have been developed utilizing these explanations to understand political participation in general and that of minorities specifically. Below we examine the most developed frameworks and their application to immigrant and minority political participation. We begin with the dominant explanatory model: the Socio Economic Status (SES) model and its refinements, the Civic Voluntarism and the Relative Education models. We next turn to models that attempt to address the shortcomings of the SES model as it relates to the participation of immigrant and minority groups: the Ethnic Group Consciousness, Pan-ethnic, and Nationality models. We then consider explanations that are complementary to the SES model, such as Rosenstone and Hansen's (1993) strong emphasis on mobilization.

The Socio-Economic Status (SES) Model

At least since Verba and Nie's research (1972) it has been a truism that explanatory models that rely on socioeconomic measures – education and income, specifically – have been most successful in accounting for differing levels of engagement in political activity across the population. Verba and Nie began from an instrumentalist perspective, where citizens engage in politics to communicate their preferences to their political representatives, including the choices of whom these representatives may be, in order to obtain from them results that may satisfy their wants and needs. Building on a substantive body of existing empirical work on participation, they outline a model in which higher levels of educational attainment, occupation and income largely "determine" how much an individual participates in political activities "through the intervening effects of a variety of 'civic attitudes' conducive to participation: attitudes such as a sense of efficacy, of psychological involvement in politics, and a feeling of obligation to participate" (1972, p. 13). This large cross-sectional study of the adult population of the United States found that higher levels of both electoral and non-electoral modes of participation were closely associated with certain civic attitudes and orientations. These in turn were strongly associated with higher levels of education and income and occupations with higher status. However, the standard SES model has not been able to explain the specific mechanisms by which socioeconomic characteristics operate and translate into robust results on participation, even through mediating factors.

The strength of this model lies nonetheless in the strong correlation between higher levels of education and income and higher rates of participation across a range of political activities.[7] The model has been particularly successful in accounting for engagement in community-oriented and campaign activity, and voting, though to a lesser extent for the latter. SES, however, has not accounted well for engagement in particularized contacting. Furthermore, while originally developed with the United States political system in mind, it has been applied across nations at varying degrees of economic and political development, and its results have been by and large validated (Verba, Nie & Kim, 1978).

Indeed, African Americans and Latinos as groups occupy lower social strata and classes than the majority white population. This would then seem to explain the differences in political participation along ethnic and/or racial lines. There are limits to this conclusion, however. The median income among whites in 1994 was $33,600; but it was only $22,644 for Latinos and $20,508 for African Americans (Oliver & Shapiro, 2001). However, for Asian Americans, the median income was $40,998.[8] Similarly, while African Americans and Latinos are as a group, less educated than whites, Asian Americans tend to be better educated than any other group. Whereas 88% of whites had graduated from high school and 28% had graduated from college, only 77% and 16% of African Americans had done so, respectively. For Latinos, only 56% had finished high school and 11% graduated from college. However, 84% Asian Americans had finished high school and 42% had graduated from college (Newburger and Curry, 2000; these data are for people in the United States 25 years of age and over).

A superficial look at these aggregate numbers would then give credence to the SES model insofar as Latinos and whites are concerned. The higher income levels and educational attainment of whites would account prima facie for their higher levels of political participation. Likewise, lower Latino income levels and educational attainment would explain lower levels of participation among them.[9] However, the model is more problematic when it involves African Americans and Asian Americans. African Americans show lower levels of activity in some forms of participation (e.g. voting, contacting elected officials, contributing money to campaigns) but they are relatively more engaged in other activities (i.e. working on political campaigns, protest activity, communal activity). On the other hand, while having higher levels of socioeconomic performance, Asian Americans do not engage in electoral politics at the levels of whites or higher as might be expected from the SES model.[10]

Refinements to the Standard Socioeconomic Model

The tendency in the participation literature to focus on socioeconomic models to explain varied levels of political activity has left scholars debating the relative influence on participation within the Latino and Asian American communities of income, education, occupation, as well as other variables, such as citizenship and age. Some scholars like Hero and Campbell (1996) and DeSipio (1996) have examined models encompassing a mix of socioeconomic factors, which show that low income, low levels of education, and relative youth are significant factors explaining diminished levels of Latino political involvement.[11] Over the short term, these constitute a series of fairly intractable variables that effectively limit Latino participation in the American political process.

Deviating from standard socioeconomic analyses, Verba, Schlozman and Brady (1995) explore the effect of a wider range of variables on Latino participation. Specifically, they incorporate education, income, and occupation into broader models examining the influence of opportunity, mobilization, and motivation on political activity. These refinements to the SES model bring attention to institutional factors that can be linked to individual and group-level socioeconomic characteristics to explain differential levels of participation. The standard SES model has only been able to demonstrate that an association exists between education, income and occupation and attitudes conducive to participation, and between these "civic attitudes" and participation. It has also shown an association between SES variables and membership in voluntary associations, and party affiliation, and community. But it still falls short of providing an explanation that traces the linkages between socioeconomic variables, institutional membership and affiliation, and participation. Later works have focused, for instance, on the civic organizations people belong to – or not – which allow them the opportunity to develop the civic skills that contribute to compensate and overcome the limitations associated with lower class status.

The Civic Voluntarism model attempts to explain involvement in political activities with a three-prong approach: by examining: (1) the resources and skills people have at their disposal, (2) how psychologically connected they may be to political affairs and the system in which these take place, and (3) the extent to which people have been recruited into political activities (Verba et al., 1995). Verba, Schlozman and Brady, however, emphasize in their account the impact that resources and psychological engagement to politics have on political participation, privileging these factors over recruitment into political activity.

Using an enormous dataset from a nationally sampled cross-sectional study, Verba and his colleagues (Verba et al., 1993, 1995) trace how education and income provide individuals with the time, the money and the "civic skills" (i.e. communication and organizational abilities) that facilitate their participation. Higher levels of formal education have a clear impact on income, which provide resources for contributing money for campaigns or to fund lobbying activities. Higher levels of formal education are also associated with more sophisticated language and communication skills in general. Higher income is associated with a greater likelihood of belonging to a non-political organization; and it also has a slightly non-linear relation with religious affiliation, where those in the middle incomes are slightly more likely to belong to a religious institution than those of higher or lower incomes. It is in these types of social institutions, in addition to the workplace, that individuals learn or further develop the ability to communicate with others more effectively as well as the organizational skills that allow for efficacious collective work. These civic skills then become assets that individuals are able to use in campaign work, or when contacting an elected official or while working towards solving a problem at the community level.

As noted above, as a group whites have both higher educational attainment levels and income levels than African Americans or Latinos. Moreover, Verba et al. (1995) find that whites score higher in measures of some civic skills, are more likely to be employed and working full-time and more likely to belong to non-political organizations. African Americans score lower than whites in these categories, but they show higher scores than Latinos, who attain the lowest scores of all groups in income, free time, educational attainment, language skills, employment status, organizational and church membership and the opportunity to exercise civic skills in these institutional settings. It is for these reasons that whites, not unexpectedly, are more active politically than Latinos in a wide array of political activities, and than African Americans in most but not all the activities that Verba and his colleagues gauged. What accounts for higher levels of participation in some activities, such as campaigning and community-oriented participation, is the unique role that institutions such as African American churches play in the political life of African Americans, which have provided the space where African Americans have been able to develop politically relevant civic skills. After all, a higher percentage of African Americans belong to a church and are able to use politically relevant civic skills in that setting than either whites or Latinos.

The importance they grant civic institutions in the political process notwithstanding, these scholars conclude that socioeconomic variables continue to emerge as the strongest predictors of low Latino political activity, with the other sets of variables contributing secondary or tertiary effects. Verba, Schlozman and Brady state that while "neither being black nor being Latino itself reduces participation [. . .] it is the fact that both groups are less well endowed with factors that foster participation that is responsible for the participation gap on the basis of race and ethnicity" (1995, p. 523).[12] Moreover, after accounting for differences in politically relevant resources, Verba, et al. (1993) found that there were no significant differences among the African Americans, whites and Latinos groups in political participation. They attributed the higher level of political activity among Cuban Americans to their higher levels of education and higher status occupations.

Verba, et al. (1993) state further that "investigations of citizen political participation in democracies around the world inevitably find a relationship between education and [political] activity," and they observe "education enhances participation more or less directly by developing skills that are relevant to politics." However, most immigrants who came to the United States during the 1960s, 70s, and 80s came from countries with little or no democratic foundation. Future research needs to consider to what extent education in a despotic and/or communist regime develops one's "sense of civic responsibility or political efficacy."

Asian Americans present a particular problem even for this refined resource model. With their high levels of education and high status occupations but lower levels of participation, Asian Americans seem to counter Verba et al.'s (1995; 1993) arguments. In order to explain the low levels of political participation of Asian Americans, researchers have offered several explanations: (1) most Asians are immigrants who are too busy earning a living and educating their children to focus on public affairs; (2) in traditional Asian fashion, they also set the welfare of their families as their chief priority, relegating civic duty to a low spot on their agenda; (3) though they may be citizens, many feel that as newcomers they are guests, who as a courtesy to their hosts, should remain silent; (4) those from countries with despotic regimes, like the Chinese and Vietnamese, either distrust government or are baffled by the democratic process; (5) as recent arrivals they are frequently riveted more on developments in their native lands than on events in America; and (6) they do not regard politics as a reputable career, an attitude that mirrors their remembrance of the corruption and venality that pervades much of public life in Asia (Karnow, 1992).

Future research needs to not only explain the low levels of political participation of Asian Americans but also to explain why these various explanations do not affect other similarly situated ethnic groups. For example, most Cuban Americans are busy earning a living, come from a despotic regime and are more "riveted" on developments in their native land. Verba et al.'s (1993), however, find that they exhibit very high levels of political participation (Harris, 1994).

One promising avenue for refining our understanding of these relationships would be to compare previous and more recent immigrants from Eastern Europe.

At a minimum, research on recent immigrants should measure not only educational attainment but also the country (or countries) in which they received their education. We may find that where one receives his or her education has as much affect on one's political development as one's level of educational attainment. In addition, since English speakers may have access to many more sources of political information, future research will need to consider the degree to which limited English capability reduces the level of political information, especially for individuals living in large metropolitan areas that have several foreign language newspapers, radio stations and even television stations.

The renewed concern over institutions has highlighted how they can become loci where capital, be it cultural or social, is acquired or developed. Putnam (2000), for instance, has tracked and analyzed the decline in meaningful associational activity and interaction over the past fifty years. He attributes to this loss of social capital (i.e. social networks, trustworthiness and associated norms of reciprocity) the parallel decline in civic and political participation. As Americans from all economic strata, race, age group, ethnicity or religious belief become more disengaged socially their political engagement falls as well.

But rather than emphasizing social capital, some alternative models have stressed the importance of politics-specific resources as more relevant factors to political participation (Fuchs et al., 2000). Thus, instead of placing greater weight on factors such as organizational and communication skills, which are learned at home and/or in school and that may be reinforced or developed further in civic organizations (such as places of worship or voluntary associations) it is "those organizational memberships, networks, structural positions and attitudes that explicitly build opportunities and capacities to participate in politics" (e.g. professional or ethnic associations, civic clubs, labor unions) that better predict political engagement (Fuchs et al., 2000, p. 8).

It is notable that when taking these political and social capital variables into account in Fuchs et al.'s political model, the effects of race and ethnicity do not appear to be statistically significant. A comment on citizenship as "political capital" is in order, however. Citizenship is undoubtedly a necessary condition for engaging in the most extended political activity – voting – but not for other activities. However, acquiring citizenship via naturalization adds a socialization dimension that may largely be missing in other citizens and may be non-existent or hardly present among alien residents and others. The actual learning process involved in becoming a citizen, as well as the actual decision and procedures to become one, politicizes people (Jones-Correa, 1998).

While Verba et al.'s (1995) and other (for example, Garcia, 1997) models represent efforts to move beyond singularly focused socioeconomic studies, they still fall short of uncovering variables that may increase Latino political engagement. Instead, their focus on resource-based variables implicitly rules out solutions to increasing Latino political involvement, barring a sudden rise in this group's social mobility. Further, by appropriating a model that has successfully accounted for white and African American participation levels in an effort to understand Latino and Asian American political inactivity, these scholars have neglected to explore whether there is a distinctive pattern to Latino and Asian American participation.

Wolfinger and Rosenstone (1980) argue that taking socioeconomic factors into account reduces voting and registration disparities. However, in response to this argument Arvizu and Garcia (1996) assert that socioeconomic variables do not have a uniformly powerful influence on Latino political activity. Instead, the authors contend that socioeconomic indexes should be unpacked, so the separate effects on participation of the component variables can be measured. In doing so, the results of their study support earlier findings that income has a much more significant effect on Latino participation than does education. While studies like Arvizu and Garcia's (1996) play a critical role by demonstrating that socioeconomic variables such as education and income are not uniformly depressing Latino participation, they fail to highlight factors that may actually draw Latinos (and other groups) into the political process.

Nie, Junn and Stehlik-Barry (1996) delve into the analysis of one of the components of socioeconomic status – education – that has been consistently identified as the strongest predictor of participation. Their objective is not to explain political participation in general, or that of minorities in particular, but in effect to respond to the puzzle whereby as the educational attainment across the population has increased over time the level of political activity has remained either stable or declined (as is the case with voter turnout). Nie and his colleagues describe how increased levels of formal education in the United States can raise levels of political tolerance (and as a result contribute to the maintenance of the extant political system), while at the same time contribute to the stratification of the political system, leading to greater political inequality. These scholars reject what they term the "absolute education model" in favor of a "relative education" model. Education, they explain,

> is of *relative*, rather than absolute, importance for qualities of political engagement and works as a sorting mechanism, allocating more central positions in the social network to citizens who have higher educational standing than those with whom they compete for political engagement. Formal education orders the distribution of political engagement among citizens on the basis of a shifting average of educational achievement in the adult population as a whole (Nie et al., 1996, p. 111. Emphasis in original).

The political system is one where political goods (e.g. public policy outcomes) are not unlimited. Rather, their availability is fixed and therefore potentially subject to scarcity. Higher educational achievement in turn is strongly associated with increased levels of political knowledge, psychological involvement in politics, participation in difficult political activities and turnout. As educational attainment throughout the population increases, participation is then expected to increase. However, the gains that may have resulted from higher educational attainment are neutralized as more people reach similar levels of education. As more individuals become more educated competition ensues given education's role as a politically relevant resource. The political edge they may have gained becomes contested, since the ability of those in positions to redistribute social goods or to be responsive has not increased. Therefore, there may be an equilibrium achieved among the more educated. Participation then would be expected to remain unchanged. At the same time, those whose educational attainment has either remained constant may have actually regressed in this competitive field of political engagement in relation to the better educated. Here education reflects, and potentially exacerbates, inequalities in the political system.

The "Relative Education model" would reasonably account for the lower position Latinos and Asian Americans as well as African Americans and American Indians occupy in a social system whose political relations are stratified by the workings of education. Being relatively low, Latino's educational attainment would have the effect of leaving them behind as competitive political players, for "the important factor in a competitive system is one's relative standing in the educational system" (Nie et al., 1996, p. 107). In the case of Asian Americans, whose educational achievement surpasses that of whites, the political clout they may have achieved (as presumed by the more "additive" Absolute Educational model) may be diffused by an increase in the number of political players in an already crowded field among the highly educated and active. In short, as competitive pressures reduce the ability of the most active to affect political outcomes, the advantage provided by education diminishes.

While Nie, Junn and Stehlik-Barry find very strong evidence for their relative educational argument, they note (but do not systematically explore) the impact race and ethnicity may have on participation. In addition to using the same cross-section study Verba et al. (1995) used to develop their Civic Voluntarism model (i.e. the Citizen Participation Study), they also test their model using longitudinal data from the National Opinion Research Center's General Social Survey and the American National Election Study. From these data, they conclude that "the results of the estimation . . . reflect the familiar finding that women and minority citizens are less likely to be engaged in politics than men and whites" (1996, p. 143).

Ethnic Group Consciousness Models: Pan-Ethnicity and Nationality

One revision to the SES model, which came about from the model's inability to account fully for the political engagement of low socioeconomic status groups, is the ethnic group consciousness model. Verba and Nie (1972) observed that "many blacks in 1967 who saw race as a social problem participated at a rate higher than those whites of comparable socio-economic status." The ethnic group consciousness model, which is derived from group interaction and competition with other groups and subgroups, may contribute to the combination of a sense of political efficacy, political mistrust and perceived deprivation which in turn induces political involvement (Olsen, 1970; Verba & Nie 1972; Sarna, 1978; Shingles, 1981; Guterbock & London, 1983; Portes, 1984; London & Giles, 1987; Bobo & Gilliam, 1990; Bobo, 1998).

The group consciousness hypothesis, developed by Verba and Nie in an attempt to address the puzzle of relative higher participation among African Americans when controlling for socioeconomic measures, was more an inference from the data than the result of direct measurement of causal mechanisms. Verba and Nie (1972) observed a stronger correlation between race and socioeconomic status than between race a political participation, and relatively higher levels of participation among African Americans as whites of the same socioeconomic status. Since African Americans who exhibited higher levels of participation were those whose awareness of race as a social, personal and national problem was noted in attitudinal measures, it was imputed that African American's self-awareness as an oppressed group accounted for their relatively higher levels of participation in some measures of political activity.

Bobo and Gilliam (1990) have confirmed the findings that African Americans indeed participate at higher rates than whites of similar social standing, and they attribute it to a particular aspect of group consciousness – empowerment. They based their conclusions on the findings of multivariate analysis that used data collected in the 1987 General Social Survey. Through empowerment, or ascension to positions of political power by members of a self-aware group, members of the group become more psychologically engaged in the political process, especially by becoming more trusting, efficacious and knowledgeable, and therefore more likely to participate.

Miller et al. (1981) extended the examination of the relationship between group consciousness and political participation to include members of a "subordinate or a dominant social group." They argued that it takes a dislike for the other social or ethnic group (polar affect) and the belief that inequities in the social system are responsible for a group's disadvantaged status in society (system blame) in order to transform "subjective group identification into participation in electoral and non-electoral activities." Uhlaner et al. (1989) "applied this extended concept of group consciousness to study the relationship between political participation and membership in social groups objectively defined by common ethnic or national origins." The study compared the political behaviors of four racial/ethnic groups in California (African American, white, Asian American, and Latino). It found that differences in socioeconomic background and the salience of ethnic and non-ethnic group problems are sufficient to explain the disparity in participation rates between whites and Latinos but not between whites and Asian Americans. Uhlaner and colleagues (1989) concluded that ethnicity does matter for political participation and they suspected that some culture-related factors may account for the distinctiveness of Asian American political participation. Alternatively, Leighley and Vedlitz (1999), using cross-sectional data from Texas, confirm the results that SES, as well as psychological involvement and social capital, are strong predictors of political participation for whites, African Americans, Mexican Americans and Asian Americans.[13] But they discount or find mixed results for the group consciousness and the group conflict model, for these tend to depress rather than enhance participation. Mangum (2000) confirms these findings as well for African Americans, in a multivariate analysis of national cross-sectional data from the 1996 National Black Election Study.

The "Pan-Ethnic" Model: Are there unique Latino or Asian American profiles of participation? Of Chinese American and Mexican American political behavior? One of the first concerns raised about research conducted on minorities is directed at the definitions used to identify and label these groups. How should the political, or for that matter the social and economic, conditions and behaviors of minority groups be studied? How are the populations to be identified? A common practice is to view and study these racialized minority groups in terms of ethnicity. Census Bureau categories traditionally have combined (under the heading "Latino" and/or "Hispanic") disparate groups such as Dominicans, Ecuadorians and Mexicans, as well as second and third generation people whose ancestors originated in the countries of Latin America. In turn, scholars have used this and other encompassing labels such "Asian and Pacific Islander" in their analyses, sometimes with little regard for the potentially significant differences among these groups. Implicitly at least, differences among the various African, Asian American and Latino subgroups are viewed as minor or otherwise insignificant (Verba et al., 1993; Henry & Munoz, 1991, Lien, 1994).

The assumption that subgroup differences among certain minority groups are less important than similarities across these groups implies the notion of "pan-ethnicity." What does "Pan-ethnic" refer to? Terms like Asian or Latino may cause confusion analytically and in social discourse because they tend to elicit variegated images in people's minds when used. Is the term a racial moniker or does it stress ethnicity? When the word Latino or Hispanic is used formally, it is intended to refer to people who originated in or who can trace their roots to Latin America (including the Spanish-speaking Caribbean). Moreover, these are terms that highlight and intend to capture a cultural milieu. However, notwithstanding efforts by the Bureau of the Census, which consistently reminds us that Hispanics can be of any race when it releases population statistics, the terms have also been racialized and identified with a prototypical (or stereotypical) image of a person of mixed (white, black and/or Amerindian) race. Asian, on the other hand, has been formally intended as a racial term, but one that is geographic-centered and therefore loaded with cultural symbolism. The more ethnic-specific term, Asian American, also contributes to the confusion because it may be used in contrast to Asian to mean native-born Americans of Asian extraction, as opposed to a first generation American (or, simply, a foreign national). While mindful of these intricacies, we narrow the use of these all-encompassing terms in this work to refer primarily, though not exclusively, to *ethnic* identity. We reserve the terms Asian, black and white to signify *racial* identity.

Examples of the "Pan-ethnic" model dominate the study of Asian American and Latino social, political and economic attitudes. For example, Verba et al. (1993) found that Latinos are substantially less politically active than whites. Henry and Munoz (1991) speak of an Asian American voter-turnout that lags significantly behind African American and whites. In terms of identifying issues, they state that Asian Americans are concerned with issues such as immigration, bilingual education, hate crimes and university admission quotas. While many of these authors acknowledge that differences exist between Asian American and Latino subgroups, they nonetheless argue that Asian American and Latino are politically meaningful categories just as African American and white.

The obvious benefits of the "Pan-ethnic" model are also its limitation – the ability to generalize about or apply characteristics to a group without identifying the differences among subgroups, as often critiqued by nationality proponents. To a large extent, reliance on Pan-ethnic labels has been due to the exigencies of research methods. Large quantitative studies, especially national studies, have resorted to aggregating groups that may fit a particular racial or supra-ethnic/national category in order to counter the problem of small group sub-samples. In the process, however, their validity and reliability might be called into question.

Leighly and Vedlitz (1999) resort to using both ethnic and Pan-ethnic labels in their test of competing models of political participation. They use a sample that collected cross-sectional data for whites, African Americans, Mexican-Americans and Asian Americans in Texas, oversampling the last three groups. The use of African Americans and Mexican-Americans seems to be appropriate for Texas, where the survey was conducted, since the majority of both African Americans and Latinos in the state are of this ethnic/national origin.[14] However, the authors rely on the larger category "Asian American" to increase the numbers for this group. The problem of "small-N" sub-samples is common enough that even well designed studies, such as the Citizen Participation Study, often fail to include in the sample American Indians or even Asian Americans.

A possible solution to this ongoing problem would be to expand the design of the Latino National Political Survey to include other ethnic/racial groups and test similarities and differences in political participation. Yet, the Latino National Political Survey itself focuses on the three largest Hispanic groups in the United States (i.e. Mexican-American, Puerto Rican, Cuban-American), and this was possible by sampling areas with high concentrations of Latinos (e.g. the Southwest, Northeast, south Florida, and the Chicago MSA). Groups such as Salvadorans, Dominicans, Guatemalans and Colombians, and Hispanics living in areas and regions such as the mid-West outside of Cook County IL, have yet to be included and studied in large national studies (Longoria, 2000).

A noteworthy fact revealed in the 2000 Census is the 6 million Latinos (17%) who identified themselves as Spanish/Hispanic/Latino but did not specify national origin (Guzmán, 2000). It may be argued that as Latinos intermarry more often across national lines, their off-springs may be reluctant to privilege one parental heritage over another and may choose a more encompassing term with which to identify. Alternately, some have argued that the large percentage of Hispanics identifying with the Pan-ethnic label is due to the way the Census Bureau posed the question rather than a conscious, pan-ethnic identification (Scott, 2001).

While the "Pan-ethnic" model may prove to be a valid approach, few studies have yet demonstrated the existence of a Pan-Asian or Pan-Latino group identity (Jones-Correa & Leal, 1996). Rather, many studies have assumed the existence of a broad, overarching group identity without providing empirical evidence that such commonalities exist. Future research needs to approach the validity of the "Pan-ethnic" models as an open question.

The "Pan-ethnic" model overlaps with the group consciousness model insofar as they both attempt to identify group identities or characteristics; however, beyond this commonality they differ fundamentally. The group consciousness model focuses specifically on the relationship of one group to another, for example, Latinos in relation to African Americans, Asian Americans in relation to whites, or within pan-ethnic categories, Filipino Americans in relation to Japanese Americans (Cruz, 2000; Lai, 2000). The inquiry is on external pressures on a particular group (or even subgroup) and how that group develops a "consciousness" as a result of the dominance or pressures from another group (Bobo & Gilliam, 1990; Bobo, 1998). An illustrative case of this form of group consciousness is Cruz's description of minority elite behavior in Hartford, CT, where he identifies "compartmentalization, racial ambivalence, paternalism, resentment and conflict over goals, interests, achievements, and status" as factors characterizing relations between African Americans and Puerto Ricans (2000, pp. 98–99).[15] Conflict arises, Cruz argues, from the following factors: "incongruent attitudinal frameworks" that are given by particular historical experiences; the "dilemma between direct and virtual representation;" the context where "minority elites represent a group that is simultaneously powerful and oppressed; "discrepancies in different minorities' intention, actions, and perceptions;" and the lack of historical memory and how both rewards and responsibilities are parceled out. However these factors may affect interminority collective behavior, they become a contextual minefield that needs to be crossed in order for common goals to be achieved.

Lai (2000) identifies socioeconomic (i.e. education and income) differences, generational issues and homeland politics as factors that have contributed to derail electoral coalitions between Filipinos and Koreans in California, diluting the "power in numbers" approach that seems so self-evident in supra-national identities in favor of a "go it alone" strategy. Lai shows how purposive action and institutions such as community-based organizations organized along ethnic lines, the ethnic media, candidate strategy, and effective symbolic leadership have been used to prevent the development of Asian-American coalitions. However, Lai also points to the growth and institutionalization of Pan-Asian organizations, the prospect of presenting candidates with broad crossover appeal and the salience of issues that resonate across racial and ethnic groups (such as hate crime legislation, affirmative action policies and immigration initiatives) as factors that could create Pan-Asian or even a broad racial-ethnic coalition.

On the other hand, the "pan-ethnic" model aggregates groups with little recognition of the interdependent processes outlined in group consciousness models. The incorporation of such contextual factors into the pan-ethnic model can create a dynamic perspective of ethnicity. For example, one could hypothesize that recent immigrants from Mexico may have strong ties to their home country that affect their social, economic, and political behavior. Over time, however, with greater levels of acculturation to the host country and psychological interaction of other racial and ethnic groups, these ties to their home country could diminish and the evolution of a Pan-Latino ethos could evolve. Gutiérrez's (1995) account of changing group identity and coalition formation among Mexican-Americans and Mexican immigrants illustrates how within the putatively same ethnic group, sharp political differences in terms of political agenda preferences (e.g. immigration policy) may arise, and how these may be overcome (e.g. intergenerational and foreign-/native-born coalition building)

As immigration has contributed to the rapid and large growth of the minority population, particularly for Latinos and Asian and Pacific Islanders, there is concern about how these new or potentially new Americans are being socialized by the political system (Cho, 1999; Jones-Correa, 1998). Nakanishi (2001) points to how with the exception of Japanese Americans, the balance within the Asian and Pacific Islander population has shifted away from being native-born to foreign-born in the twenty years since the1970 census. This fact has several implications. One is that the proportion of the Latino and Asian American population that is legally enfranchised to vote has decreased and will only increase if levels of naturalization increase. Another is the concern that, should institutions of mobilization (e.g. political parties) revert to previous practices of purposefully limiting the incorporation of immigrants into the political system, the level of participation of the first, but increasingly the second and subsequent, generations will continue to lag behind that of the majority population. This will be especially true if, as discussed above, the naturalization process itself is an important socializer for increasing political participation.

Ramakrishnan (2001) has shown how different immigrant groups are incorporated differently into the electoral process. Furthermore, Nakanishi (2001) points to the importance of year of entry into the country in accounting for higher turnout rates among long-term first generation Asian and Pacific Islanders in contrast to the foreign-born in general as well as the native-born. In all cases Ramakrishnan (2001) finds that the turnout rate among minorities, regardless of generation, remains lower than for whites of the same generation. This raises questions about how different minority groups are socialized to politics over time.

The "Nationality model": When explicitly or implicitly relying on the "pan-ethnic" model, researchers have tended to use the widest definition possible of a particular group in order to ascertain patterns that are discernible and significant. Individuals who would certainly fit the description of Asian Americans are lumped together as a race, with occasional mention that, for example, a Hmong may have little in common with a Sinhalese, or a Filipina with a Korean.

In the "nationality model," however, the national origin of specific ethnic groups is considered the key variable. Unlike the Pan-ethnic approach, each ethnic subgroup is considered to have a separate social, economic, and political identity (Cho, 1995; Nakanishi, 1991; Cain & Kiewiet, 1985; Uhlaner et al., 1989; Rogers, 2000). These studies assert the existence of politically meaningful differences among black, Asian American and Latino subgroups. Cho (1995) notes that the underlying assumption of homogeneity among Asian Americans can produce fallacious results. In fact, it is often the case that separate ethnicities act as separate groups with their own unique political perspective and identities (Lai, 2000).

Nakanishi (1991) observes that significant differences exist among Asian Americans in educational levels, affluence, party affiliation and party registration. Furthermore, Cain and Kiewit's (1985) study show significant differences within Asian American groups on issues such as bilingual education. According to the Latino National Political Survey (LNPS), 71% of Puerto Ricans and 67% of Mexican Americans identified themselves as Democrats or leaning Democratic. In contrast, 69% of Cuban Americans identified with the Republican Party (de la Garza et al., 1992). Whether the pan-ethnic or nationality model is the more accurate and under what circumstances remains an open question. However, only after surveying different groups, as the LNPS does, will the data allow for answering this question by systematically revealing dissimilarities or commonalities among the various African American, Asian American and Latino subgroups.

As another form of the Group Consciousness model, the challenge that the Nationality model poses, particularly for the Pan-ethnic model, is not exclusively conceptual in nature but methodological as well. However, if resorting to Pan-ethnic labels was a matter of methodological expediency for researchers interested in obtaining samples large enough to allow for generalizeable findings, the Nationality model faces methodological hurdles of its own. To conduct a nationwide cross sectional study that sampled large enough numbers of national groups to make valid and reliable analyses is a daunting, perhaps prohibitive task. The largest existing survey databases such as the Citizen Participation Study are limited in the empirical evidence they can provide due to the small subgroup size problem. A way to overcome some aspects of this problem is to circumscribe the geographical reach of the study to areas where the presence of the different nationality groups is substantive. This may mean narrowing the scope of the study to even smaller geopolitical units than the state (e.g. county, metropolitan area or place).

Another methodological issue to consider is language. Language proficiency certainly is a variable that affects participation (Rosenstone & Hansen, 1993), but participation in the electoral and non-electoral activities does take place in spite of the lack of knowledge of English. Sampling English-speakers may only provide a partial and even inaccurate picture of the political participation of a given group. Admittedly, however, providing translations for survey instruments in all or most languages spoken in a given area can be prohibitively expensive, and can introduce error in the comparability of questions due to the translation process or cultural differences in meaning.

Political Mobilization: An Underutilized Explanation?

The SES and the Civic Voluntarism models recognize the role of institutions both as sites where skills that are useful in political activities are learned and as sites where people may be exposed to political messages that contribute to their interest in or knowledge about politics (Verba et al., 1995; Verba & Nie, 1972). Moreover, Verba, Schlozman and Brady (1995) and Gerber and Green (2000) identify recruitment as an important element that contributes to people's political participation. In the Civic Voluntarism model recruitment is mediated through institutions. The workplace, religious institutions and non-political organizations are the targeted sites where people are asked to get involved in political activity, in addition to providing opportunities to acquire politically relevant "civic skills."

Yet, while Verba and colleagues recognize the importance of recruitment to their model of political participation, they do not emphasize it expansively because "participation can, and does, take place in the absence of specific requests for activity" (1995, p. 270). However, theories that rely on the characteristics of individuals, such as the SES model, do not seem to be able to explain changes in participation over time (Rosenstone & Hansen, 1993). Nie, Junn and Stehlik-Barry (1996), as discussed above, have offered an answer from the perspective of a highly refined socioeconomic model but it remains an answer absent a consideration of politics. While acknowledging the importance of socio-demographic characteristics, Rosenstone and Hansen propose to bring precisely such a political focus to their explanation of participation by emphasizing "the centrality of strategic mobilization," since the "public's level of activism changes more quickly than its personal characteristics do" (1993, pp. 5, 70).

Rosenstone and Hansen (1993) identify two types of strategic mobilization: direct and indirect. Direct mobilization refers to the personal appeal a citizen receives from a given political actor to become involved in a political activity (for example, when a candidate asks for a person's vote either in person at the local train station or through direct mailings, or when the President pushes for a particular legislative initiative and asks the public to contact their representative in Congress). Indirect mobilization refers to instances when the appeals are mediated by an intermediary, for example, through a petition drive or when co-workers encourage colleagues to vote for a particular candidate or ballot measure.[16] The target of strategic mobilization, according to Rosenstone and

Hansen, are those whom the mobilization agents (i.e. politicians, political parties or other activists) know, identify as centrally positioned and effective, and perceive as responsive to mobilization (1993, p. 31). These targets tend to be those who are employed and those who belong to organizations, particularly the leadership. Participation in this mobilization model then is also mediated through institutions. The timing of the mobilization depends on the calculations political leaders make as to the usefulness of such mobilization, the saliency of the issues at any given point in time and place as well as the political "calendar." Thus, Rosenstone and Hansen observe, as the level of membership in organizations has declined in the United States so has the level of political activity.

Under this mobilization model, lower minority (i.e. African American, Mexican American and Puerto Rican) political participation may once again be explained by the relatively fewer resources they have at their disposal. These range from lower educational attainment and income, lower labor force participation rate, limited English language skills, non-citizenship and so forth. But Rosenstone and Hansen (1993) add to the institutional factors that have hindered or barred minority participation such as poll taxes, literacy tests and other disenfranchising procedures that were specifically instituted to keep minorities from engaging the political system.[17] Once these were removed by the Voting Rights Act (1965) and African American voters were mobilized through voter registration drives, turnout among African Americans increased dramatically. The trend was reversed as mobilization efforts in general and voter registration drives in particular declined through the 1970s and 1980s. Rosenstone and Hansen also remark on how minorities may not be perceived by white elected officials as central to their electoral coalitions as well as the cultural or perceptual disconnect that may exist between minority constituent and white elected officials (1993, p. 78).

Wrinkle and colleagues (1996) test a model examining the influence of mobilization, culture (attachment to one's co-ethnics) and socio-economic status on Latino political involvement. The authors find that mobilization is one of the strongest predictors of Latino participation, even after controlling for socio-economic status. While this points to a variable that may promote higher levels of Latino political involvement despite this group's low socioeconomic profile, the model is problematic. The authors measure mobilization in terms of contacting public officials, engaging in collective action to solve problems, and talking to others about problems. But these independent variables are difficult to distinguish conceptually from the political acts comprising the dependent variable scale. Thus, the effects of mobilization variable may be overestimated due to the endogeneity in the model.

Diaz (1996) also constructs a model of Latino participation resting on variables beyond the typical socioeconomic indicators, but without the methodological problems complicating Wrinkle et al.'s (1996) model. Diaz explores whether organizational memberships, which have been shown to boost political activity among whites have a similarly strong, positive effect on Latino participation. Diaz (1996) finds that participation is increased among Puerto Ricans and Mexican Americans with both active and inactive organizational affiliations. The major limitation to this study is that Diaz's (1996) dependent variable measures exclusively current and past voting behavior. As numerous other studies have pointed out, Latinos tend to engage in a much broader range of political activities than voting (Garcia, 1988; Wrinkle et al., 1996; Hero & Campbell, 1996; de la Garza & DeSipio, 1994). Still, Diaz's (1996) exploration of the connection between organizational affiliation and Latino political activity contributes a great deal to the study of Latino political behavior. Shaw and colleagues (2000) estimated Latino voting rates in the 1996 presidential election by validating self-reported turnout from a post-election survey of Latinos in California, Florida, and Texas. One of the most distinctive feature of Latino voting in 1996 was that Latinos contacted by Latino political organizations were 11% more likely to vote than Latinos who were not contacted. However, the effect of being contacted by established party organizations was not significant, which suggests that targeted mobilization efforts by community-based ethnic organizations may be critical to increasing turnout and incorporating Latinos (and perhaps other ethnic groups) into the existing political system.

Barrio Ballots: Latino Politics in the 1990 Elections (De la Garza, Menchaca, & DeSipio, 1994) represents a comprehensive effort to explore factors leading Latinos to become more politically active. Conducting ethnographic studies[18] in five Latino communities across the U.S. prior to the 1990 elections, the researchers expand their scope beyond socio-economic variables to investigate how mobilization, campaign issues, and electoral variables may increase participation rates.

Generally, Latinos in the communities under investigation appeared more motivated to become active following mobilization by community-level organizations, which concomitantly educate and socialize Latinos into the political process. Motivation is also enhanced when campaign issues resonate with Latinos' daily concerns. Further, local-level elections and competitive seats contested by Latino candidates seem to enhance participation. This follows a similar trend among African Americans where African American candidates typically yield higher levels of African American political participation, even when white and Latino candidates are running on a liberal platform.

The salience of mobilization appeals from members of minority organizations to members of their own groups has also been noted (Shaw et al., 2000). However, more research is needed in this area. The consumer approach to electoral politics has emphasized the role of political parties (especially at the national level) as fund-raising machines while diminishing or abandoning altogether their function of bringing citizens into the political process. While this incorporative function traditionally had limited impact on racial and ethnic minorities (Erie, 1988; Krase & LaCerra, 1991), its more recent decline may be a contributing factor to even lower rates of minority political participation. Alternatively, appeals from highly placed elected officials, whether electoral or programmatic in nature, may promote the strategic turnout of targeted groups. Recent examples of this are the appeals of candidate and President Clinton to African Americans (e.g. affirmative action, political appointments), or those of candidate and President George W. Bush and New York Governor George E. Pataki to Latinos (e.g. on issues of immigration amnesty, the U.S. Navy's use of the island of Vieques).

The targeting of mobilization appeals to specific groups is not the only factor that seems to have a positive impact on participation. The quality or manner of the mobilization appeal elicits varying degrees of responses, some more positive than others. Gerber and Green (2000) in an experimental field study of some 30,000 registered voters in New Haven, CT, found that in contrast to direct mail appeals and telephone calls, personal canvassing had the strongest effect in bringing people out to the polls on election day. Gerber and Green inferred that it was not the overall decline of mobilization appeals in later years that has led to a decline in electoral participation, but the specific decline in personally contacting the voter.

Leighley (2001) has found that knowing the person who makes the request to participate has a powerful effect on an individual's involvement in a variety of political activities across racial or ethnic background. Political actors are more responsive to requests to participate when they come from people they know. Based on analyses of the Citizen Participation Study data, as well as data from the National Election Study and the Texas Minority Survey, Leighley finds that mobilization is a critical factor in participation, but it is structured by socioeconomic factors in such a way as to leave African Americans and, particularly, Latinos undermobilized. Moreover, campaigns tend to target their appeals to the political bases of support for particular candidates, and often just to the most consistent voters, who tend to be those of higher socioeconomic status. These efforts tend to leave unsolicited the marginal, the inconsistent or eventual voter, who tend to be those of lower socioeconomic status.

Mobilization appeals also appear to affect different ethnic groups in varying ways. For instance, the results in Fuchs et al.'s (2000) study show that Latinos and whites are more responsive to requests to register or vote than are African Americans. Latinos, furthermore, seem to be even more responsive when the appeals come from other Latinos (Shaw et al., 2000).

As political parties seem to fall short in their mobilization of minorities, a closer analysis of indigenous minority group organizations and institutions that serve as agents of mobilization is needed. There are other pertinent questions as well. What role does the ethnic press play in mobilizing co-ethnics? How successful are they in this capacity? What interests are represented in the advocacy undertaken by the ethnic press? How do community-based, social services and civic organizations operate in the mobilization of their constituencies? How are the agendas of these organizing efforts created and shaped? (Lai, 2000).

FUTURE RESEARCH

While research on the political participation of minorities has increased over the last decade, many questions remain to be answered. We reiterate the need to explore further how mobilization and recruitment affect the participation of minorities. Here we propose some areas that need attention and that we believe would contribute to elucidate further what may foster participation and what may hinder it. We emphasize the need to move beyond SES-based models to models that incorporate socialization or acculturation variables as well as other factors that stress the heterogeneity within Asian American and Latino groups (e.g. generational distance from arrival in the U.S., inter-minority group competition). We also point to the need to take into account the geographical dispersion of immigrant and minority groups throughout the country and how this may make the picture of participation even more complex; the need to distinguish the effect of jurisdiction; and the need to consider the urban/suburban divide. We highlight further aspects of the heterogeneity of minorities such as their race and their ethnicity/nationality within the all-encompassing labels that may impact both group consciousness and participation. Finally, we ask whether the rational choice framework might be applied to understand the political participation of immigrants and minorities.

Clearly, there has been an evolution in the content and sophistication of models that attempt to uncover the factors influencing Latino and Asian American participation. Most encouraging, for example, are the Wrinkle et al. (1996), Diaz (1996), de la Garza (1997), Cho (1995), Lien (1994) and Hritzuk and Park (2000) studies, which attempt to combine methodologically sound tests with theoretically expansive models of Latino and Asian American participation.

For example, Lien's (1994) examination of the political participation of Asian Americans and Mexican Americans typifies the progress made in the field of ethnic political behavior while at the same time shows the need for further research. In a re-examination of a 1984 California statewide survey of individuals 18 years of age or older, Lein (1994) found that despite a very large socioeconomic gap between Asian Americans and Mexican Americans, they have similar ethnicity and participation structures. For both groups, acculturation increases participation, attachment to homeland culture does not necessarily discourage participation and the role of group consciousness is much more complex than previously conceived. Lien (1994) states that "the extent of cognitive adaptation to the prevailing norms, beliefs, and attitudes of the American political culture can be conceived as indicated by a person's sense of civic duty, level of political information, and attitude toward immigrant issues."

While this correlation between acculturation and participation may have some validity, the questions used by Lien to measure acculturation need to be re-examined.[19] Lien (1994) states that "based on theories of group mobilization and rational choice, it is hypothesized that the identification with American social groups and the sense of being racially alienated and systematically deprived will generally mobilize ethnic group members to participate in socio-political activities." These questions used to measure an individual's group consciousness will be extremely beneficial to understand how different ethnic groups feel about one another. In particular, the Korean American-African American conflict described in the media will be an interesting ethnic group conflict to explore. Due to the speculation that the Los Angeles riots mobilized many Asian Americans, especially Korean Americans, to participate in political activities, future research needs to explore whether and how specific social, political or economic events affect different minority groups' levels of political participation.

Future research in Latino and Asian American participation should be guided by two objectives. First, to construct models that incorporate factors other than those relating to socioeconomic status and that focus on factors that may positively influence Latino and Asian American political activity despite these communities typically low levels of political participation. These models may help ascertain whether the variables explaining Latino and Asian American participation are distinct from those that account for white and African American political activity. Second, scholars need to construct scales of participatory acts beyond that of simple voting to broaden our understanding of Latino and Asian American political involvement across a wide range of activities. Beyond these general themes, a number of more specific factors need to be taken into consideration in future research.

The Ecology of Participation: Growing Geographic Dispersion

Minorities are not evenly settled throughout the country. However, as new immigrants arrive in the country and as structural shifts in the economy have made the South and the mountain and coastal West areas of population growth minorities are dispersing to parts of the country where their settlement is a new phenomenon.

Half of the Latino population may live presently in California and Texas, but in some counties of North Carolina, Georgia, Iowa, Arkansas, Minnesota and Nebraska, Hispanics represented between 6 and 25% of the county's population, far exceeding the average of the Hispanic population in those states (Guzmán, 2001). Thus, while the emphasis on the political participation of Latinos and other minorities will continue to focus on states with large proportions of given minority groups, attention must also be paid to new areas of settlement. The influx of new groups into new areas tends to change extant social and political dynamics, and consequently may provide the potential for conflict, political organization and mobilization (Cruz, 1998; Rogers, 2000).

Geographic dispersion of minority groups may also have other consequences. Historical patterns of settlement have identified particular regions of the country with, for instance, certain Hispanic groups. Mexican Americans have traditionally been by far the largest Hispanic group in the United States, but their presence has been felt largely in the Southwest. Florida, on the other hand, has been identified with Cuban émigrés and Cuban Americans, and the Northeast became synonymous with Puerto Ricans. While we may still think in these terms, conditions have in fact changed. Cuban Americans are no longer the majority Latino population in Florida nor are Puerto Ricans the majority in the Northeast, though they remain the plurality, accounting for more or less a third of the Latino population in Florida and New York, respectively (Guzmán, 2001). Therefore, national group-specific political agendas that may have prevailed for years in a given region may not be effective in mobilizing the growing Pan-ethnic group population. Parochial interests may also have the effect of diluting or neutralizing the voting strength of the larger group (Lai, 2001).

National, Regional or Local Contexts

The locale where participation takes place is an important contextual factor. For instance, the political attitudes, orientations and behavior of an individual may exhibit notable differences depending on whether such a person sees herself as member of a minority group in a town, county, state or region of the country where the group she identifies as belonging to is a small minority, a large minority or a majority of the population. Her interaction with members of her own group, as well as those she may identify as the majority and other minorities, may be influenced by the particular socio-demographic composition of the locale. If it has become evident that patterns of political participation, whether in voting, contacting elected officials or engaging in protest, among Latinos (De la Garza et al., 1992) and Asian Americans (Lien, 1994) differ within Pan-ethnic groups, it is not unreasonable to presume that participation should also vary according to the place of residence (Mollenkopf et al., 1999). Do we expect Korean-Americans to exhibit the same voting pattern in Bergen County, New Jersey as they do in Los Angeles County? Cuban-Americans in Hudson County, New Jersey, for example, have elected one of their own to the U.S. Congress as a Democrat, while those in Dade County, Florida have elected two Republicans.

There has been an over-reliance on drawing samples of minority groups from states or counties where they constitute a large proportion of the population, in order to secure a large sample size (Shaw et al., 2000; Cho, 1999; Leighley & Vedlitz, 1999). This methodology has provided us with profiles of how the majority of Latinos, Asian Americans, or African Americans behave politically. Perhaps minorities that settle in areas where their compatriots are but the smallest of minorities behave differently, but this may not be captured in the large survey studies. If, for example, a Vietnamese settles in a town where the opportunity to interact with other Vietnamese (or Asian Americans in general) is absent, one might reasonably expect that her political behavior would differ from that of other Vietnamese or Asian Americans for whom such inter-ethnic interactions are more possible. Such an individual may find it easier to assimilate and adopt the norms and ways of the majority group. Alternately, such a person may find herself even more alienated and withdrawn from the political process than her fellow co-ethnics.

Whereas African Americans are 12.3% of the country's population, they represent less than 1% in upper New England and the upper Mountain West states. Similarly Latinos range from 12.3% in Illinois to less than 2% in the Dakotas and Ohio. Does the political engagement of African Americans or Latinos vary depending on such contextual factors? Understanding the political attitudes and behaviors of minorities living in non-minority communities could provide valuable insights into the political participation of their fellow Asian

Americans, African Americans or Latinos elsewhere in the nation, as well as about the dynamics of political participation more generally.

Urban and Suburban Contexts

As whites have fled the cities to the suburbs, urban centers have become increasingly identified with minorities. Whites have driven the growth in suburbanization. Ideologically and politically, the suburbs have been identified as being more conservative and more Republican than cities. But these traits have less to do with individual-level characteristics of the population that lives in suburbs than with contextual factors specific to the suburbs (e.g. the proximity and wealth disparity between the suburb to a central city, the "age" of the suburb). " The type of community or environment in which people reside affects political behavior independently of individual socioeconomic characteristics" (Gainsborough, 2001, p. 7). There is in fact a "place effect" that impacts electoral and policy outcomes.

However, whites have not been the only ones to move to the suburbs in great numbers. The suburbanization of America may be a phenomenon driven by whites but it is not exclusive to whites. The proportion of minorities in suburbs has increased over the past decades. Hispanics account for 12% of the suburban population, with African Americans representing 9% and Asian Americans 5% (Lewis Mumford Center for Comparative Urban and Regional Research, 2001). Fifty-eight percent of Asian Americans, 49% of Latinos and 39% of African Americans now live in suburbs.

Moreover, Oliver (2000) has found that locality size matters with respect to political participation, as Verba and Nie (1972) had observed. Using data from a nationally-sampled cross-sectional study and aggregate data from the1990 Census, Oliver observed that involvement across a range of electoral and non-electoral forms of participation declines as the population size of the place of residence increases, especially in very large cities (population of one million or more). Lower levels of interest in politics and the lesser likelihood of being mobilized make residents of large cities less likely to vote or contact elected officials than small or even mid-size city dwellers. Future research should consider ecological impact as an important variable in minority political behavior (Ramírez, 2000).

The Heterogeneity of the Minority Population

The effect of ethnicity among blacks is something that necessitates further research as well. Between 1951 and 1998, just short of 1.4 million people immigrated from the non-Spanish speaking Caribbean, and 580,000 immigrated from Africa (U.S. Immigration and Naturalization Service, 2000). Furthermore, the 710,000 Hispanics who self-identified as black in the 2000 Census represented 2% of the total African American population (Grieco & Cassidy, 2001). Rogers (2000) has pointed out that while Caribbean-Americans, keenly aware of the place of race in American political society, share many social characteristics with African Americans, they may still follow a process of political incorporation different (e.g. less radical or progressive) from the latter group. Thus, while African Americans still represent the overwhelming majority of blacks in the United States, the increasing ethnic diversity among blacks requires further exploration.

In addition, race as an aspect in intra-ethnic minority dynamics has hardly received attention. The caveat that the term Hispanic is not a racial category, but refers to people of any race, does not address how black and white Hispanics think and behave politically. While the majority of Hispanics classify themselves as non-white – Asian, 0.3%, black, 2%; American Indian, 1.2%; some other race, 42.2%; two or more races, 6.3% – those who identify as white make up 48% (Grieco & Cassidy, 2001). This has led some to argue that the concerns over urban white flight may be a fallacy, with negative political implications for social policies such as affirmative action (Patterson, 2001). Race is certainly a social identity that, while partly defined by physical characteristics, is relational in nature. While an individual may choose to define him or herself one way or another, such self-definitions tend to be validated and reinforced, or discounted and rejected, through social intercourse (Thornton, 2001). Racial self-identity within minority groups, nevertheless, needs to be explored as a factor bearing on politics, particularly as coalitional strategies are considered between groups to enhance participation and policy outcomes.

Minorities as Rational Actors

To what extent might rational choice theory illuminate the observed differences in the political participation of minority and immigrant groups? Green and Shapiro (1994) note that rational choice theory fails to predict the simplest act of political participation, namely, the act of voting. While rational choice theory predicts that voter turnout should converge at or near zero, in every election millions turn out to vote. If rational choice theory fails to account for the most basic form of political participation, what, if any, utility might it have in explaining the variation in political participation among minorities and immigrants?

Moving beyond voter turnout, rational choice theory may offer an analytic framework to explain other areas of political participation, such as protests and demonstrations, as well as group competition among minorities and immigrant groups. Hechter (1986) suggests that rational choice theory should appeal to the study of minority and immigrant groups:

> Rational choice considers individual behavior to be a function of the interaction of structural constraints and the . . . preferences of individuals. The structure first determines . . . the constraints under which people act. Within these constraints, individuals face various feasible courses of action. The course of action ultimately chosen is selected rationally (Hechter, 1986, p. 286).

Since institutionalized discrimination and individual hostile acts against minorities and immigrant groups constitutes a set of obvious structural constraints, rational choice theory can and should be applied to understand the behavior of minority and immigrant groups (Ratcliffe, 2000). Chong (1991) vividly demonstrates, within a rational choice framework, how collective action was achieved among rational, self-interested, utility-maximizing African Americans during the Civil Rights movement. Chong blends formal game theory with elements of social networks (including friendship, reputation, social standing) to help explain individuals' decision to join and sustain the civil rights movement.

As Chong clearly demonstrates, rational choice has much to offer in the areas of minority and immigrant political participation. Unfortunately, works that push the boundaries of rational choice to include minority and immigrant group remain the exception instead of the rule (Leighley, 2001). We look forward to rational choice expanding beyond its traditional areas of Congress and its relationship with the bureaucracy to explore fertile areas of protest and demonstration and group conflict among minority and immigrant groups.

CONCLUSION

Verba and colleagues (1995) stress the importance for political participation of resources associated with higher socioeconomic status in part because participation takes place even in the absence of recruitment. As they describe it, higher income and educational attainment provide, and institutions mediate, resources that are key to political activity. As groups, African Americans and Latinos are over-represented among those of lower socioeconomic status as are various South East Asians groups, and they are less likely to be members of organizations or associations. Consequently, they are less likely to vote, contribute to political campaigns or contact elected officials. Their political voices are muted in the political arena. Improving their economic lot (i.e. through more education, higher income) might increase participation among minorities and individuals more generally.

As suggested by Nie and colleagues (1996), however, the gains minorities may achieve in terms of education may not translate into higher levels of political participation. As more people receive more education, the political gains that might be expected do not materialize because they are diluted by the achievement of others at any given time. Those who cannot keep up or fall behind educationally can be expected to be in worse shape politically.

These are not auspicious predictions for minorities. If the stratification structures that produced a racially and ethnically stratified society are not altered – and there is little indication that they will be – the mechanisms that may be available for minority political participation will have to be those of mobilization. Participation may "take place in the absence of specific request for activity" (Verba et al., 1995, p. 270), but mobilization determines who participates and when (Rosenstone & Hansen, 1993). Political actors, including minorities, tend to respond to requests for participation (Rosenstone & Hansen, 1993), and they tend to respond even more positively when approached by members of their own (ethnic/racial) group (Shaw et al., 2000).

What form might appeals for mobilization take? Appeals to group consciousness (i.e. co-ethnics' affinity for and identification with their group) have not been shown to be completely successful in promoting participation among minorities (Mangum, 2000), though they may decrease participation among members of the majority population (Leighly & Vedlitz, 1999). Appeals based on pan-ethnicity (e.g. "Latino/Hispanic") may be too recent and have not been studied. In practice, as the 2000 Presidential electoral campaign showed, the use of the label Latino by the Republican party was used for more targeted appeals to Mexican-Americans in Texas and Cuban-Americans in Florida. Such appeals were not made, for instance, in New York. Nationally, however, the Democratic party did so. It remains to be seen whether such a Pan-ethnic consciousness exists among Latinos and Asian Americans.

Appeals based on national origin may be more effective in smaller jurisdictions such as a county or a locality; but as the jurisdiction becomes larger, and the likelihood of a larger and more diverse minority population increases, nationality appeals may turn counter-productive and instigate inter-minority group conflict or diminished interest among the neglected groups. Inter-minority group conflict may very well increase participation in the short-run but the effects of such conflict on internal and external efficacy may result in depressed participation in the long-run. These observations, however, are speculative and await future empirical research. What is clear, however, is that as minority populations become larger, more diverse and more important constituencies in the United States, researchers interested in the dynamics of political participation can no longer afford to ignore these groups.

NOTES

1. Under the term minority we are including the following racial groups: black, Asian and Pacific Islander and Native American/American Indian. The term also includes people whose origin, or the origin of their ancestors, was in the Spanish-speaking countries of North, Central and South America and the Caribbean as well as the inhabitants of those territories acquired by the United States after the War of 1848 and the Gadsen Purchase. This group is to be interchangeably referred to as Latino or Hispanic, and it includes people of any racial group. The majority, white, group includes people of European origin or descent. The ethnic label African American will be used specifically to refer to second- or even third-generation black Americans.

2. The 2000 decennial census shows the population of the United States to be more than 281 million people, of which 12.3% identified itself as black, 1% as American Indian, Hawaiian/Pacific Islander or Alaska Native, 3.6% as Asian (Grieco & Cassidy, 2001). Another 5.5% of the population selected another race, and 2.4% indicated being of two or more races. Those identifying themselves as Latino or Hispanic made up 12.5% of the population.

3. In 2000, Latinos made up 32.4% of California's population; black 6.7%; Asians and Pacific Islanders, 11.3%; American Indian or Alaska Native, 1%; non-Hispanic whites, 46.7%. Those who marked some other race or more than one race were 21.5%. In Texas, Latinos were 32% of the state's population; black, 11.5%; Asian and Pacific Islanders, 2.8%; American Indian or Alaska Native, 0.6%; non-Hispanic whites, 52.4%. Those who marked some other race or more than one race were 14.2%. In New York, Latinos were 15.1% of the state's population; blacks, 15.9%; Asian and Pacific Islanders, 5.5%; American Indian or Alaska Native, 0.4%; non-Hispanic whites, 62%. Those who marked some other race or more than one race were 10.2%. (U.S. Census Bureau, 2001a)

4. Separation may have occurred physically and geographically, in enclaves, ghettos or reservations, or interpersonally, in subordinate relations.

5. Whereas some European groups of varied cultural or national original (e.g. Irish, southern Italians, Jews and Slavs) may not have conformed to extant Anglo-Saxon racial norm of whiteness of the nineteenth century, this social norm ultimately evolved to include them.

6. These turnout figures are higher than those reported officially. For instance, the Federal Election Commission reported the national turnout to be 96,456,345 votes or 49.08% of the voting age population in the 1996 Presidential election (Federal Election Commission, 2001). On the other hand, the total number of people reporting to vote in the same election according to the Current Population Survey for 1996 was 105,017,000. Both the Federal Election Commission and the Bureau of the Census warn that differences in totals may be the result of counting votes only for the highest office on the ballot, thus understating total number of votes cast; over-reporting and general misreporting of voting activity on the part of survey informants; survey under-coverage and general selection bias (Casper & Bass, 1998: fn.1; Federal Election Commission, 2001). Moreover, Shaw et al. (2000) have showed that, specifically in the case of Latino respondents, the *validated* turnout was much lower than the *reported* turnout for the 1996

election. These discrepancies notwithstanding, the differences in turnout across ethnic and racial groups over time are consistent and persistent.

For instance, registered voters turn out to vote in higher proportions in high profile elections such as Presidential elections. The turnout results reported by citizens in the Current Population Survey for the 1998 mid-term elections, the latest national figures on voting available, showed a marked decrease in those reporting turning out to vote when compared to the 1996 contest as well as consistently lower levels of participation among minorities. The results were as follow: non-Hispanic whites, 47.4%; Non-Hispanic blacks, 41.9%; Non-Hispanic Asian/Pacific Islanders, 32.3%; and Latinos, 32.8%; for an average of 45.3% for the citizen population as a whole (Day & Gaither, 2000). As a percentage of their numbers in the voting-age population as a whole 46.4% of non-Hispanic whites and 40% of Non-Hispanic blacks voted; but only 19.2% of the total Non-Hispanic Asian/Pacific Islanders and 20% of the Latinos.

7. It is noteworthy that these findings result from studies that use a survey research methodology. Thus, it is the respondent's account of his or her participation that is recorded. Where survey results have been validated (e.g. contrasting survey answers with actual voting records), the tendency to over-report on an activity tends to be higher "among those with a greater perceived stake in the system, such as the highly educated, efficacious, and those with a strong sense of civic duty" (Shaw et al., 2000, p. 344; Conway, 1991). This raises the question of whether the model is validated when its measurements may not be valid. If the model hypothesizes that some members of the population are more likely to be actively engaged in politics because they are more psychologically engaged, as a result of their station in life, but it turns out that those who claim to be active in fact are not but respond affirmatively because they are expected to have engaged in such activities due to social or class expectations of acceptable and proper behavior, then the argument is not only circular but spurious as well. Verba et al. (1995, Appendix E), however, dispute and discount the criticism of lack of validity due to spuriousness, it by pointing out that "social desirability does not correlate with specific characteristics of respondents" and that the basic variables of the model (e.g. civic skills and participation) are not correlated with each other. (Cf., note. 6.)

8. These income differences mean that blacks make 61 cents for every dollar whites make, and Latinos, 67 cents. The ratio for Asians is $1.22 for every dollar whites make. In terms of overall wealth, blacks have 12 cents for every dollar whites have as their median net worth, compared to 13 cents for Latinos and 67 cents for Asians. In terms of median net financial assets, blacks have 1 cent for every dollar whites have, Latinos have 3 cents and Asians, 51 cents (Oliver & Shapiro, 2001, p. 228).

9. Statistical models tend to show that Latinos, controlling for all SES variables, still lag their white counterparts in some forms of political participation.

10. Even among Asian Americans there is widespread variation in political participation. Wealth may actually be a better SES indicator than income insofar as political participation is concerned, particularly as it refers to Asians. Wealth may be capturing an effect on participation that income does not, for while Asians as a whole outperform whites in income levels, they do less well in overall wealth. This disparity may explain lower Asian participation.

11. Age exhibited a curvilinear effect on participation; that is, those in the middle-age groups (30 to 65) are much more likely to take part in political activities than the very old or the very young. However, when other sociodemographic characteristics (e.g.

marital status, work status, mobility and community roots) are controlled, participation tends to increase with age (Conway, 1991).

12. The Civic Voluntarism Model relies on resources, engagement and recruitment as factors that explain political involvement or lack thereof. Verba et al. (1995), however, emphasize the impact of time, money and civic skills as well as psychological engagement in politics over recruitment, therefore situating themselves within the SES model. Higher levels of education, income and occupation result in greater availability of money, time and organizational and communication capabilities that are conducive to participation in political activities.

13. Social capital, also described as social connectedness, was operationalized using three variables: marital status, length of residence in the community and home ownership.

14. Because of sheer numbers and the geographic concentration of nationality-specific groups, "Pan-ethnic" labels may be associated or conflated with a specific group. For instance, in the recent Presidential campaign, George W. Bush made extensive appeals to Hispanic/Latinos. But these appeals were geographically targeted. While referring to Hispanic/Latinos in Texas or Florida, it was evident that the targeted audiences were Mexican Americans and Cuban Americans. The use of the more encompassing label provided cover from criticism that the candidate was targeting one group over another. But the fact that the Republican candidate did not make similar appeals in the Northeast (with the exception of New Jersey, with its sizable Cuban American population) made it clear that Puerto Ricans, Dominicans, Colombians and other Latinos in general were not the Hispanics to be mobilized.

15. The "group consciousness" model has largely being understood in terms of the affinity among members of self-aware collectives in relation to one another, and in terms of its sense of common fate, as well as in relation to those identified as "other." Cruz's work is circumscribed to a subset of a given group's membership, i.e. its social and political elite.

16. Rosenstone and Hansen measured mobilization by asking respondents, for instance, whether he or she had worked for a political party or candidate, or had attempted to convince others to vote for a particular political candidate or party. They, however, had an expansive definition and measurements of mobilization that included not just appeals by political leaders but also mobilization around "issues" (e.g. whether there had been changes in the property tax collected, and the prevailing rate of unemployment) and "opportunities" (e.g. the number of bills up for consideration in Congress).

17. Rosenstone and Hansen (1993) use national longitudinal data from the American National Election Study, supplemented with other national cross-sectional as well as aggregate data to test their model.

18. Ethnographic methodology can be problematic because only some members of the communities studied are open to being interviewed, increasing the risk that the findings are not representative. Further rendering the results potentially unrepresentative is the small number of interviews conducted, ranging from, for example, a low of 47 informal and formal interviews in New York's El Barrio to a high of 122 informal interviews and focus groups studies in Los Angeles (Goris & Pedraza, 1994; Pachon, Arguelles & Gonzalez, 1994).

19. Indicators used to measure Acculturation:
Importance of Voting – With which of the following questions do you agree?

(a) So many people vote, it's not very important for me to vote in elections;

(b) It's only important for me to vote in those elections where the interests of people like me are affected;

(c) Whether or not the interests of people like me are affected, it's important for me to vote in elections.

Political Information (as measure of exposure to information as well).
Interviewer's assessment of respondent's general level of information about politics and public affairs.

Employer Sanction
A law making it illegal for an employer to hire immigrants who have come to the U.S. without papers. Do you favor, oppose, or have no opinion?

Bilingual ballot
Providing non-English speaking voters in an election with ballots printed in their own language. Do you favor, oppose, or have no opinion?

ACKNOWLEDGMENTS

The authors would like to thank Robert Y. Shapiro and Rodolfo de la Garza for their insightful comments and suggestions.

REFERENCES

Aldrich, J. H. (1993). Rational choice and turnout. *American Journal of Political Science, 37*(1), 246–278.

Alex-Assensoh, Y. M., & Hanks, L. J. (Eds) (2000). *Blacks and multiracial politics in America*. New York: New York University Press.

Arvizu, J. R., & Garcia, F. C. (1996). Latino voting participation: Explaining and differentiating Latino voter turnout. *Hispanic Journal of Behavioral Sciences, 18*(2), 104–128.

Banton, M. (1983) *Racial and Ethnic Competition*. Cambridge: Cambridge University Press.

Banton, M. (1985). Mixed motives and the processes of rationalization. *Ethnic and Racial Studies 8*(4), 534–547.

Banton, M. (1995). Rational choice theories. *American Behavioral Scientist, 38*(3), 478–497.

Bates, R. H. (1997). Comparative politics and rational choice: A review essay. *American Political Science Review, 91*(3), 699–704.

Bobo, L. (1998). Group conflict, prejudice, and the paradox of contemporary racial attitudes. In: P. A. Katz & D. A. Taylor (Eds), *Eliminating Racism: Profiles in Controversy* (pp. 85–114). New York: Plenum.

Bobo, L., & Gilliam, F. D., Jr. (1990). Race sociopolitical participation, and black empowerment. *American Political Science Review, 84*, 377–393.

Booth, W. (2000, August, 31). California minorities are now majorities: Non-Hispanic whites dip below 50%. *The Washington Post*.

Cain, B. E., & Kiewiet, D. R. (1985). *Minorities in California*. Public symposium of the California Institute of Technology, Division of Humanities and Social Sciences, CA.

Cain, B. E., Kiewiet, D. R., & Uhlaner, C. J. (1991). The acquisition of partisanship by Latinos and Asian Americans. *American Journal of Political Science, 35*, 390–422.

Campbell, A. (Ed.) (1996). *Elections and the political order.* New York: Wiley.

Casper L. M., & Bass, L. E., (1998, July). Voting and registration in the election of November 1996. *Current Population Report,* U.S. Census Bureau (P20–504).

Cho, W. K. T. (1995). Asians – A monolithic voting bloc? *Political Behavior, 17*(2), 223–249.

Cho, W. K. T. (1999). Naturalization, socialization, participation: Immigrants and (non-)voting. *Journal of Politics, 61*(4), 1140–1155.

Cho, W. K. T., & Cain, B. E. (2000). Asian Americans as the median voters: An exploration of attitudes and voting patterns on ballot initiatives. *Asian Americans and politics: Perspectives, experiences, prospects.* Stanford, CA, Stanford University Press.

Chong, D. (1991). *Collective action and the civil rights movement.* Chicago, IL: University of Chicago Press.

Cohen, C. J., & Dawson, M. C. (1993). Neighborhood poverty and African American politics. *American Political Science Review, 87*(2), 286–302.

Conway, M. M. (1991). *Political participation in the United States.* Washington, D.C.: Congressional Quarterly, Inc.

Cruz, J. E. (2000). Interminority relations in urban settings: Lessons from the black-Puerto Rican experience. In: Y. M. Alex-Assensoh & L. J. Hanks, (Eds), *Blacks and Multiracial Politics in America (2000).* New York: New York University Press.

Day, J. C., & Gaither, A. L. (2000, August). Voting and registration in the election of November 1998. *Current Population Report,* U.S. Census Bureau (P20–523RV).

DeSipio, L. (1996). *Counting on the Latino vote: Latinos as a new electorate.* Charlottesville, VA: University of Virginia Press.

de la Garza, R. O. (1987). *Ignored voices: Public opinion polls and the Latino community.* Austin, TX: University of Texas Press.

de la Garza, R. O., & DeSipio, L. (Eds) (1992). *From rhetoric to reality: Latino politics in the 1988 elections.* Boulder, CO: Westview Press.

de la Garza, R. O. (1996). *Ethnic ironies: Latino politics in the 1992 elections.* Boulder, CO, Westview Press.

de la Garza, R. O., & DeSipio, L. (1994). Overview: The link between individuals and electoral institutions in five Latino neighborhoods. In: R. O. de la Garza, M. Menchaca & L. DeSipio (Eds), *Barrio Ballots: Latino Politics in the 1990 Election.* Boulder, CO: Westview Press.

de la Garza, R. O. (1997). Save the baby, change the bathwater, and scrub the tub: Latino electoral participation after twenty years of Voting Rights Act coverage. In: F. C. Garcia (Ed.), *Pursuing Power: Latinos and the Political System.* Notre Dame, IN: University of Notre Dame Press.

de la Garza, R. O., DeSipio, L., Garcia, F. C., Garcia, J., & Falcón, A. (1992). *Latino voices: Mexican, Puerto Rican and Cuban perspectives on American politics.* Boulder, CO: Westview Press.

de la Garza, R. O., Falcón, A., & Garcia, F. C., (1996). Will the real Americans stand up: Anglo and Mexican-American support of core American political values. *American Journal of Political Science, 40*(2), 335–351.

de la Garza, R. O., Menchaca, M., & DeSipio L. (Eds) (1994). *Barrio ballots: Latino politics in the 1990 elections.* Boulder, CO, Westview Press.

Diaz, W. A. (1996). Latino participation in America: Associational and political roles. *Hispanic Journal of Behavioral Sciences, 18*(2), 154–173.

Eire, S. (1988). *Rainbow's end: Irish-Americans and the dilemmas of urban America, 1840–1984.* Berkeley, CA: University of California Press.

Elster, J. (2000). Rational choice history: A case of excessive ambition. *American Political Science Review, 94*(3), 685–695.

Falcón, A. (1988). Black and Latino politics in New York City: Race and ethnicity in a changing urban context. In: F. C. Garcia (Ed.), *Latinos and the political system.* Notre Dame, IN: Notre Dame University Press.

Federal Election Commission (2001, October 3). Voter Registration and turnout – 1996. http://www.fec.gov/pages/96to.htm

Fuchs, E. R., Minnite, L. C., & Shapiro, R. Y. (2000). Political capital and political participation. Paper presented at 2000 Annual Meeting of the American Political Science Association.

Gainsborough, J. F. (2001). *Fenced off: The suburbanization of American politics.* Washington, D.C.: Georgetown University Press.

Garcia, F. C. (Ed.) (1988). *Latinos and the political system.* Notre Dame, IN: University of Notre Dame Press.

Garcia, F. C. (1997). *Pursuing power: Latinos and the political system.* Notre Dame, IN: University of Notre Dame Press.

Gerber, A. S. & Green, D. P. (2000). The effects of canvassing, telephone calls, and direct mail on voter turnout: A field experiment. *American Political Science Review, 94*(3), 653–663.

Glazer, N., & Moynihan, D. P. (1963). *Beyond the melting pot: The Negroes, Puerto Ricans, and the Irish of New York City.* Cambridge, MA: MIT Press.

Green, D. P., & Shapiro, I. (1994). *Pathologies of Rational Choice Theory: Critique of Applications in Political Science.* New Haven, CT: Yale University Press.

Grieco, E. M., & Cassidy, R. C. (2001, March). Overview of race and Hispanic origin. *Census 2000 Brief.* U.S. Census Bureau, (C2KBR/01–1).

Guterbock, T., & London, B. (1983). Race, political orientation and participation: A test of four competing theories. *American Sociological Review, 48*, 191–206.

Gutiérrez, D. G. (1995). *Walls and mirrors: Mexican Americans, Mexican immigrants and the politics of ethnicity.* Berkeley, CA: University of California Press.

Guzmán, B. (2001, May). The Hispanic Population. *Census 2000 Brief.* U.S. Census Bureau (C2KBR/01–3).

Harris, D. (1994). Generating racial and ethnic conflict in Miami: Impact of American foreign policy and domestic racism. In: J. Jennings (Ed.), *Blacks, Latinos and Asians in Urban America.* Westport, CT: Praeger.

Hechter, M. (1986). Rational Choice Theory and the study of race and ethnic relations. In J. Rex & D. Mason (Eds), *Theories of Race and Ethnic Relations.* Cambridge: Cambridge University Press.

Henry, C., & Munoz, Jr., C. (1991). Ideological and interest linkages in California rainbow politics. In: B. O. Jackson & M. B. Preston (Eds), *Racial and Ethnic Politics in California.* Berkeley, CA: IGS Press.

Hero, R. E. (1992). *Latinos and the U.S. political system.* Philadelphia, PA: Temple University Press.

Hero, R. E., & Beatty, K. M. (1989). The election of Federico Pena as mayor of Denver: Analysis and implications. *Social Science Quarterly, 70*(2), 300–310.

Hero, R. E., & Campbell, A. G. (1996). Understanding Latino political participation: Exploring the evidence from the Latino National Political Survey. *Hispanic Journal of Behavioral Sciences, 18*(2), 120–141.

Hero, R. E., Garcia, F. C., Garcia, J., & Pachon, H. (2000). Latino participation, partisanship, and office holding. *PS: Political Science and Politics, 33*(3), 529–534.

Hritzuk, N., & Park, D. K. (2000). The question of latino participation: From an SES to a social structural explanation. *Social Science Quarterly, 81*(1), 151–166.

Jackman, R. W. (1993). Rationality and political participation. *American Journal of Political Science, 37*(1), 279–290.

Jones-Correa, M. (1998). *Between two nations.* Ithaca, NY: Cornell University Press.

Jones-Correa, M., & Leal, D. L. (1996). Becoming "Hispanic": Secondary pan-ethnic identification among Latin American-origin populations in the United States. *Hispanic Journal of Behavioral Sciences, 18*(2), 214–254.

Karnow, S. (1992, November 29). Apathetic Asian Americans?; Why their success hasn't spilled over into politics. *The Washington Post.*

Keiser, R. A., & Underwood, K. (Eds) (2000). *Minority politics at the millennium.* New York: Garland Publishing, Inc.

Krase, J., & LaCerra, C. (1991). *Ethnicity and machine politics.* Lanham, MD: University Press of America.

Lai, J. S. (2000). Asian Pacific Americans and the Pan-ethnic question. In: R. A. Keiser & K. Underwood (Eds), *Minority Politics at the Millennium.*

Leighley, J. E. (2001). *Strength in numbers? The political mobilization of racial and ethnic minorities.* Princeton, NJ: Princeton University Press.

Leighley, J. E., & Vedlitz, A. (1999). Race, ethnicity, and political participation: Competing models and contrasting explanations. *Journal of Politics, 61*(4), 1092–1114.

Lewis Mumford Center for Comparative Urban and Regional Research (2001). *The new ethnic enclaves in America's suburbs.* Albany, NY: Lewis Mumford Center for Comparative Urban and Regional Research, State University of New York.

Lien, P. (1994). Ethnicity and political participation: A comparison between Asian and Mexican-Americans. *Political Behavior, 16*(2), 237–65.

Lien, P. (1997). *The political participation of Asian Americans: Voting behavior in southern California.* New York: Garland Publishers.

London, B. & M. W. Giles (1987). Black participation: Compensation or ethnic identification. *Journal of Black Studies, 18*(20–44).

Longoria, Jr., T. (2000). Context, identity and incorporation: Are Latinos in the Midwest different? In: R. Keiser & K. Underwood (Eds), *Minority Politics at the Millennium.* New York: Garland Publishing Inc.

Mangum, M. (2000). Explaining black voter turnout. Paper presented at 2000 Annual Meeting of the American Political Science Association.

Miller, A. H., Gurin, P., Gurin, G., & Malanchuk, O. (1981). Group consciousness and political participation. *American Journal of Political Science, 25*, 494–511.

Mollenkopf, J., Ross, T., & Olsen, D. (1999). Immigrant political participation in New York and Los Angeles. New York, NY: The New School for Social Research, International Center for Migration, Ethnicity and Citizenship.

Myrdal, G. 1962 [1944]. *An American dilemma: The Negro problem and modern democracy.* New York: Harper and Row.

Nakanishi, D. T. (1991). The next swing vote? Asian Pacific Americans and California politics. In: B. O. Jackson & M. B. Preston (Eds), *Racial and Ethnic Politics in California* (pp. 25–54). Berkeley, IGS Press.

Nakanishi, D. T. (2001). Political trends and electoral issues of the Asian Pacific American population. In: N. J. Smelser, W. J. Wilson & F. Mitchell (Eds), *America Becoming: Racial Trends and their Consequences* (Vol. 1). Washington, D.C.: National Academy Press.

Nakanishi, D. T. (1986). The UCLA Asia Pacific America voter registrations study. *ISSR Working Papers, 2*(10).

Nie, N. H., Junn, J., & Stehlik-Barry, K. (1996). *Education and democratic citizenship in America.* Chicago, IL: University of Chicago Press.

Newburger, E. C., & Curry, A. (2000). Educational attainment in the United States. *Current Population Report*, U.S. Census Bureau, (P20–528).

Oliver, J. E. (2000). City size and civic involvement in metropolitan America. *American Political Science Review, 94*(2), 361–373.

Oliver, M. L., & Shapiro, T. M. (2001). Wealth and racial stratification. In: N. J. Smelser, W. J. Wilson & F. Mitchell (Eds), *America Becoming: Racial Trends and their Consequences* (Vol. 2).

Olsen, M. E. (1970). Social and political participation of blacks. *American Sociological Review, 35*, 682–697.

Patterson, O. (2001, May 8). Race by the numbers. *The New York Times*.

Portes, A. (1984). The rise of ethnicity: Determinants of ethnic perceptions among Cuban exiles in Miami. *American Sociological Review, 49*, 383–397.

Putnam. R. D. (2000). *Bowling alone: The collapse and revival of American community*. New York: Simon & Schuster.

Ramakrishnan, S. K. (2001). The political incorporation of immigrants and their descendants. Paper presented at the Annual Meeting of the Population Association of American.

Ramírez, R. (2000). Race, social context and referendum voting. Paper presented at Annual Meeting of the American Political Science Association.

Ratcliffe, P. (2000). 'Race,' ethnicity and housing decisions: Rational choice theory and the choice-constraints debate. In: M. Archer & J. Tritter (Eds), *Rational Choice Theory: Resisting Colonization*. London, England: Routledge.

Rogers, R. (2000). Afro-Caribbean immigrants, racial polarization, and interethnic discord. In: Y. M. Alex-Assensoh & L. J. Hanks (Eds), *Blacks and Multiracial Politics in America (2000)*. New York: New York University Press.

Rosenstone, S. J., & Hansen, J. M. (1993). *Mobilization, participation and democracy in America*. New York: MacMillan Publishing Company.

Roucek, J. S., & Eisenberg, B. (1982). *America's ethnic politics*. Westport, CT: Green Wood Press.

Sarna, J. D. (1978). From immigrants to ethnics: Toward a new theory of 'ethnicization'. *Ethnicity, 5*, 370–378.

Scott, J. (2001, June, 27). A census query is said to skew data on Latinos. *New York Times*.

Shaw, D. De la Garza, R. O., & Lee, J. (2000). Examining Latino turnout in 1996: A three-State, validated survey approach. *American Journal of Political Science, 44*, 338–346.

Shingles, R. D. (1981). Black consciousness and political participation: The missing link. *American Political Science Review, 75*, 76–91.

Smelser, N. J., Wilson, W. J., & Mitchell, F. (Eds) (2001). *America becoming: Racial trends and their consequences*, Vols. 1 and 2. Washington, D.C.: National Academy Press.

Thorton, R. (2001, March 23). What the Census doesn't count. *New York Times*.

Uhlaner, C. J. (1986). Political participation, rational actors, and rationality: A new approach. *Political Psychology, 7*, 551–573.

Uhlaner, C. J. (1989). Rational turnout: The neglected role of groups. *American Journal of Political Science, 33*, 390–422.

Uhlaner, C. J. (1991a). Perceived discrimination and prejudice and the coalition Prospects of Blacks, Latinos and Asian Americans. In: B. O. Jackson & M. B. Preston. (Eds), *Racial and Ethnic Politics in California*. Berkeley, IGS Press.

Uhlaner, C. J. (1991b). Political participation and discrimination: A comparative study of Asians, Blacks, and Latinos. In: W. Crotty (Ed.), *Political Participation and American Democracy* (pp. 139–170). Westport, CT: Greenwood.

Uhlaner, C. J., B. E. Cain et al. (1989). Political participation of ethnic minorities in the 1980s. *Political Behavior, 11*, 195–232.

U.S. Census Bureau (2000, July 19). *Current Population Report* (P20–523), http://www.census.gov/population/socdemo/voting/cps1998

U.S. Census Bureau (2001, March). *Census 2000 Redistricting File* (PL/00–1 [RV]). Summary file.

U.S. Immigration and Naturalization Service (2000). *Statistical yearbook of the Immigration and Naturalization Service, 1998.* Washington, D.C.: U.S. Government Printing Office.

Verba, S., & Nie, N. H. (1972). *Participation in America.* Chicago: University of Chicago Press.

Verba, S., Nie, N. H., & Kim, J. O. (1978). *Participation and political equality: A seven-nation comparison.* Chicago, IL: University of Chicago Press.

Verba, S., Schlozman, K. L., Brady, H. E., & Nie, N. H. (1993). Race, ethnicity and political resources: Participation in the United States. *British Journal of Political Science, 23*(4), 453–497.

Verba, S., Schlozman, K. L., & Brady, H. E. (1995). *Voice and equality: Civic voluntarism in American politics.* Cambridge, MA: Harvard University Press.

Whiteley, P. F. (1995, March). Rational choice and political participation – Evaluating the debate. *Political Research Quarterly, 48*, 211–233.

Wolfinger R. E., & Rosenstone, S. J. (1980). *Who votes?* New Haven, CT: Yale University Press.

Wrinkle, R. D., Stewart, Jr., J., Polinard, J. L. Meier, K. J., & Arvizu, J. R. (1996). Ethnicity and non-electoral political participation. *Hispanic Journal of Behavioral Sciences, 18*(2), 142–151.